Guide to Zambia

Chris McIntyre

Bradt Publications, UK
The Globe Pequot Press Inc, USA

Published in 1996 by Bradt Publications
41 Nortoft Road, Chalfont St. Peter, Bucks, SL9 0LA, England
Published in the USA by The Globe Pequot Press Inc, 6 Business Park Road,
PO Box 833, Old Saybrook, Connecticut 06475-0833

British Library Cataloguing in Publication Data
A catalogue record for this book is available in the British Library
ISBN 1 898323 50 X

Library of Congress Cataloging-in-Publication Data
McIntyre, Chris
Guide to Zambia / Chris McIntyre
p. cm. – (Bradt guides)
Includes bibliographical references (p.) and index
ISBN 0-7627-0016-5
1. Zambia – Guidebooks. I. Title. II. Series
DT3041.M38 1996
916.89404'4 – dc20 96-31871
CIP

Cover photographs
Front Victoria Falls (John Douglas, Geoslides)
Back Leopard (Mark Davison)
Colour photographs Sir Peter Holmes (PH),
Chris McIntyre (CM), Paul Mount (PM),
Zambia National Tourist Board (ZNTB)
Illustrations Edwina Hannam
Maps *Inside covers* Steve Munns *Others* Hans van Well

Typeset by Chris McIntyre
Printed and bound in Great Britain by The Guernsey Press Co Ltd

ABOUT THE AUTHOR

Chris McIntyre went to Africa in 1987, after reading Physics at Queen's College, Oxford. He taught with VSO at a rural school in Zimbabwe for almost three years, and started to travel extensively around the subcontinent. On his return to the UK, he co-authored the UK's first guide to Namibia and Botswana (also published by Bradt), now in its second edition, before spending three years as a business analyst in the city.

Chris is now concentrating on what he enjoys: Southern Africa. He runs the African operations of one of the UK's top independent tour operators, specialising in individual trips to Southern Africa, while continuing to promote responsible tourism through books, articles and talks. He lives in Notting Hill Gate, London, although he normally spends two or three months of the year travelling in Africa.

Major contributor

Judi Helmholz counts business consultant, entrepreneur, chicken farmer, and professional walking and rafting guide amongst her occupations. She lives on the banks of the Zambezi with her partner, Arthur, a rottweiler named Zulu and 4,000 chickens. From here she has explored many of Zambia's wild places, and is active in conservation and tourism – serving as one of Zambia's first female Honorary Wildlife Police and with Livingstone's Tourism Association. She provided many anecdotes for this guide and much information, especially on the Livingstone area, the Western Provinces, and Zambia's many languages.

ACKNOWLEDGEMENTS

In the course of my research, I have been helped by many people, some of whose names I have forgotten, others I never knew. This is to thank all of those who made my research in Zambia such a pleasure. I would like to start by mentioning John Coppinger, Robin Miller, and Jo and Robin Pope – not only for hospitality and help in Zambia, but also for commenting on proofs since my return.

Others who gave invaluable help include: Nick Aslin; Simon Bicknell; Anne Butler; Suzie Critchley; Grant Cummings; Lew and Dale Games; Carol and David Harvey; Roxanne Henderson; Luckson; Adrian Lush; Steve McCormack; Willard Nakutonga; Jeremy Pope; Ben Parker; Map Patel; Pierre-Dennis Plisnier; William Ruck-Keene; Mwape Sichilongo; Byron Stephenson; Andrew Sweeney; John Sweetman; Pippa Turner; Christine Wake; John Wright; Trish at Nkwali; and Craig at Nsolo.

Back in the UK, I am especially grateful to Paul Mount and Sir Peter Holmes for use of their photographs; to Noel Josephides and John der Parthog for their understanding of the time needed to write this; to Josephine Chikwenda and ZNTB London, for sponsorship of the illustrations and cover maps; and to Clare Squire, for faith that was almost endless. Last, but not least, a word of thanks to Sarah for glasses of wine, and other sustenance whilst I wrote; and to Fritz for invaluable help and support whenever the going got tough.

Finally, my immense gratitude to those who worked on the book: Tricia Hayne, Hilary Bradt, Janice Booth, Helena Smith, Edwina Hannam, Steve Munns and Hans van Well. That which is good and correct owes much to their care and attention; errors and omissions are my own.

CONTENTS

YOUNG HYENA - E.H

Introduction

Stalking lion on foot certainly focuses your attention. You think about where you walk; you see every movement; and your ears are aware of every sound. Not everyone's idea of fun, but Zambia isn't for everyone.

"Zambia: the real Africa" proclaims the tourist board's slogan. And it is right. The country feels real: unbowed, unsanitised, unpackaged, and largely unvisited. Zambia offers the best of wild Africa, in a country with very few visitors. An authentic taste of what the whole continent was like: wild, beautiful and slightly unpredictable.

For the cognoscenti, this has always been *the* place for walking safaris. Zambia's premier national park, South Luangwa, is the name to conjure with. It has top camps, Africa's best game, and many of its top guides. Throughout Africa there are khaki-uniformed attendants who drive visitors through the bush, but in South Luangwa you find expert guides to trust with your life. Such quality doesn't come cheap, but the best seldom does.

However, until now that was all that most people knew of Zambia. The rest of this huge country (twice the size of Zimbabwe) remained undiscovered, its less expensive camps unknown, its people unmentioned.

Zambia's attractions are legion, if you seek them out – and the following chapters will show you how. Whether you are arriving on an overland truck, hitchhiking with a backpack, or inside a private plane, this book can show you how to rediscover that real Africa.

Kafue National Park alone is a wilderness area the size of Wales. It is inaccessible for six months of the year, yet when its floodwaters recede, the plains flush green with grass and it fills with game – becoming one of the most fascinating areas on the subcontinent. Here you'll also find walking trips, truly remarkable leopard viewing, very few other visitors – and a variety of camps which are superb value.

Zambia's Lower Zambezi National Park isn't quite so seasonal. At any time of year large herds of elephant and buffalo can be appreciated from a leisurely canoe trip along the Zambezi. This park is remarkably empty of people, but full of game.

In the centre of Zambia lies the huge Lake Bangweulu, surrounded by the swamp that defeated Livingstone – his heart was buried nearby. This fascinating land of islands and waterways is a permanent swamp, home to the rare shoebill stork and its own endemic species of antelope, the black lechwe. The traditional communities who have lived here for centuries are now leaving their hunting to guide visitors around, as part of an eco-tourism project aided by the Worldwide Fund for Nature.

Far to the west, Liuwa Plains National Park is the venue for one of Africa's last great wildlife migrations: blue wildebeest in their thousands, plus zebra, tsessebe and buffalo, all converging on the plains for the rains. Liuwa is remote, and getting there needs planning, but the rewards are spectacular. A plain of honey-coloured grass, covered in animals, stretches as far as you can see, with no other visitors spoil the view.

Aside from its wildlife, Zambia's attractions are often dismissed by commentators, who forget the rich cultural heritage found in its more remote areas. In the ancient Lozi kingdom of Barotseland, for example, life has changed little since Livingstone first came to Zambia. The seasonal rhythm is still determined by the rains, and the whole kingdom still climbs aboard boats to move from the rich floodplains to higher ground in February or March, making one great, grand flotilla.

Those interested in Zambia's more recent history will marvel at Shiwa N'gandu – one of the subcontinent's most fascinating memorials to British rule. Here an English aristocrat built a Tucsan-style manor house and richly furnished it from Europe. He tried to carve out a utopian estate from the untamed bush, whilst helping Zambia to achieve its own independence. But Africa gradually defeated his dream and he died – to be buried with the full honours of an African chief, and a knighthood from the King of England. Shiwa's great manor still stands, offering a fascinating insight into colonial attitudes, and a palpable sense of history.

The fascination goes on. Zambia is a wonderful country if you've the time to discover it. The government is now actively encouraging tourism, providing an added reason to visit. Zambia desperately needs visitors as a source of foreign exchange, and but for such logic this guide might have remained unwritten. Many would prefer Zambia to stay as it is – a favourite place to visit, with superb wildlife, few other visitors, and Zambians who still treat travellers with kind hospitality.

Now, having committed many of Zambia's secrets to paper, I hope that those who use this guide will do so with respect. Zambia's wild areas need great care to preserve them. Local cultures are easily eroded by a visitor's lack of sensitivity, and hospitality once abused is seldom offered again. Enjoy – but be a thoughtful visitor, for the country's sake.

Chapter One

Facts and Figures

Location

Zambia is landlocked in the tropics of Southern Africa, distant from both the Atlantic and Pacific Oceans. It is at the northern edge of the region referred to as "Southern Africa", while sharing many similarities with its neighbours in East and Central Africa.

Size

Zambia is shaped like a giant butterfly, and covers about 752,610km². That is slightly smaller than the UK and France combined, and slightly larger than California and Nevada put together. In comparison with its neighbours, it is almost double the size of Zimbabwe, but only two-thirds that of South Africa.

Topography

Most of Zambia is part of the high, undulating plateau that forms the backbone of Africa. The plateau's altitude is typically 1,000-1,600m above sea level. It is deeply incised by great valleys: the Zambezi, the Kafue, the Luangwa and the Luapula.

There are several large lakes on Zambia's borders: Tanganyika and Mweru in the north, and the man-made Kariba in the south. Lake Bangweulu, and its swamps and floodplain, dominate a large area of the interior.

Climate

Zambia's climate can be split into three periods. From December to April it is hot and wet, with torrential downpours often in the late afternoon. From May to August it is dry, and fairly cool. From September to November it remains dry, but gets progressively hotter. Zambia's climate is generally moderate; only in the great valleys does it feel oppressive.

Flora and fauna

Zambia is a large country, with many large national parks, and game management areas (GMAs) where conservation and sustainable utilisation of the native wildlife is encouraged.

Miombo woodland – a mixture of grassland dotted with trees and shrubs – makes up about 70% of Zambia's natural environment, with *mopane* woodland dominating the lower-lying areas. The native fauna is classic big game found throughout East and Southern Africa. Amongst the predators, leopard seem to do exceptionally well here; lion are common but cheetah are not. Wild dog are as rare as they are anywhere else in the continent, and there are many smaller predators. Zambia's antelope are especially interesting for the range of subspecies which have evolved. Giraffe, wildebeest, waterbuck and, especially, lechwe are notable for this – each having subspecies endemic to the country.

With rich vegetation and lots of water, Zambia has a great variety of both resident and migrant birds: over 700 species in total. Wetland and swamp areas attract some specialised water-fowl, and Zambia is on the edge of the range for both Southern African and East African species.

Population

Zambia has a population of about nine million. The vast majority are of black African (Bantu) descent, though there are significant communities whose ancestors came from Europe and India.

Zambia is a large country, so its population density – around 12 people per km^2 – is about half that of Zimbabwe's, a third that of South Africa's, or about a quarter the population density of Kenya. Like much of subsaharan Africa, Zambia's population growth rate is high, at around 3% per annum.

The capital, Lusaka, is home to about 10% of the country's population, whilst the four main towns of the Copperbelt, Kitwe, Ndola, Kabwe and Mufulira, have over 1,300,000 between them. Thus the rural areas have a generally low density, and the country retains large tracts of wilderness.

Language

English is the official language in Zambia, and most urban Zambians speak it fluently. In the rural areas it is used less, though only in truly remote settlements would there be problems communicating in English.

The main vernacular languages are Bemba, Kaonde, Lozi, Lunda, Luvale, Nyanja and Tonga – though more than 72 different languages and dialects are spoken in the country.

Religion

The majority of Zambians are Christian, having been gradually converted since the first missionaries arrived in the 19th century. There is also a significant proportion of both Muslims and Hindus, originating in the Asian communities who settled whilst Zambia was under British rule. That said, traditional African beliefs are widely adhered to - even by Zambia's Christians.

History

Zambia's first Stone-Age, hunter-gatherer inhabitants were supplanted by Bantu groups from the north, who arrived with their Iron-Age culture in the first few centuries AD. These groups were taken under British rule by the Cecil Rhodes' powerful British South Africa Company around 1890.

In 1924 the territory was taken over officially by the British colonial office. In 1953 Northern Rhodesia, as Zambia was known, was joined to Nyasaland (Malawi) and Southern Rhodesia (Zimbabwe) to form the Central African Federation - though much administration still relied on the British.

Largely peaceful internal pressure, including the voices of several influential British residents, eventually led to Zambia gaining its independence in 1964, when it joined the Commonwealth.

Economy

The economy is currently in a poor state, with a huge national debt and no practical means to pay this off. Copper exports account for around 90% of the country's foreign exchange, which makes Zambia highly dependent upon the price of copper on the world's markets. Zambia's inflation rate is around 200%.

Currency

The currency here is the Zambian kwacha (Kw), which is subdivided into 100 ngwee. This is devaluing steadily, in line with the country's high inflation rate. In the few months that this guide has taken to research and publish, the exchange rate for US$1 has risen from around Kw800 to over Kw1,500. (For £1 from Kw1,200 to Kw2,250.) Thus most of the prices in this guide are in US$, and for those which are not, assume a notional rate of around US$1 for Kw1,000.

Government

The chief of state and the head of government is the president, who appoints cabinet members from those elected to the National Assembly, a chamber of 150 elected representatives.

Zambian citizens of 18 years and over are eligible to vote, and the country is split up into nine provinces for administration purposes: Central, Copperbelt, Eastern, Luapulu, Lusaka, Northern, Northwestern, Southern and Western.

The judicial system was set up according to a British model, based on English common law and customary law. Legislative acts receive judicial review in an *ad hoc* constitutional council.

Politics

From November 1991 until October 1996, the country has been run by President Frederick Chiluba, heading the government for the Movement for Multiparty Democracy (MMD). He has been liberalising the economy, which is widely appreciated as a good thing, though some of the economic measures were difficult for poorer people to live with.

In October 1996, as this book goes to press, elections are due to be held and Chiluba's MMD will be pitted against Kenneth Kaunda's United National Independence Party (UNIP), which ruled the country from independence in 1964 until losing the elections in 1991. Chiluba is certainly endorsed by the country's business community, the aid agencies, the IMF and the World Bank, but it remains to be seen if he can maintain the support of the people after the economic conditions of recent years.

Natural resources

Copper is easily the country's most important natural resource, with cobalt second. Amethyst, fluorite, feldspar, gypsum, lead, zinc, tin and gold also occur in small quantities, as well as a variety of gemstones.

Tourism

Zambia has never had many tourists: it currently receives only about 10% of the number who visit Zimbabwe. Many of these just come across the border for a daytrip, to see the Zambian side of the Victoria Falls. Others travel through Zambia as quickly as possible in overland trucks, from Malawi or Tanzania to Zimbabwe.

Few stay for long in Zambia itself, because it is perceived as expensive and/or difficult. Those few, counted in only thousands per year, come mostly for the wildlife, and the experience of staying in remote bush camps, tracking game with top guides. These numbers are growing steadily, as people seek out more remote corners of the continent, and realise that good wildlife guides are few and far between.

Independent budget travellers in Zambia are rare. Those who do come should be well prepared. Once here, they will realise that their novelty value in the rural areas ensures them a warm welcome; this alone makes Zambia a fascinating destination.

Chapter Two

History and Economy

HISTORY

Zambia's earliest inhabitants

Palaeontologists looking for evidence of the first ancestors of the human race have excavated a number of sites in Zambia. The earliest remains yet identified are Stone-Age tools dated at about 200,000 years old, which have been recovered in gravel deposits around what is now the Victoria Falls. It is thought that these probably belong to the *homo erectus* species, whose hand-axes have been dated in Tanzania to half a million years old. These were hunter-gatherer people, who could use fire, make tools, and had probably developed some simple speech.

Experts divide the Stone Age into the middle, early, and late Stone Ages. The transition from early to middle Stone Age technology - which is indicated by a larger range of stone tools often adapted for particular uses, and signs that these people had a greater mastery of their environment - was probably in progress around 125,000 years ago in Zambia.

The famous "Broken Hill Man" lived around this time. His skull was unearthed from about 20m underground during mining operations near Kabwe in 1921. He was from a species called *homo rhodesiensis*, which may have been a late survivor of *homo erectus*, or an early ancestor of us - *homo sapiens*. (Kabwe's old name was Broken Hill, explaining the origin of this name.)

The late Stone Age is normally characterised by the use of composite tools, those made of wood and/or bone and/or stone used together, and by the presence of a revolutionary invention: the bow and arrow. This first appeared in Zambia, and throughout the world, about 15,000 years ago. Skeletons found around the Kafue Flats area indicate that some of these late Stone-Age hunters had a close physical resemblance to the modern San/bushmen people, whose culture, relying on a late Stone-Age level of technology, survived intact in the Kalahari Desert until the middle of the 20th century.

The Iron Age

Around 3,000BC, late Stone-Age hunter-gatherer groups in Ethiopia, and elsewhere in north and west Africa, started to keep domestic animals, sow seeds, and harvest the produce: they became the world's first farmers.

By around 1,000BC these new pastoral practices had spread south into the equatorial forests of what is now Zaire, to around Lake Victoria, and into the northern area of the Great Rift Valley, in northern Tanzania. However, agriculture did not spread south into the rest of central/Southern Africa immediately. Only when the technology, and the tools, of iron-working became known did the practices start their relentless expansion southwards.

The spread of agriculture and Iron-Age culture seems to have been a rapid move. It was brought south by Africans who were taller and heavier than the existing small inhabitants. The ancestors of the San/bushmen people, with their simple Stone-Age technology and hunter-gatherer existence, just could not compete with these Iron-Age farmers, who became the ancestors of virtually all the modern black Africans in Southern Africa.

This major migration occurred around the first few centuries AD, and since then the San/bushmen of Southern Africa have gradually been either assimilated into the migrant groups, or effectively pushed into the areas which could not be farmed. Thus the older Iron-Age cultures persisted in the forests of the north and east of Zambia – which were more difficult to cultivate – much longer than they survived in the south of the country.

More immigrants

By the 4th or 5th century AD, Iron-Age farmers had settled throughout much of Southern Africa. As well as iron-working technology, they brought with them pottery, the remains of which are used by archaeologists to work out the migrations of various different groups of these Bantu settlers. These migrations continued, and the distribution of pottery styles suggests that the groups moved around within the subcontinent: this was much more complex than a simple north-south influx.

The origins of trade

In burial sites dating from the latter half of the first millennium, occasional "foreign" objects start to occur: the odd cowrie shell, or copper bangles in an area where there is no copper. This indicates that some small-scale bartering with neighbouring villages was beginning to take place.

In the first half of the second millennium, the pace and extent of this trade increased significantly. Gold objects appear (as well as the more common copper, iron and ivory) and shells from the Indian Ocean. The frequency of these indicates that trade was gradually developing. We know from European historical sources that Muslim traders (of Arab or possibly African origin) were venturing into the heart of Africa by around AD1400, and thus trade routes were being established.

As trade started, so the second millennium also saw the development of wealth and social structures within the tribes. The evidence for this is a number of burial sites which stand out for the quantity and quality of the goods that were buried with the dead person. One famous site, at Ingombe Ilede, near the confluence of the Lusitu and Zambezi rivers, was occupied regularly over many centuries. There is evidence that its inhabitants traded from the 14th century with people further south, in Zimbabwe, exporting gold down the Zambezi via traders coming from the Indian Ocean. Indications of cotton-weaving have also been found there, and several copper crosses unearthed are so similar that they may have been used as a simple form of currency – valuable to both the local people and the traders from outside.

By the middle of the second millennium, a number of separate cultures seem to have formed in Zambia. Many practised trade, and a few clearly excelled at it. Most were starting to develop social structures within the group, with some enjoying more status and wealth than others.

The chiefs

From around the middle of the second millennium, there is little good archaeological evidence that can be accurately dated. However, sources for the events of this period in Zambia's history are the oral histories of Zambia's people, as well as their current languages and social traditions. The similarities and differences between the modern Zambian languages can be extrapolated by linguistic experts to point to the existence of about nine different root languages, which probably existed in Zambia in the 15th century AD.

The latter half of the second millennium AD saw the first chiefs, and hence kingdoms, emerge from Zambia's dispersed clans. The title "chief" can be applied to anyone from a village headman, to a god-like king. However, this was an era of increasing trade, when local disputes were dominated by the groups with the largest resources and armies. Thus it made sense for various clans to group together into tribes, under the rule of a single individual, or chief.

One of the oldest is thought to have been the *Undi*, who came to the Luangwa area from the southern side of Lake Malawi in the 16th century. By the end of that century the *N'gandu* clan (clan of the crocodile) established a kingdom amongst the Bemba people. These people lived mostly in woodland areas, practising simple slash-and-burn types of agriculture. Perhaps because of the poverty of their lifestyle, they later earned a reputation as warriors for their raids on neighbouring peoples.

In the latter part of the 17th century the first recorded *Lozi* king is thought to have settled near Kalobo, starting a powerful dynasty which lasts to the present day. Early in the 18th century Kazemba established a kingdom around the southern end of Lake Mweru in the Luapula valley.

The growth of trade

As various cohesive kingdoms developed, their courts served as centres of trade, and their chiefs had the resources to initiate trade with other communities. Foodstuffs, iron, copper, salt, cotton, cloth, tobacco, baskets, pottery and many other items were traded within Zambia, between the various tribes.

From around the 14th century, Zambia had a trickle of trade with non-Africans: mostly Muslims exporting gold through the east coast of Africa. (This trade had started as early as the 10th century on the Limpopo River, south of Zimbabwe's gold-fields.) However, by the early 17th century the Muslims had been supplanted by the Portuguese, and by the latter half of the 17th century these Portuguese traders were operating out of Mozambique, trading gold, ivory and copper with Zambia.

Trade with the outside world escalated during the 18th century, as more and more tribes became involved, and more foreigners came to trade. Some chiefs started to trade their commodities for weapons, in attempts to gain advantage over their neighbours. Those vanquished in local conflicts were certainly used as sources of slaves – an increasingly valuable commodity of trade. These and other factors increased the pressure on Zambians to trade, and the influx of foreign traders made the picture more complex still.

By the early 19th century, Zambia was being visited with increasing frequency by both traders and slavers. These were responding to the increasing consumer demands of newly industrialised Europe and America. More trade routes were opening up, not just through Mozambique and Angola, but also to the north and south. Internal conflicts were increasing, as both the means to conduct these, and the incentives for victory, grew.

Western requirements

During the 19th century, the West (western Europe and North America) had traded with the native Africans to obtain what they wanted – commodities and slave labour – without having to go to the trouble of ruling parts of the continent. However, as the century progressed, and the West became more industrialised, it needed these things in greater quantities than the existing tribal structures in Africa could supply.

Further, there was demand for materials that could be produced in Africa, like cotton and rubber, but which required Western production methods.

Given that the West wanted a wider range and greater quantity of cheaper raw materials, the obvious solution was to control the means of supply. African political organisation was widely regarded as primitive, and not capable of providing complex and sustained trade. Inward investment would also be needed, which would be forthcoming only if white enterprises were safe from African interference. Hence the solution to Western requirements was to bring Africa, and the Africans, under European rule.

Another reason for considering the acquisition of African territory was that the world was shrinking. There were no inhabitable continents left to discover. Staking a nation's claim to large chunks of Africa seemed prudent to most of the Western powers of the time, and growing competition for these areas meant they could always be traded for one another at a later date.

Livingstone's contribution

David Livingstone's *Missionary Travels and Researches in South Africa* excited great interest in England. This account of his journeys across Southern Africa in the 1840s and 50s had all the appeal that undersea or space exploration has for us now. Further, it captured the imagination of the British public, allowing them to take pride in their country's exploration of Africa, based on an explorer who seemed to be the epitome of bravery and righteous religious zeal.

Livingstone had set out with the conviction that if the material and physical well-being of Africans were improved - probably by learning European ways, and earning a living from export crops - then they would be ripe for conversion to Christianity. He was strongly opposed to slavery, but sure that this would disappear when Africans became more self-sufficient through trade.

In fact Livingstone was almost totally unsuccessful in his own aims, failing to set up any successful trading missions, or even to convert many Africans permanently to Christianity. However, his travels opened up areas north of the Limpopo for later British missionaries, and by 1887 British mission stations were established in Zambia and southern Malawi.

The scramble for Africa

British foreign policy in Southern Africa had always revolved around the Cape Colony, which was seen as vital to British interests in India and the Indian Ocean. Africa to the north of the Cape Colony had largely been ignored. The Boers were on the whole left to their farming in the Transvaal area, and posed no threat to the colony.

However, Germany annexed South West Africa (now Namibia) in 1884, prompting British fears that they might try to link up with the Boers. Thus, to drive a wedge through the middle of these territories, the British negotiated an alliance with Khama, a powerful *Tswana* king, and proclaimed as theirs the Protectorate of Bechuanaland – the forerunner of modern Botswana.

Soon after, in 1886, the Boers discovered large gold deposits in the Witwatersrand (around Johannesburg). The influx of money from this boosted the Boer farmers, who expanded their interests to the north, making a treaty with Khama's enemy, the powerful Lobengula. This in turn prompted the British to look beyond the Limpopo, and to back the territorial aspirations of a millionaire British businessman, Cecil Rhodes. By 1888 Rhodes, a partner in the De Beers consortium, had control of the lucrative diamond-mining industry in Kimberley, South Africa. He was hungry for power, and dreamt of linking the Cape to Cairo with land under British control.

His wealth enabled Rhodes to buy sole rights to mine minerals in Lobengula's territory. Thence he persuaded the British government to grant his company – the British South Africa Company – the licence to stake claims to African territory with the authority of the British government. In 1889 Rhodes sent out several expeditions to the chiefs in the area now comprising Zimbabwe, Zambia and Malawi, to make treaties. These granted British "protection and aid" in return for sole rights to minerals in the chiefs' territories, and assurances that they would not make treaties with any other foreign powers. This effective strategy was greatly helped by the existing British influence from the missions which were already established in many of the regions. By 1891 the British had secured these areas (through Rhodes' British South Africa Company) from the other European powers, and confirmed their boundaries in treaties with the neighbouring colonial powers.

By the closing years of the 19th century, Zambia – or Northern Rhodesia as it was called – was clearly under British rule. However, this had little impact until local administrations were set up, and taxes started to be collected.

The mines

In the early years of the 20th century, the Rhodes' British South Africa Company did little in Northern Rhodesia. Its minerals were not nearly as accessible or valuable as those in Southern Rhodesia, and little protection or aid actually materialised. It became viewed by the colonials as a source of cheap labour for the mines of South Africa and Southern Rhodesia.

To facilitate this, taxes were introduced for the local people, which effectively forced them to come into the cash economy. Virtually the only way for them to do this was to find work in one of the mines further south. By 1910 a railway linked the mine at Kimberley, in South Africa, with Victoria Falls and beyond, making long-distance travel in the subcontinent more practical.

Meanwhile the costs of administering and defending the company's interests was rising, and in 1923 Southern Rhodesia became self-governing. In 1924 the British colonial office took over administration of Northern Rhodesia from the British South Africa Company, though the mining rights remained with the Company. The Colonial Office then set up a legislative council to advise on the government of the province, though only a few of its members came from outside the administration.

Shortly afterwards, in 1928, huge deposits of copper were located below the basin of the upper Kafue, under what is now known as the Copperbelt. Over the next decade or so these were developed into a number of large copper mines, working rich, deep deposits of copper. World War II demanded increased production of base metals, and by 1945 Northern Rhodesia was producing 12% of the non-communist world's copper. This scale of production required large labour forces. The skilled workers were mostly of European origin, often from South Africa's mines, whilst the unskilled workers came from all over Northern Rhodesia.

Wages and conditions were very poor for the unskilled miners, who were treated as migrant workers and expected to go home to their permanent villages every year or so to "recover." Death rates among them were high. Further, the drain of men to work the mines inevitably destabilised the villages, and poverty and malnutrition were common in the rural areas.

Welfare associations

As early as 1929 welfare associations had formed in several of the territory's southern towns, aimed at giving black Africans a voice and trying to defend their interests. These associations were often started by teachers or clerks: the more educated members of the communities. They were small at first, far too small to mount any effective challenge to the establishment, but they did succeed in raising awareness amongst the Africans, all of whom were being exploited.

In 1935 the African mineworkers first organised themselves to strike over their pay and conditions. By 1942 the towns of the African labourers in the Copperbelt were forming their own welfare associations, and by 1949 some of these had joined together as the Northern Rhodesian African Mineworkers' Union, which had been officially recognised by the colonial government as being the equal of any union for white workers.

In 1952 the union showed its muscle with a successful and peaceful three-week strike, resulting in substantial wage increases.

Central African Federation

The tiny European population in Northern Rhodesia was, on the whole, worried by the growth of the power of black African mineworkers. Most of the white people wanted to break free from colonial rule, so that they could control the pace and direction of political change. They also resented the loss of vast revenues from the mines, which went directly to the British government and the British South Africa Company, without much benefit for Northern Rhodesia.

During the 1930s and 1940s the settlers' representation on Northern Rhodesia's Legislative Council was gradually increased, and calls for self-rule became more insistent. As early as 1936 Stewart Gore-Browne (founder of *Shiwa N'gandu*, see *Chapter Thirteen*) had proposed a scheme for a Central African Federation, with an eye to Britain's future (or lack of one) in Africa. This view gained ground in London, where the government was increasingly anxious to distance itself from African problems.

In 1948 the South African Nationalist Party came to power in South Africa, on a tide of Afrikaner support. The historical enmity between the Afrikaners and the British in South Africa led the British colonials in Southern and Northern Rhodesia to look to themselves for their own future, rather than their neighbours in South Africa. In 1953 their pressure was rewarded and Southern and Northern Rhodesia were formally joined with Nyasaland (which is now Malawi), to become the independent Central African Federation.

The formation of the Federation did little to help the whites in Northern Rhodesia, though it was so strongly opposed by the blacks, who feared that they would then lose more of their land to white settlers. Earlier, in 1948, the Federation of African Societies – an umbrella group of welfare associations – changed its name at an annual general meeting into an overtly political "Northern Rhodesian Congress". This had branches in the mining towns and the rural areas, and provided a base upon which a black political culture could be based. A few years later, it was renamed as the Northern Rhodesia African National Congress.

Independence

Despite the Federation, Northern Rhodesia actually remained under the control of the Colonial Office. Further, the administration of the Federation was so biased towards Southern Rhodesia that the revenues from its mines simply flowed there, instead of to Britain. Thus though the Federation promised much, it delivered few of the settlers' wishes in Northern Rhodesia.

A small core of increasingly skilled African mineworkers gained better pay and conditions, whilst poverty was rife in the rest of the country. By the 1950s small improvements were being made in the provision of education for black Zambians, but widespread neglect had demonstrated to most that whites did not want blacks as their political or social equals. Thus black politics began to focus on another goal: independence.

In 1958 elections were held, and about 25,000 blacks were allowed to vote. The Northern Rhodesia African National Congress was divided about whether to participate or not, and eventually this issue split the party. Kenneth Kaunda, the radical Secretary General, and others founded the Zambia African National Congress (ZANC). This was soon banned, and Kaunda was jailed during a state of emergency.

Finally, in 1960, Kaunda was released from jail, and greeted as a national hero. He took control of a splinter party, the United National Independence Party (UNIP), and after a short campaign of civil disobedience forced the colonial office to hold universal elections. In October of 1962, these confirmed a large majority for UNIP. In 1963 the Federation broke up, and in 1964 elections based on universal adult suffrage gave UNIP a commanding majority. On October 24 1964 Zambia became independent, with Kenneth Kaunda as its president.

Zambia under Kaunda

President Kenneth Kaunda took over a country whose income was controlled by the state of the world copper market, and whose trade routes were entirely dependent upon Southern Rhodesia, South Africa, and Mozambique. He also inherited a Kw50,000,000 national debt from the colonial era, and a populace which was largely unskilled and uneducated. (At independence, there were fewer than one hundred Zambians with university degrees, and fewer than a thousand who had completed secondary school.)

In 1965, shortly after Zambia's independence, Southern Rhodesia made a Unilateral Declaration of Independence (UDI). This propelled Zambia's southern neighbour further along the same path of white rule which South Africa had adopted. Sanctions were then applied to Rhodesia from the rest of the world. Given that most of Zambia's trade passed through Rhodesia, these had very negative effects on the country's economy,

As the black people of Rhodesia, South Africa and South West Africa (Namibia) started their liberation struggles, Kaunda naturally wanted to support them. Zambia became a haven for political refugees, and a base for black independence movements. However ideologically sound this approach was, it was costly and did not endear Zambia to its economically dominant white-ruled neighbours. The apartheid government in South Africa also began a policy of destabilising the black-ruled countries around the subcontinent – so civil wars and unrest became the norm in Mozambique and Angola, squeezing Zambia's trade routes further.

The late 1960s and early 1970s saw Zambia try to drastically reduce its trade with the south. Simultaneously it worked to increase its links with Tanzania – which was largely beyond the reach of South Africa's efforts to destabilise. With the help of China, Tanzania and Zambia built excellent road and rail links from the heart of Zambia to Dar es Salaam, on the Indian Ocean. However, Tanzania was no match as a trading partner for the efficiency of South Africa, and Zambia's economy remained sluggish.

During these difficult years Zambia's debt did not reduce, but grew steadily. The government's large revenues from copper were used in efforts to reduce the country's dependence on its southern neighbours, and to improve standards of living for the majority of Zambians. Education was expanded on a large scale, government departments were enlarged to provide employment, and food subsidies maintained the peace of the large urban population. Kaunda followed Julius Nyerere's example in Tanzania in many ways, with a number of socialist policies woven into his own (much promoted) philosophy of "humanism".

In retrospect, perhaps Kaunda's biggest mistake was that he failed to use the large revenues from copper either to reduce the national debt, or to diversify Zambia's export base – but his choices were not easy.

In the early 1970s, the world copper price fell dramatically. Simultaneously the cost of imports (especially oil) rose, the world economy slumped and the interest rates on Zambia's debt increased. These factors highlighted the fundamental weaknesses of Zambia's economy, which had been established to suit the colonial powers rather than the country's citizens.

The drop in the price of copper crippled Zambia's economy. Efforts to stabilise the world copper price – through a cartel of copper-producing countries, similar to the oil-producing OPEC countries – failed. Kaunda borrowed more money, betting on a recovery in copper prices which never arrived.

In the 1970s and 1980s Kaunda's government became increasingly intertwined with the International Monetary Fund (IMF) in the search for a solution to the country's debt. None was found. Short-term fixes just made things worse, and the country's finances deteriorated. The West did give Zambia aid, but mostly for specific projects, which usually had strings attached. What Zambia most needed (and still does) was help with the enormous interest payments that it was required to make to the West.

Various recovery plans, often instituted by the IMF, were tried. In 1986 food subsidies were sharply withdrawn, starting with breakfast meal, one of the country's staple foods. This hit the poor hardest, and major riots broke out before subsidies were hastily reintroduced to restore calm. In 1988 Zambia applied to the United Nations for the status of "least developed nation" in the hope of obtaining greater international assistance.

It was rejected. By the end of the decade Zambia's economy was in tatters. The official exchange rate bore little relation to the currency's actual worth, and inflation was rampant.

Despite Kaunda's many failures with the economy, his policies did encourage the development of some home-grown industries to produce goods to replace previously imported items. It created systems for mass education, which were almost entirely absent when he came to power: there are now primary and secondary schools for everyone, and a university in Lusaka.

Zambia in the late 1980s was one of the world's poorest countries, with a chronic debt problem, high inflation, and a weak currency. A reputation for corruption, reaching to the highest levels of the government, did little to encourage help from richer nations.

Current politics

These economic problems, the lack of obvious material benefits for the majority of Zambians, gradually fomented opposition. UNIP's tendency to become authoritarian in its demands for unity also led to unrest. Kaunda's rule was finally challenged successfully by the capitalist Movement for Multiparty Democracy (MMD) led by Frederick Chiluba. This received widespread support during the late 1980s, on a platform of liberalisation and anti-corruption measures.

Kaunda agreed to an election, apparently certain that he would win. In the event, UNIP was resoundingly defeated by the MMD (16% to 84%), and Chiluba became Zambia's second elected president in November 1991. Kaunda accepted the results with grace – he continues to live in Zambia and to head UNIP (a rare, and very encouraging, co-existence in the volatile world of modern African politics).

When elected, Frederick Chiluba faced enormous economic problems, which he has attempted to tackle. He has succeeded in liberalising and privatising much of the economy. There is now a freely floating market for the kwacha, and policies to attract inward investment. However, the country's debt has not reduced. In 1995 this stood at US$6.25 billion, and debt service payments were some 40% of the gross national product – equivalent to about US$600/£400 per capita per annum. One of Chiluba's highest priorities has, necessarily, been to try to get the major industrialised nations to write off large chunks of this. Zambia owes US$3.1 billion to the World Bank and the IMF alone.

The IMF's latest scheme is an Enhanced Structural Adjustment Facility (ESAF), which allows the world's poorest nations to pay lower interest rates on the money that they owe. Zambia may join this, though it is criticised by experts as being of more benefit to the IMF than to Zambia, as Zambia will first have to repay all its arrears to date.

So, Zambia's economy remains unbalanced by its dependence upon copper, and severely weakened by debt. Chiluba has gained the confidence of some Western donors since coming to power in 1991, but his reforms are long term, and much of their success depends on the willingness of international donors to help him.

Certainly the general attitude towards visitors has changed under Chiluba: Zambia is a more welcoming country now than it was under Kaunda's reign. Tourism is recognised as a very direct and helpful source of jobs and foreign currency, and the climate of suspicion of Kaunda's Zambia has been replaced with a warmer welcome.

Chiluba's attention has, necessarily, been focused on the country's unbalanced economy and the huge debt burden. Observers have noted that Zambia's absence from the world's headlines in the early 1990s was an example of "no news being good news".

Chiluba having remained in power for the last five years, presidential elections are due in October 1996 – as this book goes to press. Kenneth Kaunda still heads the UNIP, and is expected to contest the elections and seek a return to power, claiming new economic policies which are more market-oriented.

ECONOMY

Aside from mining, which is covered below, Zambia's other industries are small in comparison. They include construction, chemicals, textiles and fertiliser production. Agriculture accounts for about 12% of Zambia's GDP, and about 85% of its workforce – most of whom are working in small, subsistence farms. The main crops are maize (the staple food for most people), sorghum, rice, peanuts, sunflowers, tobacco, cotton, sugarcane, cassava, cattle, goats, beef and eggs.

The country receives much economic aid, and all Zambia's regional centres are home to at least a few aid-agency staff. However, what the country most needs is a reduction in its debt – which isn't forthcoming.

Zambia remains one of the world's poorest countries, with a major national debt, inflation at around 200%, much corruption, and a very weak currency.

Zambia's mining industry

Zambia's economy is totally dependant upon its mining sector, and particularly its copper mines. Mining contributes about 20% of the country's GDP and about 90% of its export earnings. It employs perhaps 15% of the country's workforce.

Copper

Zambia is the world's fourth largest copper-producer. It has large, high-quality deposits of copper ore which currently yield about 310,000 tons per annum. This has declined from around 700,000 tons in the late 1970s.

All the mines are owned by Zambia Consolidated Copper Mines (ZCCM), which in turn is jointly controlled by the Zambian Government and Anglo American Corporation. At present the government is trying to sell off its controlling stake in the mines to investing institutions. The Zambian Privatisation Agency is currently looking at privatising ZCCM, and attracting inward investment in the industry. With this there are plans for a "Konkola Deep" project which would increase production by about 180,000 tons per year.

As yet there are no major secondary industries which use copper, and so the metal is exported as copper ingots to the USA, UK, Japan, Malaysia, Thailand, Indonesia and Europe.

Cobalt

Zambia is the world's largest producer of cobalt, producing around 5,000 tons per annum of this valuable, strategic metal: around 20% of the world's total production. In one recent deal, a private mining company was granted rights to extract cobalt and copper from the "Nkana Slag Dump" – the slag heap of an old mining operation. This company estimates that this still has about 56,000 tons of cobalt and 86,000 tons of copper within it, so Zambia's output is expected to remain high.

Coal

Zambia has only one coal mine, at Maamba, where production has been declining for some time. It is currently running at about 300,000 tons per annum, though it is thought that this could increase by 60% if modern machinery and more efficient practices were introduced. Similarly, it is in the throes of being privatised.

Other mineral resources

Zambia has natural resources of amethyst, fluorite, feldspar, gypsum, aquamarine, lead, zinc, tin and gold – as well as a variety of gemstones. All are on a small scale, and few are being commercially exploited. An exception is emeralds, which are said to be among the highest quality in the world. These are being mined to the order of about US$200 million per year. However, about half of them are thought to be smuggled out of the country, so the actual figures are uncertain.

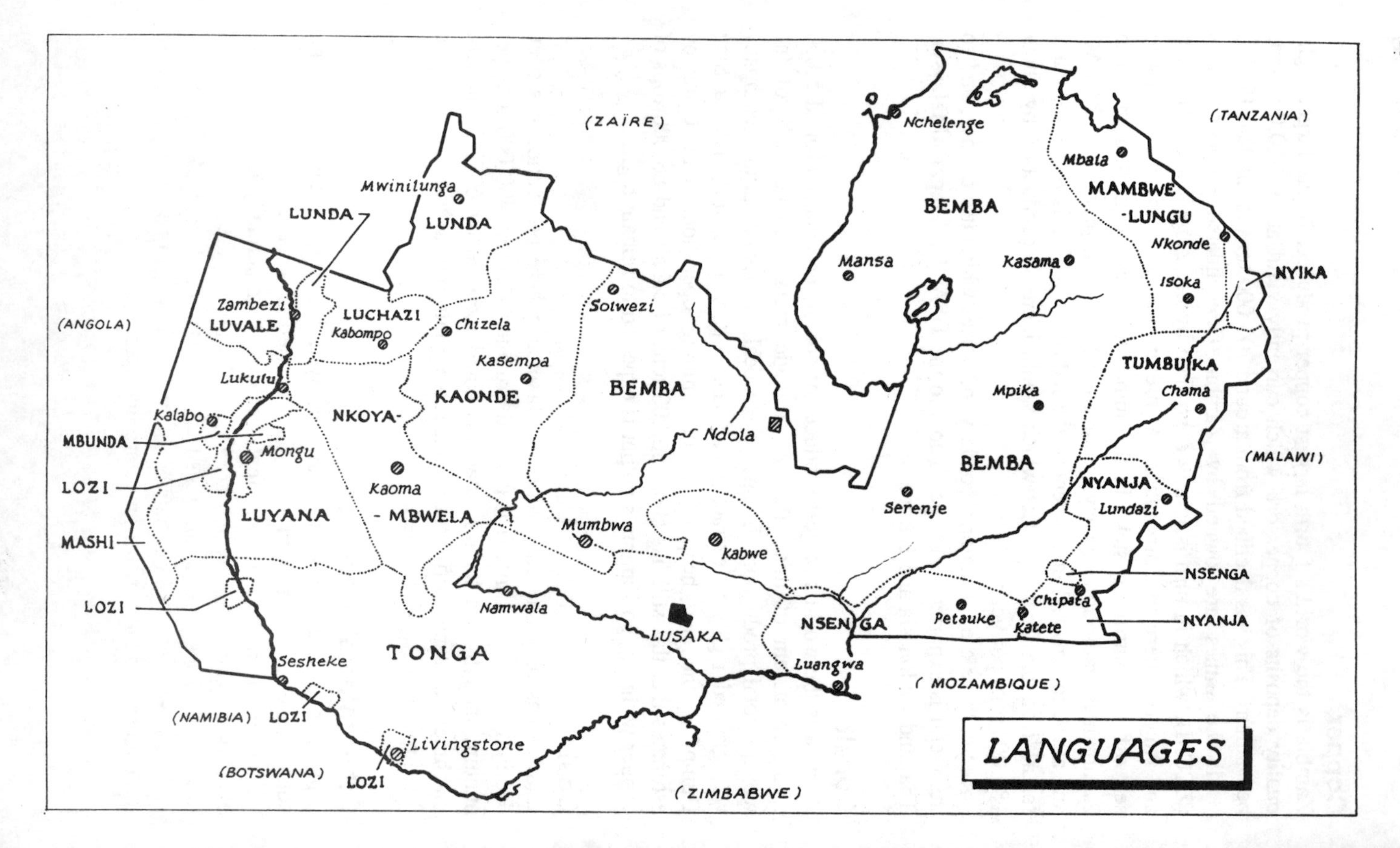
(ZAÏRE)
(TANZANIA)
(ANGOLA)
(MALAWI)
(MOZAMBIQUE)
(NAMIBIA)
(BOTSWANA)
(ZIMBABWE)
Nchelenge
Mbala
MAMBWE
-LUNGU
BEMBA
Mwinilunga
LUNDA
LUNDA
Nkonde
Mansa
Kasama
Isoka
NYIKA
Zambezi
LUVALE
LUCHAZI
Kabompo
Chizela
Solwezi
Kasempa
TUMBUKA
Lukulu
KAONDE
BEMBA
Mpika
Chama
Kalabo
NKOYA-
Ndola
MBUNDA
Mongu
BEMBA
Kaoma
NYANJA
LOZI
Lundazi
Serenje
LUYANA
- MBWELA
Mumbwa
MASHI
Kabwe
NSENGA
LOZI
Namwala
Chipata
Petauke
Katete
NSENGA
NYANJA
LUSAKA
Sesheke
TONGA
Luangwa
LOZI
Livingstone
LOZI
LANGUAGES

Chapter Three

People and Culture

PEOPLE

The population

Recent statistics suggest that Zambia's population stands at about nine million, and this is increasing by around 3% per year. About 49% of Zambia's population are under 15 years of age, whilst some 73% of those above age 15 are literate. About 10% of Zambians live in Lusaka.

Statistics indicate that the average life expectancy for a Zambian is 44 years. Around 99% of the population are black African in origin, and the remaining 1% are mostly people of European or Indian origin.

However, the statistics say nothing of the warmth that the sensitive visitor can encounter. If you venture into the rural areas, take a local bus, or try to hitchhike with the locals, you will often find that Zambians are curious about you. Chat to them openly, as fellow travellers, and you will find most Zambians to be delightful. They will be pleased to help you where they can, and as keen to help you learn about them and their country as they are interested in your lifestyle and what brings you to Zambia.

A note on "tribes"

The people of Africa are often viewed, from abroad, as belonging to a multitude of culturally and linguistically distinct tribes – which are often portrayed as being at odds with each other. Whilst there is certainly an enormous variety of different ethnic groups in Africa, most are closely related to their neighbours in terms of language, beliefs and way of life. Modern historians eschew the simplistic tags of "tribes", noting that such groupings change with time.

Sometimes the word tribe is used to describe a group of people who all speak the same language; it may be used to mean those who follow a particular leader or to refer to all the inhabitants of a certain area at a given time. In any case, tribe is a vague word which is used differently for different purposes. The term "clan" (blood relations) is a smaller, more precisely defined, unit – though rather too precise for our broad discussions here.

Certainly, at any given time, groups of people or clans who share similar language and cultural beliefs do band together and often, in time, develop "tribal" identities. However, it is wrong to then extrapolate and assume that their ancestors will have had the same groupings and allegiances centuries ago.

In Africa, as elsewhere in the world, history is recorded by the winners. Here the winners, the ruling class, may be the descendants of a small group of intruders who achieved dominance over a larger, long-established community. Over the years, the history of that ruling class (the winners) usually becomes regarded as the history of the whole community, or tribe. Two "tribes" have thus become one, with one history – which will reflect the origins of that small group of intruders, and not the ancestors of the majority of the current tribe.

Zambia is typical of a large African country. Currently historians and linguistics experts can identify at least 16 major cultural groupings, and more than 72 different dialects are spoken in the country. As you will see, there are cultural differences between the people in different parts of the country. However, these are no more pronounced than those between the states of the USA, or the different regions of the (relatively tiny) UK.

There continues to be lots of inter-marriage and mixing of these peoples and cultures – perhaps more so than there has ever been, due to the efficiency of modern transport systems. Generally, there is very little friction between these communities (whose boundaries, as we have said, are indistinct) and Zambia's various peoples live peacefully together.

African language groups

Below are detailed some of the major language groups, arranged alphabetically. This is only a rough guide to the many languages and dialects of Zambia's people. Although these different language groupings do loosely correspond to what many describe as Zambia's tribes, the distinctions are blurred further by the natural linguistic ability of most Zambians. Whilst it is normal to speak English plus one local language, many Zambians will speak a number of local languages fluently.

When the colonial powers carved up Africa, the divisions between the countries bore only a passing resemblance to the traditional areas of these various ethnic groups. Thus many of the groups here are split between several countries. Note that the estimates of populations quoted below are based on surveys done during the 1980s, and average estimated population growth rates since then.

Bemba

Bemba is the first language of about two and a quarter million Zambians: almost a quarter of the country's population. It is spoken in the rural areas of northern Zambia, from the Luapula River eastwards to Mpika, Kasama and beyond. Because people from these areas were the original workers in the mines of the Copperbelt, Bemba has subsequently achieved the status of *lingua franca* in the major urban areas of the Copperbelt and Lusaka.

It is recognised for administration and educational purposes within Zambia, whilst outside its borders Bemba is also spoken by over 150,000 people in Zaire, and around 37,000 in Tanzania.

Kaonde

Kaonde-speakers live mostly around the northern side of Kafue National Park, centring on the small towns of Kasempa and Chizela, and extending southeast as far as Mumbwa. They are one of Zambia's larger language groups, and probably number about 200,000.

RICH LANGUAGES

By Judi Helmholz

When considering where languages are at their richest and most descriptive, it is often noted that Eskimos have many ways of saying "snow". Each of their words describes a slightly different type of snow – the differences being too subtle to express so concisely in English. In a similar vein, Bantu languages have areas where they are more descriptive and colourful than plain English. For example, in Lozi no less than 40 words are used to mean "woman". All have slightly different implications. These include:

Liombe	a tall, beautiful woman
Cebucebu	a crafty, old woman
Katubaminzi	a woman who destroys village life by bad behaviour
Likula	a woman with many husbands
Kamundendule	a woman who speaks loudly and carelessly
Mumbulu	a doddering old woman
Namukuka	a woman not presently married
Njakati	a woman with a voracious appetite
Licenkenene	a stall, stout woman
Muketa	a thin, old woman.
Mubala	a newlywed, just arrived in her husband's village
Mushuwi	a woman fishing with a basket net
Njimikati	a woman who cultivates a lot

Lozi

There are about 500,000 Lozi-speakers in Zambia, concentrated in the western and southern provinces, around Barotseland and Livingstone. The centre of Lozi culture is the rich agricultural floodplain around the upper Zambezi River – and it is here that the Ku-omboka (see *Festivals*, page 25) takes place each year.

Luchazi

This language has only a small number of speakers, perhaps 70,000 in the west of Zambia – less than 1% of the country's population. There are thought to be a similar number of Luchazi-speaking people in Angola.

Lunda

Not to be confused with Luunda, which is a dialect of Bemba, Lunda is the first language of about 230,000 Zambians and is spoken in areas of the Copperbelt, as well as nearby Zaire and Angola. It is officially taught in primary schools, and can occasionally be heard on radio or seen in newspapers in the area.

Luvale

Luvale is an important language in Angola, where it is spoken by almost one million people. In Zambia there are only about 215,000 people whose first language is Luvale, and they live in the northwestern and western provinces of Zambia.

Luyana

The Luyana-speaking people are a small group, perhaps numbering 130,000 in total. Their language has not been well documented, though it is spoken in Zambia, Angola, Namibia and also Botswana. In Zambia it is found almost exclusively in the western province.

Mambwe-Lungu

These are other languages that need further study – so far they appear to differ from each other only slightly, as dialects would. In total about 280,000 Zambians count them as their first language – about 3% of the population. Their stronghold is in the northeast of the northern province, south of Lake Tanganyika. As you might expect, they are also spoken in Tanzania.

Mashi

Mashi seems to be spoken by only a tiny number of Zambians, perhaps only 25,000 people, who are often nomadic within a southwestern area of the western province. Little has been documented about this language –

though it has been noted that virtually all the native speakers of Mashi follow traditional religious practices, rather than the more recently introduced Christian beliefs.

Mbunda

The first language of about 130,000 Zambians, Mbunda is spoken in the north of Barotseland and the northern side of western Zambia – as well as in Angola.

Nkoya-Mbwela

Nkoya and Mbwela are two closely related languages. Mbwela is often referred to as a dialect of Nkoya, though here we have grouped them together as equals. They also have only a tiny number of speakers around 80,000 people – who are found around the Mankoya area, in Zambia's western and southern provinces.

Nsenga

There are thought to be over 330,000 people speaking Nsenga as their first language, of whom the vast majority live in Zambia. These are clustered around the area of Petauke – near to the borders with Zimbabwe and Mozambique, across which the language is also spoken.

Nyanja

Nyanja is the Bantu language most often encountered by visitors in Zambia. It is widely used in much of the country, including the key cities of Lusaka and Livingstone. Nyanja is sometimes described as not being a language *per se*, but rather a common skill enabling people of varying tribes living in Eastern, Central and Southern parts of Zambia and Malawi to communicate without following the strict grammar of specific local languages. In other words, like *Swahili* other "universal" languages, Nyanja is something of a *lingua franca* for Zambia.

Nyanja is certainly the official language of the police, and is widely used for administrative and educational purposes. About a million Zambians use Nyanja as their first language – mostly in the eastern and central areas of the country – and there may be double that number using the language in Malawi. Then there are around 330,000 Nyanja-speakers in Zimbabwe, and perhaps 500,000 in Mozambique. A total of approaching four million people in the subcontinent speak Nyanja as a first language.

Nyika

Also known as Nyiha, Nyika is spoken most widely in Tanzania, and also in Malawi. In Zambia it is used around the Isoka and Chama areas, across to the Malawi border. (It may be the same language as that known as Ichilambya in Tanzania and Malawi.)

Tonga

Tonga is the language of a small minority of Zimbabweans, many of whom were displaced south by the creation of Lake Kariba (see page 165). However, in Zambia it is the first language of around one million people, about 11% of the country's population, and is widely used in the media. Tonga is distributed throughout the south of the country, with its highest concentration in the middle Zambezi valley.

Tumbuka

Zambia has about 430,000 people who speak Tumbuka as a first language, mostly living on the eastern side of the country. Outside Zambia many Tumbuka-speakers live in Malawi and Tanzania, bringing the total number to about two million.

Other ethnic groups

White Zambians

There are a small number of white Zambians, very different from the expat community (see below) who are often white but simply working in the country on a temporary basis. Many white Zambians will trace their families back to colonial immigrants who came over during British rule, but most will regard themselves as Zambian rather than, say, British. This is generally an affluent group of people, and many of the country's businesses, and the vast majority of the safari companies, are owned and run by white Zambians.

Asian Zambians

Like the white Zambians, many people of Asian origin came here during the colonial period. Whilst the British ruled African colonies like Zambia as well as India, there was movement of labour from Asia to Africa. Now, like the white Zambians, this is generally an affluent group. On the whole, Zambians of Asian descent retain a very strong sense of Asian identity and culture, and many are traders or own small shops.

Expatriates

Distinct from Zambians, there is a large "expat" community in Zambia. These foreigners usually come to Zambia for two or three years, to work on short-term contracts, often for either multi-national companies or aid agencies. Most are highly skilled individuals who come to share their knowledge with Zambian colleagues – often teaching skills which are in short supply in Zambia.

CULTURE

Festivals

Zambia has several major cultural festivals which, on the whole, are rarely seen by visitors. If you can get to one, then you will find them to be very genuine occasions, where ceremonies are performed for the benefit of the local people and the participants, and not for the odd tourist who is watching.

Bear in mind that, like most celebrations worldwide, these are often accompanied by the large-scale consumption of alcohol. To see these festivals properly, and to appreciate them, you will need a good guide: someone who understands the rituals, can explain their significance, and can instruct you on how you should behave. After all, how would you feel about a passing Zambian traveller who arrives, with curiosity, at your sibling's wedding (a small festival), in the hope of being invited to the private reception?

Photographers will find superb opportunities at such colourful events, but should behave with sensitivity. Before you brandish your camera, remember to ask permission from anyone who might take offence.

The Ku-omboka

This is the most famous of the ceremonies, and takes place in the western province, around February or March, often on a Thursday, just before full moon. The precise date will only be known a week or so in advance, as it is decided upon by the Lozi king.

The Lozi Kingdom is closely associated with the fertile plains around the Upper Zambezi River. When dry, this well-defined area affords good grazing for livestock, and its rich alluvial soil is ideal for cultivation. It contrasts with the sparse surrounding woodland, growing on poor soil typical of the rest of western Zambia. So for much of the year, these plains support a dense population of subsistence farms.

However, towards the end of the rains, the Zambezi's water levels rise. The plains then become floodplains, and the settlements gradually become islands. The people must leave them for the higher ground, at the margins of the floodplain. This retreat from the advancing waters – known as the Ku-omboka – is traditionally led by the king himself, the Litunga, from his dry-season abode at Lealui, in the middle of the plain. He retreats with his court to his high-water residence, at Limulunga, on the eastern margins of the floodplain.

The Litunga's departure is heralded by the beating of three huge old royal war drums – Mundili, Munanga, and Kanaono. These continue to summon the people from miles around until the drums themselves are loaded above the royal barge: a very large wooden canoe built around the turn of the century and painted with vertical black-and-white stripes. The royal barge is then paddled and punted along by about one hundred polers, each sporting a skirt of animal skins and a white vest. Their scarlet hats are surmounted by tufts of fur taken from the mane of unfortunate lions.

The royal barge is guided by a couple of "scout" barges, painted white, which search out the right channels for the royal barge. Behind it comes the Litunga's wife, the Moyo, in her own barge, followed by local dignitaries, various attendants, many of the Litunga's subjects, and the odd visitor lucky enough to be in the area at the right time.

The journey takes most of the day, and the flotilla is accompanied by an impromptu orchestra of local musicians. When the royal barge finally arrives at Limulunga, the Litunga steps ashore sporting the uniform of an old English admiral, to spend an evening of feasting and celebrations, with much eating, drinking, music and traditional dancing.

Likumbi Lya Mize

The Luvale people of western Zambia have an annual "fair" type of celebration, which takes place for four or five days towards the end of August. "Likumbi Lya Mize" means "Mize day" and the event is held at the palace of the senior chief – at Mize, about 7km west of Zambezi.

This provides an opportunity for the people to see their senior chief, watch the popular Makishi dancers, and generally have a good time. As you might expect, there is also lots of eating and drinking, plus people in traditional dress, displays of local crafts, and singing.

Umutomboko

This is nothing to do with the *Ku-omboka*, described above. It is an annual celebration, performed in the last weekend of July, whereby the Senior Chief Kazeme celebrates his ancestral war dance. It is held in a specially prepared arena, close to the Ng'ona River, and accompanied by feasting and celebrations.

Shimungenga

This traditional gathering is held on the weekend of a full moon, in September or October, at Maala on the Kafue Flats – about 40km west of Namwala. Then the Ila people (whose language is closely related to Tonga) gather together as an act of devotion to their ancestors.

The N'cwala

On 24 February there is a thanksgiving festival at Mutenguleni village, near Chipata. This large celebration was recently revived, after 80 years of not being practised. Then traditional dancing and beer-drinking accompanies the first tasting the year's produce by Chief Mpezeni.

THATCHING A BUSH LODGE - E.H

Cultural guidelines

Comments here are intended to be a general guide, just a few examples of how to travel more sensitively. They should not be viewed as blueprints for perfect Zambian etiquette.Cultural sensitivity is really a state of mind, not a checklist of behaviour - so here we can only hope to give the sensitive traveller a few pointers in the right direction.

When we travel, we are all in danger of leaving negative impressions with local people that we meet. It is easily done - by snapping that picture quickly, whilst the subject is not looking; by dressing scantily, offending local sensitivities; by just brushing aside the feelings of local people, with the high-handed superiority of a rich Westerner. These things are easy to do, in the click of a shutter, or flash of a dollar bill.

However, you will get the most representative view of Zambia if you cause as little disturbance to the local people as possible. You will never blend in perfectly when you travel - your mere presence there, as an observer, will always change the local events slightly. However, if you try to fit in and show respect for local culture and attitudes, then you may manage to leave positive feelings behind you.

One of the easiest, and most important, ways to do this is with greetings. African societies are rarely as rushed as Western ones. When you first talk to someone, you should greet them leisurely. So, for example, if you enter a bus station and want some help, do not just ask outright, "Where is the bus to ..." That would be rude. Instead you will have a better reception (and better chance of good advice) by saying:

Traveller: "Good afternoon."
Zambian: "Good afternoon."
Traveller: "How are you?"
Zambian: "I am fine, how are you?"
Traveller: "I am fine, thank you. *(pause)* Do you know where the bus to ..."

This goes for approaching anyone - always greet them first. For a better reception still, learn these phrases of greeting in the local language (see pages 306-7). English-speakers are often lazy about learning languages, and, whilst most Zambians understand English, a greeting given in an appropriate local language will be received with delight. It implies that you are making an effort to learn a little of their language and culture, which is always appreciated.

Occasionally, in the town or city, you may be approached by someone who doesn't greet you, but tries immediately to sell you something, or even hassle you in some way. These people have learned that foreigners aren't used to greetings, and so have adapted their approach accordingly. An effective way to dodge their attentions is to reply to their questions with a formal greeting, and then politely – but firmly – refuse their offer. This is surprisingly effective.

Another part of the normal greeting ritual is handshaking. As elsewhere, you would not normally shake a shop-owner's hand, but you would shake hands with someone to whom you are introduced. Get some practice when you arrive, as there is a gentle, three-part handshake used in Southern African which is easily learnt.

Your clothing is an area that can easily give offence. Skimpy, revealing clothing is frowned upon by most Zambians, especially when worn by women. Shorts are fine for walking safaris, but dress conservatively and avoid short shorts, especially in the more rural areas. Respectable locals will wear long trousers (men) or long skirts (women).

Photography is a tricky business. Most Zambians will be only too happy to be photographed – provided you ask their permission first. Sign language is fine for this question: just point at your camera, shrug your shoulders, and look quizzical. The problem is that then everyone will smile for you, producing the type of "posed" photograph which you probably do not want. However, stay around and chat for five or ten minutes more, and people will get used to your presence, stop posing and you will get more natural shots of them (a camera with a quiet shutter is a help).

Note that special care is needed with photography near government buildings, bridges, and similar sites of strategic importance. You must ask permission before photographing anything here, or you risk people thinking that you are a spy.

The specific examples above can only be taken so far – they are general by their very nature. But wherever you find yourself, if you are polite and considerate to the Zambians you meet, then you will rarely encounter any cultural problems. Watch how they behave, and if you have any doubts about how you should act, then ask someone quietly. They will seldom tell you outright that you are being rude, but they will usually give you good advice on how to make your behaviour more acceptable.

INEXPLICABLE ZAMBIA

Judi Helmholz

There are always challenges to be overcome when living, working or travelling in a foreign country. One day we asked an old colonial farmer for advice. He was 60 years old, born and raised here. "How long do you have to be here before you can truly understand this country," we queried, hoping for some words of wisdom. "I can't answer that, you'll have to ask someone who has been here longer," he replied in a matter-of-fact tone.

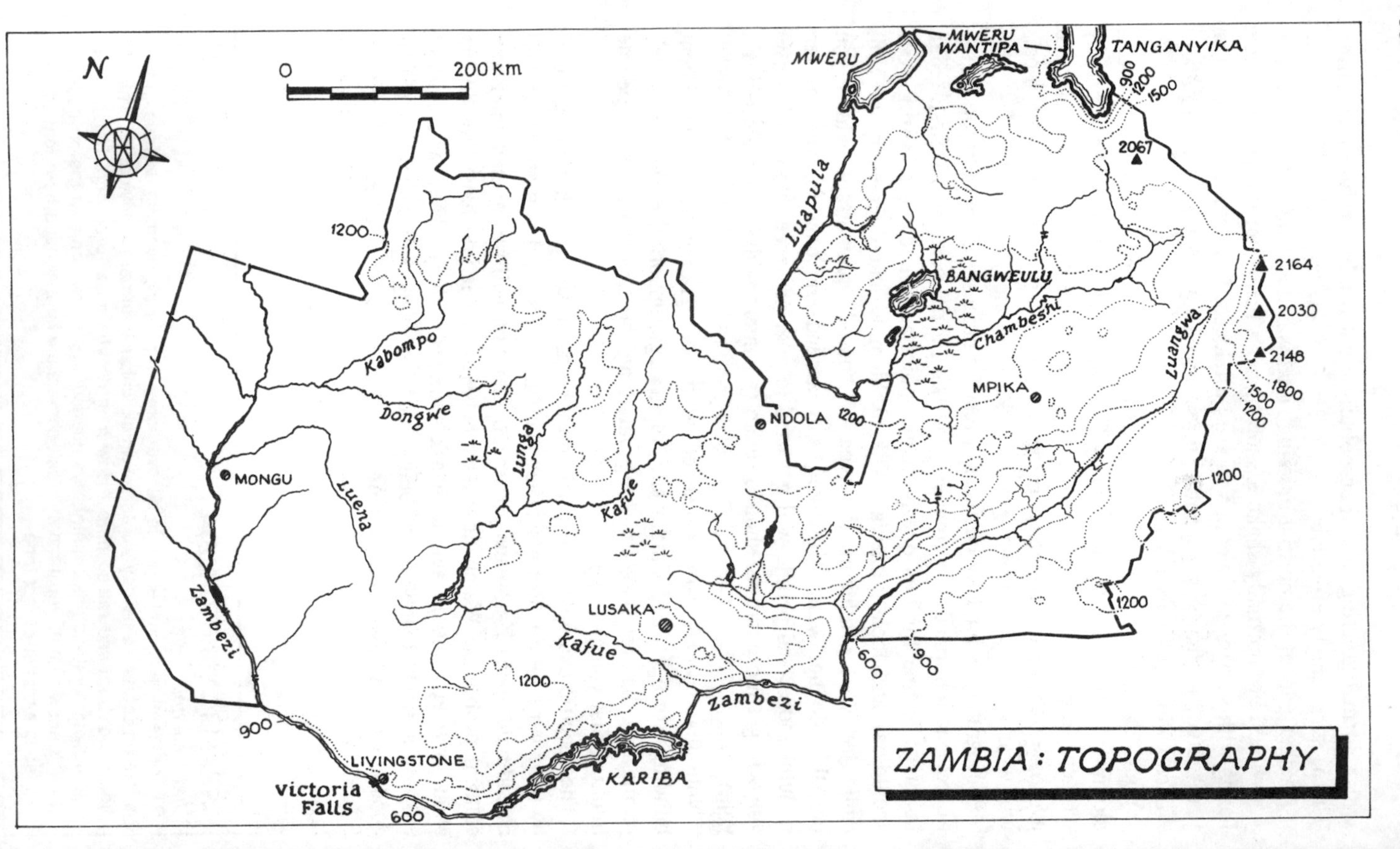
ZAMBIA : TOPOGRAPHY
N
0
200 km
MWERU
MWERU WANTIPA
TANGANYIKA
900
1200
1500
2067
2164
2030
2148
1800
1500
1200
1200
1200
Luapula
BANGWEULU
Chambeshi
Luangwa
MPIKA
NDOLA
1200
1200
Kabompo
Dongwe
Lunga
MONGU
Luena
Kafue
LUSAKA
Kafue
1200
600
900
Zambezi
Zambezi
900
LIVINGSTONE
KARIBA
Victoria Falls
600

Chapter Four

The Natural Environment

PHYSICAL ENVIRONMENT

Geology and topology

Zambia lies landlocked between the Tropic of Capricorn and the Equator, shaped like a giant butterfly and covering about 752,610km². Most of this is part of the high, undulating plateau that forms the backbone of the African continent. Most of Zambia has an altitude of between 1,000m and 1,600m, whilst only a few of the low-lying rift valleys sit below 500m.

Zambia's oldest rocks, known as the Basement Complex, were laid down at an early stage in the pre-Cambrian era – as long as 2,000 million years ago. These were extensively eroded and covered by sediments which now form the Katanga system of rocks, dating from around 1,000 to 620 million years ago. These are what we now see near the surface in most of northeast and central Zambia, and they contain the important mineral deposits of the Copperbelt. Later still, from about 300 to 150 million years ago, the karoo system of sedimentary rocks was deposited: sandstones, mudstones, conglomerates and even coal. Towards the end of this era, molten rock seeped up through cracks in the crust, and covered areas of western Zambia in layers of basalt – the rock that is seen cut away by the Zambezi River in the gorges below Victoria Falls.

About 150 million years ago, during the Jurassic era of the dinosaurs, Africa was still part of Gondwana – a super-continent which included South America, India, Australasia and Antarctica. Since then Zambia's highlands have been eroded down from an original altitude of over 1,800m (Nyika Plateau is still at this altitude), to their present lower levels.

Very recently, perhaps only a few million years ago, the subcontinent had a dry phase which saw sands from the Kalahari Desert blow far across southern Africa, and much of western Zambia now lies beneath a covering of Kalahari sand... as will becomes evident the moment you try to drive in western Zambia.

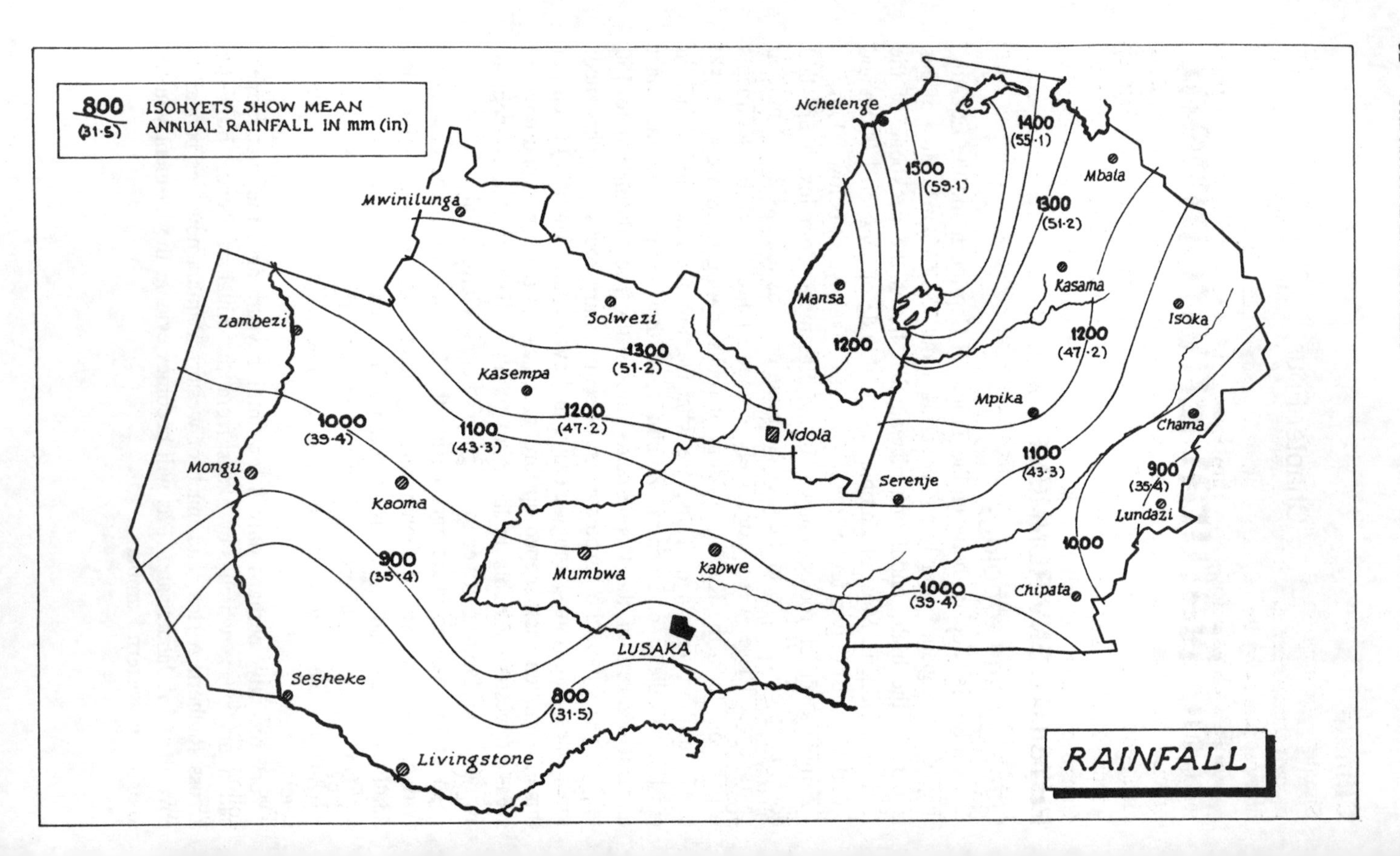
800 (31·5) ISOHYETS SHOW MEAN ANNUAL RAINFALL IN mm (in)
Nchelenge
1400 (55·1)
Mbala
1500 (59·1)
1300 (51·2)
Mwinilunga
Mansa
Kasama
Isoka
Zambezi
Solwezi
1200
1300 (51·2)
1200 (47·2)
Kasempa
Mpika
1000 (39·4)
1100 (43·3)
1200 (47·2)
Ndola
Chama
1100 (43·3)
Mongu
900 (35·4)
Kaoma
Serenje
Lundazi
1000
900 (35·4)
Mumbwa
Kabwe
1000 (39·4)
Chipata
LUSAKA
Sesheke
800 (31·5)
Livingstone
RAINFALL

Climate

Situated squarely in the tropics, Zambia gets lots of strong sunlight, though the intense heat normally associated with the tropics is moderated in most places by the country's altitude, and its rainfall.

Zambia's climate follows a similar pattern to most of southern Africa, with rainfall when the sun is near its zenith, from November to April. The precise timing and duration of this is determined by the interplay of three air-streams: the moist "Congo" air-mass, the north-eastern monsoon winds, and the south-eastern trade winds. The water-bearing air is the Congo air-mass, which normally brings rain when it moves south into Zambia from Central Africa. This means that the northern areas, around Lakes Tanganyika and Mweru, receive the first rainfall – often in early November. This belt of rain will then work south, arriving in southern Zambia by the end of November or the start of December.

As the sun's intensity reduces, the Congo air-mass moves back north, leaving southern Zambia dry by around late March, and ceasing rain in the north by late April or May. Most areas receive their heaviest rainfall in January, though some of the most northern areas have two peaks: one in December and one in March. This twin-peak cycle is more characteristic of central and eastern Africa. The heaviest total rainfall is found in the north, and the lightest in the south.

Lusaka's climate statistics are typical of the pleasant climate found in the higher areas of southern and central Zambia:

	Temp°C		Temp°F		Humidity%		Rainfall
	max	min	max	min	am	pm	mm
Jan	26	17	78	62	84	71	231
Feb	26	17	78	62	85	80	191
Mar	26	17	78	62	83	56	142
Apr	26	15	78	59	71	47	18
May	25	12	77	52	59	37	3
Jun	23	10	73	50	56	32	0
Jul	23	9	73	48	54	28	0
Aug	25	12	77	53	46	26	0
Sep	29	15	84	59	41	19	0
Oct	31	18	87	64	39	23	15
Nov	29	18	84	64	57	46	91
Dec	27	17	80	62	76	61	150

The lower-lying valleys, including the Luangwa and Lower Zambezi, follow the same broad pattern but are considerably hotter throughout the year. In October, which is universally the hottest month, temperatures there will often reach over 45°C in the shade.

FLORA AND FAUNA

Vegetation types

As with animals, each species of plant has its favourite conditions. External factors determine where each species thrives, and where it will perish. These include temperature, light, water, soil type, nutrients, and what other species of plants and animals live in the same area. Species with similar needs are often found together, in communities which are characteristic of that particular environment. Zambia has a number of different such communities, or typical "vegetation types" within its borders – each of which is distinct from the others. The more common include:

Mopane woodland

The dominant tree here is the remarkably adaptable mopane (*Colophospermum mopane*), which is sometimes known as the butterfly tree because of the shape of its leaves. It is very tolerant of poorly drained or alkaline soils, and those with a high clay content. This tolerance results in the mopane having a wide range of distribution throughout southern Africa; in Zambia it occurs mainly in the hotter, drier, lower parts of the country, including the Luangwa and Zambezi valleys.

Mopane trees can attain a height of 25m, especially if growing on rich, alluvial soils. However, shorter trees are more common in areas which are poor in nutrients, or have suffered from extensive fire damage. Stunted mopane will form a low scrub, perhaps only 5m tall. All mopane trees are deciduous, and the leaves turn beautiful shades of yellow and red before falling in September and October.

Ground cover in mopane woodland is usually sparse, just thin grasses, herbs and the occasional bush. The trees themselves are an important source of food for game, as the leaves have a high nutritional value – rich in protein and phosphorus – which is favoured by browsers and is retained even after they have fallen from the trees. Mopane forests support large populations of rodents, including tree squirrels (*Peraxerus cepapi*), which are so typical of these areas that they are known as "mopane squirrels".

Miombo woodland

Without human intervention, the natural vegetation of most of Zambia (about 70%) is miombo woodland and its associated *dambos* (see below). This exists on Zambia's main plateau, and its adjacent escarpments, where the acid soils are not particularly fertile and have often been leached of minerals by the water run-off.

Miombo woodland consists of a mosaic of large wooded areas and smaller, more open spaces, dotted with clumps of trees and shrubs.

Dominant trees are *Brachystegia*, *Julbernardia* and *Isoberlinia* species – most of which are at least partially fire-resistant. There is more variation of species in miombo than in mopane woodland, and the ground cover is less sparse.

Munga woodland

The word "munga" means thorn, and this is the thorny woodland which occurs when open grassland has been invaded by trees and shrubs – normally because of some disturbance like cultivation, fire or overgrazing. *Acacia*, *Terminalia* (bearing single-winged seeds) and *Combretum* (bearing seeds with four or five wings) are the dominant species, but many others can be present.

Teak forest

In a few areas of south-western Zambia (including the southern part of Kafue National Park), the Zambezi teak, *Baikaea plurijuga*, forms dry semi-evergreen forests on a base of Kalahari sand. This species is not fire-resistant, so these stands only occur where slash-and-burn type cultivation methods have never been used. Below the tall teak is normally a dense, deciduous thicket of vegetation, interspersed with sparse grasses and herbs in the shadier spots of the forest floor.

Moist evergreen forest

In the areas of higher rainfall (mostly in the north of Zambia), and near rivers, streams, lakes and swamps, where a tree's roots will have permanent access to water, dense evergreen forests arc found. Many species occur, and this lush vegetation is characterised by having three levels: a canopy of tall trees, a sub-level of smaller trees and bushes, and a variety of ground-level vegetation. In effect, the environment is so good for plants that they have adapted to exploit the light from every sunbeam.

This type of vegetation is sometimes further subdivided into *montane* forests, found on the lower slopes of mountains where the rainfall is high; *swamp* forests, near to some of Zambia's permanent swamps (see Kasanka National Park for some excellent examples); and *riparian* forests (sometimes called riverine forests), which line Zambia's major rivers.

Dambo

A dambo is a shallow grass depression, or small valley, that is either permanently or seasonally waterlogged. This corresponds closely to what is known as a "vlei" in other parts of the subcontinent. These open, verdant dips in the landscape often appear in the midst of miombo woodlands and support no bushes or trees. In higher valleys amongst hills, they will sometimes form the sources of streams and rivers. Because of their permanent dampness, they are rich in species of grasses, herbs and flowering plants, like orchids – and are excellent grazing (if a little exposed) for antelope. Their margins are usually thickly vegetated by grasses, herbs and smaller shrubs.

Floodplain

Floodplains are the low-lying grasslands on the edges of river, streams, lakes and swamps which are seasonally inundated by floods. Zambia has some huge areas of floodplain most obviously beside the Kafue River, in the Barotseland area around the Zambezi, and south of the permanent Bangweulu Swamps. These contain no trees or bushes, just a low carpet of grass species which can tolerate being submerged for part of the year.

Montane grassland

More common in other areas of Africa, montane grassland occurs on mountain slopes at higher altitudes where the precipitation is heavy and the climate cool. Zambia's best examples of this are on Nyika Plateau.

Pan

Though not an environment for rich vegetation, a pan is a shallow, seasonal pool of water with no permanent streams leading into it or out of it. The bush is full of small pans in the rainy season, most of which will dry up soon after the rains cease.

Animals

Zambia's large mammals are typical of the savannah areas of east and (especially) southern Africa. The large predators are here: lion, leopard, cheetah, wild dog and spotted hyena, although cheetah and wild dog are relatively uncommon.

Elephant and buffalo occur in large herds in protected national parks, and in small, furtive family groups where poaching is a problem. Black rhino are probably, sadly, extinct in Zambia, though there are white rhino in the small, well protected, Mosi Oa Tunya National Park at Livingstone.

Antelope are well represented, with puku and impala being numerically dominant in the drier areas. There are several interesting, endemic subspecies found in Zambia, including the Angolan and Thornicroft's giraffe, Cookson's wildebeest, and two unusual subspecies of lechwe – the black and the Kafue Flats lechwe – occurring in very large numbers in some of the country's more marshy areas.

Because Zambia is a wet country, with numerous marshy areas, its natural vegetation is lush and capable of supporting a high density of game. The country has a natural advantage over drier areas, and this accounts for the sheer volume of big game to be found in its better parks.

Birdlife

Much of Zambia is still covered by original, undisturbed natural vegetation, and hunting is not a significant factor for most of Zambia's 733 recorded species of birds. Thus, with a range of verdant and natural habitats, Zambia is a superb birding destination.

Whilst the animal species differ only occasionally from the "normal" species found in southern Africa, the birds are a much more varied mix of those species found in southern and in eastern and even central Africa. The obvious celebrity is the ungainly shoebill stork - which breeds in the Bangweulu Swamps, and only one or two other places in central Africa. However, there are many other unusual, rare and beautifully coloured species that attract enthusiasts to Zambia.

In addition to its resident bird species, Zambia receives many migrants. In September and October the Palaearctic migrants appear (ie: those that come from the northern hemisphere - normally Europe), and they remain here until around April or May. This is also the peak time to see the intra-African migrants, which come from further north in Africa.

The rains from December to around April see an explosion in the availability of most birds' food: seeds, fruits and insects. Hence this is the prime time for birds to nest, even if it is also the most difficult time to visit the more remote areas of the country.

Field guides

Finding good, detailed field guides to plants, animals and birds in Zambia is tricky. Some excellent, very comprehensive guides on the flora and fauna of both East and Southern Africa have been written, which are often invaluable in Zambia. However, for total coverage and certainty of identification, you will need both sets of books - because Zambia's natural environment contains species which are typical of both areas, existing at the edge of their range in Zambia.

For the traveller with less space, some smaller, less detailed guides to the more common species found in Zambia are now being produced by the Wildlife Conservation Society of Zambia (see page 102), which are ideal for more general game viewing and bird watching. See *Further Reading*, page 308-9, for recommendations and more details.

CONSERVATION

A great deal has been written about conservation in Africa, much of which is over-simplistic and intentionally emotive. As an informed visitor you are in the unique position of being able to see some of the issues at first hand, and to appreciate the perspectives of local people. So abandon your preconceptions, and start by appreciating the complexities of the issues involved. Here I shall try to develop a few ideas common to most current thinking on conservation; ideas to which the text in the rest of the book only briefly alludes.

Firstly, *conservation* must be taken within its widest sense if it is to have meaning. Saving animals is of minimal use if the whole environment is degraded, so we must consider conserving whole areas and ecosystems, not just the odd isolated species.

Observe that land is regarded as an asset by most societies, in Africa as it is elsewhere. To "save" the land for the animals, and use it merely for the recreation of a few privileged foreign tourists – whilst the local people remain in poverty – is a recipe for huge social problems. Local people have hunted game animals for food for centuries. They have always killed those which threatened them, or ruined their crops. If we now try to proclaim animals in a populated area as protected, without addressing the concerns of the people, then our efforts will fail.

The only pragmatic way to conserve Zambia's wild areas is to see the *development* of the local people, and the conservation of the animals and the environment, as two inter-linked goals.

In the long term one will not work without the other. Conservation without development leads to resentful locals who will happily, and frequently, shoot, trap and kill animals. Development without conservation will simply repeat the mistakes that most developed countries have already made: it will lay waste a beautiful land, and kill off its natural heritage. Look at the tiny areas of natural vegetation which survive undisturbed in the UK, the USA, or Japan, to see how unsuccessful they have been at long-term conservation over the last 500 years.

As an aside, the local people in Zambia are often wrongly accused of being the only agents of degradation. Observe the importation of tropical hardwoods by the Western world to see the problems that the West's demands place on the natural environment in the developing world.

In conserving some of Zambia's natural areas, and developing her people, the international community has a vital role to play. It could effectively encourage the Zambian government to practise sustainable long-term strategies, rather than grasping for the short-term fixes which politicians seem universally to prefer. But such solutions must have the backing of the people themselves, or they will fall apart when the foreign aid budgets eventually wane.

In practice, to get this backing from the local communities, it is not enough for a conservation strategy to be compatible with development. Most Zambians are more concerned about where they live, what they can eat, and how they will survive, than they are about the lives of small, obscure species of antelope that taste good when roasted.

To work in Africa, conservation must not only be compatible with development, it must actually promote it, and help the local people to improve their own standard of living. If that situation can be reached, then local communities can be mobilised behind long-term conservation initiatives.

Governments are the same. As Luangwa's famous conservationist Norman Carr once commented, "governments won't conserve an impala just because it is pretty". But they will work to save it *if* they can see that it is worth more to them alive than dead.

The best strategies tried so far on the continent attempt to find lucrative sustainable ways to use the land. They then plough much of the revenue back into the surrounding local communities. Once the local communities see revenue from conservation being used to help them improve their lives – to build houses, clinics and schools, and to offer paid employment – then such schemes rapidly get their backing and support.

Carefully planned, sustainable tourism is one solution that can work effectively. For success, the local communities must see that the visitors pay because they want the wildlife. Thus, they reason that the existence of wildlife directly improves their income, and they will strive to conserve it.

It isn't enough for people to see that the wildlife helps the government to get richer; that won't dissuade a local hunter from shooting a duiker for dinner. However, if he is directly benefiting from the visitors, who come to see the animals... then he has a vested interest in saving that duiker.

It matters little to the Zambian people, or ultimately to the wildlife, whether these visitors come to shoot the wildlife with a camera or with a gun – as long as any hunting is done on a sustainable basis (ie: only a few of the oldest "trophy" animals are shot each year, and the size of the animal population remains largely unaffected). Photographers may claim the moral high-ground, but should remember that hunters pay far more for their privileges. Hunting operations generate large revenues from few guests, who demand minimal infrastructure and so cause little impact on the land. Photographic operations need more visitors to generate the same revenue, and so may cause greater negative effects on the country.

National parks and GMAs

In practice, there is room for both types of visitors in Zambia: the photographer and the hunter. The national parks are designated for photographic visitors, where no hunting is allowed, and around these are large areas designated as Game Management Areas. GMAs contain settlements, but hunting is meant to be controlled and practised sustainably. They are used by both local and overseas hunters, and the latter pay handsomely for the privilege.

The theory of GMAs is good, but unfortunately their administration is difficult. In many of them hunting by the local people is uncontrolled and has effectively wiped out much of the game. There are projects which aim to reverse this trend... but much more needs to be done if there is to be any country-wide, long-term effect.

Tourism

Zambia lies in the heart of sub-Saharan Africa. To the northeast lie the "original" safari areas of East Africa: Kenya and Tanzania. Some of their best parks are now rather crowded, though their wildlife spectacles are still on a very grand scale. South of Zambia are the more subtle attractions of Zimbabwe, Botswana and Namibia. Each country draws its own type of wildlife enthusiasts, and all have an element of wilderness that can seem difficult to find in East Africa today.

All have embraced tourism in different ways. Zambia is fortunate in having addressed this question later than the others, with the chance to learn from the mistakes of its neighbours. It is hoped that sustainable "eco" tourism can be a saviour of Zambia's economy as well as its wildlife, though there is a long way to go before tourism contributes a sizeable slice of the country's revenue.

Tourism is helping Zambia - both in economic terms, and with conservation. It is providing employment and bringing foreign exchange into the country, which gives the politicians a reason to support the preservation of the parks. That said, many of the Zambian safari operators have yet to realise that greater efforts must be made towards the development objectives of the local people. Many of the lodges in the rest of southern Africa, and especially the "campfire" schemes in Zimbabwe, show excellent models for how things could be developed. Zambia would be wise to learn fast.

The visitor on an expensive safari is, by his or her mere presence, making some financial contribution to development and conservation in Zambia. Perhaps the single greatest thing that they can do further is to ask their safari operator, in the most penetrating of terms: what do *they* do to help local development initiatives? How much of *their* revenue goes directly back to the local people? How do the local people benefit directly from the visitors at *this* camp? How much of a say do the local people have in what goes on in the area in which *these* safaris are operated?

If enough visitors did this, it would make a big difference. All Zambia's operators would start to place development initiatives higher on their list of priorities. At present most operators have some form of small "charity" donation to the local communities, but few get locals involved in any meaningful way beyond employment as camp workers and scouts. If they would look to the inspiring projects in the rest of southern Africa, and wake up to the fact that the local people must benefit more (and more directly) from tourism if conservation is going to be successful in Zambia.

Hunting

Big game hunting, where visiting hunters pay large amounts to kill trophy animals, is a practical source of revenue in the long term for people living in the country's GMAs. In a few areas this is already working, though in many there is just not enough game to attract the big-spending international clients that this type of system requires. Several aid agencies, including the World Wide Fund for Nature (WWF), are working to help sustainable schemes develop.

Poaching

After tales of government corruption and complicity with poachers, those travellers who have not ventured into Zambia can be forgiven for asking, "Is there any game left in Zambia?" The answer is a definitive "yes."

The 1970s and especially 1980s saw rampant hunting in the GMAs, and considerable poaching of Zambia's National Parks - partly small-scale hunting for food by local people, and partly large commercial poaching operations. The government reaction to this was a mixture of indifference and, allegedly, complicity. The only national park with an appreciable number of foreign visitors, South Luangwa, was effectively defended from all but the persistent infiltrations of specialist rhino-poachers. Other parks were, to various extents, neglected. Most still suffer from the results of that past neglect even now.

However, various parks and GMAs are now, once again, being developed for visitors. With that development comes a reason to protect the parks (as well as a financial motivation - see *Conservation*, above). Kafue's game populations are almost back to normal, as are those in the Lower Zambezi National Park. Both Kasanka and North Luangwa are being effectively protected with the help of two very different private conservation initiatives, and the WWF is working hard to help the local people earn an income from the sustainable utilisation of wildlife around the Bangweulu Swamps. Camps are opening up along the upper reaches of the Zambezi, and the remote parks of Sioma Ngwezi and Liuwa Plain are once again receiving the odd organised safari.

So the message from Zambia is upbeat. The main parks have excellent game populations, and many more are gradually recovering. Unlike much of Africa, Zambia has not generally been ravaged by overgrazing, and so even the parks that have suffered from poaching have usually managed to retain their natural vegetation in pristine condition. This gives hope that excellent game populations can eventually be re-established, and that these vast tracts of land can once again be returned to their natural state.

SECRETARY BIRD – E.H

Chapter Five

Planning and Preparations

GETTING THERE

By air

Since Zambia Airways went into liquidation in December 1994, flights have been the most difficult aspect of a trip to Zambia. The main flights from Europe to Lusaka are with British Airways or KLM. BA flies non-stop from London once a week, and via Harare twice. KLM operates directly from Amsterdam twice a week. These routes are mainly business traffic and pre-booked holidays; cheap "bucket-shop" tickets are uncommon. Expect to pay a minimum of £650/US$1,000 for a return flight. Tour operators have access to cheaper seats, but you will only be able to buy these if you are buying a complete holiday from them.

If you want a cheap flight, then consider using one of the nearby regional centres, and connecting through to Zambia. Harare is easily reached using various carriers including Air Zimbabwe, KLM, British Airways and Lufthansa. Expect London-Harare prices from about £500/US$750. There are frequent flights from Harare to Victoria Falls, as well as Lusaka – or you can easily travel overland by bus.

Windhoek, in Namibia, has good international connections with Air Namibia to London and Frankfurt – and operates an excellent regional service to Livingstone and Lusaka.

Johannesburg is very well served internationally, by South African Airways and many other carriers – including Virgin Airlines and several charter companies from the UK. From Johannesburg, SAA has connections to Zambia, as does Zambia Express and Aero Zambia.

Similarly from Nairobi: Kenya Airways and Aero Zambia have connections; from Lilongwe, Air Malawi will connect through; and from Dar, Air Tanzania has the flights.

If you are coming from the US then you will probably need to stop at London, Amsterdam or Johannesburg to make connections to Zamibia, as there are no direct flights. Booking everything in the US may not save you money – investigate the flight prices in comparison to those available in London.

However you get to the subcontinent, if you do not fly directly to Lusaka then try to book your intercontinental flight with a carrier who can offer you a regional flight into Zambia. Booking the whole trip together, you can often find reasonably cheap deals available (eg: Windhoek-Livingstone or Windhoek-Lusaka with London-Windhoek on Air Namibia, or Harare-Victoria Falls with London-Harare on Air Zimbabwe).

Note that there is a US$20 departure tax for all international flights from Lusaka or Livingstone - payable at departure only in US$, cash.

Crossing borders

Most borders open from about 06.00 to 18.00, although this is less rigidly adhered to at the smaller, more remote posts.

To/from Zimbabwe

Zambia's greatest flow of visitors come from Zimbabwe, over the Livingstone-Victoria Falls border. Many come over for just a daytrip, so this is usually a very relaxed, swift border crossing. The crossings over the Kariba Dam and at Chirundu are also straightforward, and the latter is especially good for hitchhiking on long-distance lorries, which ply the route from Harare to Lusaka.

To/from Botswana

Despite its territory only meeting at a point with Zambia, Botswana does have one border crossing with Zambia: a reliable ferry across the Zambezi linking Kazungula with the corner of Botswana, which costs about US$25/£17 per vehicle.

To/from Namibia

There is a ferry crossing, again costing about US$25/£17 per vehicle, between Zambia and Katima Mulilo in Namibia. This can be linked with the Kazungula ferry by a relatively smooth drive through Namibia and Botswana, to provide an alternative route between Sesheke and Kazungula. Though it takes much longer, and involves several border crossings, using the ferries does avoid the terrible road on the Zambian side of the Zambezi. See *The road to Sesheke*, in *Chapter Ten*, for more details.

To/from Angola

Angola is, at the time of writing, still not regarded as a safe country to visit. The easiest border post with Angola is near Chavuma, northwest of Zambezi town...elsewhere in western Zambia there is a danger of accidentally wandering into Angola, as the border has few markings.

To/from Zaire

There are numerous crossings between Zambia and Zaire, especially around the Copperbelt. Otherwise there is a good track leading into Zaire at Jimbe Bridge, reached via Mwinilunga and Kalene Hill.

To/from Tanzania

Many visitors from Tanzania (and a few from Burundi or Zaire) enter Zambia by ferry boat across Lake Tanganyika, into Mpulungu. The main alternative is the land border, either by road crossing or by TAZARA train, crossing east of Tunduma. See *Chapter Fifteen*, and the section on *Kapiri Mposhi*, for more details of TAZARA's important rail link between Zambia and Dar es Salaam.

To/from Malawi

The main crossing between Zambia and Malawi is east of Chipata. This would also be the swiftest way to reach the Nyika Plateau, as the roads in Malawi are better than those to Nyika in Zambia.

To/from Mozambique

There is a land crossing between Zambia and Mozambique south of Katete, west of Chipata, though this is not often used. A more common route would be via Malawi or Zimbabwe.

ENTRY REQUIREMENTS

Citizens of Commonwealth countries do not require visas, except those from Cyprus, Ghana, India, Nigeria, Sri Lanka and Pakistan. Most EC citizens do require visas, except for the UK, Ireland and Denmark. US citizens need visas, whilst most citizens of neighbouring Southern African countries (including South Africa) do not. That said, it is best to check the situation with your local embassy, high commission, or tourist board office (see below) before you travel, as these rules and exemptions do change from time to time.

The maximum length of stay normally awarded is 3 months. You may be asked to show an onward ticket, or at least that you can support yourself as you pass through the country (credit cards are invaluable).

When Kaunda ruled the country, Zambia effectively discouraged visitors. The government fostered a paranoia about foreign press and spies, and so visitors were routinely treated with suspicion – especially those with cameras. Fortunately this has now changed, and the prevailing attitude amongst both the government and the people is very welcoming. Visitors are seen as good for the country because they spend valuable foreign currency – so if you look respectable then you will not find any difficulties in entering Zambia.

Given this logic, and the conservative nature of local Zambian customs, the converse is also true. If you dress very untidily, looking as if you've no money, when entering via an overland border, then you may be questioned as to how you will be funding your trip. Dressing respectably in Zambia is not only courteous, but it can also make your life easier.

Zambia's diplomatic missions abroad

Australia: Zambian High Commission, Box 517, Canberra Rex Hotel, Canberra City Act 2601, Canberra

Botswana: Zambian High Commission, Zambia House, Plot 1118, The Mall, Box 362, Gaborone. Tel: 351951; fax: 353952

Canada: Zambian High Commission, 130 Albert Street, STL, 1610 Otawa, Ontario K1P5G4

France: Zambian Embassy, 76 Avenue o'Jena 75116, Paris

India: Zambian High Commission, 14 Jor Bagh, New Delhi 110003

Japan: Zambian Embassy, 9-19 Ebisu 3-Chrome, Shibuya-Ku, CPO Box 1738, Tokyo

Kenya: Zambian High Commission, City Hall Annex, Box 48741, Nairobi

Malawi: Zambian High Commission, Box 30138, Capital Hill, Lilongwe

Tanzania: Zambian High Commission, Box 2525, Plots 5 and 9, Ohio Street, Sokoine Street Junction, Dar es Salaam

UK: Zambian High Commission, 2 Palace Gate, London W2. Tel: 0171 589 6655

USA: Zambian Embassy, 2419 Massachusetts NW, Washington DC 20008. Tel: 202 265 9717; fax: 202 265

Zimbabwe: Zambian High Commission, Zambia House, 48 Union Avenue, Box 4698, Harare. Tel: 04 790851/5; fax: 04 790856

Zambia National Tourist Board offices

Australia: c/o Orbitair International, 36 Clarence Street, Sydney, NSW 2000. Tel: 02 9299 5300; fax: 02 9290 2665

Italy: c/o Relazioni Turishche, Via Mauro Macchi 42, 20124 Milan. Tel: 02 6690341; fax: 02 66987381

Hungary: c/o CRS International, Radnoti Miklos U 40, H-1137 Budapest. Tel: 01 269 5092; fax: 01 131 3960

South Africa: Finance House, Ernest Oppenheimer Road, Johannesburg. Tel: 011 622 9206/7; fax: 011 622 7424

UK: 2 Palace Gate, Kensington, London W8 5NG. Tel: 0171 589 6343; fax: 0171 225 3221

USA: 237 East 52nd Street, New York, NY 10022. Tel: 212 308 2155; fax: 212 758 1319

WHEN TO GO

Weather

See the section on *Climate*, page 33, for a detailed description of the weather that can be expected, and note that Zambia's rainy season occurs between the end of November and the start of May. This makes travel in the more remote areas very difficult, sometimes impossible, and accounts for the fact that most of Zambia's safari camps are seasonal: they close down in the rainy season.

So, from June to October is the easiest time to travel, though visiting any of the low-altitude places (like the Luangwa, the Lower Zambezi valley, or Lake Tanganyika) can get very hot towards the end of this period. October is referred to as "suicide month" in these areas with good reason.

Game

During the wet season, the foliage goes wild and there are pools of water throughout the bush. Both these factors make game viewing difficult. Seeing the animals is easiest when the bush is thinner, and when the animals have fewer places to drink they are forced to concentrate more. This gives viewers better chances of spotting them at one of the obvious water sources – like the rivers.

So for good game viewing, come to Zambia in the dry season, towards the end if possible. If October's heat puts you off, then August and September are very good substitutes: cooler but still with good game. In June and July the game-viewing probably isn't quite as good – but you'll have the company of even fewer visitors, and the landscape is greener and, arguably, more photogenic.

That said, most larger mammals choose the rainy season to have their young. So if you do find a way to get out into the bush during the rains, then you should be rewarded with some wonderful sightings of baby animals.

Birdlife

The birdlife in Zambia is best when the foliage is most dense, and the insects are thriving: in the wet season. This is also when the Palaearctic migrants are found here, and when many of the resident birds are nesting. That said, the profusion of greenery does not make for easy identification of species, so spotting them can be even harder than it is in the dry season.

MONEY

Black market

Until recently there used to be a "black market" in foreign currency in Zambia, where US$1 used to be worth much more if you surreptitiously changed it with a shady (and illegal) street dealer than if you changed it at a bank. This was a result of the official (government decreed) exchange rate for the kwacha not corresponding to the true market value of the currency.

Now this has changed. Financial reforms have forced the government to value the kwacha at a floating, free-market rate, wiping out the black market. The odd shady character on the street who still hisses "change money" as you pass is now more likely to be a con-man relying on sleight of hand than a genuine money-changer.

Budgeting

Zambia is not a cheap country to visit; and, if you want to see some of the national parks, then it can be expensive. This is not because the park fees are high: on the contrary, US$10-15/£7-10 per day is very reasonable by African standards. Rather, it is because most of Zambia's safari camps are expensive. (Being seasonal and small, their supply logistics are difficult and the cost is shared between few visitors.) For European or American visitors, these camps present the only practical bases for a visit to Zambia, and so it is an expensive destination. Budget for an all-inclusive cost of about US$200-260/£130-170 per person per day when staying in a camp.

If you have your own rugged 4WD, and the experience to use one, then you will be able to camp at designated sites in the parks, which can dramatically cut costs, down to US$15-20/£10-12 per person per day for both park fees and camping fees.

The cost of food depends heavily on where you buy it, as well as what you buy. If you can shop in Lusaka for your camping supplies then you will save money and have a wider choice than elsewhere, provided that you don't go for expensive imported foods. In any event, it will be cheaper than eating at most safari camps that you pass. If you are sensible, then US$10-15/£7-10 per day would provide you with a good, varied diet...including the odd treat.

If you are staying in Lusaka, or one of the main cities, then the bigger hotels are about US$50-60/£30-40 per person sharing, whilst a smaller (and often much less impressive) local place will cost around US$30-

40/£20-27. Camping at organised sites on the outskirts of the cities is, again, a good bet if you have the equipment and transport. It will cost an almost universal US$5/£3.50 per person per night.

Restaurant meals in the towns are cheap compared with Europe or America: expect to pay US$10-15/£7-10 for a good evening meal, including a local beer or two. Imported beers are expensive (around US$3/£2 per bottle), as are South African wines, so avoid them if you are on a tight budget. European wines and spirits, as you might expect, are ridiculously priced - and so are an excellent gift if you are visiting someone here. You will pay well over US$100/£65 for a bottle of champagne in Lusaka!

How to take your money

If you are changing money at one of the main banks, in a major town, then there is no difference in the rates between presenting a travellers cheque, or presenting pounds sterling or US dollars in cash. This perhaps makes travellers cheques preferable from a security point of view, as they are refundable if stolen. (AMEX travellers cheques are probably the most widely recognised.)

However, if you are likely to need to use a bureau dc change at any time, then you will need cash - as they will often not even consider taking travellers cheques.

If you are bringing cash then carry it in convenient denominations of US dollars, or pounds sterling: perhaps US$10, US$20 and US$50; and £10 or £20 notes. Larger denomination notes are regarded with suspicion, as many forgeries are in circulation. South African rand arc also accepted, though not quite as widely as dollars or pounds. Sometimes you can pay for hotels and services in US dollars directly, as you would with kwacha, however this gets less common away from the bigger towns. The western provinces are perhaps an exception to this rule, as there rand are more commonly acceptable than further east or north.

Note that, although most safari camps accept credit cards, if park fees are not included then they will sometimes need to be paid directly at the park gate in US$ cash.

Around Livingstone there is a keen market for buying Zimbabwean dollars and selling kwacha (due to the availability of consumables in Victoria Falls, and the constant demand for Zimbabwe dollars to use on shopping trips over the border). However, the money-changers near the border are notorious for their dishonesty. Finding a way to change money safely is difficult and even street-wise locals get ripped off by these con-men. It is better to try changing money in Livingstone town, at the banks, or even at one of the shops run by the Asian community.

WHAT TO BRING

This is an impossible question to answer fully, as it depends on how you intend to travel and exactly where you are going. If you are flying in for a short safari holiday then you need not pack too ruthlessly – provided that you stay within your weight allowance. That said, note that smaller, privately chartered planes may specify a maximum weight of 10kg for hold luggage, to be packed in a soft, squashable bag.

If you are backpacking then weight becomes much more important, and minimising it becomes an art form. Each extra item must be questioned: is its benefit worth its weight?

If you have your own vehicle then neither weight nor bulk will be so vital, and you will have a lot more freedom to bring what you like. Here are some general guidelines:

Clothing

For most days all you will want is light, loose-fitting cotton clothing. Pure cotton, or at least a cotton-rich mix, is cooler and more absorbent than synthetic materials, making it more comfortable in the heat.

For men shorts (not too short) are fine in the bush, but long trousers are more socially acceptable in the towns and rural villages. (You will rarely see a respectable black Zambian man wearing shorts outside a safari camp.) For women a knee-length skirt or culottes is ideal. Zambia's dress code is generally conservative: a woman wearing revealing clothing in town implies that she is a woman of ill repute, whilst untidy clothing suggests a poor person, of low social standing.

These rules are redundant at safari camps, where dress is casual, and designed to keep you cool and protect skin from the sun. Green, khaki and dust-brown cotton is *de rigueur* at the more expensive camps, and the ones specialising in serious walking trips – and amongst visitors out to demonstrate how well they know the ropes. At the less committed (and less expensive) camps you will see a smattering of brighter coloured clothes amongst these dull bush colours – usually worn by visitors who are less familiar with the specific fashion styles of upmarket safari camps. Note that washing is done daily at virtually all camps, so only a few changes of clothes are necessary.

A squashable hat and a robust pair of sunglasses with a high UV-absorption are essential.

Finally avoid anything which looks military – especially camouflage patterns. Wearing camouflage is asking for trouble anywhere in Africa. You are likely to be stopped and questioned by the genuine military, or at least the police, who will assume that you are a member of some militia... so may question exactly what you are doing in Zambia.

Footwear

If you plan to do much walking, either on safari or with a backpack, then lightweight walking boots (with a high ankle support if possible) are essential. This is firstly because the bush is not always smooth and even, and anything which minimises the chance of a twisted ankle is worthwhile; and secondly because it will reduce still further the minute chance of being bitten by a snake, or other creepy-crawly, whilst walking.

Because of the heat, bring the lightest pair of boots you can find - preferably go for canvas, or a breathable Goretex-type material. Leather boots are too hot for wearing in October, but a thin single-skin leather is bearable for walking in July and August. *Never* bring a new pair, or boots which aren't completely worn in, and always bring several pairs of thin socks. Two thin pairs of socks are more comfortable than one thick pair, and will help to prevent blisters.

Camping equipment

If you are coming on an organised safari, then a "tented camp" will mean large walk-in tents with en suite shower and even a toilet. However, without camp attendants to erect and maintain these, and a large back-up vehicle in which to carry them, such luxury is beyond independent visitors.

Here are some observations on various essentials. Note that very little kit is available in Zambia, so buy high-quality equipment before you arrive if you can, as it will save you a lot of trouble over time.

Tent

During the rains a good tent is essential in order to stay dry, whilst even during the dry season they are useful if there are lion or hyena around. If backpacking, invest in a high-quality, lightweight tent. Make sure that it is very well ventilated with fine-mesh mosquito netting - just a corner of mesh at the top of the tent is not enough for comfort. I have been using the same *Spacepacker* tent (manufactured by *Robert Saunders Ltd*, Five Oaks Lane, Chigwell, Essex IG7 4QP, UK) for almost ten years - a dome tent with fine mesh doors on either side which allows a through draft for ventilation, making all the difference when the temperatures are high. The alternative to a good tent is a mosquito net, which is fine unless it is raining or you are in a big game area.

Sleeping bag

A lightweight, "three-season" sleeping bag is ideal for Zambia, unless you are heading up to the Nyika Plateau in winter where the nights get cold. Down is preferable to synthetic fillings for most of the year, as it packs smaller, is lighter, and feels far more luxurious to sleep in. That said, when down gets wet it loses its efficiency, so bring a good synthetic bag if you are likely to encounter much rain.

Ground mat

A ground mat of some sort is essential. It keeps you warm and comfortable, and it protects the tent's ground sheet from rough or stony ground (put it underneath the tent). Closed cell foam mats are widely available outside Zambia, so buy one before you arrive. The better mats cost double or treble the cheaper ones, but are stronger, thicker and warmer – well worth the investment. Therm-a-Rests, the combination air-mattress and foam mats, are strong, durable and also worth the investment...but take a puncture repair kit with you just in case of problems.

Sheet sleeping bag

Thin cotton sheet sleeping bags (eg: as designed for youth hostels) are small, light, and very useful. They are easily washed and so are normally used like a sheet, inside a sleeping bag, to keep the bag itself clean. Alternatively, if it is hot, they can be used on their own: to cover you whilst you lie on top of the sleeping bag.

Stove

"Trangia" type stoves which burn methylated spirits are very simple to use, light to carry, and cheap to run. They come with a set of aluminium pans – which are equally useful when you have a fire and don't need a stove. Methylated spirits is cheap and widely available, even in the rural areas, but bring a tough (purpose made) fuel container with you as the bottles in which it is sold will soon crack and spill all over your belongings.

The normal alternative is a gas stove – but the pressurised canisters for these are difficult to buy, and you will probably be banned from carrying them on an aircraft. Stoves which burn petrol or kerosene (very weight-efficient fuels) are more powerful than a Trangia. However, these are more complex, and invariably more temperamental and messy than a simple Trangia, which has no moving parts at all.

Torch (flashlight)

Bring one that is small, tough and preferably waterproof. Head-mounted torches leave your hands free, which is useful when you are cooking or mending the car, but some find them bulky and uncomfortable to wear. The *Maglite* range of small, strong torches is excellent, but bring several spare bulbs with you as you will not find these in Zambia.

Those with vehicles will find a strong spotlight, powered by the car's battery (perhaps through the socket for the cigarette lighter), is invaluable for impromptu lighting and game drives at night.

Water containers

If you are backpacking then bring a one or two litre container, for normal drinking, whilst you are travelling. Also consider a collapsible water-bag for camping, perhaps about 5-10 litres in size which will reduce the number of trips that you need to make from your camp to the water source. Drivers will want to carry a number of large containers of water, especially if venturing into the Kalahari sand in western Zambia, where good surface water is not common.

Other useful items

Obviously no list is comprehensive, and only travelling will teach you what you need, and what you can do without. That said, here are a few of my own favourites and essentials, just to jog your memory. For visitors embarking on an organised safari, camps will have most things but useful items include:

- "Leatherman" knife – an amazing tool: never go into the bush without one
- Electrical insulating tape – remarkably useful for general repairs
- Sunblock and lipsalve – for vital protection from the sun
- Binoculars – totally essential for game-viewing
- Camera – long lenses are vital for good shots of animals
- Basic sewing kit – with at least some really strong thread for repairs
- Cheap waterproof watch (leave expensive ones, and jewellery, at home)
- Couple of paperback novels
- Large plastic "bin-liner" (garbage) bags, for protecting your luggage from dust
- Simple medical kit and insect repellent

And for those driving or backpacking, useful extras are:

- Concentrated, biodegradable washing powder
- Long-life candles – as Zambian candles are often soft, and burn quickly
- Nylon "paracord" – bring 20m for emergencies and washing lines
- Hand-held GPS navigation system – for expeditions to remote areas
- Good compass and a whistle
- More comprehensive medical kit

MAPS AND NAVIGATION

Zambia has an excellent range of detailed "Ordnance Survey" type maps available cheaply in Lusaka, from the basement office of Mulungushi House. See *Lusaka*, page 114, for details. There are also a few maps of the parks, aimed at tourists, which are useful to supplement these – including an excellent 1989 map of South Luangwa's landscape and vegetation. If you are driving yourself around, then go there to buy all the maps for your trip at the start.

Navigation by these maps gets more difficult as your location becomes more remote, as expecting all the information on these maps to be accurate is unrealistic – though they are usually very close.

GPS systems

If you are heading into one of the more remote parks in your own vehicle, then consider investing in a hand-held GPS: a Global Positioning System. Under an open, unobstructed sky, these can fix your latitude, longitude and elevation to within about 100m, using 24 American military satellites which constantly pass in the skies overhead. They will work anywhere on the globe.

Commercial units now cost around US$300-900/£200-600 in Europe or the USA, although their prices will fall as the technology matures. I use one of the less expensive models, the Garmin GPS 38, which will store "waypoints", enabling you to build up an electronic picture of an area, as well as working out basic latitude, longitude and elevation. So, for example, you can store the position of your campsite, and the nearest road, enabling you to leave with confidence and be reasonably sure of navigating back. This is invaluable in remote areas.

Whilst they are no substitute for good map work and navigation, they will help you to recognise your minor errors before they are amplified into major problems (and they are fantastic "toys" to play with). All these units use lots of battery power, so bring spares with you – and do not to rely on them too much, or you will be unable to cope if your GPS fails.

PHOTOGRAPHY AND OPTICS

Don't expect to find any reasonably priced or reasonably available optical equipment in Zambia – so bring everything that you will need with you.

Cameras

35mm SLR cameras with interchangeable lenses offer you the greatest flexibility. For general photography, a mid-range zoom lens (eg: 28-70mm) is best – much more useful than the standard (50mm) lens. For wildlife photography you will need at least a 200mm zoom lens, otherwise most animals and birds will look like mere dots on the horizon.

Compact cameras are fine for shots of people and landscapes, but of little use for pictures of the wildlife.

Auto-focus zoom lenses are a godsend for capturing animals and birds which might move in the time that it takes to focus manually, but they need extra care to ensure that they remain dust-free. A few grains of sand or dust in the wrong place will render some such lenses useless.

Binoculars

For a safari holiday, especially if you are doing much walking, a good pair of binoculars will bring you far more enjoyment than a camera. They make the difference between merely seeing an animal or bird at a distance, and being able to observe its markings, movements and moods closely.

There are two styles: the small "pocket" binoculars, perhaps 10-12cm long, which account for most popular modern sales – and have only been in production since the 1980s. These were popularised by the makers of compact and auto-focus cameras, and are now often made in the Far East. Then there are larger, heavier styles, double or triple that size, which have been manufactured for years. Many of the remaining manufacturers of these are in the CIS, Germany or Austria.

The small ones are now mass-produced at around US$150/£100, whilst the larger ones vary widely in cost and quality. If you are buying a pair, then consider getting the larger style. The smaller ones are fine for spotting animals; but are difficult to hold steady, and very tiring to use for extensive periods. You will only realise this when you are out on safari, by which time it is too late.

Around 8 x 30 is an ideal size for field observations, as most people need some form of rest, or tripod, to hold the larger 10 x 50 models steady. Get the best quality ones you can for your money. The cheapest will be about US$60/£40, but to get a decent level of quality consider spending at least US$300/£200. You will be able to see the difference when you use them.

Accessories

The bush is very dusty, so bring plenty of lens-cleaning cloths, and a blow-brush. Take great care not to get dust into the back of any camera, as a single grain on the back-plate can be enough to make a long scratch which ruins every frame taken.

Tripods are useful, though they are inconvenient at times. Consider taking a small bean-bag for resting the camera on the window-sill.

Film

Film is expensive in Zambia, and the choice is very limited - so bring a large supply of anything that you will want to use. The range of film speeds should be dependent upon the type of photography that most interests you. For most landscape shots, where you will have plenty of light, a slow film (100ASA or less) will give the highest quality of results. For wildlife photography, you will probably need a faster film: 200 or even 400ASA.

Pictures taken around dawn and dusk will have the richest, deepest colours, whilst those taken in the middle of the day, when the sun is high, will seem pale and washed-out by comparison. Beware of the very deep shadows and high contrast which are typical of tropical countries - film just cannot capture the sheer range of colours and shades that our eyes can. If you want to take pictures in full daylight, and capture details in the shadows, then you will need a good camera, and to spend some time learning how to use it fully. By restricting your photography to mornings, evenings and simple shots you will encounter fewer problems.

Especially after exposure, film deteriorates rapidly in the heat. Aim to keep all your film away from direct sunlight, somewhere shady and cool.

VEHICLE HIRE

With difficult roads, which seem to vanish completely in some of the more remote areas, driving around Zambia is not easy. The big car-hire firms do have franchises in Lusaka, but they concentrate their small efforts on business-people who need transport around the city. They insist that most foreigners hiring cars also hire a chauffeur...and just do not cater for visitors in search of recreation.

A basic model like a Toyota Corolla from, say, AVIS will cost around US$60/£40 per day, with 50km "free" per day, and a 50c/35p charge per kilometre thereafter. See *Car hire* in *Chapter Nine* for the relevant contact details. It is not possible to hire reliable 4WD vehicles in Zambia, so the only option is to bring them in from outside, or arrange for a safari company to take you around on a (very costly) private mobile safari.

Hiring outside Zambia

If you want to explore Zambia in your own 4WD, then you must bring it into the country. If you do not have a vehicle in Southern Africa, then the best place to hire one from is Kessler 4x4 Hire, of Namibia (PO Box 20274, Windhoek; Tel: 00 264 61 233451, fax: 00 264 61 224551. Email: kessler@iwwn.com.na). Kessler are based in Windhoek but can deliver and collect a car conveniently from Victoria Falls, adjacent to Livingstone; or Katima Mulilo.

They will charge a few hundred dollars for the delivery and collection from the Falls, and you will need to arrange for an insurance which covers the vehicle in Zambia, but they have easily the subcontinent's best range of 4x4 vehicles. These are mostly sturdy twin and single cab Toyota Hiluxs – some with optional roof tents – as well as a couple of Land Rover models. There are other 4x4 hire companies in Windhoek and Johannesburg which are cheaper, but Kessler have earned an enviable reputation for quality – which is what you need most when you rely so heavily on a vehicle.

ORGANISING A SAFARI

Most visitors who come to Zambia for few weeks' safari stay at some of the established safari camps, perhaps combining a week in South Luangwa with a few days around the Falls, and a few days canoeing on the Lower Zambezi. Such trips are expensive, but not difficult to arrange through a good operator. If you have favourite camps, or a tight schedule, then organise this as far in advance as you can. Bear in mind that most camps are small (and so easily filled), and organise their logistics with military precision. Finding space at short notice is difficult.

To arrange everything, you are recommended to use a reliable, independent tour operator based in your own country. Although many operators sell trips to Zambia, few really know the country well; insist on dealing directly with someone who does. Zambia changes so fast that detailed local knowledge is vital in putting together a trip that runs smoothly and suits you. Make sure that whoever you book with is fully bonded, so that your money is protected if they go broke; and, ideally, pay with a credit card. Never book a trip from someone who doesn't know Zambia personally: you are asking for problems.

Safaris in Zambia are, by their nature, expensive. Expect to pay US$1,500-4,500/£1,000-3,000 per person for a couple of weeks, plus airfares. This high cost means that you can expect a good level of service from the operator whilst you are considering the options and booking the trip: if you don't get it, then go elsewhere.

Booking directly with Zambian safari operators or agencies is possible, but communication can be difficult – and you will have no recourse if anything goes wrong. European/US operators usually work on commission for the trips that they sell, which is deducted from the basic cost that the visitor pays. Thus you should end up paying the same whether you book through an overseas operator or talk directly to a camp in Zambia, but the former is a lot easier.

Tour operators

Zambia is something of a touchstone for tour operators to Southern Africa. Many operators feature Zambia, but few have spent much time here, and fewer still can give first-hand guidance on a good range of camps. Don't be talked into thinking that there are only three decent safari camps and one national park in Zambia, just because they are the only ones that your operator knows. If your operator doesn't know that there is a good range of choice, then change to one who does. The better operators to Zambia are invariably the better operators to the rest of Southern Africa, and include:

In the UK

Abercrombie & Kent Sloane Square House, Holbein Place, London, SW1W 8NS
Tel: 0171 730 9600; fax: 0171 730 9376

Art of Travel 21 The Bakehouse, 119 Altenberg Gardens, London, SW11 1JQ
Tel: 0171 738 2038; fax: 0171 738 1893

Cazenove & Lloyd Unit 1, 39 Tadema Road, London, SW10 0PY
Tel: 0171 376 3746; fax: 0171 376 5237

Grenadier Safaris 11/12 West Stockwell Street, Colchester, CO1 1HN
Tel: 01206 549585; fax: 01206 561337

Hartley's Safaris 3 Bailgate, Lincoln, LN1 3AE
Tel: 01522 511577; fax: 01522 511372

Sunvil Discovery 7&8 Upper Square, Old Isleworth, Middlesex, TW7 7BJ
Tel: 0181 568 4499; fax: 0181 568 8330; Email: discovery@sunvil.itsnet.co.uk

Wildlife Worldwide 170 Selsdon Road, South Croydon, Surrey, CR2 6PJ
Tel: 0181 667 9158; fax: 0181 667 1960

In the USA

African Travel tel: 908 870 0223; fax: 908 870 0278

African Wildlife Travel tel: 800 432 9968/914 693 8909; fax: 914 693 8916

Safari Centre International tel: 800 223 6046/310 546 4411; fax: 310 546 8540

Wildlife Safari tel: 800 221 8118/510 376 5595; fax: 510 376 5059

In Australia

Adventure World tel: 02 956 7766; fax: 02 956 7707

Africa Wildlife Safaris tel: 03 9696 2899; fax: 03 9696 4937

In Canada

East African Travel Consultants tel: 416 967 1613

Exotic Tours tel: 800 316 1007

In the Netherlands

Africa Holidays tel: 023 421334; fax: 023 421574

Angeli Safari tel: 04950 40155; fax: 04950 41275

Chapter Six

Health and Safety

There is always great danger in writing about health and safety for the uninitiated visitor. It is all too easy to become paranoid about exotic diseases that you may catch, and all too easy to start distrusting everybody you meet as a potential thief – falling into an unfounded us-and-them attitude toward the people of the country you are visiting.

As a comparison, imagine an equivalent section in a guidebook to a Western country – there would be a list of possible diseases and advice on the risk of theft and mugging. Many Western cities are very dangerous, but with time we learn how to assess the risks, accepting almost subconsciously what we can and cannot do.

It is important to strike the right balance: to avoid being excessively cautious or too relaxed about your health and your safety. With experience, you will find the balance that best fits you and the country you are visiting.

BEFORE YOU GO

Travel insurance

Visitors to Zambia must take out a comprehensive medical insurance policy to cover them for emergencies, including the cost of evacuation to another country within the region. Such policies come with an emergency number (often on a reverse-charge/call collect basis). You would be wise to memorise this – or indelibly tattoo it in as many places as possible on your baggage.

Personal effects insurance is also a sensible precaution, but check the policy's fine print before you leave home. Often, in even the best policies, you will find a limit per item, or per claim – which can be well below the cost of a replacement. If you need to list your valuables separately, then do so comprehensively. Check that receipts are not required for claims if you do not have them, and that the excess which you have to pay on every claim is reasonable.

Annual travel policies can be excellent value if you travel a lot, and some of the larger credit card companies do excellent policies. That said, often it is better to get your valuables named and insured for travel using your home contents insurance. These year-round policies will try harder to settle your claim fairly as they want your business in the long term.

Inoculations

Having a full set of inoculations takes time, normally at least six weeks, although excellent protection can be had by visiting your doctor even as late as just a few days before you travel. Ideally, see your doctor early on to establish an inoculation time-table. Equally, it is worth having a dental check-up before you go – you could be several painful days from the nearest dentist. If you wear glasses, bring a spare pair. The same goes for those who wear contact lenses – they should bring spare lenses, and also a pair of glasses in case the sand and dust prove too much for the lenses. If you take regular medication (including contraceptive pills) then bring a large supply with you – it is most unlikely that you will easily find your usual drugs available in Zambia.

UK vaccination clinics

Note that getting vaccinations at these specialist centres can be more costly than using your GP, but often their specialists will be more up to date on the latest advice.

British Airways Travel Clinics There are over thirty throughout the country. Call 0171 831 5333 to find your nearest.

MASTA (Medical Advisory Services for Travellers) working with the London School of Hygiene and Tropical Medicine has a touch-tone advice line (0891 224 100). This will advise you on your particular trip, and send you further written advice. There is no clinic here.

Hospital for Tropical Diseases, 4 St Pancras Way, London NW1 0PE. This also has a touch-tone advice line, with information prepared by the Malaria Reference Laboratory. Tel: 0891 600350.

Trailfinders Immunisation Centre, 194 Kensington High Street, London W8 7RG. Tel: 0171 938 3999. This centre has a doctor on site, and most vaccinations are available immediately.

Nomad Travel Pharmacy & Vaccination Centre, 3-4 Wellington Terrace, Turnpike Lane, London, N8 0PX. Tel: 0181 889 7014. This private pharmacy, specialising in travel medicine, is linked to the next-door centre selling travel equipment.

Legal requirements

No inoculations are required by law for entry into Zambia unless you are entering from an area where cholera or yellow fever is endemic – eg: Zaire. In that case, vaccination certificates may be required.

Recommended precautions

Check that you are protected against polio and tetanus, as you should be whether you are at home or travelling abroad. Vaccinations against cholera and typhoid may be recommended by your doctor, although most now regard the cholera vaccination as ineffective and only worth having if you need the certificate to enter a country – which you don't for Zambia.

Hepatitis A is not a common disease in Zambia, but it is very unpleasant. Limited protection (for three or six months) is conferred by a jab of gamma-globulin, which is a general booster to the body's immune system. However, the HAVRIX vaccine is now widely available and gives complete coverage for ten years. This is well worth having. Note that complete protection requires two shots several months apart.

Vaccination against rabies is unnecessary for most visitors, but would be wise for those who travel for extended periods, or stay in rural areas.

Malaria prophylaxis (prevention)

Malaria is the most dangerous disease in Africa, and the greatest risk to the traveller. It is common throughout Zambia, and so it is essential that you take all possible precautions against it.

Prophylaxis regimes aim to infuse your bloodstream with drugs that inhibit and kill malaria parasites which are injected into you by a biting mosquito. This is why you must take the drugs before you arrive in a malarial area – so that the drugs are established in your bloodstream from day one. Unfortunately, the malaria parasites continually adapt to the drugs which we use to combat them – so the recommended regimes have to adapt and change in order to remain effective. None is 100% effective, and all require time to kill the parasites – so keeping up the prophylaxis regime for weeks after you leave the infected area is usually recommended.

Currently recommended regimes include two drugs taken in combination: Proguanil (Paludrine) – two tablets (200mg base each) every day after food, and Chloroquine (Nivaquine) – two tablets (300mg base each) at the same time every week. A few people find that the pills make them nauseous. This feeling can be lessened by taking the pills after your evening meal and sleeping through the worst effects.

Prophylaxis does not stop you catching malaria, only stopping the mosquitoes biting will do that (see *Avoiding insect bites* below). However, it significantly reduces your chances of fully developing the disease and, if it does develop, it will lessen its severity. Falciparum (cerebral) malaria is the most common in Africa, and usually fatal if untreated, so it is worth your while trying to avoid it.

Because the strains of malaria, and the drugs used to combat them, change frequently, it is important to get the latest advice before you travel. Normally it is better to obtain this from a specialist malaria laboratory rather than a local doctor, who may not be up to date with the latest drugs and developments. In the UK, call the recorded message at the Malaria Reference Laboratory in London (tel: 0891 600350). In the USA call the Center for Disease Control in Atlanta, Georgia (tel: 404 332 4559).

Medical kit

Pharmacies in Zambia often lack medicines and general supplies, and you will find very little in the rural areas. So you must take with you anything that you expect to need. If you are on an organised trip, an overlanding truck, or staying at hotels, lodges or safari camps, then you will not need much as these establishments normally have comprehensive emergency kits. In that case, just a small personal medical kit might include:

- antihistamine tablets
- antiseptic cream
- aspirins and paracetamol
- condoms and contraceptive pills
- lip-salve (ideally containing a sunscreen)
- malaria prophylaxis
- micropore tape (for closing small cuts - and invaluable for blisters)
- moisturising cream
- sticking plasters (a roll is more versatile than pre-shaped plasters)
- sunscreen

However, if you are going to be travelling on your own for much of the time, and likely to end up in very remote situations, then you should also consider taking the following:

- burn dressings (burns are a common problem for campers)
- injection swabs, sterile needles and syringes
- lint, sterile bandage and safety pins
- oral rehydration sachets
- steristrips or butterfly closures
- strong painkiller (*codeine phosphate* – also use for severe diarrhoea)
- tweezers (perhaps those on a Swiss army knife)
- water purification equipment (2% tincture of iodine and dropper is ideal)
- several different malaria treatment courses and broad-spectrum antibiotics – plus a good medical manual.

STAYING HEALTHY

Food and storage

Throughout the world, most health problems encountered by travellers are contracted by eating contaminated food or drinking unclean water. If you are staying in safari camps or lodges which rely on overseas visitors for their existence, then you are unlikely to have problems. However, if you are backpacking and cooking for yourself, or relying on local food, then you need to take more care. Tins, packets, and fresh green vegetables (when you can find them) are least likely to cause problems – provided that clean water has been used for washing the vegetables and preparing the meal. In Zambia's warm climate, keeping meat or animal products unrefrigerated for more than a few hours is asking for trouble.

Water and purification

Whilst piped water in the major towns is unlikely to harbour any serious pathogens, it will almost certainly cause upset stomachs for an overseas visitor. In more rural areas, the water will generally have had less treatment, and therefore will be even more likely to cause problems. Hence, as a general rule, ensure that all water used for drinking or washing food in Zambia is purified.

To purify water yourself, first filter out any suspended solids – perhaps passing the water through a piece of closely woven cloth, or something similar. Then either vigorously boil it for a minimum of two minutes, or sterilise it chemically. Boiling is much more effective, provided that you have the fuel available.

Tablets sold for purification are based on either chlorine or iodine, and normally adequate. Just follow the manufacturer's instructions carefully. Iodine is most effective, especially against the resilient amoebic cysts which cause amoebic dysentery.

A cheaper alternative to tablets sold over the counter is to travel with a small bottle of medical-quality tincture of iodine (2% solution) and an eye dropper. Add four drops to one litre of water, shake well, and leave to stand for ten minutes. If the water is very cloudy – even after filtering – or very cold, then either double the iodine dose, or leave to stand for twice as long.

Note that this tincture of iodine can also be used as a general external antiseptic, but it will stain things deep purple if spilt – so seal and pack its container exceedingly well.

Heat and sun

Heat stroke, heat exhaustion and sunburn are often problems for travellers to Africa, despite being easy to prevent. To avoid them, you need to remember that your body is under stress and make allowances for it. Firstly, take things gently - you are on holiday after all. Next, keep your fluid and salt levels high: lots of water and soft drinks, but go easy on the caffeine and alcohol. Thirdly, dress to keep cool with loose fitting, thin garments - preferably of cotton, linen or silk. Finally, beware of the sun. Hats and long-sleeved shirts are essential. If you must expose your skin to the sun, then use sun blocks and high factor sun screens (the sun is so strong that you will still get a tan).

Avoiding insect bites

The most dangerous biting insects in Africa are mosquitoes, because they can transmit malaria, yellow fever, and a host of other diseases. Research has shown that using a mosquito net over your bed, and covering up exposed skin (by wearing long-sleeved shirts, tucking trousers into socks) in the evening, are the most effective steps towards preventing bites. Mosquito coils and chemical insect repellents will help, and sleeping in a stream of moving air, eg: under a fan, will help to reduce your chances of being bitten.

Visitors on safari are also exposed to bites during the day from tsetse flies. These large dark flies (bigger than house flies) bite during the day and are especially attracted both to the scent of cattle and to dark colours. Dark blue seems to be their favourite, so avoid wearing that and don't forget your insect repellents even during the day. (See *Sleeping sickness,* page 68-9.)

DEET (diethyltoluamide) is the active ingredient in almost all repellents, so the greater the percentage of DEET, the stronger the effect. However, DEET is a strong chemical. It will dissolve some plastics and synthetic materials, and may irritate sensitive skin. Because of this, many people use concentrated DEET to impregnate materials, rather than applying it to themselves. Mosquito nets, socks, and even cravats can be impregnated and used to deter insects from biting. Eating large quantities of garlic, cream of tartar, or taking yeast tablets are said to deter some biting insects, although the evidence is anecdotal - and the garlic may affect your social life.

Snakes, spiders and scorpions...

Encounters with aggressive snakes, angry spiders or vindictive scorpions are really more common in horror films than in Africa. Most snakes will flee at the mere vibrations of a human footstep whilst spiders are far more interested in flies than people. You will have to seek out scorpions if you wish to see one. If you are careful about where you place your hands and feet, especially after dark, then there should be no problems. Simple precautions include not putting a pair of boots on without shaking them empty first, and always checking the back of your backpack before putting it on.

Snakes do bite occasionally, and you ought to know the standard first aid treatment. First, and most importantly, *don't panic*. Remember that only a tiny minority of bites, even by highly poisonous species, inject enough venom to be dangerous. Even in the worst of these cases, the victim has hours or days to get to help, and not a matter of minutes. He/she should be kept calm, with no exertions to pump venom around the blood system, whilst being taken rapidly to the nearest medical help. The area of the bite should be washed to remove any venom from the skin, and the bitten limb should be immobilised. Paracetamol may be used as a pain killer, but never use aspirin because it may cause internal bleeding.

If the bite is both serious and venomous, then splint the limb, and apply a crêpe bandage firmly over the length of the effected limb. Forget cutting out the wound, sucking and spitting, or any of the commercial anti-snake bite kits – which vary from being a waste of time to being positively dangerous. Equally, a tourniquet will probably do more harm than good unless it is administered by a experienced doctor. The only real treatment is for a specific antivenom to be medically administered. Identification of the snake is very helpful, so killing it and taking it along with you is a good idea if at all possible.

When deep in the bush, heading for the nearest large farm or camp may be quicker than going to a town – it may have a supply of antivenom, or facilities to radio for help by plane.

DISEASES AND WHEN TO SEE A DOCTOR

Traveller's diarrhoea

There are almost as many names for this as there are travellers' tales on the subject. Firstly, do resist the temptation to reach for the medical kit as soon as your stomach turns a little fluid. Most cases of traveller's diarrhoea will resolve themselves within 24 to 48 hours with no treatment at all. To speed up this process of acclimatisation, eat well but simply: avoid fats in favour of starches, and keep your fluid intake high. Bananas and papaya fruit are often claimed to be helpful. If you urgently need to stop the symptoms, for a long bus ride for example, then Lomotil, Imodium or another of the commercial anti-diarrhoea preparations will do the trick – but they will not cure the problem.

When severe diarrhoea gets continually worse, or the stools contain blood or pus, or it lasts for more than ten days, you must seek medical advice. There are as many possible treatments as there are causes, and a proper diagnosis involves microscopic analysis of a stool sample – so go straight to your nearest hospital. The most important thing, especially in Zambia's climate, is to keep your fluid intake up. The body's absorption of fluids is assisted by adding small amounts of dissolved sugars, salts and minerals to the water. An ideal ratio is eight level teaspoons of sugar and one level teaspoon of salt dissolved in one litre of water. Palm syrup or honey make good substitutes for sugar, and fresh citrus juice will not only improve the taste of these solutions, but also add some valuable minerals like potassium.

If you are likely to be more than a few days from qualified medical help, then come equipped with a good health manual and the selection of antibiotics which it recommends. *Bugs, Bites & Bowels* by Dr Jane Wilson Howarth (see *Further Reading*) is excellent for this purpose.

Malaria

You can still catch malaria even if you are taking anti-malarial drugs. Classic symptoms include headaches, chills and sweating, abdominal pains, aching joints and fever - some or all of which may come in waves. It varies tremendously, but often starts like a bad case of flu. If anything like this happens, you should first suspect malaria and seek immediate medical help. A definite diagnosis of malaria is normally only possible by examining a blood sample under the microscope. However, note that any anti-malarial drugs, whether taken for prophylaxis or treatment, will hamper this diagnosis - so don't treat yourself if you can easily reach a hospital first.

If (and only if) medical help is unavailable, then self-treatment is fairly safe, except for people who are pregnant or under twelve years of age. Fansidar, mefloquine, high dose chloroquine (preferably intravenous), and quinine can all be used in the treatment of malaria. Ideally take several different courses of tablets with you, and rely on experienced local advice to tell you which will be the most effective.

Quinine is very strong, but often proves to be an effective last defence against malaria. Include it in your medical kit, as rural clinics will often have the expertise to treat you, but not the required drugs. Treatment consists of taking two quinine tablets (600mg) every eight hours for up to seven days, until the fever abates. Quinine's side effects are disorientating and unpleasant (nausea and a constant buzzing in the ears), so administering this whilst on your own is not advisable.

AIDS

AIDS is spread in exactly the same way in Africa as it is at home - through body secretions, blood, and blood products. This means that it can be spread through close physical contact, such as sexual intercourse, through blood transfusions using infected blood, or through unsterilised needles which have been used on an infected person.

In Zambia, by far your greatest chance of getting AIDS is through sexual intercourse. Using condoms will reduce this risk considerably, but not eliminate it. Conservative estimates suggest HIV infection rates in Zambia of 30%, although the infection rate of high-risk groups, like prostitutes, is far greater.

Hepatitis

This is a group of viral diseases which generally start with Coca-Cola-coloured urine and light-coloured stools. It progresses to fevers, weakness, jaundice (yellow skin and eyeballs) and abdominal pains caused by a severe inflammation of the liver. There are several forms, of which the two most common are typical of the rest: Type A (formerly infectious hepatitis) and Type B (formerly viral hepatitis).

Type A is spread by the faecal-oral route, that is by ingesting food or drink contaminated by excrement or urine. It is avoided as you would generally avoid stomach problems, by careful preparation of food and by only drinking clean water. There is now an excellent vaccine against Type A, HAVRIX, which lasts for ten years and is certainly worth getting before you travel. See *Inoculations* on pages 60-1.

In contrast, the more serious but rarer Type B is spread in the same way as AIDS (by blood or body secretions), and is avoided the same way as one avoids AIDS. There is a vaccine which protects against hepatitis B, but this is expensive and not always successful. It is usually only considered necessary for medical workers, and others with a high risk of exposure.

There are no cures for hepatitis, but with lots of bed rest and a good low-fat, no-alcohol diet most people recover within six months. If you are unlucky enough to contract hepatitis of any form, use your travel insurance to fly straight home.

Rabies

Rabies is contracted when broken skin comes into contact with saliva from an infected animal. The disease is almost always fatal when fully developed, but fortunately there are excellent post-exposure vaccines. It is possible, albeit expensive, to be immunised against rabies before you travel, but not really worthwhile unless your risk of exposure to it is high (eg: if you are working with animals). Even if you have been immunised, it is standard practice to treat all cases of possible exposure with a full course of post-exposure vaccine.

Rabies is rarely a problem for visitors, but these small risks are further minimised by avoiding dogs in the towns and small carnivores in the bush. If you are bitten then clean and disinfect the wound thoroughly by scrubbing it with soap under running water for five minutes, and then applying a disinfectant (gin, whisky or brandy will do). Then seek medical advice.

The incubation period for rabies is the time taken for the virus to travel from the area of bite to the brain. This varies with the distance of the bite from the head - from a week or so, to as much as a year. Thus it is vital to get medical attention, and post-exposure vaccine, even if this is days or weeks after you are bitten.

The later stages of the disease are very unpleasant - spasms, personality changes and hydrophobia (fear of water). Thus animals acting strangely, be they mad dogs in town or friendly jackals in the bush, should be given a very wide berth.

Bilharzia

Bilharzia is an insidious disease, contracted by coming into contact with infected water. It is caused by an infestation of parasitic worms which damage the bladder and/or intestine. Often the parasites are present in the local population who have built up a measure of immunity over time, but the visitor who becomes infected may develop a severe fever for weeks afterwards. A common indication of an infection is a localised itchy rash - where the parasites have burrowed through the skin - and symptoms of a more advanced infection will probably include passing bloody urine. Bilharzia is readily treated by medication, and only serious if it remains undetected (the symptoms may be confused with malaria) and untreated.

The life-cycle of the parasites starts when they are urinated into a body of water. Here they infect particular species of water-snails. They grow, multiply, and finally become free-swimming. Then they leave the snails to look for a human, or primate, host. After burrowing through the skin of someone coming into contact with the water, they migrate to the person's bladder or intestine where they remain - producing a large number of eggs which are passed every day in the urine, so continuing the cycle.

The only way to avoid bilharzia infection completely is to stay away from any bodies of fresh water. Obviously this is restrictive, and would make your trip less enjoyable. More pragmatic advice is to avoid slow moving or sluggish water, and ask local opinion on the bilharzia risk, as not all water is infected. Generally these snails do not inhabit fast-flowing water, and hence rivers are free from infection. However, dams and standing water, especially in populated areas, are usually heavily infected. If you think you have been infected, don't worry about it - just get a test done on your return.

Sleeping sickness or trypanosomiasis

This is really a cattle disease, which is occasionally caught by people. It is spread by bites from the distinctive tsetse fly - which is slightly larger than a house fly, and has pointed mouth-parts designed for sucking blood. These flies are easily spotted as they bite during the day, and have distinctive wings which cross into a scissors shape when they are resting.

Prevention is easier than cure, so avoid being bitten by covering up. Chemical insect repellents are also helpful. Dark colours, especially blue, are favoured by the flies, so avoid wearing these if possible.

Tsetse bites are nasty, so expect them to swell up and turn red – that is a normal allergic reaction to any bite. The vast majority of tsetse bites will just do this. However, if the bite develops into a boil-like swelling after five or more days, and a fever two or three weeks later, then seek immediate medical treatment to avert permanent damage to your central nervous system. The name "sleeping sickness" refers to a daytime drowsiness which is characteristic of the later stages of the disease.

Because this is a rare complaint, most doctors in the West are unfamiliar with it. If you think that you may have been infected – draw their attention to the possibility. Treatment is straightforward, once a correct diagnosis has been made.

Some Africans view the fly positively, referring to it as a guardian of wild Africa, because fear of the disease's effect on cattle has prevented farming, and hence settlement, encroaching on many areas of wild bush. In recent years the tsetse fly has been subject to relentless spraying programmes in much of the sub-continent, designed to remove the last natural barrier to cattle farming. Then material screens, impregnated with a chemical attractant derived from cattle and an insecticide, are hung in shady areas under trees in order to attract and kill any remaining flies.

Tsetse flies are common in many areas of Zambia – including most of the national parks – although cases of sleeping sickness amongst visitors are exceedingly rare.

RETURNING HOME

Many tropical diseases have a long incubation period, and it is possible to develop symptoms weeks after returning home (this is why it is important to keep taking anti-malaria prophylaxis for six weeks after you leave a malarial zone). If you do get ill after you return home, be certain to tell your doctor where you have been. Alert him/her to any diseases that you may have been exposed to. Several people die from malaria in the UK every year because their doctors are not familiar with the symptoms, and so waste time in making a correct diagnosis.

If problems persist, get a check-up at one of the hospitals which specialise in tropical diseases. Note that to visit such a hospital in the UK, you need a letter of referral from your doctor.

For further advice or help in the UK, ask your local doctor to refer you to the London Hospital for Tropical Diseases, 4 St Pancras Way, London NW1; tel: 0171 387 4411.

SAFETY

Zambia is not a dangerous country. If you are travelling on an all-inclusive trip and staying at lodges and hotels, then problems of personal safety are exceedingly rare. There will always be someone on hand to help you.

Even if you are travelling on local transport, perhaps on a low budget, you will not be attacked randomly just for the sake of it. A difficult situation is most likely to occur if you have made yourself an obvious target for thieves, perhaps by walking around at night. The answer then is to give them what they want, and cash in on your travel insurance. Heroics are not a good idea.

For women travellers, especially those travelling alone, it is doubly important to rapidly learn the local attitudes, and how to behave acceptably. This takes some practice, and a certain confidence. You will often be the centre of attention, but by developing conversational techniques to avert over-enthusiastic male attention, you should be perfectly safe. Making friends of the local women is one way to help avoid such problems.

Theft

Theft is a problem in Zambia's urban areas. Given that a large section of the population is living below the poverty line and without any paid work, it is surprising that the problem is not worse. Despite Lusaka's reputation, in the author's experience theft is no more of a problem here than it is in Harare – while the centre of Johannesburg is significantly more dangerous than either.

How to avoid it

Thieves in the bigger cities usually work in groups – choosing their targets carefully. These will be people who look vulnerable and who have items worth stealing. To avoid being robbed, try not to fit into either category – and certainly not into both. Observing a few basic rules, especially during your first few weeks in Zambia's cities, will drastically reduce your chances of becoming a target. After that you should have learnt your own way of assessing the risks, and avoiding thefts. Until then:

- Try not to carry anything of value around with you.
- If you must carry cash, then use a concealed money-belt for your main supply – keeping smaller change separately and to hand.

- Try not to walk around alone. Move in groups. Take taxis instead.
- Try not to look too foreign. Blend in to the local scene as well as you can. Act like a street-wise expat rather than a tourist, if you can.
- Rucksacks, and large, plump, new bags are bad. If you must carry a bag, choose an old battered one. A local plastic carrier bag is ideal.
- Move confidently and look as if you know exactly what you are doing, and where you are going. Lost foreigners make the easiest targets.
- Never walk around at night – that is asking for trouble.

If you have a vehicle then don't leave anything in it, and avoid leaving it parked in a city. One person should always stay with it, as vehicle thefts are common. Armed gangs doing American-style vehicle hijacks are much rarer, but not unknown – and their most likely targets are new 4WD vehicles. If you are held up then just surrender: you have little choice if you want to live.

Reporting thefts to the police

If you are the victim of a theft then report it to the police – they ought to know. Also try to get a copy of the report, or at least a reference number on an official-looking piece of paper, as this will help you to claim on your insurance policy when you return home. That said, reporting anything in a police station can take a long time, and do not expect any speedy arrests for a small case of pick-pocketing.

SAFETY FOR WOMEN TRAVELLERS

Janice Booth

When attention becomes intrusive, it can help if you are wearing a wedding ring and have photos of "your" husband and children, even if they are someone else's. A good reason to give for not being with them is that you have to travel in connection with your job – biology, zoology, geography, or whatever. (But not journalism – that's risky.)

Pay attention to local etiquette, and to speaking, dressing and moving reasonably decorously. Look at how the local women dress, and try not to expose parts of yourself that they keep covered. Think about body language. In much of Southern Africa direct eye-contact with a man will be seen as a "come-on"; sunglasses are helpful here.

Don't be afraid to explain clearly – but pleasantly rather than as a put-down – that you aren't in the market for whatever distractions are on offer. Remember that you are probably as much of a novelty to the local people as they are to you; and the fact that you are travelling abroad alone gives them the message that you are free and adventurous. But don't imagine that a Lothario lurks under every bush: many approaches stem from genuine friendliness or curiosity, and a brush-off in such cases doesn't do much for the image of travellers in general.

Take sensible precautions against theft and attack – try to cover all the risks before you encounter them – and then relax and enjoy your trip. You'll meet far more kindness than villainy.

Arrest

To get arrested in Zambia, a foreigner will normally have to try quite hard. During the Kaunda regime, when the state was paranoid about spies, every tourist's camera became a reason for suspicion and arrest. Fortunately that attitude has now vanished, though as a precaution you should still ask for permission to photograph near bridges or military installations. This simple courtesy costs you nothing, and may avoid a problem later.

One excellent way to get arrested in Zambia is to try to smuggle drugs across its borders, or to try to buy them from "pushers". Drug offences carry penalties at least as stiff as those you will find at home - and the jails are a lot less pleasant. Zambia's police are not forbidden from using entrapment techniques and "sting" operations to catch criminals, so buying, selling or using drugs in Zambia is just not worth the risk.

Failing this, arguing with any policeman or army official - and getting angry into the bargain - is a sure way to get arrested. It is *essential* to control your temper and stay relaxed when dealing with Zambia's officials. Not only will you gain respect, and hence help your cause, but you will avoid being forced to cool off for a night in the cells.

If you are careless enough to be arrested, you will often only be asked a few questions. If the police are suspicious of you, then how you handle the situation will determine whether you are kept for a matter of hours or days. Be patient, helpful, good-humoured, and as truthful as possible. Never lose your temper, it will only aggravate the situation. Avoid any hint of arrogance. If things are going badly after half a day or so, then start firmly, but politely, to insist on seeing someone in higher authority. As a last resort you do, at least in theory, have the right to contact your embassy or consulate, though the finer points of your civil liberties may end up being overlooked by an irate local police chief.

Bribery

Bribery is certainly a fact of life in Zambia, though it is a difficult subject to write about. There are many different points of view on how to deal with it.

Some argue that it is present already, as an unavoidable way of life, and so must be accepted by the practical traveller. They view using bribery as simply getting used to one of the local customs. Another school of thought regards paying bribes as a totally unacceptable step towards condoning an immoral practice. Thus any bribe should be flatly refused, and requests to make them never acceded to.

Whichever school of thought you would naturally tend towards, bribery is an issue in Zambia which you should consider. It is not as widespread, or on the same large scale, as you will find in countries further north -

but low-level bribery is not uncommon. A large "tip" is often expected for a favour, and acceptance of small fines from police for traffic offences will often mean avoiding proceedings which may appear to be deliberately time-consuming.

Many pragmatic travellers will only accede to using a bribe as a very last resort, and only then when it has been asked for repeatedly. Never attempt to bribe someone unsubtly, or use the word "bribe". If the person involved hasn't already dropped numerous broad hints to you that money is required, then offering any sort of bribe would be a great insult. Further, even if bribes are being asked for, an eagerness to offer will encourage any person you are dealing with to increase their price.

Never simply say "here's some dollars, now will you do it?" Better is to agree, reluctantly, to pay the "on-the-spot-fine" that was requested; or to gradually accept the need for the extra "administration fee" that was demanded; or to finally agree to help to cover the "time and trouble" involved... provided that the problem can be overcome.

BUSH CAMPING – E.H

Chapter Seven

In the Wilds

DRIVING

Driving around Zambia isn't for the novice, or the unprepared. Long stretches of the tarred roads are extensively potholed, and some of the secondary gravel roads are in very poor repair. If you plan on exploring in the more rural areas, and remote parks, then you will need at least two sturdy, fully-equipped 4WD vehicles. It is interesting to note that several of Zambia's car hire companies only rent vehicles (saloons for use only in the towns) if you take a local driver – it says something of the roads in general.

Equipment and preparations

Fuel

Petrol and diesel are available in most of the towns, and shortages are now rare. However, for travel into the bush you will need long-range fuel tanks, and/or a large stock of filled jerry cans. It is essential to plan your fuel requirements well in advance, and to carry more than you expect to need.

Remember that using the vehicle's 4WD capability, especially in low ratio gears, will significantly increase your fuel consumption. Similarly, the cool comfort of a vehicle's air conditioning will burn your fuel reserves swiftly.

Spares

Zambia's garages do not generally have a comprehensive stock of vehicle spares – though bush mechanics can effect the most amazing short-term repairs, with remarkably basic tools and raw materials. Spares for the more common makes are easiest to find, so most basic Land Rover and Toyota 4WD parts are available somewhere in Lusaka, at a price. So if you are arriving in Zambia with a foreign vehicle, it is best to bring as many spares as you can.

Navigation

See the section on *Maps and navigation* in *Chapter Five*, for detailed comments, but there are good maps available, and you should seriously consider taking a GPS system if you are heading off the main roads in the more remote areas of the country.

Coping with Zambia's roads

Tar roads

Many of Zambia's tar roads are excellent, and a programme of tarring is gradually extending these good sections. However, within these tar sections there are occasional potholed patches. These often occur in small groups – making some short stretches of tar very slow going indeed. If you are unlucky, or foolish, enough to hit one of these sections after speeding along a smooth stretch of tar, then you are likely to blow at least one tyre and are in danger of having a serious accident. For this reason, if for no other, even the tar roads that look good are worth treating with caution. It is wiser never to exceed about 80kph.

Strip roads

Occasionally there are roads where the sealed tar surface is only wide enough for one vehicle. This becomes a problem when you meet another vehicle travelling in the opposite direction...on the same stretch of tar. Then local practice is to wait until the last possible moment before you steer left, driving with two wheels on the gravel adjacent to the tar, and two on the tar. Usually, the vehicle coming in the opposite direction will do the same, and after passing each other both vehicles veer back onto the tar. If you are unused to this, then slow right down before you steer onto the gravel.

Gravel roads

Gravel roads can be very deceiving. Even when they appear smooth, flat and fast (which is not often) they still do not give vehicles much traction. You will frequently put the car into small skids, and with practice at slower speeds you will learn how to deal with them. Gravel is a less forgiving surface on which to drive than tar. The rules and techniques for driving well are the same for both, but on tar you can get away with sloppy braking and cornering which would prove fatal on gravel.

Further, in Zambia you must always be prepared for the unexpected: an animal wandering on to the road, a rash of huge potholes, or an unexpected corner. So it is verging on insane to drive over about 80kph on any of Zambia's gravel roads. Other basic driving hints include:

Slowing down If in any doubt about what lies ahead, always slow down. Road surfaces can vary enormously, so keep a constant look-out for potholes, ruts or patches of soft sand which could put you into an unexpected slide.

Passing vehicles When passing other vehicles travelling in the opposite direction, always slow down to minimise both the damage that stone chippings will do to your windscreen, and the danger in driving through the other vehicle's dust cloud.

Using your gears In normal driving, a lower gear will give you more control over the car – so keep out of high "cruising" gears. Rather stick with third or fourth, and accept that your revs will be slightly higher than they normally are.

Cornering and braking Under ideal conditions, the brakes should only be applied when the car is travelling in a straight line. Braking whilst negotiating a corner is dangerous, so it is vital to slow down before you reach corners. Equally, it is better to slow down gradually using a combination of gears and brakes, than to use the brakes alone. You are less likely to skid.

Driving at night

Never drive at night unless you have to. Both wild and domestic animals frequently spend the night by the side of busy roads, and will actually sleep on quieter ones. Tar roads are especially bad as the surface absorbs all the sun's heat by day, and then radiates it at night – making it a warm bed for passing animals. A high-speed collision with any animal, even a small one like a goat, will not only kill the animal, but will cause very severe damage to a vehicle, with potentially fatal consequences.

Driving techniques

To drive anywhere outside of the main towns, and linking arteries, you need at least a high-clearance vehicle, and preferably one with four-wheel drive. The latter will extend your range considerably, and becomes essential to reach much of the country in the rainy season. However, no vehicle can make up for an inexperienced driver – so make sure that you are confident of your vehicle's capabilities before you venture into the wilds with it.

Driving in convoy is a sensible precaution on the quieter tracks in the bush, in case one vehicle gets stuck or breaks down. If that does happen then larger local farms (if there are any) often have extensive workshops. You will be amazed at the effective repairs that local "bush mechanics" can make: Zambians are masters at keeping their vehicles on the road.

Driving in sand

If you start to lose traction in deep sand, then stop on the next piece of solid ground that you come to. Lower your tyre pressure until there is a distinct bulge in the tyre walls (having first made sure that you have the means to re-inflate them when you reach solid roads again). This will help your traction greatly, but increase the wear on your tyres. Pump them up again before you drive on a hard surface at speed, or they will be badly damaged.

Where there are clear, deep-rutted tracks in the sand, don't fight the steering wheel – just relax and let your vehicle steer itself. Driving in the cool of the morning is easier than later in the day because when sand is cool it compacts better and is firmer. (When hot, the pockets of air between the sand grains expand and the sand becomes looser.)

If you do get stuck, despite these precautions, don't panic. Don't just rev the engine and spin the wheels – you'll only dig deeper. Instead stop. Relax and asses the situation. Now dig shallow ramps in front of all the wheels, reinforcing them with pieces of wood, vegetation, stones, material or anything else which will give the wheels better traction. Lighten the vehicle load (passengers out) and push. Keep the engine revs high as you engage your lowest ratio gear, and use the clutch to ensure that the wheels don't spin wildly and dig themselves further into the sand.

Sometime rocking the vehicle backwards and forwards can build up momentum to break you free. This can be done by intermittently applying the clutch and by getting helpers who can push and pull the vehicle at the same frequency. Once the vehicle is moving, the golden rule of sand driving is to keep up the momentum: if you pause, you will sink and stop.

Driving in mud

This is difficult, though the theory is the same as for sand: keep going and don't stop. That said, even the most experienced drivers get stuck. Some areas of Zambia have very fine soil known as "black-cotton" soil, which can become totally impassable when wet. Hence many of the more remote camps will close down during the wet season, as the only way to reach them would be to walk.

Rocky terrain

Have your tyre pressure higher than normal and move very slowly. If necessary passengers should get out and guide you along the track to avoid scraping the undercarriage on the ground.

Crossing rivers

The first thing to do is to stop and check the river. You must assess its depth, its substrate (type of river bed) and its current flow; and determine the best route to drive across it. This is best done by wading across the river – but watch out for hippos and crocodiles. Beware of water that's too deep for your vehicle, or the very real possibility of being swept away by a fast current and a slippery substrate.

If everything is OK then select your lowest gear ratio and drive through the water at a slow but steady rate. Note that your vehicle's air intake must be above the level of the water to avoid your engine filling with water. It's not worth taking risks, so remember that a flooded river will often subside to much safer levels by the next morning.

Many rivers in Zambia have hand-operated pontoons. There are often, but not always, local people around who can help you with these, for a small tip.

Handy hints

Grass seeds In areas of tall grass keep a close watch on the water temperature gauge. Grass stems and seeds will get caught in the radiator grill and block the flow of air, causing the engine to overheat and the grass to catch fire. You should stop and remove the grass seeds every few kilometres also, depending on the conditions.

If the engine has overheated then the only option is to stop and turn the engine off. Don't open the radiator cap to refill it until the radiator is no longer hot to the touch. Even then keep the engine running, and the water circulating, while you refill the radiator – otherwise you run the risk of cracking the hot metal by suddenly cooling it. Flicking droplets of water on to the outside of a running engine will cool it.

Push-starting when stuck If you are unlucky enough to need to push-start your vehicle whilst it is stuck in sand or mud, then there is a remedy. Raise up the drive wheels, and take off one of the tyres. Then wrap a length of rope around the hub and treat it like a spinning top – with one person (or more) pulling the rope to make the axle spin, whilst the driver lifts the clutch, turns the ignition on, and engages a low gear to turn the engine over – the equivalent of a push start. This may be difficult, but it's probably your only option.

Decanting petrol If you need to transfer petrol from a jerry can to the petrol tank, and you haven't a proper funnel, then roll up a piece of paper into a funnel shape – it will work just as well.

Driving near big game

In the game parks the only animals which pose any major threat to vehicles are elephants – and only really elephants which are totally familiar with vehicles. So, treat them with the greatest respect and don't "push" them by trying to move ever closer. Letting them approach you is much safer, and they will feel far less threatened and more relaxed. Then, if the animals are relaxed, you can afford to turn the engine off, sit quietly, and just watch as they pass you by.

If you are unlucky, and foolish, enough to unexpectedly drive yourself into the middle of an herd, then don't panic. Keep your movements, and those of the vehicle, slow and measured. Back off steadily. Don't be panicked, or overly intimidated, by a mock charge – this is just their way of frightening you away.

BUSH CAMPING

Many "boy scout" type manuals have been written on survival in the bush, usually by military veterans. If you are stranded with a convenient multi-purpose knife, then these useful tomes will describe how you can build a shelter from branches, catch passing animals for food, and signal to the inevitable rescue planes which are combing the globe looking for you – whilst avoiding the attentions of hostile forces.

Here in Zambia, bush camping is usually less about surviving than about being comfortable. You will usually have much more than the knife: at least you will have a bulging backpack, if not a loaded 4WD. Thus the challenge is not to camp and survive, it is to camp and to be as comfortable as possible. Only practice will teach you this, but a few hints might be useful for the less experienced African campers:

Where you can camp

In national parks which get frequent visitors, there are designated camping sites which you must use, as directed by the local game scouts. Elsewhere the rules are less obvious, though it is normal to ask the scouts, and get their permission, for any site that you have in mind.

Outside of the parks, you should ask the local landowner, or village head, if the are happy for you to camp on their property. If you explain patiently and politely what you want, then you are unlikely to meet anything but warm hospitality from most rural Zambians They will normally be as fascinated with your way of life, as you are with theirs – and company by your camp fire is virtually assured.

Choosing a site

Only experience will teach you how to choose a good site for pitching a tent, but a few points may help you avoid a lot of problems:

- Avoid camping on what looks like a path through the bush, however indistinct, as it may be a well-used game trail.

- Beware of camping in dry river beds: dangerous flash floods can arrive with little or no warning.
- In marshy areas camp on higher ground to avoid cold, damp mists in the morning and evening.
- Camp a reasonable distance from water: near enough to walk to it, but far enough to avoid animals which arrive to drink.
- If a lightning storm is likely, make sure that your tent is not the highest thing around.
- Finally, choose a site which is as flat as possible - you will find sleeping much easier.

Camp fires

Camp fires can create a great atmosphere and warm you on a cold evening, but they can also be damaging to the environment and leave unsightly piles of ash and blackened stones. Deforestation is a cause for major concern in much of the developing world, including some parts of Zambia, so if you do light a fire then use wood as the locals do - sparingly. If you have a vehicle, then consider buying firewood in advance from people who sell it at the roadside.

If you collect it yourself, then take only dead wood, nothing living. Never just pick up a log - always roll it over first, checking carefully for snakes or scorpions.

Experienced campers build small, highly efficient fires by using a few large stones to absorb, contain and reflect the heat, and gradually feeding just a few thick logs into the centre to burn. Cooking pots can be balanced on the stones, or the point where the logs meet and burn. Others will use a small trench, lined with rocks, to similar effect. Either technique takes practice, but is worth perfecting. Whichever you do, bury the ashes, take any rubbish with you when you leave, and make the site look as if you had never been there.

Don't expect an unattended fire to frighten away the wild animals - that works in Hollywood, but not in Africa. A fire may help your feelings of insecurity, but lion and hyena will disregard camp fires with stupefying nonchalance.

Finally, do be hospitable to any locals who appear - despite your efforts to seek permission for your camp, you may effectively be staying in their back gardens.

Using a tent (or not)

Whether to use a tent or to sleep in the open is a personal choice, dependent upon where you are. If you are in an area where there are predators around (specifically lion and hyena) then you should use a tent. Then sleep *completely* inside the tent, as a protruding leg may seem like a tasty take-away to a hungry hyena. This is especially true at organised campsites, where the local animals have got so used to humans that they have lost much of their inherent fear of man.

Outside game areas, you will be fine sleeping in the open, or preferably under a mosquito net, with just the stars of the African sky above you. On the practical side, sleeping under a tree will reduce the morning dew that settles on your sleeping bag. If your vehicle has a large, flat roof then sleeping on this will provide you with peace of mind, and a star-filled outlook. Kessler 4x4 hire (see page 56) even has 4WD vehicles with built-on roof-tents.

Animal dangers for campers

Camping in Africa is really *very* safe, though you may not think so from reading this. If you have a major problem whilst camping, it will probably be because you did something stupid, or because you forgot to take a few simple precautions. Here are a few basics:

Big animals

Big game will not bother you if you are in a tent – provided that you do not attract its attention, or panic it. Elephants will gently tip-toe through your guy ropes whilst you sleep, without even nudging your tent. However, if you wake up and make a noise, startling them, they are far more likely to panic and step on your tent. Similarly, scavengers will quietly wander round, smelling your evening meal in the air, without any intention of harming you.

- Remember to go the toilet before you go to bed, and avoid getting up in the night if possible.
- Scrupulously clean everything used for food which might smell good to scavengers. Put these utensils in a vehicle if possible, suspend them from a tree, or pack them away in a rucksack *inside* the tent.
- Do not pack any smelly foodstuffs, like meat or citrus fruit, in your tent. Their smells may attract unwanted attention.
- Do not leave anything outside that could be picked up – like bags, pots, pans, etc. Hyenas, amongst others, will take anything. (They have been known to crunch a camera's lens, and eat it.)
- If you are likely to wake in the night, then leave the tent's zips a few centimetres open at the top, enabling you to take a *quiet* peek outside.

Creepy crawlies

As you set up camp, clear stones or logs out of your way with great caution: underneath will be great hiding places for snakes and scorpions. Long moist grass is ideal territory for snakes, and dry, dusty, rocky places are classic sites for scorpions.

If you are sleeping in the open, it is not unknown to wake and find a snake lying next to you in the morning. Don't panic, it has just been attracted to you by your warmth. You will not be bitten if you gently edge away without making any sudden movements. (This is one good argument for using at least a mosquito net!)

Before you put on your shoes, shake them out. Similarly, check the back of your backpack before you slip it on. Just a curious spider, in either, could inflict a painful bite.

WALKING IN THE BUSH

Walking in the African bush is a totally different sensation to driving through it. You may start off a little unready – perhaps even sleepy for an early morning walk – but swiftly your mind will awake. There are no noises except the wildlife, and you. So every noise that isn't caused by you must be an animal; or a bird; or an insect. Every smell and every rustle has a story to tell, *if* you can understand it.

With time, patience, and a good guide you can learn to smell the presence of elephants, and hear when impala are alarmed by a predator. You can use oxpeckers to lead you to buffalo, or vultures to help you locate a kill. Tracks will record the passage of animals in the sand, telling what passed by, how long ago, and to where it was heading.

Eventually your gaze becomes alert to the slightest movement; your ears aware of every sound. This is safari at its best. A live, sharp, spine-tingling experience that's hard to beat and very addictive. Be careful: watching game from a vehicle will never be the same again for you.

Walking trails and safaris

One of Zambia's biggest attractions is its walking safaris, which can justly claim to be the best in Africa. The concept was pioneered here, in the Luangwa Valley, by Norman Carr – who founded Kapani Lodge, and trained several of the valley's best guides. It was he who first operated walking safaris for photographic guests, as opposed to hunters. The Luangwa still has a strong tradition of walking – which, in itself, fosters excellent walking guides. Several of the camps are dedicated to walking safaris, and guiding standards are generally very high.

One of the reasons behind the valley's success is the stringent tests that a guide must pass before he, or she, will be allowed to take clients into the bush. Walking guides have the hardest tests to pass; there is a less demanding exam for guides who conduct safaris from vehicles.

The second major reason for excellence is Zambia's policy of having a safari guide and an armed game scout accompany every walking safari. If a problem arises with an aggressive animal, then the guide looks after the visitors – telling them exactly what to do – whilst the scout keeps his sights trained on the animal, just in case a shot is needed. Fortunately such drastic measures are needed only rarely. This system of two guides means that Zambia's walks are very safe, and few shots are ever fired.

Contrast this with other African countries where a single guide (who may, or may not, be armed) watches out for the game *and* takes care of the visitors at the same time. The Zambian way is far better.

Etiquette for walking safaris

If you plan to walk then avoid wearing any bright, unnatural colours, especially white. Dark, muted shades are best; greens, browns and khaki are ideal. Hats are essential, as is sun-block. Even a short walk will last for two hours, and there's no vehicle to which you can retreat if you get too hot.

Cameras and binoculars should be immediately accessible - ideally in dust-proof cases strapped to your belt. They are of much less use if buried at the bottom of a camera bag.

Walkers see the most when walking in silent single file. This doesn't mean that you can't stop to whisper a question to the guide; just that idle chatter will reduce your powers of observation, and make you even more visible to the animals (who will usually flee when they sense you).

With regard to safety, your guide will always brief you in detail before you set off. S/he will outline possible dangers, and what to do in the event of them materialising. Listen carefully: this is vital.

Face-to-face animal encounters

Whether you are on an organised walking safari, on your own hike, or just walking from the car to your tent in the bush, it is not unlikely that you will come across some of Africa's larger animals at close quarters. Invariably, the danger is much less than you imagine, and a few basic guidelines will enable you to cope effectively with most situations.

Firstly, don't panic. Console yourself with the fact that animals are not normally interested in people. You are not their normal food, or their predator. If you do not annoy or threaten them, you will be left alone.

If you are walking to look for animals, then remember that this is their environment not yours. Animals have been designed for the bush, and their senses are far better attuned to it than yours. To be on less unequal terms, remain alert and try to spot them from a distance. This gives you the option of approaching carefully, or staying well clear.

Finally, the advice of a good guide is more valuable than the simplistic comments noted here. Animals, like people, are all different. So whilst we can generalise here and say how the "average" animal will behave - the one that's glaring over a small bush at you may have had a *really* bad day, and be feeling much more grumpy than average.

That said, here are a few general comments on how to deal with some potentially dangerous situations:

Buffalo

This is probably the continent's most dangerous animal to hikers, but there is a difference between the old males, often encountered on their own or in small groups, and large breeding herds.

The former are easily surprised. If they hear or smell something amiss, they will charge without provocation – motivated by a fear that something is sneaking up on them. Buffalo have an excellent sense of smell, but fortunately they are short-sighted. Avoid a charge by quickly climbing the nearest tree, or by side-stepping at the last minute. If adopting the latter, more risky, technique then stand motionless until the last possible moment, as the buffalo may well miss you anyhow.

The large breeding herds can be treated in a totally different manner. If you approach them in the open, they will often flee. Sometimes though, in areas often used for walking safaris, they will stand and watch, moving aside to allow you to pass through the middle of the herd.

Neither encounter is for the faint-hearted or inexperienced, so steer clear of these dangerous animals wherever possiblc.

Black rhino

Unfortunately there are few, if any, black rhino left in Zambia. However, if you are both lucky enough to find one, and then unlucky enough to be charged by it, use the same tactics as you would for a buffalo: tree climbing or dodging at the last second. (It is amazing how even the least athletic walker will swiftly scale the nearest tree when faced with a charging rhino.)

Elephant

Normally elephants are only a problem if you disturb a mother with a calf, or approach a male in musth (state of arousal). So keep well away from these. Lone bulls can usually be approached quite closely when feeding. If you get too close to any elephant they will scare you off with a "mock charge": head up, perhaps shaking – ears flapping – trumpeting. Lots of sound and fury. This is intended to be frightening, and it is. But it is just a warning and no cause for panic. Just freeze to assess the elephant's intentions, then back off slowly.

When elephants really mean business, they will put their ears back, their head down, and charge directly at you without stopping. This is known as a "full charge". There is no easy way to avoid the charge of an angry elephant, so take a hint from the warning and back off very slowly as soon as you encounter a mock charge. Don't run. If you are the object of a full charge, then you have no choice but to run – preferably round an anthill, up a tall tree, or wherever.

Lion

Tracking lion can be one of the most exhilarating parts of a walking safari. Sadly, they will normally flee before you even get close to them. However, it can be a problem if you come across a large pride unexpectedly. Lion are well camouflaged; it is easy to find yourself next to one before you realise it. If you had been listening, you would probably have heard a warning growl about twenty metres ago. Now it is too late.

The best plan is to stop, and back off slowly, but confidently. If you are in a small group, then stick together. *Never* run from a big cat. Firstly, they are always faster than you are. Secondly, running will just convince them that you are frightened prey, and worth chasing. As a last resort, if they seem too inquisitive and follow as you back off, then stop. Call their bluff. Pretend that you are not afraid and make loud, deep, confident noises: shout at them, bang something. But do not run.

John Coppinger, one of Luangwa's most experienced guides, adds that every single compromising experience that he has had with lion on foot has been either with a female with cubs, or with a mating pair, when the males can get very aggressive. You have been warned.

Leopard

Leopard are very seldom seen, and would normally flee from the most timid of lone hikers. However, if injured, or surprised, then they are very powerful, dangerous cats. Conventional wisdom is scarce, but never stare straight into the leopard's eyes, or it will regard this as a threat display. (The same is said, by some, to be true with lion.) Better to look away slightly, at a nearby bush, or even at its tail. Then back off slowly, facing the direction of the cat and showing as little terror as you can. As with lion – loud, deep, confident noises are a last line of defence. Never run from a leopard.

Hippo

Hippo are fabled to account for more deaths in Africa than any other animal (ignoring the mosquito). Having been attacked and capsized by a hippo whilst in a dug-out canoe, the author finds this very easy to believe. Visitors are most likely to encounter hippo in the water, when paddling a canoe (see *Canoeing*, page 88), or fishing. However, as they spend half their time grazing on land, they will sometimes be encountered out of the water. Away from the water, out of their comforting lagoons, hippos are even more dangerous. If they see you, they will flee towards the water – so the golden rule is never to get between a hippo and its escape route to deep water. Given that a hippo will outrun you on land, standing motionless is probably your best line of defence.

Snakes

These are really not the great danger that people imagine. Most flee when they feel the vibrations of footsteps; only a few will stay still. The puff adder is responsible for more cases of snake bite than any other venomous snake in Zambia because, when approached, it will simply puff itself up and hiss as a warning, rather than slither away. This makes it essential to always watch where you place your feet when walking in the bush.

Similarly, there are a couple of arboreal (tree dwelling) species which may be taken by surprise if you carelessly grab vegetation as you walk. So don't.

Spitting cobras are also encountered occasionally, which will aim for your eyes and spit with accuracy. If the spittle reaches your eyes, you must wash them out *immediately* and thoroughly with whatever liquid comes to hand: water, milk, even urine if that's the only liquid that you can quickly produce.

CANOEING

The Zambezi – both above the Falls and from Kariba to Mozambique – is in constant use for canoeing trips. One good operator, Remote Africa Safaris (see page 202-3), even features adventurous canoeing/rafting trips down the Luangwa when it is in flood. Thus canoeing along these beautiful, tropical rivers is as much a part of Zambia's "safari scene" as are open-top Land Rovers.

Most operators use large, two-person Canadian-style fibreglass canoes, which have kit in the centre and a person at either end. The heavier, more powerful person will normally be at the back. Though no previous experience is demanded, it takes a while to get into a comfortable style of rowing, so is worth doing for at least three days and two nights if you are going at all.

In most of the commercial operations you can expect to join a party of about seven canoes, one of which will contain a guide. S/he should know the stretch of river well, and will canoe along it very regularly. The actual distances completed on the two/three night trips are quite short. All the trips run downstream and a day's canoeing could actually be completed in just three hours with a modicum of fitness and technique.

Like other guides, there is a professional licence which the "river guides" must possess in order to be allowed to take paying guests canoeing. Only a few of the best river guides also hold licences to conduct walking safaris. These all-rounders normally have a wider and deeper understanding of the game than the ones who are only "river guides".

However, this type of guide commands a higher price and they are usually found in the smaller, more upmarket operations. They often run their own small canoeing and/or safari company, some of which are poorly marketed overseas.

The safety record of river trips is excellent, though accidents do happen occasionally – usually when the group gets strung out and separated. The main dangers are:

Hippo

Hippos are strictly vegetarians, and will usually only attack a canoe if they feel threatened. The standard technique for avoiding hippo problems is firstly to let them know that you are there. If in doubt, bang your paddle on the side of the canoe a few times (most novice canoeists will do this constantly anyhow).

During the day, hippopotami will congregate in the deeper areas of the river. The odd ones in shallow water – where they feel less secure – will head for the deeper places as soon as they are aware of a nearby canoe. Avoiding hippos then becomes a fairly simple case of steering around the deeper areas, where the pods will make their presence obvious. This is where experience, and knowing every bend of the river, becomes useful.

Problems arise when canoes inadvertently stray over a pod of hippos, or when a canoe cuts a hippo off from its path of retreat into deeper water. Either situation is dangerous, as hippos will overturn canoes without a second thought, biting them and their occupants. Once in this situation, there are no easy remedies. It is essential to avoid them in the first place.

Crocodiles

Crocodiles may have sharp teeth and look prehistoric, but are of little danger to a canoeist...unless you are in the water. Then the more you struggle and the more waves you create, the more you will attract their unwelcome attentions. There is a major problem when canoes are overturned by hippos – making it essential to get out of the water as soon as possible, either into another canoe or on to the bank.

When a crocodile attacks an animal, it will try to disable it. It normally does this by getting a firm, biting grip, submerging, and performing a long, fast barrel-rolling. This will disorient the prey, drown it, and probably twist off the limb that has been bitten. In this dire situation, your best line of defence is probably to stab the reptile in its eyes with anything sharp that you have. Alternatively, if you can lift up its tongue and let the water into its lungs whilst it is underwater, then a crocodile will start to drown and will release its prey.

Jo Pope reports that a man survived an attack in the Zambezi recently when a crocodile grabbed his arm and started to spin backwards into deep

Above: *Victoria Falls and its gorges seen from a microlight* (CM)

Below: *Fishing at sunset* (PM)

Above: *The old Manor at Shiwa N'gandu* (CM)

Below: *Children playing* (ZNTB)

Above: *Thatching a bush lodge near Livingstone* (CM)
Below left: *Boys with home-made toys* (ZNTB)
Below right: *Women preparing maize, the staple food of most Zambians* (ZNTB)

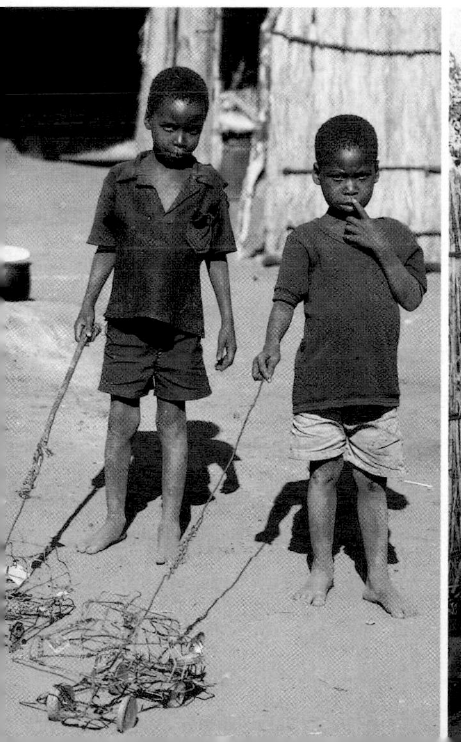

Above: *Open-bill stork on a tributary of the Kafue* (PM)
Below left: *Fish eagles are common throughout Zambia* (PM)
Below right: *Male masked weaver bird* (Ploceus velatus) *under its nest* (PH)

water. The man wrapped his legs around the crocodile, to spin with it and avoid having his arm twisted off. As this happened, he tried to poke his thumb into its eyes, but this had no effect. Finally he put his free arm into the crocodile's mouth, and opened up the beast's throat. This worked. The crocodile left him and he survived with only a damaged arm. Understandably, anecdotes on this topic, of tried and tested methods of escape, are rare.

MINIMUM IMPACT

When you visit, drive through, or camp in an area with minimum impact, that area is left in the same condition - or better than when you entered it. Whilst most visitors view minimum impact as being desirable, spend time to consider the ways that we contribute to environmental degradation, and how these can be avoided.

Driving

Use your vehicle responsibly. If there's a road, or a track, then don't go off it - the environment will suffer. Driving off-road leaves unsightly tracks which detract from the "wilderness" feeling for subsequent visitors.

Hygiene

Use toilets if they are provided, even if they are basic long-drop loos with questionable cleanliness. If there are no toilets, then human excrement should always be buried well away from paths, or groundwater, and any tissue used should be burnt and then buried.

If you use rivers or lakes to wash, then soap yourself near the bank, using a pan for scooping water from the river - making sure that no soap finds its way back into the water. Use biodegradable soap. Sand makes an excellent pan-scrub, even if you have no water to spare.

Rubbish

Biodegradable rubbish can be burnt and buried with the camp fire ashes. Don't just leave it lying around: it will look very unsightly and spoil the place for those who come after you.

Bring along some plastic bags with which to remove the rest of your rubbish, and dump it at the next town. Items which will not burn, like tin cans, are best cleaned and squashed for easy carrying. If there are bins, then use them, but also consider when they will next be emptied, and if local animals will rummage through them first. Carrying out all your own rubbish may still be the sensible option.

Host communities

Whilst the rules for reducing impact on the environment have been understood and followed by responsible travellers for years, the effects of tourism on local people have only recently been considered. Many tourists consider it their right, for example, to take intrusive photos of local people – and even become angry if the local people object. They refer to higher prices being charged to tourists as a rip off, without considering the hand-to-mouth existence of those selling these products or services. They deplore child beggars, then hand out sweets or pens to local children with outstretched hands.

Our behaviour towards "the locals" needs to be considered in terms of their culture, with the knowledge that we are the uninvited visitors. We visit to enjoy ourselves, but this should not be at the expense of local people. Read *Cultural guidelines* (page 28-9) and aim to leave the local communities better off after your visit.

Chapter Eight

Zambia Today

TOURISM IN ZAMBIA

Tourists still come to Zambia in small numbers, and largely restrict themselves to a few of the main towns and national parks. Away from these centres, visitors are regarded with mild curiosity and often shown great warmth and hospitality. Zambia is a genuinely friendly country which (perhaps Lusaka excepted) has not yet had sufficient bad experiences of visitors to lower its opinion of them.

Zambia's attitude to tourism has changed considerably over the last few years, and visitors are now generally seen as good for the country because they spend valuable foreign currency and create employment. Tourism is helping Zambia's economy and its conservation policy, by making a major contribution to the preservation of the national parks.

Northeast of Zambia are the "original" safari areas of east Africa: Kenya and Tanzania, where many of the national parks are now rather too crowded. To the south are the more subtle attractions of Zimbabwe, Botswana and Namibia – each appealing to its own type of wildlife enthusiasts, and all having an element of wilderness remaining. It is hoped that sustainable "eco" tourism can be a saviour of Zambia's economy as well as its wildlife, though there is a long way to go.

COST OF LIVING

Like anywhere else, the cost of visiting Zambia varies with the style in which you travel, and the places where you spend your time. However, unlike many countries, Zambia's lack of infrastructure leads to a "polarisation" of travelling styles.

If you plan a week or two to visit the parks, staying at small private safari camps, then the costs are high. You may need to take the odd private charter flight, and an average US$225-375/£150-250 per day, including all meals and activities, would be expected. This is typical for an exclusive safari in a pristine and remote corner of Africa – the kind of trip at which Zambia excels.

At the other end of the spectrum, if you travel through Zambia on local buses, camping and staying in local (and sometimes rather seedy) resthouses, then Zambia is not expensive. A budget of US$30-45/£20-30 per day for food, accommodation and transport would suffice. However, most backpackers who undertake such trips are simply "in transit" between Malawi and Zimbabwe. They see little of the wildlife and few of the national parks, missing out on even Zambia's cheaper attractions.

Finding a trip of medium expenditure, between these two extremes, is difficult. Hiring a vehicle is one way, as then you can buy food, camp and drive yourself around – though this requires driving expertise, and is not something to undertake lightly. The easier option would be to make use of the odd medium-priced safari camp. Lufupa/Shumba in northern Kafue and the Wildlife Camp in South Luangwa are obvious options, whilst Chundukwa's trips from Livingstone into the Nanzhila Plains of southern Kafue promise impressive value for small, active groups. If you are hitchhiking, then Kasanka is a super park: cheap and vastly under-visited.

Creatively using these options, being prepared to pay where necessary, you might spend only US$150/£100 per day whilst seeing some of the very best that the country has to offer.

Currency and inflation

Zambia's unit of currency is the kwacha. Theoretically each kwacha is divided into 100 ngwee, although one ngwee is now worth so little that these subdivisions are never used. The old practices of strict exchange control and unrealistic exchange rates have now gone – as has the black market for currency that these policies created.

As the result of the present free market, US dollars and UK pounds sterling are easily changed, and it is sometimes possible to spend US dollars directly.

On 18 September 1996 the **exchange rates** were £1=Kw1,950; US$1=Kw1,260.

Inflation has been running at between 100% and 200% since at least 1989. It is now towards the lower end of that band, but is showing signs that it might drop down to double figures. This makes thinking and calculating in US dollars the easiest way to plan, and explains why we have used US$ for most of the prices in this guide.

Banks

If you need to change foreign currency, receive bank drafts, or do any other relatively complex financial transactions, then the larger cities (ideally Lusaka) are your best option. Opening hours are generally 08.15-14.45 on Monday, Tuesday, Wednesday and Friday, and 09.00-11.00 on

Thursdays. A few of the bigger banks in Lusaka will also open from 09.00-11.00 on Saturdays. Cash-point (ATM) machines do not exist in Zambia.

GETTING AROUND

By air

If you want to fly internally in Zambia, but do not have the money to charter your own light aircraft, then there are a few possibilities. Several local companies use the routes vacated by Zambia Airways, but they are still finding their feet commercially. They are very reliable if you book just a few days in advance, but their schedules do change regularly. The services that I have encountered are high-quality operations, so you need have few worries about safety. However, if you book an internal flight a long time in advance, you should re-check its timing (and existence) every few months, especially if you have connections to make. Cancellation at short notice is unlikely, though taking a philosophical attitude towards the possibility of this would be wise.

The companies from which you can find the latest information are:

Aero Zambia Zambia Insurance Brokers House, Kimathi Road, P Bag 8717, Lusaka. Tel: 226192/3/4; fax: 226147

Air Malawi at Pamodzi Hotel. Tel: 254455
Promise a convenient service linking Lusaka, Mfuwe and Lilongwe.

Proflight PO Box 30536, Lusaka. Tel: 264439 or 263686 or 263687; airport tel: 271437; fax: 222888/262379
Currently notable for Lusaka-Mfuwe links which connect with the international BA flights. Expect to pay about US$135/£90 one-way; US$216/£145 return.

SafariLink PO Box 22, Kasane, Botswana. Tel: (267) 650505; fax: (267) 650352; tlx: 2901 BD
From their base in Botswana, they fly Kasane–Victoria Falls–Livingstone–Mfuwe. This costs about US$340/£220 one-way Kasane-Mfuwe.

Staravia PO Box 34273, Lusaka. Tel: 291962; airport tel: 271038

Tropic Air P Bag 7405, Chisipite, Harare, Zimbabwe. Tel: 304800 or 302350; fax: 302693; tlx: 22393 EXAIR
Links Harare with Mfuwe for US$175/£115 one-way.

Roan Air PO Box 310277, Lusaka International Airport. Tel: 271066; tlx: ZA 40410

Zambia Express tel: 222060 or 271208; fax: 227964; Email: zamex@zamnet.zm

If you want to fly into, or out of, Mfuwe International Airport, then you can normally find a scheduled way. However, getting anywhere else is often a matter of chartering your own plane. This isn't for the backpacker's budget, but if you plan to stay at private safari camps then it will be within your price range.

If you decide to arrange your own plane, then expect a five-seater to cost around US$1.30/£0.85 per kilometre, including any mileage to/from its base. Thus rough round-trip mileages would be:

Lusaka – Mfuwe	880km
Lusaka – Livingstone	810km
Lusaka – Kafue	500km

By rail

There are two totally separate rail systems of train in Zambia: ordinary trains and TAZARA trains. Zambia's ordinary trains have a limited network and are slow and uninteresting, so few travellers use them as a means of transport.

In contrast the TAZARA service is very popular with backpackers and runs from Kapiri Mposhi to the Indian Ocean, at Dar es Salaam in Tanzania. This is a reliable international transport link which normally runs to time and is by far the fastest way between Zambia and Tanzania with the exception of flying. See *Chapter Fifteen*'s section on *Kapiri Mposhi* for more details of this service.

By bus

Zambia's local buses are cheap, frequent and a great way to meet local people, although they can also be crowded, uncomfortable and noisy. In other words they are similar to any other local buses in Africa, and travel on them has both its joys and its frustrations.

In the main bus stations, there are two different kinds: the smaller minibuses, and the longer, larger "normal" buses. Both will serve the same destinations, but the smaller ones go faster and stop less. They may also be a little more comfortable. Their larger relatives will take longer to fill up before they leave the bus station (because few buses ever leave before they are full), and then go slower and stop at more places. For the smaller, faster buses there is a premium of about 20% on top of the price.

Then there are a few "postbuses" which operate between the post offices in the main towns, taking both mailbags and passengers as they go. These conform to a more fixed schedule, and tickets are booked in advance – thus restricting passenger numbers. They can be booked in advance from the post offices involved, and by telephoning Ndola (02) 615864, Kitwe (02) 223396, or Lusaka (01) 225795.

By coach

There used to be one or two luxury coach services which connect Lusaka to Livingstone, Harare and even Johannesburg. These were privately run, and usually arranged through the local travel agents in Lusaka. However, latest reports are that these have closed down. Ask around for the latest information on this.

By taxi

Taxis are common and very convenient, in Lusaka, Livingstone and the main towns of the Copperbelt, whilst elsewhere they are uncommon. They can be hailed down from the street, and never have meters. They all have typed sheets of the "minimum" rates to and from various local places, though charges can be higher if their customers appear affluent. Rates should always be agreed before getting into the vehicle. If you are unsure of the route then rates per kilometre, or per hour, are easy to negotiate.

Postboats

Rather like the postbuses, postboats operate on the Upper Zambezi and the waters of Lake Bangweulu during the rainy season, transporting cargo, passengers and even vehicles. Contact them by telephoning Samfya (02) 830254, Ndola (02) 617740, or Mongu (07) 221175.

Driving

Driving in Zambia is on the left, based on the UK's model. However, the standard of driving is generally poor, matched only by the quality of some of the roads. Most roads in the cities, and the major arteries connecting these, are tar. These vary from silky-smooth recently laid roads, to pot-holed routes that test the driver's skill at negotiating a "slalom course" of deep holes. Inconveniently, the smooth kind of road often changes into the holed variety without warning, so speeding on even the good tar is a dangerous occupation. Hitting a pothole at 40-60km/h will probably just blow a tyre; any faster and you risk damaging the suspension, or even rolling the car.

Away from the main arteries the roads are gravel and usually badly maintained. During the dry season these will often need a high-clearance vehicle: a 4WD is welcome here, but not strictly vital. (The exceptions being areas of western Zambia standing on Kalahari sand, which always require 4WD.) During the wet season Zambia's gravel roads are less forgiving, and they vary from being strictly for 4WDs, to being totally impassable. Travel on anything except the tar roads is very difficult during the rains.

Hitchhiking

Hitchhiking around Zambia is a very practical way to get around – especially in the more remote areas. Most of Zambia's poorer citizens will get buses between the major centres, and then hitchhike on the smaller roads.

Hitching has the great advantage of allowing you a one-to-one audience to talk with a whole variety of people, from local business-people and expats, to truck-drivers and farmers. Sometimes you will be cramped on to the back of a windy pick-up with a dozen people and as many animals, while occasionally you will be comfortably seated in the back of a plush Mercedes, satisfying the driver's curiosity as to why you are in Zambia at all. It is simply the best way to get to know the country, through the eyes of its people, though it is not for the lazy or those pressed for time.

Waiting times can be long, even on the main routes, and getting a good lift can take six or eight hours. Generally, on such occasions, the problem is not that lots of potential vehicles refuse to take you. The truth is that there are sometimes very few people going your way with space to spare. If you are in a hurry then combining hitchhiking with taking the odd bus can be a very speedy way to travel.

The essentials for successful hitching in Zambia include a relatively neat set of clothes, without which you will be ignored by some of the more comfortable lifts available. A good ear for listening and a relaxed line in conversation are also assets, which spring naturally from taking an interest in the lives of the people that you meet. Finally, you must always carry a few litres of water and some food with you, both for standing beside the road, and for lifts where you can't stop for food.

Dangers of drunk driving

Unfortunately, drunk driving is common in Zambia. It is more frequent in the afternoon/evening, and towards the end of the month when people are paid. Accepting a lift with someone who is drunk, or drinking and (simultaneously) driving, is foolish. Occasionally your driver will start drinking on the way, in which case you would be wise to start working out how to disembark politely.

An excuse for an exit, which I used on one occasion, was to claim that some close family member was killed whilst being driven by a driver who had been drinking. Thus I had a real problem with the whole idea, and had even promised a surviving relative that I would never do the same... hence my overriding need to leave at the next reasonable town/village/stop. This gave me an opportunity to encourage the driver not to drink any more, and when that failed (which it did), it provided an excuse for me to disembark swiftly. Putting the blame on my own psychological problems like this avoided blaming the driver too much, which might have caused a difficult scene.

Safety of hitchhiking

Not withstanding the occasional drunk driver, Zambia is generally a very safe place to hitchhike for a robust male traveller, or couple travelling. It is safer than the UK, and considerably safer than the USA. Having said that, hitchhiking still cannot be recommended for single women, or even two women travelling together. This is not because of any known horror stories, but because white women hitching would evoke intense curiosity amongst the local people. Local people might view a white woman hitching as asking for trouble, whilst some would associate them with the "promiscuous" behaviour of white women seen on imported films and TV programmes. The risk seems too high – so stick to buses.

ACCOMMODATION

Hotels

Hotels in Zambia tend to be large concrete blocks with pretensions to an "international" standard, or small, run-down places catering to Zambians that are not very particular about quality.

The former are restricted to Lusaka and the Copperbelt – the areas that attract businessmen – and have little to distinguish them from each other. They will, however, have clean modern rooms, good communications, and all the facilities that international business people expect. Their prices will reflect this, at around US$60/£40 per person sharing a room. The smaller, cheaper places vary tremendously, but very few are good and many seem over-priced. Zambian hotels are a very uninspiring bunch on the whole, so most visitors spend as little time in them as possible.

The exception to this rule are a few game-lodge-cum-hotels which are within reach of Lusaka, like Lilayi or Lechwe Lodge. These are much more interesting if you want somewhere pleasant to stay near Lusaka.

Government resthouses

These are dotted around the country in virtually every town: a very useful option for the stranded backpacker. They are usually run by a town or district council and, although a few have degenerated into brothels, others are excellent for a brief overnight stop. The sheets are usually clean, and most have rooms with private facilities. These are normally clean, though rarely spotless.

Bush camps and lodges

Zambia's camps in the bush are a match for the best in Africa. As befits a destination for visitors who take their game-viewing and bird-watching seriously, the camps are very comfortable but seldom luxurious. En suite showers and toilets are almost universal, the accommodation is fairly spacious, the organisation smooth, and food invariably excellent. However, few forget that their reputations are won and lost by the standards of their individual guides.

Expect a maximum of twenty guests, and close personal care at most. But beware: if you seek a safari for its image, wanting to sleep late and then be pampered in the bush; or to dine from silverware and sip from cut-glass goblets... then perhaps Zambia isn't for you after all.

FOOD AND DRINK

Food

Zambia's native cuisine is based on *nshima,* a cooked porridge made from ground maize. This is usually made thin, perhaps with sugar, for breakfast, then eaten thicker – the consistency of mashed potatoes – for lunch and dinner. For these main meals it will also normally be accompanied by some tasty relish, perhaps made of meat and tomatoes, or dried fish. (In Zimbabwe this is *sadza*, in South Africa *mealie-pap*.)

You should taste this at some stage when visiting, as it is available in small restaurants in all of the towns. Often these will have only three items on the menu: nshima and chicken; nshima and meat; and nshima and fish – and they can be very good.

That said, camps, hotels and lodges that cater to overseas visitors will serve a very international fare, and the quality of food prepared in the most remote camps amazes most visitors.

If you are driving yourself around, and plan to cook, then get most of your supplies in Lusaka, as there you will find a good range of foodstuffs (at the best prices). Elsewhere, in Zambia's smaller towns, availability is limited to products popular locally. These include bread, flour, rice, soups and various tinned vegetables, meats, and fish. This is fine for subsistence, but you may get bored with the selection in a week or two.

Alcohol

Local Zambians usually drink bottled beer – *Castle, Lion, Mosi* or *Rhino* – if they are fairly affluent, or alternatively *Chibuku* (alias *Shake-shake*) if they are less so. Castle, Lion, Mosi and Rhino are similar brands, and the first two of these are found all over the subcontinent, often in the same kind of bottles. They are at their best when cold, and are then a match in thirst-quenching for any overseas beer. Note that the bottles have "deposit" on them, like those of soft drinks. The contents will cost about US$1/£0.65 from a shop, or about US$3.00/£2.00 in a hotel bar.

Chibuku is much cheaper and totally different. This is a commercial version of traditional beer, brewed from grain. It appears like a watery, alcoholic muesli, and is certainly an acquired taste. Locals will buy a bucket of it, and then pass this round for everyone to drink from. It would be unusual for a visitor to drink this, so try some if you are offered it: you will greatly amuse your Zambian drinking companions.

Soft drinks

Soft drinks are available everywhere, which is fortunate when the temperatures are high. Choices are often limited, though the ubiquitous *Coca-Cola* is usually there. Diet drinks are rarely seen in the rural areas – which is no surprise for a country where malnutrition is a problem.

Try to buy up at least one actual bottle in a city before you go travelling: it will be invaluable. Because of the cost of bottle production, and the "deposit" system, you will often be unable to buy full bottles of soft drinks in the rural areas without simultaneously supplying empty ones in return. The alternative is to stand and drink the contents where you buy a drink, and leave the empty behind you. This is fine, but can be inconvenient if you have just dashed in for a drink while your bus stops for a few minutes.

Water

Water in the main towns is usually purified, provided there are no shortages of chlorine, breakdowns, or other mishaps. The locals drink it, and are used to the relatively innocuous bugs that it may harbour. If you are in the country for a long time, then it may be worth acclimatising yourself to it – though be prepared for some days spent near a toilet. However, if you are in Zambia for just a few weeks, then try to drink only bottled, boiled, or treated water in town.

Out in the bush, most of the camps and lodges use water from bore-holes. These underground sources vary in quality, but are normally free from bugs. Sometimes it is sweet to drink, at other times bore-hole water is a little alkaline or salty. Ask the locals if it is suitable for an unacclimatised visitor to drink, then take their advice.

Tipping

In the cities tipping is used widely and often expected, though the amounts are small. Helpers with baggage might expect US$0.50/30p equivalent, whilst sorting out a problematic reservation would be US$2-3/£1.50-2.00. Restaurants will sometimes add an automatic service charge to the bill, in which case a tip is not obligatory. If they do not do this, work on 10%.

A tip is seen, by some, as a polite way to reward someone for a favour, and thus can sometimes be used as a bribe for services rendered. See the general comments on *bribery*, at the end of *Chapter Six*.

WHAT TO BUY

Zambia's best bargains are handicrafts: carvings and baskets made locally. The curio stall near the border to the Falls has an excellent selection, but prices are cheaper if you buy within Zambia, in Lusaka or at some of the roadside stalls. *Kabwata Cultural Centre*, page 124, is an obvious place to do some shopping. Wherever you buy handicrafts, don't be afraid to bargain. Expect an eventual reduction of about one quarter to one third of the original asking price, and always be polite and good-humoured. After all, a few cents will probably make more difference to the person with whom you are bargaining than it will mean to you.

Note that you will often see carvings on sale in the larger stalls which have been imported from Kenya, Tanzania, Zaïre and Zimbabwe. Assume that they would be cheaper if purchased in their countries of origin, and try to buy something Zambian as a memento of your trip.

Occasionally you will be offered "precious" stones to buy - rough diamonds, emeralds and the like. Expert geologists may spot the occasional genuine article amongst hoards of fakes, but most mere mortals will end up being conned. Stick to the carvings if you want a bargain.

ABOUT CIGARETTES & BEER

Willard Nakutonga & Judi Helmholz

There are several types of beer or *Mooba* (meaning "beer" in Nyanja) produced in Zambia, including the following brews:

Mosi Lager is a bottled beer reflecting the local name for Victoria Falls – "Mosi Oa Tunya", meaning the "Smoke that Thunders". It is one of the most popular beers in Zambia. **Rhino Lager** is another bottled beer, produced and distributed throughout Zambia. You can ask for it by saying *Nifuna mooba wa Rhino* – I want rhino beer.

Chibuku or **Shake-Shake** is a much cheaper, opaque beer. Resembling an alcoholic milkshake, it is an acquired taste and a favourite amongst more traditional and less affluent Zambians.

Kachusuis the name for the main illicit beer – akin to "moonshine". It is brewed in villages or at *shebeens*, and it is wise never to agree to drink this. Not only is it illegal, so you may be arrested for just drinking it, but it may also damage your liver and kidneys.

Cigarettes, or *Fwaka* in Nyanja, can be purchased almost anywhere. In local markets, you can find big bins of raw tobacco, or tobacco shavings, on sale for those who like to roil their own. The most popular brand available in Zambia is Peter Stuyvesant, affectionately referred to as "Peters". Don't even think about trying *mbanje* or *dagga* (marajuana); if arrested there is no bail, and the penalty is five years in prison with hard labour.

ORGANISING AND BOOKING

Public holidays

New Year's day	January 1
Youth day	March 12 (and 13)
Good Friday	
Holy Saturday	
Labour day	May 1
Africa freedom day	May 25
Heroes' day	first Monday of July
Unity day	first Tuesday of July
Farmers' day	first Monday of August
Independence day	October 24
Christmas day	December 25
Boxing day	December 26

National parks

Head office

All of Zambia's national parks fall under the control of the National Parks and Wildlife Service – known simply as the NPWS – which is a department of the Ministry of Tourism. They set the rules and administer the parks from their head office near Chilanga, about 20km south of Lusaka.

Address written requests to the Chief Warden, Private Bag 1, Chilanga – though telephoning (01 278366) or calling in person will be much more effective. If you want to do anything unusual, or to go to any of the more remote parks, then it will make your trip easier if you buy your permits in advance from Chilanga. Clear your trip with them, and get some written permission that looks official: a letter from Chilanga and the appropriate permits work wonders at even the most remote scout camps.

The next best option is to try to get permission at the regional NPWS offices – which will probably be easier than negotiating with the scouts on the gate. See the country chapters for the locations of these.

Entry permits

Most organised trips will include park entry fees in their costs, but if you are travelling on your own then you must pay these directly, either at NPWS offices or in the parks. There is a scale of entry fees, and separate charges for camping in the parks. Currently South Luangwa costs US$15/£10 per person per day, whilst Kafue, Lower Zambezi, Lochinvar and Sumbu are US$10/£7. The rest cost US$5/£3.50 per person per day. On top of these, vehicles are charged US$5/£3.50 per entry, and camping within the park is another US$15/£10 per person per night.

Guides

For more adventurous trips to remote parks, hire a game scout from the nearest camp to act as your guide. This will save wasted driving time, and probably personal anguish over navigational puzzles. You may have to feed the scout, but even then this can still be an inexpensive way to get a local guide who may be able to add a whole new dimension to your trip.

Wildlife Conservation Society of Zambia (WCSZ)

This is an excellent society which supports environmental education in Zambia. It sponsors various conservation activities; runs some innovative children's conservation clubs – like the Chongololo clubs; publishes a number of good, inexpensive field guides specific to Zambia (see *Further Reading*; and is even responsible for several simple camps in the National Parks (eg: Kafwala and David Shepherd camps in Kafue, and the Wildlife Camp at Mfuwe).

Bookings for these camps can be made in person or by post, through the Wildlife Conservation Society of Zambia, PO Box 30255, Lusaka; tel: 254266; Email: wcsz@zamnet.zm.

To find out more, visit the WCSZ offices off Saddam Hussein Boulevard, near Longacres Lodge. They are also involved with the Wildlife Shop, near the corner of Cairo and Church roads – which is a good place to buy both WCSZ publications and other guide/wildlife books.

COMMUNICATIONS AND MEDIA

Post

The post is neither cheap nor fast, though it is fairly reliable for letters and postcards. The charges are increased to keep pace with the devaluations of the kwacha, but generally it costs around US$0.60/£0.40 to send a postcard and US$1/£0.65 for a letter.

Using the express mail is a practical but expensive way of increasing the chance that your letter will be delivered quickly. As an example, an express letter weighing less than 100g would costUS$30/£20 to send to the UK, or US$37.50/£25 to send to the USA. Couriers are another practical option – costing similar amounts, see under *Lusaka*, page 129.

Telephone

The Zambian telephone system is overloaded, and has difficulty coping. Getting through to anywhere can be hard, and this difficulty generally increases in proportion to the remoteness of the place that you are trying to contact. If you must use the phone, then persistence is the key – just keep on trying and eventually you should get a line that works.

To dial into the country from abroad, the international access code for Zambia is 260. From inside Zambia, you dial 00 to get an international line, then the country's access code (eg: 44 for the UK, or 1 for the USA).

New lines are difficult to acquire from the state-owned company which has a monopoly over the phone system, and old ones can take time to repair. Thus having up to five different numbers for one company is very common. Just try them all until one works for you.

Fax

If you are trying to send a fax to, or within, Zambia then always use a manual setting to dial (and redial, and redial...) the number. Listen for a fax tone on the line yourself. Only when you finally hear one should you press the "start" button on your machine to send the fax.

Regional codes in Zambia

There are only 12 regional codes in Zambia, most of which cover large regions of the country. The main towns associated with these codes are:

01 Chilanga; Chirundu; Chisamba; Chongwe; Kafue; Luangwa; Lusaka; Mumbwa; Namalundu Gorge; Nampundwe; Siavonga

02 Chambishi; Chililabombwe; Chingola; Itimpi; Kalulushi; Kawambwa; Kitwe; Luanshya; Mansa; Masaiti; Mufulira; Mwense; Nchelenge; Ndola; Samfya

03 Livingstone

032 Choma; Gwembe; Itezhi-Tezhi; Kalomo; Maamba; Mazabuka; Monze; Namwala; Pemba

04 Chinsali; Isoka; Kasama; Luwingu; Mbala; Mpika; Mporokoso; Mpulungu; Mungwi; Nakonde

05 Chibombo; Kabwe; Kapiri Mposhi; Mkushi; Serenje

062 Chadiza; Chipata; Katete; Mfuwe; Sinda

063 Nyimba; Petauke

064 Chama; Lundazi

07 Kalabo; Kaoma; Lukulu; Mongu; Senanga

08 Kabompo; Kasempa; Mufumbwe; Mwinilunga; Solwezi; Zambezi

Telex

Telex machines are not common in Zambia, but where they do exist they provide communication which you can instantly verify. You need not worry if your message has arrived, as the answer-back code will confirm that for you.

Email and the internet

Contrary to what you may have expected, the internet community in Zambia is quite large. Although there are few web-sites, there are many Email addresses. Because of telephone problems, this is an excellent way of communicating with some of the country's more remote spots. Virtually all addresses and sites are accessed through the University of Zambia's "zamnet" server.

Newspapers, radio and TV

There are six major papers in Zambia: the *Post*, the *Daily Mail*, *The Sun*, the *Times of Zambia*, the *Daily Express* and the *Financial Mail*. These are generally free in what they print, and one or two will criticise the government without much restraint - the Post is perhaps the most outspoken and interesting of them. The others seem to voice their criticisms less freely.

Radio is limited, though Radio Mulungushi does broadcast a popular range of music and chat on 95.6 FM, which can be received around the larger cities. Those with short wave radios have more choice, including the BBC World Service, the Voice of America, and Radio Canada.

Zambia National Broadcasting Corporation, ZNBC, broadcasts only in the evenings - and their panel debates can be fascinating. Most of the larger hotels with TVs will also subscribe to CNN, and/or the South African cable network, M-Net.

MISCELLANEOUS

Electricity

The local voltage is 220V, delivered at 50Hz. Sockets fit three square pins, like the current design in the UK.

Embassies

Angolan Embassy: 6660 Mumana Road, Olympia Road Ext, PO Box 31598, Lusaka. Tel: 291142/290346; fax: 292592

Belgian Embassy: Anglo American Building, 74 Independence Avenue, Woodlands, PO Box 320021, Lusaka. Tel: 252344/252512/252906; tlx: ZA 40000

Botswana High Commission: 2647 Haile Selassie Avenue, PO Box 31910, Lusaka. Tel: 250555/250019/253903; fax: 253895

Brazilian Embassy: Anglo American Building, 74 Independence Avenue, Woodlands, PO Box 34470, Lusaka. Tel: 250400; fax: 251652; tlx: ZA 40102

British High Commission: Diplomatic Triangle, Independence Avenue, PO Box 50050, Lusaka. Tel: 251133; fax: 253798; tlx: ZA 41150.

Bulgarian Embassy: 4045 Lukulu Road, PO Box 32896, Lusaka. Tel: 263295

Canadian High Commission: 5119 United Nations Avenue, PO Box 31313, Lusaka. Tel: 250833; fax: 254176; tlx: ZA 25416

Chinese Embassy: 7430 Haile Selassie Ave (corner of Pandit Nehru), PO Box 31895, Lusaka. Tel: 253770; fax: 253001; tlx: ZA 41360

Cuban Embassy: 5574 Magove Road, PO Box 33132, Lusaka. Tel: 251381

Cyprus Consulate: PO Box 32925, Lusaka. Tel: 262931/263004

Danish Embassy: Second Floor, Ndeke House Annex, Haile Selassie Ave., PO Box 50299, Lusaka. Tel: 254182/253750/254277; fax: 254618; tlx: ZA 40272

Egyptian Embassy: Pandit Nehru Road, Lusaka. Tel: 254149; tlx: ZA 40021

Finnish Embassy: Anglo American Building, 74 Independence Avenue, PO Box 50819, Lusaka. Tel: 251988; fax: 254981; tlx: ZA 43460

French Embassy: 4th Floor, Anglo American Building, 74 Independence Avenue, PO Box 30062, Lusaka. Tel: 251332; tlx: ZA 41430

German Embassy: 5209 United Nations Avenue, PO Box 50120, Lusaka. Tel: 250644; fax: 254014; tlx: ZA 41410

Greek Consulate: 54 Joseph Mwilwa Road, Fairview, PO Box 31587, Lusaka. Tel: 211120; fax: 231061; tlx: ZA 40280

Indian High Commission: 5220 Haile Selassie Avenue, PO Box 32111, Lusaka. Tel: 253066; fax: 245171

Irish Embassy: 6663 Katima Mulilo Road, Olympia Park Extension, PO Box 34923, Lusaka. Tel: 290482; tlx: ZA 43110

Italian Embassy: 5211 Embassy Park, Diplomatic Triangle, PO Box 31046, Lusaka. Tel: 250755/260382; fax: 214664; tlx: ZA 43380

Japanese Embassy: 3218 Haile Selassie Avenue, PO Box 34190, Lusaka. Tel: 251555; tlx: ZA 41470

Kenyan High Commission: 5207 United Nations Avenue, PO Box 50298; Lusaka. Tel: 250722

Korean Embassy: 8237 Nangwenya Road, Rhodes Park, PO Box 34030, Lusaka. Tel: 252978/252994; fax: 261476

Malawian High Commission: 5th Floor, Woodgate House, Cairo Road, PO Box 50425, Lusaka. Tel: 228296

Mozambique Embassy: Villa 46, Mulungushi Village, PO Box 34877, Lusaka. Tel: 290451; tlx: ZA 45900

Namibian High Commission: 6968 Kabanga Road, Rhodes Park, Lusaka. Tel: 252250

Netherlands Embassy: 6717 Chiwalamabwe Road, PO Box 31905, Lusaka. Tel: 292310/253819; fax: 250200; tlx: ZA 40211

Nigerian High Commission: Findeco House, Cairo Road, PO Box 32598, Lusaka. Tel: 253177; fax: 250622

Norwegian High Commission: 65 Birdcage Walk, Haile Selassie Avenue, PO Box 34570, Lusaka. Tel: 252188; fax: 253915; tlx: ZA 25119

Portuguese Embassy: Kudu Road, PO Box 33871, Lusaka. Tel: 253720; fax: 253896; tlx: ZA 40010

Russian Embassy: Diplomatic Triangle, PO Box 32355, Lusaka. Tel: 252120; fax: 253582; tlx: ZA 40341

Saudi Arabian Embassy: 4896 Los Angeles Boulevard, PO Box 33441, Lusaka. Tel: 253266; fax: 253582; tlx; ZA 40341

Somalian Embassy: 377A Kabulonga Road, PO Box 34051, Lusaka. Tel: 262119; tlx: ZA 40270

South African High Commission: 4th Floor, Bata House, Cairo Road, Lusaka. Tel: 225829; fax: 223268

Swedish Embassy: Haile Selassie Avenue (opposite Ndeke House), PO Box 30788, Lusaka. Tel: 251711; fax: 254049; tlx: ZA 41820

Tanzanian High Commission: Chancery Ujaama House, United Nations Avenue, PO Box 31219, Lusaka. Tel: 253320/253222; fax: 254861

United Kingdom – see *British High Commission*, above

United States Embassy: Independence Avenue (corner of United Nations Avenue), PO Box 31617, Lusaka. Tel: 250955; fax: 252225

Zaire Embassy: 1124 Perirenyatwa Road, PO Box 71234, Lusaka. Tel: 213343 /229044. (There is also a Consulate in Ndola – tel: 614247.)

Zimbabwean High Commission: 4th Floor, Memaco House, Cairo Road (south end), Lusaka. Tel: 229382

Hospitals and dentists

Should you need one, there are good hospitals in Zambia. However, the public health system is over-stretched and under-funded – so unless your illness is critical, it will take time for you to be attended to and treated.

There are better-funded private hospitals which cater for both affluent Zambians and expats/diplomatic staff. These are a much better bet if you have a good health insurance scheme (as you should have).

Pharmacies in Lusaka have a basic range of medicines, though specific brands are often unavailable. So bring with you all that you will need, as well as a repeat prescription for anything that you might run out of. Outside of Lusaka, and perhaps in the larger cities of the Copperbelt, you will be lucky to find anything other than very basic medical supplies. Thus you should carry a very comprehensive medical kit if you are planning on heading off into the wilds.

Imports and exports

There is no problem in exporting normal curios, but you will need an official export permit from the Department of National Parks to take out any game trophies. Visitors are urged to support the letter and the spirit of the CITES bans on endangered species, including the ban on the international trade in ivory. This has certainly helped to reduce ivory poaching, so don't undermine it by buying ivory souvenirs here. In any case, you will probably have big problems in importing them back into your home country.

Maps

Excellent maps covering the whole of Zambia are available in Lusaka and the major cities, if you can find them. The best place is the main government map office at the Ministry of Lands, in the basement of Mulungushi House. See page 114 in the chapter on *Lusaka*.

BUFFALO – E.H

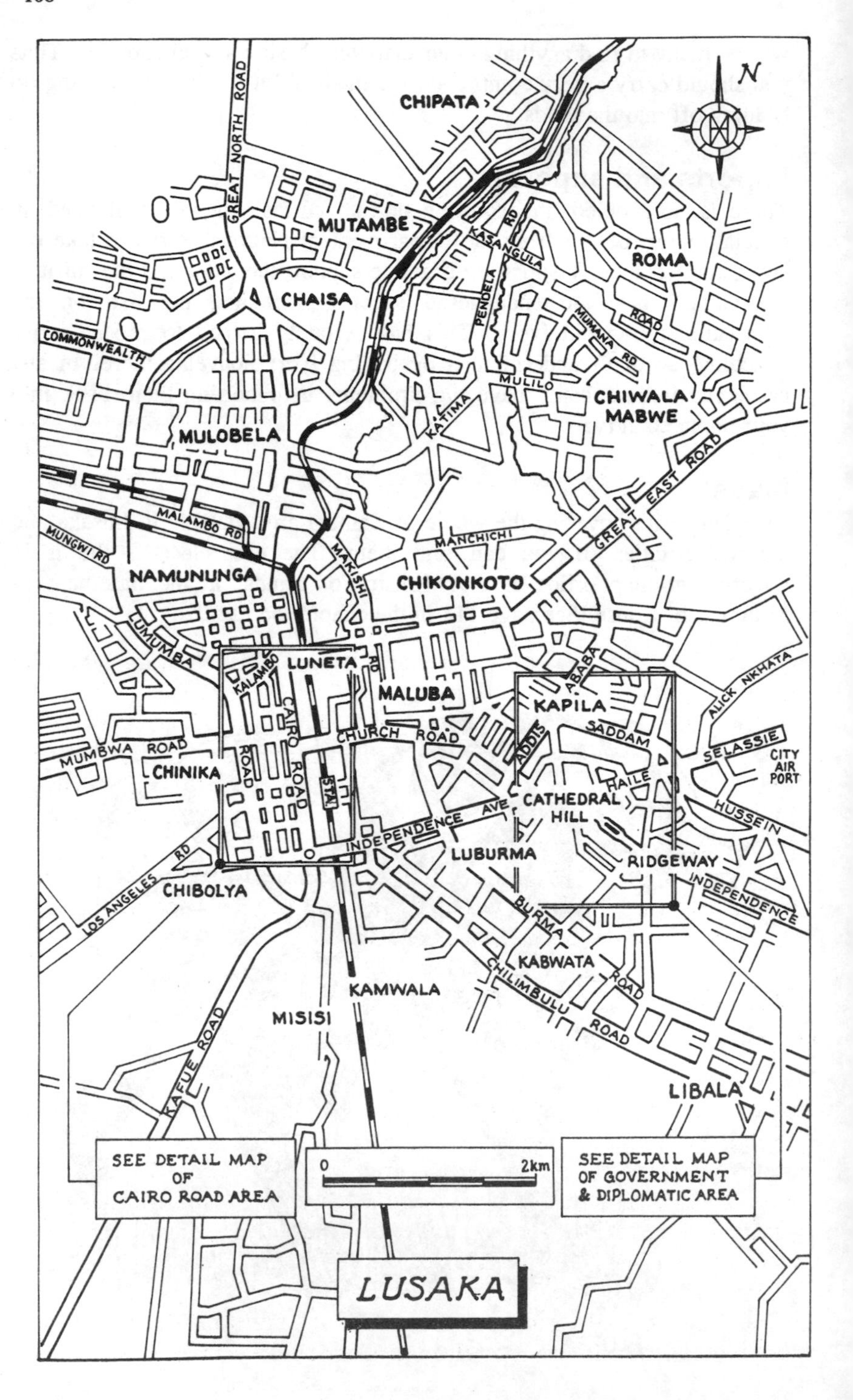
N
CHIPATA
GREAT NORTH ROAD
MUTAMBE
ROMA
KASANGULA
RD
PENDELA
CHAISA
MUMANA RD
ROAD
COMMONWEALTH
MULILO
KATIMA
CHIWALA
MABWE
MULOBELA
GREAT EAST ROAD
MALAMBO RD
MUNGWI RD
MANCHICHI
MAKISHI RD
NAMUNUNGA
CHIKONKOTO
LUMUMBA
KALAMBO
LUNETA
MALUBA
KAPILA
ADDIS ABABA
SADDAM
ALICK NKHATA
CAIRO ROAD
CHURCH ROAD
SELASSIE
CITY AIR PORT
MUMBWA ROAD
CHINIKA
HAILE
STN.
CATHEDRAL HILL
HUSSEIN
INDEPENDENCE AVE
LUBURMA
RIDGEWAY
LOS ANGELES RD
CHIBOLYA
INDEPENDENCE
BURMA
KABWATA
CHILIMBULU ROAD
ROAD
KAMWALA
MISISI
KAFUE ROAD
LIBALA
SEE DETAIL MAP OF CAIRO ROAD AREA
0
2km
SEE DETAIL MAP OF GOVERNMENT & DIPLOMATIC AREA
LUSAKA

Chapter Nine

Lusaka

Despite the assertions of the tourist board, Lusaka is still not high on Zambia's list of major attractions. Its wide tree-lined boulevards can be pleasant, but the traffic is chaotic, many of the suburbs are sprawling and dirty, and finding a good place to stay that is reasonably priced is almost impossible. However, Lusaka is no worse than London, New York, or any number of other big cities. Like them, it has a fascination because it is unmistakably cosmopolitan, alive and kicking. As home to one-tenth of Zambia's people, it has a discernible heartbeat which smaller and more sanitised cities lack. So if you go to Zambia with an interest in meeting a cross-section of its people, Lusaka should figure on your itinerary.

In my experience, the city's bad reputation for crime is exaggerated. It is certainly unsafe for the unwary - but probably less so than Nairobi or Johannesburg. Walking around at night is positively stupid, and during the day pickpockets will strike if you keep valuables anywhere accessible. However, visitors to Lusaka who allow their paranoia to elevate the city's dangers to the dizzy heights of Lagos are deluding themselves. It isn't *that* dangerous, if you are careful.

The rest of this chapter aims to provide you with some useful contact details, help you find places to stay and eat that will suit your budget, and suggest options for spending your spare time.

GETTING THERE AND AWAY

By air

Lusaka is well served by international flights, though regional flights catering to overseas visitors sometimes by-pass the city to serve Livingstone and/or Mfuwe instead. Currently British Airways and KLM are the main intercontinental carriers from Europe direct to Zambia, but other carriers are possible if you use neighbouring African capitals as gateways to the region. See *Planning and Preparations,* page 43, for more details of the best fares to Zambia, and *Zambia Today,* page 93, for general comments on getting around the country by air.

The airport is well signposted, if isolated, at 25km from the centre, off the Great East Road. Transport there is either by the courtesy buses of the big hotels (Intercontinental, Holiday Inn or Taj Pamodzi), or by private taxi. A taxi should cost around US$20/£14 between the airport and the city, though this is the route for which the drivers will charge most imaginatively.

International airlines represented in Lusaka include:

Air Angola PO Box 37731, Lusaka. Tel: 222401/221684; tlx: ZA 40550

Air Botswana c/o Steve Blagus Travel, Nkwazi Rd, PO Box 31530. Tel: 227739/40 or 227285 or 221445; fax: 223724; tlx: ZA 43320

Air France Chindo Rd, Woodlands. Tel: 264930/36; airport tel: 271212; Fax: 264950; tlx: ZA 41390

Air India 1st Floor, Shop 4, Findeco House, Cairo Rd, PO Box 34471. Tel: 223128 or 229563 or 226349

Air Malawi at Pamodzi Hotel. Tel: 254455

Air Namibia c/o Inter Continental Travel, Mukuba Pension House, Dedan Kimathi Rd, (near Woodlands Shopping Centre), PO Box 30851. Tel: 223839/43 or 220910 or 223842; fax: 222904; airport tel: 271427; tlx: ZA 40398

Air Tanzania 3rd floor, Bata House, Cairo Road, PO Box 32635. Tel: 228295 or 224798 or 222347

Air Zimbabwe 2 Kalidas Building (next to Society House), Cairo Rd, PO Box 35191. Tel: 225431 or 215540

British Airways Findeco House, PO Box 32006. Tel: 228337; airport tel: 271231; fax: 223826; tlx: ZA 42440

Kenya Airways Findeco House, PO Box 31856. Tel: 228484-6; tlx: ZA 40460

KLM at Pamodzi Hotel. Tel: 254455

South African Airways 3rd Floor, Bata House, Cairo Rd, PO Box 34150. Tel: 223655-7 or 221508; fax: 221509

The charter companies and local airlines based in Lusaka include:

Aero Zambia Zambia Insurance Brokers House, Kimathi Road, P Bag 8717, Lusaka. Tel: 226192/3/4; fax: 226147

Proflight PO Box 30536, Lusaka. Tel: 264439 or 263686 or 263687; airport tel: 271437; fax: 222888/262379

Staravia PO Box 34273, Lusaka. Tel: 291962; airport tel: 271038

Roan Air PO Box 310277, Lusaka International Airport. Tel: 271066; tlx: ZA 40410

Zambia Express tel: 222060 or 271208; fax: 227964; Email: zamex@zamnet.zm

By bus

Local buses

The Intercity Bus Terminal is a noisy, bustling station which shelters under a large purpose-built roof, on the western side of Dedan Kimathi Road. It is not a place to go idly strolling at night, or to display your valuables, but it is the obvious place to catch a bus to virtually any of Zambia's main towns. Locals are paranoid about thieves who frequent the area, so expect warnings about safety. However, if you keep your belongings with you and are careful, then you should have no problems.

Despite the apparent confusion which greets you, there is some order to the Terminal's chaos. The buses sitting in bays are grouped roughly by their eventual destinations, as indicated by the white boards displayed next to the driver. If you can't see the name you want, then ask someone – most people will go out of their way to help.

Generally there are two different prices for any given place: a higher one to travel in a smaller, faster minibus, and a lower rate for the larger, slower normal buses. Expect about a 20% premium for a minibus.

Most (big or small) will not leave until they are full, which can take hours. If possible, it is better not to pay until the bus has started on its way, as you may want to swap buses if another appears to be filling faster and hence is likely to depart earlier.

Buses to some destinations leave frequently, others weekly – dependent upon demand. The only way to find out is to come and ask. Just a few of the many options include:

To Livingstone 2/3 buses per day, leaving between 07.00 and 11.00, costs Kw8,000 for a minibus or Kw6,500 for an ordinary bus.

To Kitwe Numerous departures, mostly in the morning and early afternoon, costs Kw6,500 for a minibus or Kw5,000 for an ordinary bus.

To Kapiri Mposhi Numerous departures throughout the day, costs Kw4,500 for a minibus or Kw4,000 for an ordinary bus.

A few international buses also leave from here to Zimbabwe, including:

To Harare Run by Dzimiri Special Buses, departing once a day, Sun-Fri, between about 10.30 and 12.30, costs Kw10,000.

To Bulawayo Run by Mazhandu Family Buses, departs Thursdays 06.00, costs Kw11,000.

Postbuses

The post office runs a very limited number of scheduled buses for mail, which only stop at post offices. Seats can be booked in advance for passengers. These are quicker and less crowded than the normal local buses (they claim to run to a timetable), though not more comfortable.

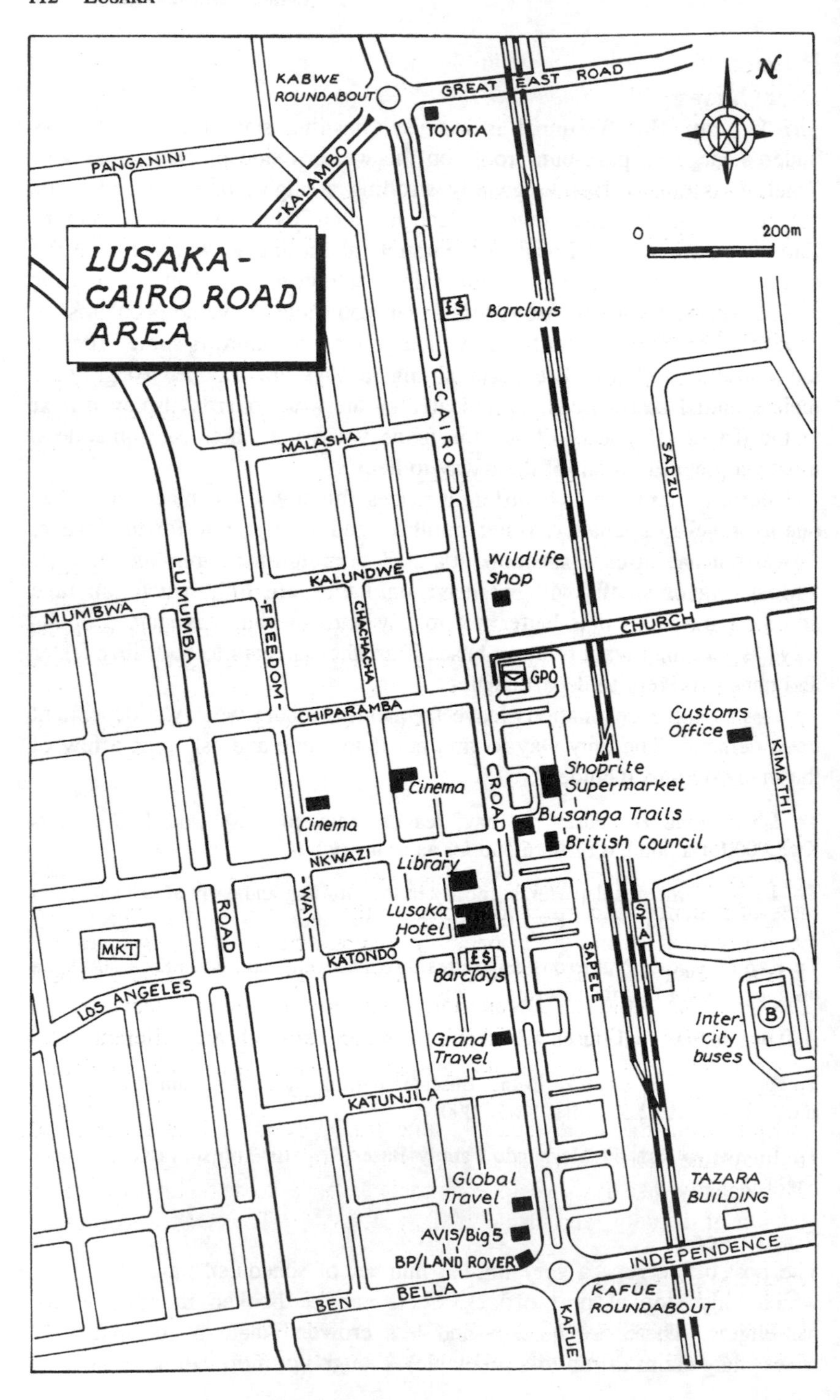
LUSAKA - CAIRO ROAD AREA
N
0
200m
KABWE ROUNDABOUT
GREAT EAST ROAD
TOYOTA
PANGANINI
KALAMBO
Barclays
CAIRO
SADZU
MALASHA
Wildlife Shop
KALUNDWE
MUMBWA
LUMUMBA
FREEDOM
CHACHACHA
CHURCH
GPO
CHIPARAMBA
Customs Office
KIMATHI
Shoprite Supermarket
Cinema
Cinema
C ROAD
Busanga Trails
British Council
NKWAZI
Library
WAY
Lusaka Hotel
STA
ROAD
MKT
KATONDO
Barclays
SAPELE
LOS ANGELES
Inter-city buses
B
Grand Travel
KATUNJILA
Global Travel
TAZARA BUILDING
AVIS/Big 5
BP/LAND ROVER
INDEPENDENCE
BEN BELLA
KAFUE ROUNDABOUT
KAFUE

The booking office for postbuses is at their depot, behind the main post office, off Cairo Road and Dar-es-Salaam Place. Book three days before departure for either of their three routes:

To Kasama costs Kw7,500 and stops at Kabwe, Kapiri Mposhi, Mkushi, Serenje, Mpika and Kanona. Departs Wednesday at 07.00.

To Mongu costs Kw5,500 and stops at Mumbwa and Kaoma. Departs Saturday at 07.00.

To Chipata costs Kw6,000 and stops at Nyimba, Petauke, Sinda and Katete. Departs Monday at 07.30.

The above costs reduce proportionately if you alight at a town en route. These buses return to Lusaka on the day following their outward journey. Tickets can be booked at local post offices where they stop, but note that these buses cannot be hailed from the roadside.

Luxury coaches

Coach operators seem to come and go, so ask around Cairo Road's travel agents for the latest news. Global Travel (tel: 227508), at the south end of Cairo Road, currently runs a luxury service to Johannesburg, complete with videos and music. This is booked in advance from Global Travel and departs from outside their office at 12.00 every Wednesday. It takes about 25 hours, and costs Kw110,000 single. The return journey departs on Saturday at 12.00 from the Protea Gardens Hotel, in Hillbrow, and arrives in Lusaka on Sunday afternoon.

By train

Few travellers use Zambia's ordinary trains for transport, but if you have lots of patience, and a few good books, then try them. Lines link Lusaka with Livingstone and the Copperbelt. Express trains to Livingstone leave at 19.30 every Monday, Wednesday and Friday, taking about 12 hours. Slower trains, which stop even more frequently, leave every morning.

The regular, efficient TAZARA trains to Tanzania are different. They leave from Kapiri Mposhi, not Lusaka, so see pages 256-7 for details. Despite this, their main office is here in Lusaka. Take Independence Avenue from the south end of Kafue Road, over the bridge across the railway line. The main TAZARA office is in the building on your left. This usually displays the current timetable on a notice-board outside, on the left of the door, and inside you buy tickets for TAZARA in advance.

ORIENTATION

Lusaka is a large, spread-out city, so buy a map when you first arrive (see *Maps* section, below). Its focus is the axis of Cairo Road, which runs roughly north–south. This is about six lanes of traffic wide, 4km long, and has a useful pedestrian island which runs like a spine down its centre. Parallel to Cairo Road, to the west, is Chachacha road – a terminus for numerous local minibuses, and home to a lively market. Cairo Road is always bustling with people during the day as it is the city's commercial centre, and location for most large shops.

Completely separate, about 2km to the east, is the much larger, more diffuse, "Government Area". It is linked to Cairo Road by Independence Avenue, and centres on the areas of Cathedral Hill and Ridgeway. Here you will find the big international-standard hotels, government departments and embassies set in a lot more space. It has a different atmosphere from the bustle of Cairo Road: the quiet and official air that you often find in diplomatic or administrative corners of capitals around the world.

Maps

Excellent, detailed maps covering the whole of Zambia can be bought cheaply from the main government map office at the Ministry of Lands. This is in the basement of Mulungushi House, by the corner of Independence Avenue and Nationalist Road. Prices are very good, at around Kw3-5,000 per map. Aside from the normal "Ordnance Survey" type maps, there are several special tourist maps available. To see what's in stock, browse through the maps on the right of the door before finally choosing. Include in your purchase the detailed street map of Lusaka. This is essential for navigating around the capital, and comes complete with an alphabetical street index.

A limited selection of Zambia's most useful maps can also be found at the Wildlife Shop, on the east side of Cairo Road, just north of the main Post Office, or at *Drumbeat* in the Pamodzi Hotel. These outlets are more convenient than Mulungushi House, but the same maps cost more.

WHERE TO STAY

There is little to choose between Lusaka's international-standard hotels – which are functional and efficient, if expensive and rather soulless. You might just ask yourself if you need to be near the centre, or can afford to stay beyond the suburbs, at somewhere like Lilayi Lodge. This is a lot more pleasant than being in town, but transport can be a problem.

Those on a budget should choose their lodgings with care, as price is often a poor guide and the quality of the budget hotels varies considerably. Ask around if you can, as new places are opening all the time. If your budget is very tight (though there are a few rather seedy cheap hostels) you would be better to consider camping.

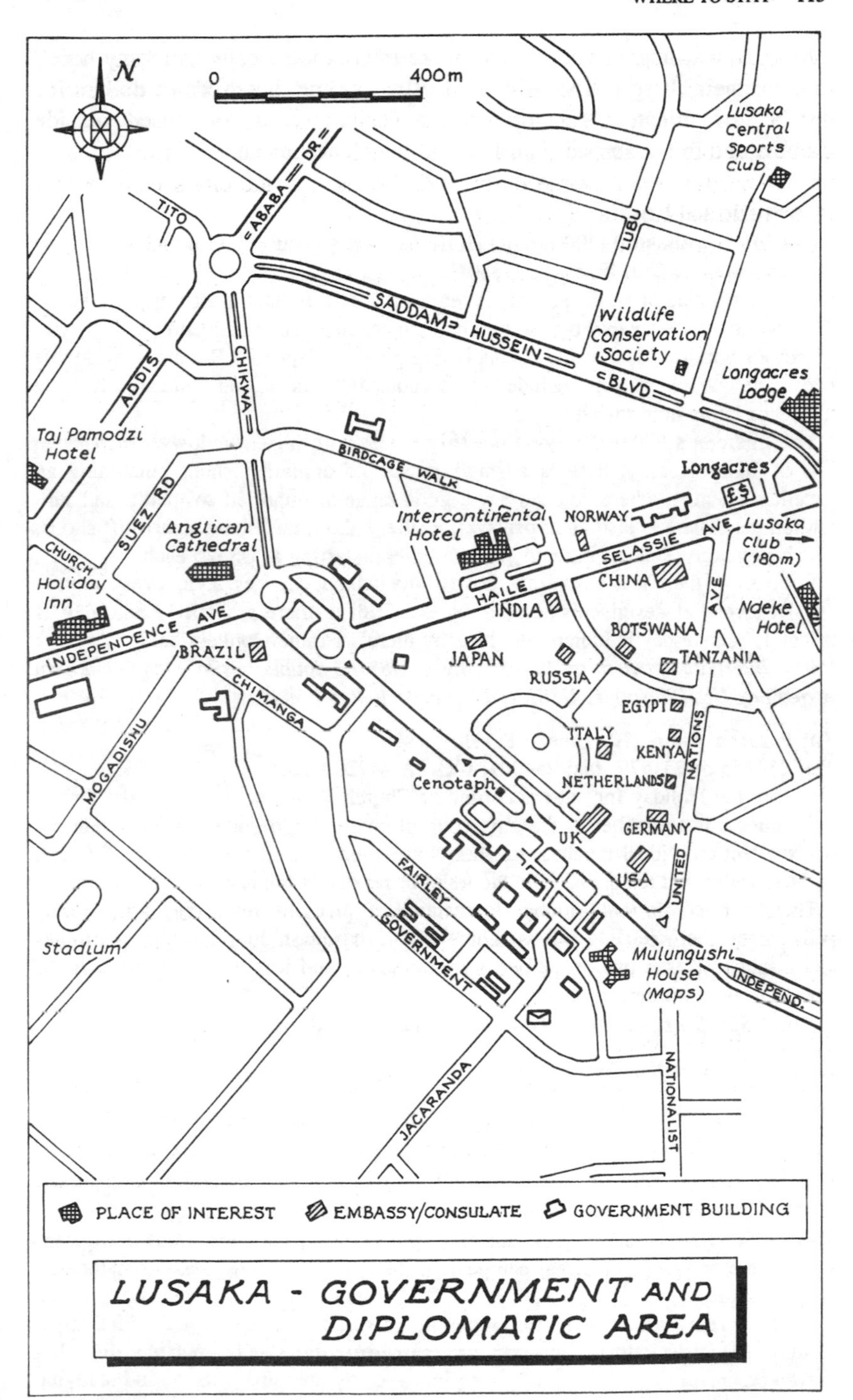

N
0
400m
Lusaka Central Sports Club
TITO
ABABA DR
LUBU
SADDAM HUSSEIN BLVD
Wildlife Conservation Society
Longacres Lodge
ADDIS
CHIKWA
Taj Pamodzi Hotel
BIRDCAGE WALK
Longacres
SUEZ RD
Anglican Cathedral
Intercontinental Hotel
NORWAY
HAILE SELASSIE AVE
Lusaka Club (180m)
CHURCH
Holiday Inn
CHINA
INDIA
AVE
Ndeke Hotel
INDEPENDENCE AVE
BRAZIL
JAPAN
BOTSWANA
TANZANIA
RUSSIA
CHIMANGA
EGYPT
ITALY
KENYA
NATIONS
MOGADISHU
Cenotaph
NETHERLANDS
UK
GERMANY
USA
UNITED
FAIRLEY
GOVERNMENT
Stadium
Mulungushi House (Maps)
INDEPEND.
NATIONALIST
JACARANDA
PLACE OF INTEREST
EMBASSY/CONSULATE
GOVERNMENT BUILDING
LUSAKA - GOVERNMENT AND DIPLOMATIC AREA

Just one warning: if you plan to make international calls from any hotel, find out their charges first. Bills will often run into hundreds of dollars for just a few minutes. An international calling card, organised outside Zambia and billed abroad, is usually a much cheaper alternative.

International hotels

Hotel Intercontinental (200 rooms) Haile Selassie Avenue, PO Box 32201
Tel: 250600-1 or 250148; fax: 251880
On the north side of Haile Selassie Avenue, this is Lusaka's most imposing hotel. The rooms are reasonably big, so you can expect an en suite bath/shower, TV with M-Net (a South African cable channel), fridge and telephone. Rooms with double beds have enough space to include both a couch and a desk, and you can rely upon the decor being uninspiring.

The Intercon's lobby is a good meeting place, with huge windows which let in lots of light. Nearby there is a small arcade of upmarket shops, including an excellent chemist, where you can buy a good range of imported cosmetics and sun-tan lotions. There is also an expensive jewellery shop, and some smart gift shops. The best quality T-shirts in town are found here, starting at US$25 each.

For eating there's a restaurant downstairs which changes style every day: a regular cycle of seven cuisines per week. Fridays there's a BBQ, Saturday is oriental, Wednesday is Indian, etc. Nearby there's a rather soulless bar.
Rates: International visitors US$155 single, US$180 double; visitors from Southern Africa pay US$100 single, US$120 double, including breakfast

Taj Pamodzi Hotel (202 rooms) PO Box 35450
Tel: 254455 or 251579; fax: 254005; tlx: ZA 44720 PAMHO
Opposite the Holiday Inn, at the corner of Church Road and Addis Ababa Drive, the Pamodzi is a member of the Taj group of hotels, but despite this has a number of excellent individual touches. Its rooms are good, with a bath/shower, TV with M-Net, fridge and telephone, and the level of service is impressive.

There's a comfortable lobby downstairs, a pleasant restaurant and a bar. Adjacent to the hotel is a fitness centre with two squash courts, a gym, aerobics and a sauna. This is one of the best gyms in town, and it is popular with many of Lusaka's more affluent residents.
Rates: US$120 single, US$130 double, including breakfast

Holiday Inn Garden Court (155 rooms) PO Box 30666
Tel: 251666; fax: 253529; tlx: ZA 42510
Situated at the corner of Independence Avenue and Church Road the Holiday Inn occupies the site of the old Ridgeway Hotel. Its air-conditioned rooms are not as spacious as either the Intercon or the Pamodzi, and show no more imagination either. They are functional though, with showers and baths, telephones, colour TVs (with M-Net), razor plugs, and tea/coffee making facilities. Beds are queen-size double or twin. For a real pampering, the beautician here does aromatherapy and massage.

On the ground floor there are a couple of restaurants and a bar. McGinty's Traditional Irish Pub is as good as most expat-type pubs outside the UK. However, instead of gazing into your pint here, try stepping outside and studying the beautiful colony of masked weavers nesting over the ornamental pond. A few yards away is the Spur Restaurant – a steak and chips place with good salads, burgers and attentive service which attracts many Lusaka residents in the evening.

You will also find an outdoor pool, a curio shop and the main branch of *Bushwackers Travel Agency* (see page 131) here at the Holiday Inn.

Rates: US$85 single, US$110 double, including breakfast

Lilayi Lodge (12 rooms & 5 suites) PO Box 30093
Tel: 228682/3 or 230611 or 230326; fax: 222906; tlx: ZA 40536 LILAYI
If you can arrange the transport, then Lilayi is the most pleasant, and the best value, of the upmarket options in Lusaka. It is on a game farm about 20 minutes drive from the centre of town off the Kafue Road.

To get there head south on Cairo Road and continue over the Independence Avenue roundabout. Turn left after about 11km, then right at the T-junction, where the police training college is in front of you. Then next left and continue straight to the Lodge. It is about 10km off the main road.

Lilayi's accommodation is in very comfortable, well-furnished brick rondavels spread out over green lawns. Five of the rondavels are suites, which have a bedroom, spacious lounge, and en suite bath, shower and toilet. The other six rondavels have two bedrooms in them, with en suite showers and toilets, and they share a lounge. (If the hotel is not full, then they may give you a suite for the price of a normal room.)

The main building has a large bar and dining area overlooking a large pool, plus another upstairs lounge and an excellent small library for reference. The restaurant is excellent, and often complemented by a popular outdoor braai.

Lilayi is set on a large farm criss-crossed by game-viewing roads. It has been well-stocked with most of Zambia's antelope - including some of the less common species – like roan, sable, defassa waterbuck, tsessebe and giraffe. So if you failed to sight something in one of the parks, walk around here for a few hours before you leave. Horse-riding is also possible here, for experienced riders, at about US$25 per person. There are also facilities for badminton and volleyball.

Rates: US$80/US$120 standard/suite single, US$90/130 double, bed & breakfast

Budget hotels

Even "budget" hotels can be expensive in Lusaka, but if you have Kw20-40,000 (US$20-40) per night to spend then there is quite a choice. The best are described here, whilst others are simply listed with their contact details:

Andrews Motel (84 rooms) PO Box 30475. Tel: 272102 or 273532; fax: 214798
Andrews Motel is about 8km from the Independence Avenue roundabout on the Kafue Road. Despite the impression of a fading motel being neglected by over-relaxed staff, Andrews remains popular with locals– perhaps because its facilities include two tennis courts and a spacious pool, with adjacent bar and snack area.

Being out of the centre, it has the space for a layout typical of a motel, with a security guard on the gate and parking bays in front of rooms. This should reassure those concerned about the safety of vehicles. The rooms are a little dingy, but all have air-con units, twin beds and baths, though no showers. Note that this

is the base for Acacia Safaris, and the venue for regular reggae concerts (keep an eye out for bill posters around town) during weekends.
Rates: Kw 42,000 per twin; Kw 67,000 for a family room for 4 persons, including a basic breakfast of cereals and fruit.

Chainama Hotel (28 rooms) PO Box 51033. Tel: 292452/3/4/5/6; fax: 290809
On the south side of the Great East Road, about 7km from the centre of town, Chainama Hotel has quite spacious rooms. These have tables and chairs, plenty of space, as well as telephones, fans, and remote-control TVs with M-net and CNN. A picture window takes up one wall of most of the rooms, and the en suite bathrooms have showers but not baths.
Rates: Kw 45,000 for a single or a twin; non-Zambians pay US$60/£40

Lusaka Hotel (70 rooms) PO Box 30044. Tel: 229049 or 221833; fax: 225726; tlx: ZA 41921
Some decades ago the Lusaka Hotel was the only hotel in Lusaka, right at the centre of town (just a few metres from Cairo Road) on the bustling Katondo Road. Now the area around the hotel's entrance is always busy with people loitering suspiciously, and if you stay here you should be careful with your belongings.

Inside the hotel feels old, small and noisy, but clean. The standard rooms have tea/coffee makers, M-net television, a telephone, a fan and an en suite toilet/-shower room. The deluxe rooms are a little larger with baths as well as showers, and air-conditioning instead of fans.
Rates: Singles KW33,000 Std, Kw39,000 Dlx; Doubles Kw41,000 Std, Kw49,000 Dlx – all include a basic continental breakfast

Fairview Hotel (30 rooms) PO Box 33200 Tel: 212954; fax: 218432; tlx: ZA 40572
The Fairview is a long way out of town on Church Road, and a little run-down. The rooms all have private facilities and colour TVs, but are otherwise unimpressive.
Rates: Kw 35,000 per twin, including a basic breakfast

Belvedere Lodge Tel: 263680
On the east side of the city, close to Kabulonga shopping centre, Belvedere stands at the corner of Leopard's Hill Road and Chindo Road. Inside the rooms are small, uninspiring and outdated – though fairly clean; they do have an en suite toilet and bathroom. It is often booked up by visiting officials, so if you plan to stay here ring ahead to see if there is space before you arrive.
Rates: Kw30-42,000 for a twin room, including dinner, bed & breakfast. There is no bed & breakfast tariff here

Longacres Lodge c/o Hostels Board of Management, PO Box 50100 Tel: 251761
This government-run hostel is sparsely furnished, though reasonably clean and good value. The rooms have a basic twin beds, an en suite toilet, bath and basin, and perhaps a dressing table or wardrobe. Generally the plumbing seems to work, despite its appearance.

The Lodge is situated on Saddam Hussein Boulevard, about 100m north of Haile Selassie Avenue. If you come from town, then that's about 600m past the Intercontinental Hotel.
Rates: Kw 24,000 for a single or a double room, including breakfast

Zamearth Lodge Plot 5520, Magoye Road, Kalundu, P Bag 107, Woodlands. Tel/fax: 294680
Run by Mr Emmanuelle Nikupula, Zamearth opened in 1992. It still has only seven rooms, which are often full with long-term visitors working for aid agencies. The comfortable rooms are all serviced every day and have clean carpets and soft furnishings – comforts usually missing from Zambia's budget hotels. There is one telephone for guests, and the main complaint is the expense of the Lodge's laundry service.

The Lodge is well signposted in side-streets to the north of the Great East Road, after the showgrounds but before the University of Zambia. It is probably the best value accommodation in town.
Rates: Kw27,000 single, Kw35-42,000 double, including a full breakfast. Other meals available, including a 3-course dinner for Kw6,600

Barn Motel Great East Road (50 rooms) Tel: 282890/2; fax: 228949; tlx: ZA 48670
On the Great East Road beyond the airport turn-off, about 20km from the city, the Barn has little to recommend it.
Rates: about Kw25-32,000 double, including breakfast.

Garden House Hotel (50 rooms) Mumbwa Road, PO Box 30815.
Tel: 287337 or 787328
About 5km from the city on the Mumbwa road, the Garden House is ideal if you arrive late from Kafue. Otherwise, there's no reason to seek it out.
Rates: about Kw25-35,000 double, including breakfast

Hillview Hotel (10 rooms) Makeni PO Box 30815. Tel: 278554; fax 229074
About 15km from the city, take the Kafue road and turn right shortly after Andrews Motel. The Hillview is about 5km down the tar road, and an airy, almost colonial atmosphere.
Rates: about Kw35-42,000 double, including breakfast

Ndeke Hotel (45 rooms) Chisidza Crescent, PO Box 30815.
Tel: 261100; fax: 229074
Near the roundabout of Haile Selassie Avenue and Saddam Hussein Boulevard, the Ndeke is an old hotel with a slightly offbeat atmosphere that has made it a favourite with budget travellers. It is a short walk from Longacres Lodge, on the eastern side of the main government area.
Rates: about Kw30-38,000 double, including breakfast

Hostels and camping

Fringilla Farm Tel: 611199; fax: 611213
Situated about 50km north of Lusaka on the Great North Road, Fringilla makes a good base if you have transport, though it is far if you want to spend much time in Lusaka itself. There are chalets to rent and camping available, as well as farm meals and activities like pony rides. The camp-site is fine and there are good hot showers and ablutions. Ideal if you are arriving from the north at night – much safer than searching for a hotel in the city.

Salvation Army Hostel
On the south side of Chishango Road, just off the Great North Road, is the Salvation Army's hostel – which used to be one of the best places in the city to find a welcoming floor or camp-site for the night. When last visited, it had ceased to accept travellers.

YWCA Tel: 252726
South of Ridgeway, on the main Nationalist Road opposite the teaching hospital – between Chire Close and Dama Close – the YWCA is easy to find. It accepts both men and women to stay. However, the rooms are small and very basic. The cooking, washing and toilet facilities are all shared, and none are very clean.
Rates: Kw10,000 per person per night. Bring your own food.

Sikh Temple
On a bend on the northeast side of the quiet Mumbwa Road, behind gates with clear yellow-and-gold insignia, lies the calm of a Sikh Temple. Whilst meant for pilgrims, travellers are welcomed provided that they do not smoke, drink alcohol or cook meat whilst here. There are twin rooms here for which there is no charge, but it is customary to leave a donation.

Eureka Tel: 272351
Lusaka's best camp-site is on a private farm, on the eastern side of Kafue Road, about 7km from the Independence Avenue roundabout. This was started in 1992, with the aim of attracting budget travellers. It now has a large area for campers and a thatched bar with easy chairs, a darts board and a pool table for their use. There are a few permanent tents for hire, and plans to build basic A-frame chalets. This is Lusaka's best place for budget travellers.
Rates: Kw 4,500 (£3/US$5/Zim$40/SAR18) per person per night.

WHERE TO EAT

During the day there are a number of fast-food places on Cairo Road, but otherwise the supply of cheap and good eats is limited. Shopping centres and supermarkets are obvious places to start catering for yourself, so see the *Shopping: food and drink* section for details of these. Equally there are street-food stalls and people selling snacks from baskets around the markets and bus stations – though judge their standards of hygiene carefully: food cooked as you watch is by far the best, but not very common.

If your budget is more flexible, and you seek a better meal, then you need to be mobile and go out of the centre. The **Intercon**, **Pamodzi** and **Lilayi Lodge** have good restaurants, while the **Spur** steak house at the Holiday Inn is very popular. Expect to pay around US$12-15 for dinner with a few drinks at any of these.

Other places to note include the Showgrounds, beside the Great East Road. Here the **Marco Polo Restaurant** serves fairly elaborate fare, with simpler eats found at the **Polo Grill**. This is popular amongst the young-and-privileged crowd, serving a range of bites with a better selection of drinks. The **Calabash Restaurant** has a good reputation for seafood (and a more diverse clientele) while near the east gate of the grounds is the relaxed **Oasis Restaurant**. The Showgrounds area as a whole is worth an evening visit when its restaurants and bars come to life.

Away from the Showgrounds, **Mike's Car Wash Centre**, on the left about 5km out of town on the Kafue Road, is the unlikely setting for Mike's Restaurant & Take-away, which is also a popular spot for an evening of drinking and eating. Expect a bill of around Kw10-15,000 for a good meal with a few beers.

There are several restaurants spread around the suburbs, like **Gringos** on Lubu Road, between Addis Ababa Drive and Saddam Hussein Boulevard. Like most of Lusaka's restaurants, this steak restaurant has an enclosed car-park. Virtually all of its diners will drive here in the evening – nobody walks at night. **Arabian Nights**, on the Great East Road, east of Addis Ababa Drive, has a similar arrangement, but this is a large and very flamboyant Indian/Middle Eastern restaurant, where a meal with drinks costs about Kw20,000 each.

Ask around for what's new in town, but an enduring favourite is the **Lusaka Club**, near the corner of Saddam Hussein Boulevard and Haile Selassie Avenue. The atmosphere of this old sports club is colonial and almost seedy. Walk past the doorman, and towards the back of the club house you'll find what seems like an uninspiring café. However, it serves some of the best (and best value) food in town. The menu isn't fancy, but the food is good quality. At about Kw6,600 including vegetables, the sizeable pepper steaks are a renowned speciality. Don't miss them.

GETTING AROUND

Lusaka is quite large. Without your own vehicle, you will probably want to use a taxi or one of the small minibuses which ply between the outer suburbs/townships and the centre. If you are careful, then these are very useful and quite safe. The other possibility is to note that car hire firms usually supply their cars with a driver – who can act as a convenient guide for a short business trip.

Taxis

Lusaka's taxis are mostly small, decrepit Datsun 120Y or 1200 models, held together by remarkable roadside mechanics and lots of improvisation. The licensed ones will have a large number painted on their side, and even these will have no fare meter. When taking a taxi, you should agree a rate for the journey before you get into the vehicle. If you know roughly what it should cost, then most drivers recognise this and don't try to overcharge. As a last resort when bargaining, all licensed taxis should have a rate-sheet, giving the "standard" prices for waiting time and various common journeys – though drivers will not admit to having one if the bargaining is going their way. Typical fares are:

Kw3,000	between Ridgeway (big hotels) and Cairo Road
Kw20,000	between the airport and town
Kw8-12,000	between the centre of town and the inner suburbs
Kw7,000	per hour of additional waiting time

If you need a vehicle all day, then consider hiring a taxi with its driver. Start by making a clear deal to pay by the hour or the kilometre, and record the time or the mileage reading. Around Kw5,000 per hour, or Kw500 per kilometre, is fair, though a tough negotiator would pay less.

Minibuses

These are the packed transport that the city's poorer commuters use to travel between the outer, satellite suburbs to the centre of town. There are many different routes, so if you want to find out which to use then go down to Chachacha Road, which is the unofficial terminus for most of them. These are an especially good way to reach the farther flung suburbs, or to get a lift along one of the main routes out to a good hitching spot. Fares are not normally dependent upon distance, and expect to pay less than Kw1,000 per journey. Minibuses usually have regular stops, but can sometimes just be flagged down if they're not full and you are lucky.

BANKS AND MONEY

American Express

Eagle Travel, the recently de-nationalised travel agents, are Zambia's official AMEX representative. Find them in Findeco House, at the southern end of Cairo Road. If you have an AMEX card or travellers cheques, then this is a more secure maildrop than using Post Restante at the main post office. Eagle also have offices in Chingola, Kabwe, Kitwe, Livingstone, Luanshya, Mufulira, and Ndola.

Banks

The main banks generally have their head offices along Cairo Road. These are the best ones to use if you are dealing with foreign currency or transfers. Their contact details are:

African Commercial Bank PO Box 30097, Superannuation House, Ben Bella Road. Tel: 229482; fax: 227495

Barclays Bank of Zambia Kafue House, Cairo Road. Tel: 228858/66 or 227859/63; fax: 222519

Chase Trust Bank Third Floor, Memaco House, Sapele Road. Tel: 221255 or 226405

Citibank Chachacha Road. Tel: 229025; fax: 226254

Commerce Bank Limited PO Box 32393, 627 Cairo Road. Tel: 229948/57; fax: 223769

Credit Africa Bank Anchor House, Cairo Road. Tel: 220201; fax: 220196

Finance Bank Lusaka Square, Cairo Road. Tel: 229739/40; fax: 224450

Prudence Bank Society House, Cairo Road. Tel: 225936 or 225739; fax: 223691

Standard Chartered Bank Cairo Road. Tel: 228127; fax: 222092

Bureaux de change

These can be found along Cairo Road (watch for the touts who entice punters inside) and also in the main hotels. The former are invariably busy, and seem to do little to safeguard the privacy of transactions and hence the security of their customers. (As an aside, they will not exchange travellers cheques.) The latter generally offer poor rates, or charge steep commissions – and may insist that you are a guest of the hotel. Changing money on the street does not confer a better exchange rate, but does open you to a much greater risk of being ripped off. Use a bank whenever you can, or a hotel when you cannot.

WHAT TO SEE AND DO

Perhaps the most fun to be had around town is simply people-watching, and talking with those who live here. From the poor street-vendors to the taxi drivers and aid-agency expats in the larger hotels, you'll find that people are usually happy to chat. They will comment freely on politics and the issues of the day, and probably ask you how you view things as a foreigner.

These conversations can be fascinating, but be mindful that there aren't debating points to be earned, just new points of view to learn. Try not to expound your prejudices, or to jump to hasty conclusions on issues with which you are not familiar, and you'll have much longer and more interesting conversations. Other ways to spend your time in Lusaka include:

Local markets

Several of the markets are fascinating to wander around, but pay attention to your safety and don't take anything valuable with you. Think twice before wandering around with a backpack, which is inviting theft, and if you have a safe place to leave your money belt, then don't bring that either.

The more relaxed of the two main markets to visit is about 500m east of the south end of Cairo Road. Walk over the railway on the Independence Avenue bridge, and you can't miss it on your right. Here is the country's centre for the sale of clothing donated by charities from the west. This trade, known as *salaula*, has badly affected Zambia's indigenous clothes industry – which previously thrived on the production and sale of printed cotton fabrics, like the common *chitenjes*. This is why salaula's long-term value as a form of aid is hotly debated.

On the western side of Cairo Road, the **Soweto** market is found between the Katondo and Nkwazi Roads. This is a teeming maze of small trading stalls, where you can buy almost anything. However, it is a place to be wary of, not well suited to single or less confident foreign travellers. Again, dress down for a visit and don't even think of taking those valuables with you.

Bazaars

Somewhat different in character to the markets are a couple of genteel, upmarket bazaars. The atmosphere is equally interesting, although totally different.

The **Dutch Reformed Church** has a bazaar on the last Saturday of each month from 09.00. Find it about 4km east of Ridgeway on Kabulonga Road, past Bishop's Road and towards Ibex Hill. Expect gifts and crafts, house plants, home-made jams, etc.

Very nearby, **Shantina's**, in the Alstone Cottage Shopping Area on Bishops Road, has a similar but much smaller function every Saturday from 09.00-12.00.

Places to visit

Kabwata Cultural Centre

On Burma Road, just north-west of Jacaranda Road, is probably the city's best spot for buying hand-carved crafts and curios. Set back a little from the road are a number of rondavels, many of which shelter stone- and wood-carvers. Large wooden hippos (around Kw10,000) are cheaper than equivalent carvings near Livingstone's bridge over the Zambezi. The prices and quality of the carvings are good. There are tribal dances here at 15.00 on Sundays during the winter.

Kalimba Reptile Park

Kalimba is gradually becoming worth the journey. It now has quite good displays of crocodiles, snakes and chameleons, plus ponds for anglers, and drinks and snacks are available. There are plans for crazy golf and

even a children's playground. To get there, head out of town on the Great East Road, then take a left on to District Road at the Caltex station, about 1km before the Chelstone Water Tower. This heads towards the east side of Ngwerere. Follow this road, the D564, about 11km to a T-junction, turn right and park about 1km later on the right.
Open: daily, 09.00-17.00. Rates: adults Kw2,000, children Kw1,000

National Archives

A good library on Africa, and also an exhibition of photographs to be seen. Drop in if you're passing, they are found on Government Road and also maps are for sale here.
Open: daily, 08.00-17.00

Political Museum

Tel: 228805
Situated at the Mulungushi International Conference Centre, this displays some interesting, if slightly unimaginative, exhibits on the country's struggle for independence
Open: daily, Mon-Fri 09.00-16.30. Admission free

Zintu Community Museum

Tel: 223183
Houses a good cultural exhibition with some excellent arts and crafts from all over the country in its building on Panganini Road.
Open: daily, Mon-Fri 10.00-15.00. Admission free

Parliament Buildings

Guided tours are organised around the National Assembly, on Nangwenya Road (off Addis Ababa Drive), on the last Thursday of the month.
Open: normally Friday afternoons only

Moore Pottery Factory

Tel: 221814; fax: 237417
On the eastern side of Kabelenga Road, between the Great East Road and Church Road, Moore Pottery is well worth the 15-minute walk from Cairo Road for its excellent selection of beautiful ceramics. Most are for sale and, although many are expensive, their quality is good and they would cost more abroad.

Mpapa Gallery

On the quiet, residential Joseph Mwilwa Road (between the Great East Road and Church Road) next to the Bell Cross Farm vegetable shop, is a private gallery the size of a large house. This usually has a good range of pieces by Zambian artists for sale, and sometimes hosts small exhibitions on various art forms from jewellery to sculpture and painting. Worth a look if you're passing, but you won't find any bargains here.

Munda Wanga Zoo and Botanical Gardens

On Kafue Road, about 15km from the centre, just after the turn off for Lilayi Lodge, this is frequently cited as a tourist attraction. For most overseas visitors, the zoo's caged collection of unfortunate animals is very depressing. The Botanical Gardens have more potential for a picnic or a laze in the sun, if the litter has been kept to a minimum.

Open: daily until 17.00

Rates: non-resident Kw1,650 per person and also per camera

Nightlife

The period that a nightclub remains in fashion, and hence remains in business, is even shorter than the life of most restaurants. So recommendations in this section will, by their very nature, be out of date quickly. Better to ask the locals about the best places, and go with the recommendations. You should always be mindful of your safety, not take much cash to a club with you, and not linger anywhere which feels uncomfortable.

Current favourites include **Chez Ntemba**, behind the Kamwala market, which has a cover charge of Kw2,500 and plays mainly rumba. The bar is good and on Friday and Saturday nights it continues to party until dawn – but there's no food available. Elsewhere the **Cosmo Club** (tel: 273020) on Kafue Road is somewhat more chic – described by one punter as "where the rich go". At the other end of the scale, the **Theatre Club**, opposite the Pamodzi, is a fascinating place to chat to the locals, and a few doors down is an even more relaxed bar, which is ideal for a drink and a game of pool. Nearby, **The Nook** is more basic still, with a lively dance floor.

Other possibilities include **Go Bananas**, on Panganini Road, **Grasshopper Inn** (tel: 213627), **Lotus Inn** (tel: 226965), **Moon City Night Club** on the second floor of Findeco House (tel: 213771 or 225118), and **Mr. Pete's Steakhouse** on Panganini Road (tel: 223428 or 291192).

SHOPPING

Lusaka's main shopping centre is Cairo Road, but identifying the right place for what you want to buy can be difficult. Lusaka does, to some extent, remain in a time-warp. It has been a capital of cramped corner-shops until now. Most of Lusaka's residents have been innocent of those consumer-friendly hypermarkets where wide, ergonomically designed aisles are lined with displays of endless choice. However, this is starting to change. If you are prepared to look, then you can buy most things that you will need for your travels, and there are signs that modern supermarkets will be thriving before long.

Food and drink

If you need food and supplies, then there are several obvious places. The first is beside Lusaka Square, in the centre of Cairo Road, on the eastern side. *Checkers*, alias *Shoprite*, is the first venture into the country of a large South African chain of supermarkets. In late 1995, Checkers arrived with a largely alien culture of large volume, low margins and good levels of pay to reward honest employees. This rocked Lusaka's existing, mainly Asian, shop-owning community - who had always gone for the high-margin corner-shop approach. Rumours were rife of the ways in which Checkers' arrival was resisted, and even blocked by the capital's existing business community. Checkers now seems to have found its feet, and is the best supermarket in the country.

Outside the centre, there are a couple of smaller supermarkets, supplying good quality, if quite expensive, produce which is mostly imported. **Melissa Minimarket** is probably the best, situated just off the Great East Road in Northmeads, behind the Mobil petrol station. It isn't cheap, but if you crave a carton of exotic fruit-juice, or a choice of diet drinks, then drop in. Several delis and a bakery or two have sprung up around the minimarket (*Jimmy's Deli* has a good choice of yoghurts) and opposite it is a small craft market selling some good malachite bracelets, necklaces and a wide selection of carvings.

Kabulonga Shopping Centre is similar, though not quite as upmarket. Found at the corner of Twin Palms and Chindo Roads, it is very convenient if you are staying at Belvedere Lodge.

Fresh vegetables can also be picked up from various street-sellers, like the excellent stall at the BP station on the south side of the Great East Road. **BC Farms**, on Joseph Mwilwa Road, a few blocks northwest of the Pamodzi, has excellent fresh farm produce and an interesting notice-board if you want to buy/sell something from/to the expat or UN residents.

Other supplies

For **cosmetics**, **toiletries** or **sun creams**, try the pharmacies and curio shops in the Holiday Inn, Pamodzi, and (especially) Intercontinental Hotels. Don't expect bargain prices, but you should find something which is close to what you are seeking.

For **books** try Bookworld, either at the north end of Cairo Road or in Kabulonga shopping centre. Alternatively, from Wed-Fri 09.30-17.00 or on Saturday 09.30-12.30, try Mary's Book Shop, on Leopard's Hill Road,

1km beyond the end of the tarmac. The Video Shop, on Bishop's Road in Kabulonga, also stocks a small selection of second-hand books – which tends to be a more interesting and eclectic range than the new books which are available.

For **camping and fishing supplies**, again try BC Farms, on Joseph Mwilwa Road. Open: Mon-Fri 08.30-14.00, Sat 08.30-12.00.

Basic **camera supplies** can be found at Phoenix Photographics and Royal Art Studios, which are adjacent on Cairo Road, near Society House. Alternatively try Fine Art Studios, on Chachacha Road. Don't expect to find a great range of anything at any of these.

Car repairs and **spare parts** can be difficult to arrange, as spare parts are often in poor supply. However, start at either the Impala Service Station (tel: 243890; fax: 243876) on the Great North Road just past the roundabout at the end of Cairo Road, or AutoWorld (tel: 223207; fax: 223323) on Freedom Way, near the corner with Ben Bella Road.

Souvenirs and curios

For typical **African carvings, basketware and curios**, you probably won't get better value or a wider selection than at Kabwata Cultural Centre, on Burma Road (see *What to see and do* above). However, you could also try African Relics, at the airport; The Gift Box, on Chachacha Road; the outdoor market at Northmeads opposite Melissa Minimarket; or Shantina's Crafts, on Bishop's Road in Kabulonga.

Aside from these, Lusaka is not a shopper's paradise, though if you want pirate music cassettes then the stalls on Chachacha Road have some cheap buys.

If you can transport it safely, there is good value (if not actually cheap) **pottery** to be had at Moore Pottery on Kabulonga Road, or Bente Lorentz Pottery, off Los Angeles Boulevard behind Longacres Market.

Gems and jewellery can be found in expensive shops at the Intercontinental, Pamodzi or Holiday Inn, though don't expect any bargains. More original (but alas, not cheaper) creations in silver can be found at Kalipinde, on Panganini Road.

For a more practical and much cheaper souvenir get a *chitenje* for about Kw2,300-2,700 – there are shops in the smallest of towns. You will see these 2m-long sections of brightly patterned cotton cloth everywhere, often wrapped around local women. Whilst travelling use them as towels, sarongs, picnic mats or – as the locals do – simply swathed over your normal clothes to keep them clean. When back home, you can cut the material into clothes, or use them as coverings. Either way, you will have brought a splash of truly African colour back home with you.

INFORMATION AND ADDRESSES

British Council

If you are in Lusaka for any length of time then the British Council runs a good library, with lending and reference sections, from its offices in Heroes Place off Cairo Road. Joining fee is £4 (US$6) for books, and £10 (US$15) for videos.

Car hire

See *Vehicle hire* in *Chapter Five* for advice and a guide to typical rates. Lusaka's car hire companies normally insist upon foreign drivers using a chauffeur. They include:

Hertz PO Box 32591, 25/26 Nkwazi Road. Tel: 229944/7, fax: 229947. They have other branches in Ndola and Kitwe

Zungulila Zambia PO Box 31475, TAZ House Annex, corner of Chiparamba Road & Chachacha Road. Tel: 227730 or 223234 or 220251 or 220121, fax: 227729

AVIS/Big 5 PO Box 35371, Cairo Road (near the southern roundabout). Tel: 271058 or 274420 or 220191 or 229237 or 221098, fax: 271262 or 221978

Couriers

If you need to send something valuable, or send it rapidly, then do not trust the postal service. A courier is by far the best way, so start phoning around:

DHL (Zambia) Tel: 229768 or 225558
Express Courier Tel: 228988
Karnak Couriers Tel: 221686
Mercury Courier Tel: 217989
Sky Couriers Tel: 227127

For post and packages within Zambia, Express are probably the best, as they also have offices in Chipata (tel: 21471), Kitwe (tel: 217110), Livingstone (tel: 320704), Mpulungu (tel: 455011) and Ndola (tel: 650597).

Emergencies

For a serious medical condition, see *Chapter Six*, *Health and Safety*, and don't hesitate to use the emergency number given with your medical insurance. Your embassy or hotel can be of help, as both will be able to recommend a doctor. A sick foreign traveller will usually be accepted by one of the well-equipped clinics used by the city's more affluent residents.

Proof of comprehensive medical insurance will make this all the more speedy, so try:

Primary Care Services Ltd Katopola Road and the Great East Road. Tel: 253858 or 251034

Monica Chiumya Memorial Clinic off Buluwe Road, near Lake Road, Kabulonga. Tel: 260491

Alternatively, the University Teaching Hospital has probably the city's best Emergency Department (tel: 254113).

Post, telephone, fax and telex

Lusaka's busy main post office is in the centre of Cairo Road, on the corner with Church Road. The main hall on the ground floor has a row of assistants in cubicles - above which the occupant's responsibilities are detailed.

Upstairs on the first floor, you will find the telegraph office (open Mon-Fri 08.30-16.30, Sat 08.00-12.00). Here you can send a telex or a fax, or even make an international phone call. It is often crowded and conversations are anything but private, but they can be accomplished surprisingly fast. Time is metered in three-minute units, and a call will be cut off automatically unless you instruct the operators otherwise. A three-minute call to Zimbabwe costs Kw9,737, and to the UK or USA Kw19,127.

Travel agents

Cairo Road seems lined by travel agents, as if the capital's residents do little but travel. At the last count, there were 35 different agencies in Lusaka's yellow pages telephone directory. However, attentive and efficient service isn't so common, and only a few are used to the demands of overseas clients. Here, in alphabetical order, are a few of the agencies which are better adapted to helping overseas visitors with local travel arrangements:

The Adventure Centre PO Box 35058, Ben Bella Road (100m from Cairo Road, next to the BP station). Tel: 220112-5, fax: 220116, tlx: ZA 40675
This is really the Lusaka HQ of **Wilderness Trails,** which owns Chibembe and Nsefu Camps in South Luangwa. However, they can arrange more extensive itineraries all over the country.

African Tour Designers PO Box 31802, Amandra House, Ben Bella Road (south side, about 300m from Cairo Road). Tel: 224248, fax: 224265, tlx: ZA 40143
This small independent agency has a good reputation and close relations with Lechwe Lodge, Puku Pans Camp and Barotseland Fishing Tours & Safaris.

Busanga Travel & Tours PO Box 37538, Cairo Road (1st floor of building on south side of Lusaka Square) Tel: 220897 / 274196 / 223628 / 224971 / 221683 or 221694; fax: 222075 / (home) 274253
Synonymous with Busanga Trails, they have a long association with northern Kafue. Busanga run Lufupa and Shumba camps, to which clients are transferred by minibuses from Lusaka.

Bushwackers PO Box 320712, Holiday Inn Hotel, Ridgeway. Tel: 250310 / 253869 / 253906, fax: 223568 / 253790, tlx: ZA 42510 RIDGE
A good independent agency, Bushwackers are an obvious choice to arrange trips anywhere in Zambia. They have particularly close links with some of the Luangwa valley's better camps.

Eagle Travel PO Box 34530, Findeco House, Cairo Road (by the southern roundabout). Tel: 228604/5 / 229540/1, fax: 221031 / 221817
With eight offices spread around the country, Eagle Travel are the country's largest agency and, until 1993, they were state-owned. Now it can be difficult to find the level of expertise here that is available at some of smaller agencies.

Grand Travel and Tours PO Box 35211, Grand Building, Cairo Road (southern side, opposite Bank Square). Tel: 223113 / 224464 / 226073 / 223110, fax: 223648 / 223048, tlx: ZA 42850
Grand is another excellent independent agent. Close links to Shiwa N'gandu, and hence North Luangwa, make them a good choice to organise a tour of this part of the country.

Further information

There are few really useful sources of information about Lusaka, other than the concise listings in *Lusaka at a Glance*. This excellent little black-and-white booklet, published by the Tour Operators' Association, lists names, addresses and contact numbers under useful headings from air charter companies, through chemists, libraries and restaurants to travel agents and finally the Zambian National Tourist Board. It is fairly comprehensive, but not descriptive, and although some of the phone numbers are incorrect, annual updates are promised. If you're spending any time in Lusaka then do get hold of a copy. It is available from the Wildlife Shop (near the corner of Cairo and Church roads) and big hotels.

THE NEXT EDITION

Our readers play a vital role in updated books for the next edition. If you have found changes, or new and exciting places, or have a story to share do write. The most helpful contributions will receive a free book. Write to:
"Zambia", Bradt Publications, 41 Nortoft Road, Chalfont St. Peter, Bucks, SL9 0LA, UK

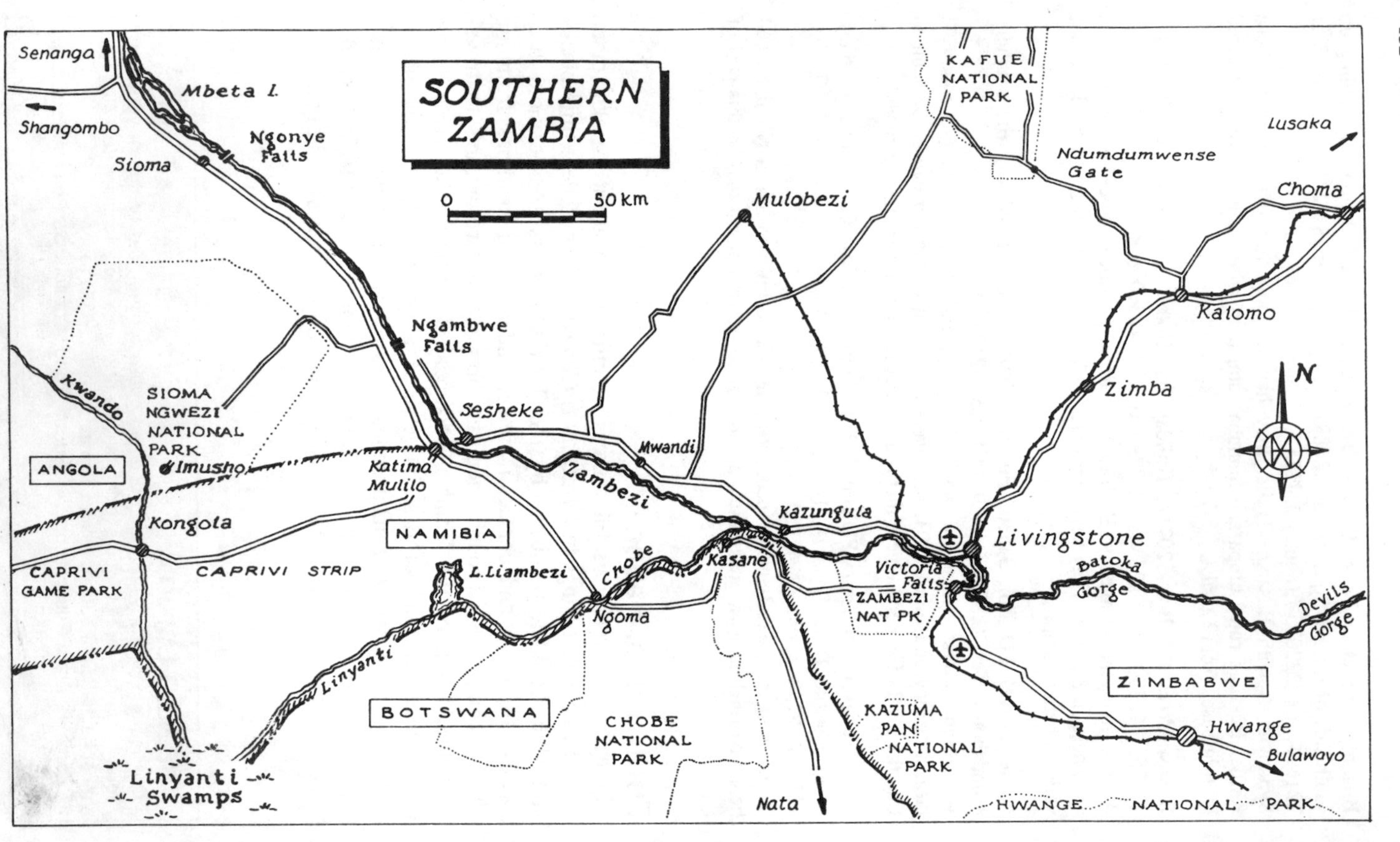
SOUTHERN ZAMBIA
0
50 km
Senanga
Shangombo
Mbeta I.
Ngonye Falls
Sioma
KAFUE NATIONAL PARK
Lusaka
Ndumdumwense Gate
Choma
Mulobezi
Kalomo
Ngambwe Falls
N
Zimba
Kwando
SIOMA NGWEZI NATIONAL PARK
Sesheke
Mwandi
ANGOLA
Imusho
Katima Mulilo
Zambezi
Kongola
NAMIBIA
Kazungula
Livingstone
CAPRIVI GAME PARK
CAPRIVI STRIP
L. Liambezi
Chobe
Kasane
Victoria Falls
Batoka Gorge
ZAMBEZI NAT PK
Ngoma
Devils Gorge
Linyanti
ZIMBABWE
BOTSWANA
CHOBE NATIONAL PARK
KAZUMA PAN NATIONAL PARK
Hwange
Bulawayo
Linyanti Swamps
Nata
HWANGE NATIONAL PARK

Chapter Ten

Livingstone and Victoria Falls

Livingstone is probably better oriented towards visitors than any other corner of Zambia. However, visitors travelling north from Zimbabwe are attracted simply by the Victoria Falls, and Livingstone often remains unseen. Some even view it with suspicion, being bigger and less well known than the small Zimbabwean town which shares the name of the waterfall.

This chapter aims to give details of both sides of the river: Zambian and Zimbabwean. Both have different views of the waterfall, as both have different attractions for visitors. Just as it is worth seeing both sides of the Falls to appreciate the whole waterfall, you will almost certainly find attractions that interest you in both Livingstone and Victoria Falls.

Tourism on the Zambian side of the Falls still lags behind that on the Zimbabwe side by about a decade. But while Livingstone may not be quite so well prepared for visitors, it also feels pleasantly less commercial.

History

We can be sure that the Falls were well known to the native peoples of Southern Africa well before any European "discovered" them. After the San/bushmen hunter-gatherers, the Tokaleya people inhabitcd the area, and it was probably they who christened the Falls "Shongwe". Later, the Ndebele knew the Falls as the "aManza Thunqayo", and after that the Makololo referred to them as "Mosi-oa-Tunya".

However, their first written description comes to us from Dr David Livingstone, who approached them in November 1855 from the west – from Linyanti, along the Chobe and Zambezi rivers. Livingstone already knew of their existence from the locals, and wrote:

> "I resolved on the following day to visit the falls of Victoria, called by the natives Mosioatunya, or more anciently Shongwe. Of these we had often heard since we came into the country: indeed one of the questions asked by Sebituane [the chief of the Makololo tribe] travelling was, 'Have you the smoke that sounds in your country?' They did not go near enough to examine them, but, viewing them with awe at a distance, said, in reference

> to the vapour and noise, 'Mosi oa tunya' (smoke does sound there). It was previously called Shongwe, the meaning of which I could not ascertain. The word for a 'pot' resembles this, and it may mean a seething caldron; but I am not certain of it."

Livingstone continues to describe the river above the Falls, its islands and their lush vegetation, before making his most famous comment about sightseeing angels, now abused and misquoted by those who write tourist brochures to the area:

> "Some trees resemble the great spreading oak, others assume the character of our own elms and chestnuts; but no one can imagine the beauty of the view from anything witnessed in England. It had never been seen before by European eyes; but scenes so lovely must have been gazed upon by angels in their flight. The only want felt is that of mountains in the background. The falls are bounded on three sides by ridges 300 or 400 feet in height, which are covered in forest, with the red soil appearing amongst the trees. When about half a mile from the falls, I left the canoe by which we had come down this far, and embarked in a lighter one, with men well acquainted with the rapids, who, by passing down the centre of the stream in the eddies and still places caused by many jutting rocks, brought me to an island situated in the middle of the river, on the edge of the lip over which the water rolls."
>
> from the autobiographical *Journeys in Southern Africa*

Those who bemoan the area's emphasis on tourism should note that there must have been sightseeing boat trips ever since David Livingstone came this way.

Being the most eastern point reachable by boat from the Chobe or Upper Zambezi rivers, the area of the Falls was a natural place for European settlement. Soon more traders, hunters and missionaries came into the area, and by the late 1800s a small European settlement had formed around a ferry crossing called the Old Drift, about 10km upstream from the Falls. However, this was built on low-lying marshy ground near the river, buzzing with mosquitoes, so malaria took many lives.

By 1905 the spectacular Victoria Falls bridge had been completed, linking the copper deposits of the Copperbelt and the coal deposits at Wankie (now Hwange) with a railway line. This, and the malaria, encouraged the settlers to transfer to a site on higher ground, next to the railway line at a place called Constitution Hill. It became the centre of present-day Livingstone, and many of its original buildings are still standing. A small cemetery, the poignant remains of Old Drift, can still be seen on the northern bank of the Zambezi within the Mosi-oa-Tunya National Park.

In 1911 Livingstone became the capital of Northern Rhodesia (now Zambia), which it remained until 1935, when the administration was transferred to Lusaka.

Geology

The Falls are, geologically speaking, probably a very recent formation. About a million years ago, the Zambezi's course is thought to have been down a wide valley over a plateau dating from the karoo period, until it met the Middle Zambezi rift – where the Matetsi River mouth is now.

Here it fell about 250m over an escarpment. However, that fast-falling water would have eroded the lip of the waterfall and gouged out a deeper channel within the basalt rock of the escarpment plateau – and so the original falls steadily retreated upstream. These channels tended to follow some existing fissure – a crack or weakness, formed when the lava first cooled at the end of the karoo period. At around the Batoka Gorge these fissures naturally run east–west in the rock, parallel to the course of the valley.

By around the Middle Pleistocene period, between 35,000 and 40,000 years ago, this process had formed the Batoka Gorge, carving it out to within about 90km of the present falls.

However, as water eroded away the lip of the falls, its valley gradually turned north, until it was almost at right-angles to the basalt fault lines which run east–west. Then the water began to erode the fissures and turn them into walls of rock stretching across the valley, perpendicular to it, over which gushed broad curtains of water.

Once such a wall had formed, the water would wear down the rock until it found a fault line behind the wall, along which the water would erode and cause the rock subsequently to collapse. Thus the new fault line would become the wall of the new falls, behind the old one. This process resulted in the eight gorges that now form the river's slalom course after it has passed over the present Falls. Each gorge was once a great waterfall.

Today, on the eastern side of the Devil's Cataract, you can see this pattern starting again. The water is eroding away the rock of another fault line, behind the line of the present falls, which geologists expect will form a new waterfall a few thousand years from now.

LIVINGSTONE

Orientation

Livingstone town itself is compact, and surrounded by several small township suburbs just a few kilometres from its centre. Navigation is easy, even without a map, though signposts are often missing.

Livingstone's main street is the important Mosi-oa-Tunya Road. Sections of this are lined with classic colonial buildings – corrugated iron roofs and wide wooden verandas. Drive north on the main street out of the city, and it becomes Lusaka Road leading to the capital.

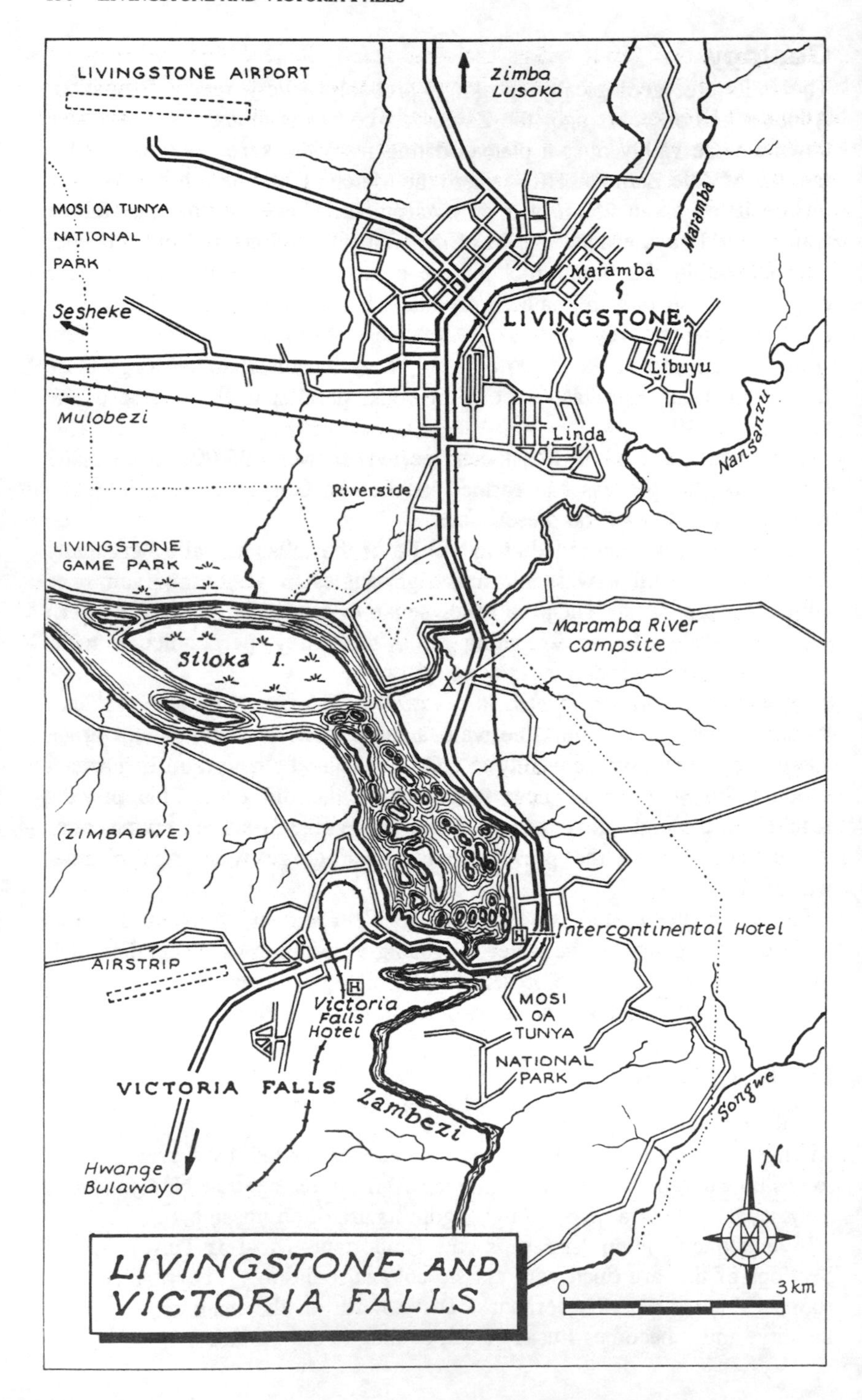
LIVINGSTONE AIRPORT
Zimba
Lusaka
MOSI OA TUNYA
NATIONAL
PARK
Maramba
Maramba
LIVINGSTONE
Libuyu
Sesheke
Mulobezi
Linda
Nansanzu
Riverside
LIVINGSTONE
GAME PARK
Maramba River
campsite
Siloka I.
(ZIMBABWE)
Intercontinental Hotel
AIRSTRIP
Victoria
Falls
Hotel
MOSI
OA
TUNYA
NATIONAL
PARK
VICTORIA FALLS
Zambezi
Songwe
Hwange
Bulawayo
N
0
3 km
LIVINGSTONE AND
VICTORIA FALLS

Head south for about 10km and you reach the Zambezi river and Victoria Falls themselves. There are some places to stay around here, a border post to cross the Zambezi into Zimbabwe, a small museum, and an excellent curio stand selling locally produced souvenirs.

Travel west from town on Nakatindi Road and you soon find yourself parallel to the Zambezi, following its north bank upstream. Signposts point left, to small, exclusive lodges, perched at picturesque spots on the river's bank.

Getting there and away

By air

Livingstone's international airport is just 5km northwest of the centre on Libala Drive. It is served by several regional carriers, although its actual runway is a little too bumpy for some airlines. If you are trying to fly into the Falls area, then landing at Livingstone Airport is as convenient as Victoria Falls Airport.

Amongst others, Livingstone is has regular links with Lusaka, and weekly flights by Air Namibia from Windhoek. The latter flights usually include a free transfer to any hotel, on either side of the border, if you remember to ask for it when you book.

By bus

The main terminus for local buses is Kapondo Street, just on Mosi-oa-Tunya Road, opposite the main post office. Here a range of buses gather in the early morning. Most head towards Lusaka, though one or two will go west to Sesheke. Expect the first to leave around 06.30, and the last around 11.00, depending upon demand. A seat to Lusaka on a large bus costs around Kw6,500, on a small minibus around Kw8,000. If you are backpacking, then expect the attentions of bus touts. Whilst waiting, stay towards the top end of Kapondo Road, near Mosi-oa-Tunya Road, to minimise this.

By train

There is a railway station with regular trains to Kitwe via Lusaka, but it is not used much by travellers. It is well signposted about 1km south of the centre on the way to the Falls, on the eastern side of the Mosi-oa-Tunya Road.

Express trains to Lusaka depart from Livingstone at 19.00 on Sundays Tuesdays and Thursdays, and arrive at around 07.00 on the following morning. There are daily trains departing at 09.00 which stop everywhere and so take even longer. A 15.00 train to Victoria Falls is scheduled to connect with the excellent overnight train to Bulawayo. However, check this connection before relying upon it as it is probably more reliable to take a taxi to the border then walk to the Zimbabwean railway station from there.

Driving west

If you have a vehicle and intend to head west, into Namibia's Caprivi Strip, Botswana, or Western Zambia, then Nakatindi Road continues past the lodges by the river and on to Kazungula – where Namibia, Botswana, Zimbabwe and Zambia all meet at a notional point. Here you can continue northwest, within Zambia to Sesheke, or take the ferry across the Zambezi into Botswana, near Kasane. The road to Sesheke is currently in a very bad state of repair, and large, frequent potholes make the drive very slow and uncomfortable.

The less bumpy option is to cross the Zambezi into Botswana, drive through Kasane and on to an excellent gravel road to the Namibian border at Ngoma, where you cross the Chobe River into Namibia. From there the good gravel road to Katima Mulilo is now being tarred, and from Katima you can drive across into Zambia. There is a small village on the Zambian side of the border, also called Katima Mulilo, and a ferry across the Zambezi to Sesheke. This is a longer drive, and has half-a-dozen border posts at which you must complete border formalities – which means lots of time standing around and filling in forms. However, the driving is much more comfortable, and both Kasane and Katima have good supplies and communications.

This route also involves purchasing a Botswana road insurance, for about 20 Botswana Pula or 25 South African Rand (US$ or UK£ are not accepted) on entry into Botswana. As a deterrent to car thieves, if you have a South African registered vehicle then you may also need to obtain police clearance at Katima Mulilo to take the vehicle out of Namibia.

Where to stay

There is no lack of accommodation in Livingstone, or across the river in Victoria Falls. The problem is finding good quality accommodation at a reasonable price.

In town

Wasawange Lodge (13 rooms) PO Box 60278. Tel: 324066 or 324077/8; fax: 324067

Situated on the Libala Road – the way to the airport – just on the edge of town, Wasawange Lodge is a comfortable small hotel with a few ethnic touches. Its rooms are individual rondavels with en suite facilities and satellite TV. It is popular with business visitors and has a good restaurant, a pool, sauna and jacuzzi, a conference room, and is convenient for town. Because of its popularity and small size, you will often need to book in advance to get a room.

Rates: US$70 single, US$100 double, bed and breakfast

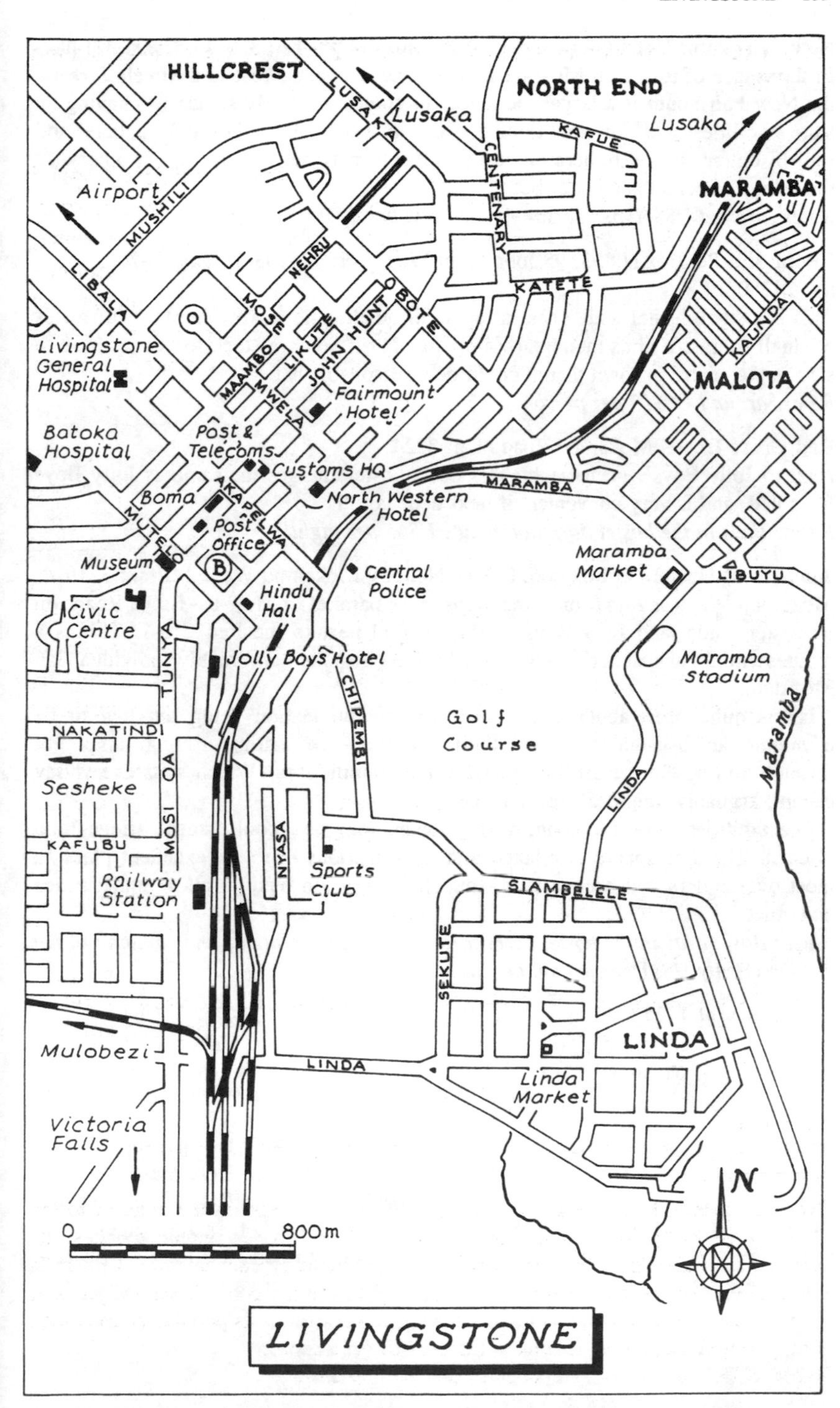
HILLCREST
NORTH END
Lusaka
Lusaka
LUSAKA
KAFUE
CENTENARY
Airport
MUSHILI
MARAMBA
NEHRU
OBOTE
KATETE
LIBALA
MOSE
HUNT
JOHN
LIKUTE
KAUNDA
Livingstone General Hospital
MAAMBO
MWELA
Fairmount Hotel
MALOTA
Batoka Hospital
Post & Telecoms
Customs HQ
MARAMBA
Boma
AKAPELWA
North Western Hotel
MUTELO
Post office
Museum
B
Central Police
Maramba Market
LIBUYU
Hindu Hall
Civic Centre
Jolly Boys Hotel
Maramba Stadium
TUNYA
CHIPEMBI
Golf Course
Maramba
NAKATINDI
Sesheke
MOSI OA
LINDA
KAFUBU
NYASA
Sports Club
Railway Station
SIAMBELELE
SEKUTE
LINDA
Mulobezi
LINDA
Linda Market
Victoria Falls
N
0
800m
LIVINGSTONE

New Fairmount Hotel (84 twin rooms) PO Box 60096. Tel: 320723-8; fax: 321490
In the centre of town, on Mosi-oa-Tunya Road between Mose and Mwela Streets, the New Fairmount is a large, old hotel. Its rooms are fairly standard – having en suite facilities and air-conditioning, but in need of a thorough update and refurbishment. If you're here on business then it may be convenient, but otherwise the Intercontinental is a better bet.
Rates: around US$40 per person for bed and breakfast.

Living Inn PO Box 60853, 95 John Hunt Way. Tel: 324203-5; fax: 324206; tlx: 24380 ZA
This is a small hostel with a central open-air quadrangle surrounded by two stories of small rooms. It aims mainly at Zambians, but if you are stuck for somewhere to stay in the centre of town then it could be a reasonable bet.
Rates: around US$15 per person

Red Cross Hostel Mokambo Road. Tel: 32247
Next to Jolly Boys', on its right, this basic hostel charges the same as Jolly Boys for a bed, and is very convenient if next door is full.
Rates: Beds in the hostel dormitories are US$5 per night.

Jolly Boys' Hostel PO Box 60611, Plot No. 559 Mokambo Way. Tel/fax: 321924
Mokambo Way (or *Road*, on some maps) runs parallel to Mosi-oa-Tunya Road, on its eastern side, and Jolly Boys is easy to find next to the Red Cross. This is a quintessential backpacker's lodge, run by the outspoken and highly individual Ian McAdam.

Ian is quite open about these rates for accommodation being too low to be economic, and asks guests to book their activities – like rafting or bungi jumping – through him so that he can benefit from the commission. (Which suits everybody except, arguably, the local travel agents.)

The facilities here are good, with a telephone, fax, pool, sauna, fridge, and kitchen. The atmosphere is relaxed and unpretentious – it's an excellent place to meet overlanders and backpackers, though usually too busy to allow much peace and quiet.
Rates: Basic beds in the hostel dormitories are US$5 per night, and camping in the garden is only US$1 per person per night.

Zambezi Motel (25 twin rooms) PO Box 60700. Tel: 321511-2 or 321996
Just south of Livingstone, on the way to Victoria Falls, the Zambezi Motel is well located next to Mosi-oa-Tunya Road. However, with so many interesting places to stay, this uninspiring motel has little to recommend it.

Busika Guest Accommodation PO Box 60694. Tel: 322467; fax: 322468
About 10km northeast of town, Busika is situated on a farm. Here there is a large bunkhouse sleeping up to eight, a couple of basic wooden chalets, and a campsite. To get there head north through town on the main road, then turn right on to Katete Avenue – where Mosi-oa-Tunya Road begins to bend left towards Lusaka. From there just follow the signs over the railway line to the farm.

By the Zambezi

Kubu Cabins (5 chalets) PO Box 60748. Tel: 324093; fax: 324091 (also telephone and answer machine)

Kubu Camp is the furthest camp from Livingstone and is well signposted. Leave town on the Nakatindi Road and continue for about 30km, until the camp is indicated off to the left. Follow the signs, and the lodge will appear after a further 5km of sandy track. (This last 5km needs careful driving with a low-slung car.)

The cabins have a beautiful site, opposite the Zambezi National Park in Zimbabwe. Kubu's bar-lounge area is friendly and comfortable - built under thatch, on a wooden deck overlooking the river. "Kubu" means hippo, which are common here, and there is an extensive collection of drums and xylophones if you wish to accompany their nocturnal grunts.

Kubu's normal chalets are solid wood and thatch structures, thoroughly mosquito-proofed, with twin beds, en suite facilities, mains lights and electricity. There are also two more spacious "honeymoon suites" which have double beds, sunken baths and one side open to the river. These are great rooms in which to stay, and worth paying the extra few dollars.

Canoeing is easily organised on the river, as *Makora Quest* (see page 163) are less than a kilometre downstream, and horse riding is available through nearby *Chundukwa*. This is an excellent place to relax by the river, and the food is very good. However, if you wish to make a lot of trips into the falls, for sight-seeing or activities, then you need your own vehicle.

Rates: around US$150 per person for full board including drinks, laundry, and a return transfer to Livingstone or Victoria Falls.

Kubu Camping (camping sites) PO Box 60748. Tel: 324093; fax: 324091 (also telephone and answer machine)

As well as its chalets, downstream Kubu has a good grass campsite set under false ebony, marula and teak trees by the river. There is a kitchen area, clean toilets and hot showers - all watched over by an attendant.

Rates: US$10 per person including firewood. Owners are very helpful about transport to town and the Falls - though finding vehicles is not easy.

Chundukwa River Camp (4 chalets) PO Box 61160. Tel: 324006; fax: 324006 or 323224; tlx: 24043 ZA

Owned and run by Doug Evans, this is the base camp for *Chundukwa Adventure Trails* (see page 162 for details) - it is not really a place to just drop into for a few nights.

The camp is out on the main Nakatindi Road, just before Kubu Cabins, and has just three twin-bedded chalets, and one larger for honeymoon or family use. Each is divided in two: the bedroom and a small veranda perch on stilts amongst the waterberry trees above the river, whilst the private toilets and showers are just a few yards away (over a wooden walkway) on the river bank. A novel and cosy design.

Rates: Expect an average of US$150 per person per night (full board and all activities) for an adventure trip including walking safaris, canoeing, horse riding and a few days here.

Mosi-O-Tunya Intercontinental Hotel (100 rooms) PO Box 60151. Tel: 321121 or 321122; fax: 321128; tlx: ZA 24221
Affectionately known as the "Intercon", the Mosi-O-Tunya Intercontinental is a few hundred metres from the border post, and certainly the closest hotel to the Falls. Most passing travellers stop here for a cold drink by the (excellent) pool, after the long hot walk from Zimbabwe.
If you're staying longer, then this is a good base for exploring the Falls, with the facilities that you'd expect from a big hotel (plus tennis courts and a squash court). The rooms aren't very imaginative, but they are your best chance of finding air-conditioning on the Zambian side anywhere near the river. The food is good, the service relaxed and friendly, and if you are looking for a "normal" hotel, rather than a bush lodge, then this is ideal.
Rates: US$90 per person sharing, or US$145 single, including breakfast

Rainbow Lodge PO Box 60090. Tel: 321806; fax: 320236; tlx: ZA 24080
Situated on a stunning site by the Zambezi, just north of the Intercon, the old Rainbow Lodge was government run and becoming rather dilapidated. The site was put up for tender in late 1995, and soon it is expected that a private company will take it over, renovate it, and once again make it an excellent place to stay. Until then there are camping facilities here, but these are not very secure – so better to go a further 5km to the Maramba River Campsite.

Thorn Tree Lodge (6 twin-bed tents) PO Box 60420. Tel: 320823; fax: 320277 or 320732
Thorn Tree Lodge is owned and managed by Di and John Tolmay and, rather like Chundukwa, it is the base for a safari company, *Across Africa Overland* (see page 162).
That said, the lodge has lots of space and welcomes non-safari visitors to stay. To find it take the main Nakatindi Road, and turn left at the signpost to *Melrose Farm*. This is well before Chundukwa. Thorn Tree Lodge's large Meru-style tents are very comfortable – built on a brick base under a thatched roof, with en suite electricity and showers. There's a very comfortable bar and dining area, from which you can watch the elephants hopping between the islands in the Zambezi.
Rates: US$125 per person per night full board, including drinks

Tongabezi (5 twin-bed tents and 3 double houses) P Bag 31. Tel: 323235; fax: 323224; tlx: ZA 25043
Run by Will and Ben, two well-spoken Englishmen, this is perhaps the most expensive place to stay on the north side of the river. The accommodation is good, with excellent attention to detail and the usual en suite facilities. Choose between tented twin-bedded chalets, or one of the three suites: the Bird House, the Tree House or the Honeymoon Suite (often cited as "worth getting married for"). Each suite is well designed, with a large double bed, impressive bath, and one side completely open on to the river. This is more private than it might appear.

Tongabezi is a quiet, reserved, and very English place to stay, where the food is excellent, and the staff will pander to your every wish. Guided sunrise and sunset boat trips, canoeing, fishing and even tennis are included. Tongabezi oozes style and quality, though can sometimes feel formal.

The camp uses two London taxis for transport – unmistakable in these parts. Very few of the guests here are local, so if you want to stay, then contact the town office in Nakatindi Road (200m from the junction with Mosi-oa-Tunya Road). It is better to arrange your stay from overseas before you arrive. There are also options to sleep on one of the islands in the river, or have a champagne breakfast on Livingstone Island – but these should be booked in advance.
Rates: US$210 per person per night, including drinks, transfers and most activities

Taita Falcon Lodge PO Box 60012. Tel/fax: 321850
This new lodge is perched overlooking rapid number 17 in the Batoka Gorge, downstream of the Falls. It is a 45-minute drive from Livingstone, following the road normally used to bring rafters back from the river. Taita Falcon Lodge is named after a rare falcon found in the area, and was due to start operating in 1996, though at the time of going to press few details were available. One unique attraction here is a hiking trail down into the gorge, which takes several days to complete. Hikers must have all of their own equipment, though maps are provided.
Rates: US$120 per person full board including transfers

Maramba River Caravan and Campsite PO Box 60957. Tel: 324189; fax: 324266
Between the border post and Livingstone town, about 5km from each, lies the friendliest campsite in Zambia. Maramba River is run by Judi (whose contributions form an integral part of this guide), Arthur, and a large dog named Zulu – who is generally very friendly. Firewood and braai (BBQ) packs are available, and for a little extra, you can sleep on a wooden platform in one of the trees. Judi and Arthur can also arrange any activity or excursion bookings from here.

The showers and toilets are absolutely spotless, and security guards patrol during the night, making this one of the safest sites in the area. The site is within the Mosi-oa-Tunya National Park, so expect hippos, crocodiles, antelope and the occasional elephant to be around. It's an excellent and original alternative to the crowded site in Victoria Falls.
Rates: US$10 per person per night

Where to eat

Take-away

There are several take-aways in town, including Magic Take-Away, Shambas and Eat Rite. For a few thousand kwacha, these serve the usual fare of pre-packaged chips, burgers, sandwiches and soft drinks. They are all in the centre of town, near where the buses stop – around the intersection of Kapondo Street and Mosi-oa-Tunya Road. There is a good supermarket – its stock is extensive though largely imported, and hence expensive.

If you're near the border, then go for the Intercon's civilised terrace, where good poolside snacks and chilled drinks are served.

Restaurants

All Livingstone's better restaurants are attached to the hotels and lodges. If you've got a vehicle, then the food at Kubu Cabins is worth the drive (you must book in advance). Otherwise try Wasawange Lodge, the Intercon, or even the New Fairmount Hotel.

Getting around

Livingstone town is small enough to walk around, as is the Falls area. However if you are travelling between the two, or going to the airport, or in a hurry, then use one of the plentiful taxis. A taxi between town and either the border or the airport will cost around Kw8,000. From the airport to the border is about Kw16,000. Most drivers are unfamiliar with the riverside lodges, and will be reluctant to take you there cheaply as they will not find a passenger for the return journey.

VICTORIA FALLS (the Zimbabwean side)

Orientation

The buzzing town of Victoria Falls is less than 2km south of the Zambezi, the border with Zambia. It feels smaller than Livingstone, and is currently more of a centre for tourists. The heart of the town is small, comprising shops, offices and a campsite within a few metres of the landmark Wimpy restaurant on the corner. Those that are not either travel agencies or take-aways seem to sell curios, camping equipment or at least T-shirts. Few remain oblivious to the potential of the tourist dollar.

Between the town and the Falls, the railway station stands opposite the old, and still gracious, Victoria Falls Hotel – now adjoined by the less colonial Makasa Sun, with its roof-top restaurant and casino.

Head south from the Wimpy, away from the Falls, and you soon pass the main township on the left. Later, some 25km from the centre, comes Victoria Falls airport, as you begin the long road south to Bulawayo.

Go northeast, following the Zambezi upstream, and the scenery rapidly opens out to bush. You pass several hotels before reaching the National Park's riverside restcamp and campsite, on your right, and then entering the Zambezi National Park.

Getting there and away

By air

Victoria Falls airport is busier than Livingstone's, with daily Air Zimbabwe flights connecting to Hwange, Kariba and Harare. Their office is on Livingstone Way, opposite the Makasa Sun Hotel (tel: (13) 4136). Other airlines flying here include South African Airways, who have convenient non-stop connections to Jo'burg and Cape Town, Air Namibia

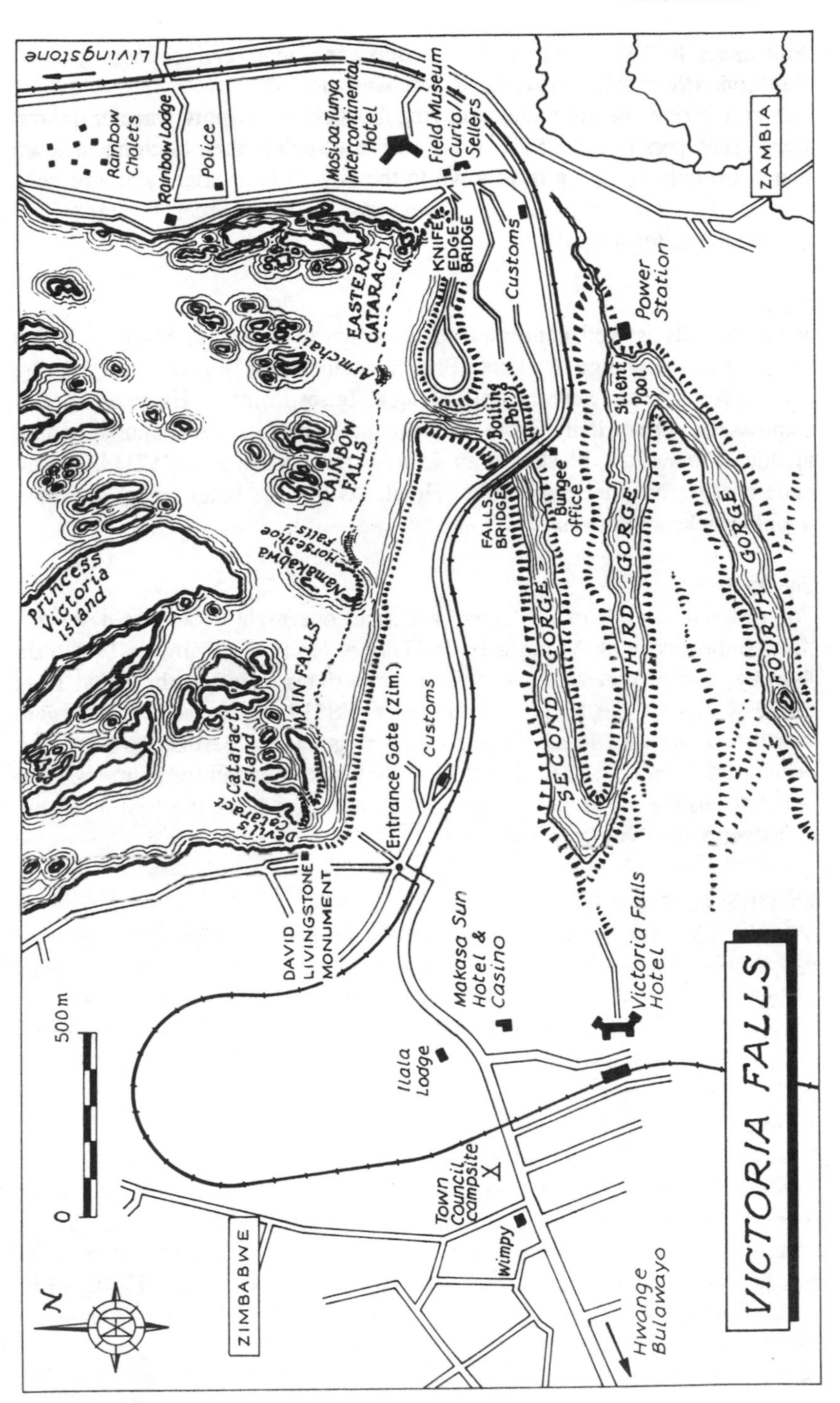
VICTORIA FALLS
N
ZIMBABWE
ZAMBIA
0
500 m
Livingstone
Hwange
Bulawayo
Rainbow Chalets
Rainbow Lodge
Police
Mosi-oa-Tunya Intercontinental Hotel
Field Museum
Curio/ Sellers
KNIFE EDGE BRIDGE
Customs
Power Station
EASTERN CATARACT
Armchair
Boiling Pot
Silent Pool
RAINBOW FALLS
FALLS BRIDGE
Bungee Office
Princess Victoria Island
Namakabwa
Horseshoe Falls
MAIN FALLS
SECOND GORGE
THIRD GORGE
FOURTH GORGE
Cataract Island
Devil's Cataract
Entrance Gate (Zim.)
Customs
DAVID LIVINGSTONE MONUMENT
Makasa Sun Hotel & Casino
Victoria Falls Hotel
Ilala Lodge
Town Council Campsite
Wimpy

with links to Windhoek, and Air Botswana who can connect you to Gaborone (their office is near Air Zimbabwe).

If you arrive by air without having booked an airport transfer (about US$12 per person, or US$70 for a whole vehicle), then hitching to town is not difficult. Hitching from town to the airport is trickier, you will need to walk to a spot opposite the Sprayview Hotel in order to start. It is worth paying for a transfer.

By bus

Victoria Falls is well connected to the town of Hwange, Hwange Safari Lodge (near Hwange National Park's Main Camp), and Bulawayo by good bus services. Several normal local buses, run by Hwange Special Expresses, depart daily from the car park behind the main shopping arcade. The swifter, plusher Ajay Express (tel: Bulawayo 62521) buses go once a day from the Makasa Sun Hotel. Ask at the hotel reception about booking tickets in advance.

By train

For those in search of nostalgia, a classic overnight steam train service links Bulawayo with Victoria Falls. This is easily Zimbabwe's best train journey, and a great way to arrive at (or perhaps to leave) the Falls. First class, with four berths per cabin, costs US$30 per person – a bargain worth booking well in advance. Second class has six berths per cabin and costs US$17 per person. Third class has only (uncomfortable) wooden benches costing US$8 per person. Treat yourself: book the best available and sleep whilst you travel in style.

Where to stay

Victoria Falls has many hotels, catering for a very international crowd. All except the **Sprayview** charge substantial amounts in US$. If your budget is limited, don't forget your camping kit. Also remember that having a vehicle opens up possibilities on the outskirts of town, giving you more options than just the town council's crowded campsite in the centre.

Hotels

Whereas Zambia has a number of excellent bush lodges along the Zambezi river-front, the hotels near the Falls on the south side of the river are more conventional. Most are quite large, but their atmosphere differs widely. None are really bush lodges – despite the claims of one or two. Included here are only those lodges within about 10km of the Falls, all of which have en suite facilities, and all except Ilala have air-conditioning.

Victoria Falls Hotel (141 rooms) PO Box 10
Started in 1905, with its back facing the train station, the Victoria Falls Hotel has a stunning position overlooking the second cataract and the railway bridge. The almost Edwardian ambience of the town's oldest and most famous hotel retains a strong colonial hint - as close to Singapore's old Raffles Hotel as you can find in Africa. In the 1950's Laurens van ver Post wrote:

> "... this hotel in the bush on one of the great rivers of the world has been like a second home to me. I have known it since boyhood and seen it grow into one of the most remarkable establishments in Africa. Before many a long expedition I have spent the night there, and enjoyed celebrating the successful end of many another with a hot bath, dinner jacket, and civilised dinner."
>
> from *The Lost World of the Kalahari*

It remains the most prestigious place to stay south of the river, and the *Livingstone Room* restaurant is easily the most stylish venue in town for dinner. That said, while the rooms are comfortable, they are the town's most expensive and short on the luxury that you might expect. The Victoria Falls Hotel is either absolutely charming, or far too colonial, depending upon your taste - but not impressive value which ever view you hold.
Rates: US$188 single, US$290 double, including breakfast

Elephant Hills Hotel (276 rooms)
Elephant Hills is a large brick complex of very modern design. It has superb facilities and a view over the Zambezi in the distance a few kilometres east of the Falls - just follow the road to the Zambezi National Park. Elephant Hills has risen, phoenix-like, from the ashes of a hotel that was burned down during the struggle for independence. The facilities include three restaurants, several bars, a casino, an 18-hole golf course and several swimming pools. Each room has fans, air-con, local and CNN TV, lots of space, and a balcony. It is all very impressive, though too big and modern to be charming.
Rates: US$160 single, US$250 double, including breakfast

Makasa Sun Hotel (97 rooms) PO Box 4275
Next to the Victoria Falls Hotel, the Makasa Sun is run by the same group - Zimbabwe Sun Hotels - and has the most convenient location of any of the town's hotels. It has a very unpretentious Zimbabwean atmosphere, and good facilities including a large pool, two restaurants, and a casino. Its rooms are similar to those in the Victoria Falls Hotel, with slightly older decor at a more reasonable cost.
Rates: US$120 single, US$170 double, including breakfast

Victoria Falls Safari Lodge (141 rooms)
The Victoria Falls Safari Lodge aims for the thatch-and-wood feel of a traditional bush lodge, yet within reach of the Falls. It is too big to achieve the intimacy of such lodges, but does have a relaxed, rural atmosphere away from the bustle of town. It is very comfortable, and if you don't want to venture out then the rooms overlook a water-hole which attracts game from the nearby Zambezi National Park. Its restaurant has a good reputation, and the bar is quite a meeting place.
Rates: US$170 single, US$250 double, including breakfast

Ilala Lodge (16 rooms) Livingstone Way, PO Box 18. Tel: 4203
A good small lodge in the heart of Victoria Falls, on Livingstone Way opposite the AVIS garage and Makasa Sun. Don't be fooled by the noisy pre-rafting briefings that occur in the front bar in the early evening; behind this façade there are cool green lawns and a quiet, intimate atmosphere. This excellent small lodge is in a very convenient position and invariably needs to be booked in advance.
Rates: US$130 single, US$200 double, including breakfast

A'Zambezi Rainbow Hotel (95 rooms) Tel: 4561
About 5km out of town on Park Way, the A'Zambezi is a few hundred yards outside the gates to the Zambezi National Park. The rooms all overlook the river from within a large, semi-circular thatched building. There is the usual pool, bars and restaurant, and a convenient courtesy bus to whisk you in and out of town. Consider taking the more adventurous walk into town via the path by the river (see page 158).
Rates: about US$105 single, US$150 double, including breakfast

Rainbow Hotel (44 rooms) PO Box 150
On the corner of Park Way and Courtenay Selous Drive, the Rainbow has been built, it is claimed, in Moorish style. Hence the architect's fondness for arches. That aside, it has pleasant gardens and a large pool which boasts a bar that you can swim up to.
Rates: about US$105 single, US$150 double, including breakfast

Sprayview Hotel (45 rooms) PO Box 70
Efficiently run by a delightful couple from the north of England, the Sprayview is by far the best value hotel in Victoria Falls. Situated just out of town, on the road to Bulawayo, its atmosphere is bright and cheerful, without the pretensions (or the prices) of the others. The rooms are clean and organised like a motel - with easy access for vehicles. The restaurant is cheap and cheerful, and there is even a courtesy bus into town and the Falls - though these are only twenty or thirty minutes' walk away. Note that this hotel is invariably full: if you don't book at least six months in advance, then you will be looking for a cancellation.
Rates: US$65 single, US$85 double, including breakfast

Camping

In many ways the Zambian sites are better - at Maramba River, Kubu Cabins or Jolly Boys' - but if you must be south of the river then there are two options:

Victoria Falls Town Council Campsite
As befits the attractions of Victoria Falls, this is probably the busiest campsite in Southern Africa. This makes it great for meeting other budget travellers, but lousy if you seek any space to yourself, peace and quiet, or even sleep. Large numbers of people, often disgorged from enormous trucks, seem to arrive and depart at perplexing hours of the night. All try hard to cause the maximum possible noise and disturbance. That said, it is very central and hence convenient.
Rates: US$12 per person camping, US$30 in dormitories

Zambezi National Park Restcamp
For those with a vehicle, this is about 6km out of town, on Park Way, which leads to the Zambezi National Park. There is a caravan and camping park, on the right of the road, next to the river. Then a kilometre or so later is the site for the chalets next to the entry gate to the National Park.

The chalets have four beds in each - excellent value for small groups - and have self-catering facilities and braais. Their lawns lead down to the river, so keep a careful watch for the local wildlife. You can book these in advance either in Harare or in the National Parks office on Livingstone Way.

The campsite is slightly nearer to town, but still too far away to be convenient if you are walking. With a vehicle this is a good place to camp, being much quieter than the campsite in town.
Rates: US$40 per chalet, US$10 per person camping

Where to eat

If you're looking to splash out on an expensive meal, then the best restaurants are all in the hotels. More frugal travellers should seek a take-away in town, or cook for themselves.

Take-away

There's not a great choice of take-aways, but all are within two minutes' walk of the Wimpy - go into the shopping arcade by Shearwaters. Some never get beyond Wimpy's, but Naran's take-away is definitely worth a try, as is the excellent ice-cream bar between the supermarket and Wimpy. If you've time for a leisurely breakfast, then consider the Victoria Falls Hotel, or Makasa Sun - both do all-you-can-eat buffets for about US$12.

Restaurants

The most impressive is the Livingstone Room at the Victoria Falls Hotel, which serves classic European dishes, à la carte, in a formal jacket-and-tie atmosphere. You'll understand why Laurens van der Post donned his dinner jacket here. Outside, on the terrace, there is a large, popular all-you-can-eat buffet under the stars: a must for any visit to the Falls.

The Makasa Sun, on its roof terrace, has a good restaurant concentrating on fish and seafood. This is small, quiet, and informal - and makes a good stop before dropping into the Makasa's casino.

Further out of town, the Elephant Hills and the Safari Lodge both have good restaurants, both in keeping with their different styles. The Safari Lodge's bar is the best place for a drink at sundown, as the animals all come to the water-hole.

Getting around

Victoria Falls is quite small: walking from the Wimpy corner to the Falls entry gate takes only about ten minutes. The hotels which are further away all have courtesy bus services; check the precise details with their receptions.

If you are in a hurry then hail a taxi. These are inexpensive and convenient, despite their usual poor state of repair. Bargain before getting into the vehicle, and expect a fare around Z$5 per kilometre.

Car hire

This is expensive, working out at about US$60 per day for a short hire. It is the best way if you want to visit Hwange National Park independently, but isn't worthwhile for just getting around town. Note that Zimbabwean car hire firms will not yet let their cars into Zambia, Botswana or South Africa. (Although firms from South Africa and Botswana will sometimes let their vehicles into Zimbabwe.)

Contact AVIS (tel: 13 4532), situated in the garage opposite the Makasa Sun, or Hertz (tel: 13 4267 or 13 4268) through UTC in the shopping centre next to the Wimpy. If you are planning a trip from the UK, then Sunvil Discovery (see page 58) offers a unique 100% Collision Damage Waiver (CDW) insurance as part of their excellent fly-drive trips.

Bicycle hire

This is an excellent, practical option for getting around and is highly recommended. It will cost around US$10 per day, and bicycles can be taken across the border into Livingstone.

Several companies rent bicycles, including the AVIS garage, opposite the Makasa Sun, or *Michael's* in Park Way.

THINGS TO SEE AND DO

The Falls area has been a major crossroads for travellers for the last hundred years. From the early missionaries and traders, to the back-packers, overland trucks and package tourists of the last few decades – virtually everyone passing through the region from overseas has stopped here. Recently this has created a thriving tourism industry, mostly based south of the river. Apart from simply marvelling at one of the world's greatest waterfalls, there are now lots of ways to occupy yourself. Some are easily booked after you arrive, one or two are better pre-arranged.

The last decade has witnessed a gradual shift in the town's atmosphere. Visitors used to be from Southern Africa, with perhaps the odd intrepid backpacker and the fortunate few who could afford an upmarket safari. Now the sheer volume of visitors to the Falls has increased massively. This increase, especially noticeable in the proportion of younger visitors, has fuelled the rise of more active, adventurous pursuits like white-water rafting and (most recently) bungee-jumping.

A genteel cocktail at the Victoria Falls Hotel is no longer the high point of a visit for most people. You are more likely to return home with vivid memories of the adrenaline rush of shooting rapids in a raft, or the buzz of accelerating head-first towards the Zambezi with only a piece of elastic to save you.

The Falls

The Falls are 1,688m wide and average just over 100m in height. Around 550 million litres (750 at peak) cascades over the lip every minute, making this one of the world's greatest waterfalls.

Closer inspections shows that this immense curtain of water is interrupted by gaps, where small islands stand on the lip of the falls. These effectively split the Falls into smaller waterfalls, which are known as (from west to east) the Devil's Cataract, the Main Falls, the Horseshoe Falls, the Rainbow Falls and the Eastern Cataract.

Around the Falls is a genuinely important and interesting rainforest, with plant species (especially ferns) rarely found elsewhere in Zimbabwe or Zambia. These are sustained by the clouds of spray which blanket the immediate vicinity of the Falls. You'll also find various small antelope, monkeys and baboons here, whilst the lush canopy shelters Livingstone's Lourie amongst other birds.

The flow, and hence the spray, is greatest just after the end of the rainy season – around March or April, dependant upon the rains. It then decreases gradually until about December, when the rains in western Zambia will start to replenish the river. During most of the year a light raincoat is very useful for wandering between the viewpoints: otherwise the spray will soak you in seconds. Similarly, anything that you want to keep dry must be wrapped in several layers of plastic.

The Falls never seem the same twice, so try to visit several times, under different light conditions. At sunrise, both danger point and knife-edge point are fascinating – position yourself carefully to see your shadow in the mists, with three concentric rainbows appearing as halos. (Photographers will find polarising filters invaluable in capturing the rainbows on film – as the light from the rainbows at any time of day is polarised.)

Moonlight is another fascinating time, when the Falls take on an ethereal glow and the waters blend into one smooth mass which seems frozen over the rocks.

On the Zambian side, viewing the Falls could not be easier. Simply follow the signs and your nose along the paths from in front of the field museum and curio stalls. One track leads upstream for a while. If you visit when the river is at its lowest, towards the end of the dry season, then the channels on the Zambian side may have dried up. Whilst the Falls will be less spectacular then, you can sometimes walk from this track across the bed of the Zambezi as far as Livingstone Island, before you are stopped by a channel which is actually flowing. Looking down on the Falls from their lip does afford a totally different perspective - just don't slip!

The main path leads along the cliff opposite the Falls, then across the swaying knife-edge bridge to the farthest west of the Zambian viewpoints. A third descends right down to the water's edge at the boiling pot, which is often used as a raft launch-site. Coming back up from here is a long, hot climb.

Viewing the Falls by moonlight is not restricted, though consider carefully the safety of wandering around at night.

From the Zimbabwean side, viewing the Falls is more regulated. There is now a small ticket booth and display at the entrance gate to the Falls, which is a few hundred yards from the Zimbabwean border post. A ticket costs US$5 per person, and you can return for no extra cost during the same day.

Technically this area is within the Victoria Falls National Park - and you will find a map of the paths at the entrance. Start at the western end, by Livingstone's statue - inscribed with "Explorer, Missionary and Liberator", and overlooking the Devil's Cataract.

Visiting the viewpoints in order, next is the Cataract View. If water levels are low, and the spray not too strong, after clambering down quite a steep stairway you will be greeted by views along the canyon of the Falls. Climbing back up, wander from one viewpoint to the next, eastwards, and you will eventually reach the slippery-smooth rocks at Danger Point.

Few of these viewpoints have anything more than brushwood fences and low railings to guard the edges - so going close to the edge is not for those with vertigo. Viewing the Falls by moonlight is possible by special arrangement.

Museums

Given its history, it is no surprise that Livingstone has several good museums. The main Livingstone Museum is the most important of these, and certainly one of the best in the country.

Livingstone Museum

In a prime position on the crest of Mosi-oa-Tunya Road, in the middle of town, this museum is worth exploring for a few hours. There are exhibits covering the area's prehistory and history as well as a collection of

Livingstone's personal possessions and a fascinating exhibition on witchcraft. Don't miss it.
Rates: entry fee Kw5,000

Railway Museum

This is a specialist museum situated on Chishimba Falls Road, towards the southwest side of town. There's a good collection of old steam locomotives, appropriate for a town where a railway was built in 1905.
Rates: entry fee Kw5,000

Field Museum

Much smaller than the main museum in town, this is next to the curio stands by the border and concentrates on the origin of the Falls, and the development of man in the area.
Rates: entry fee Kw5,000

Local culture

South of the river you will find practised, if commercial, tribal dances held just before dinner, at around 6pm, behind the Victoria Falls Hotel. If you want something more sensitive to the local cultures, not to mention authentic, then look north, to Livingstone, and Shungu Mufu.

Shungu Mufu Tours PO Box 60403. Tel: (03) 324092, fax: (03) 324094
Run by Cilla and Graham Young, Shungu Mufu are the best, and the most established, operators of day-trips on the Livingstone side. They collect and drop off their participants from either the Livingstone hotels, or the border post with Zimbabwe.

Amongst their tours is an excellent full day trip encompassing the Falls, a local village, lunch and a game drive. It begins with a guided walk around the Zambian side of the Falls, followed by a fascinating visit to the Mukuni village – just east of the Falls. This typical Zambian settlement is home to about 7,000 people, and you will be taken around by a guide who lives here. This is probably the closest you will get to an insight into the life of normal Zambians – an excellent chance to see how the local people live, and to talk with them.

After Mukuni, lunch is normally a picnic at the Youngs' home, followed by a short safari around the Mosi-oa-Tunya National Park.

These tours have been run for years, and part of their beauty is that a small percentage of their cost is automatically paid to the Mukuni village. Thus the villagers are happy to see strangers strolling around, accompanied by a local guide, and you will not encounter any begging or hassle.
Rates: US$70 per person for a full day, or US$45-50 for a half day. Book direct, or through any local agent

Maramba Cultural Village

This normally deserted kraal stands beside the main road between the border and Livingstone town, about 5km from each. Each Saturday and Sunday, between about 15.00 and 17.00, cultural dances are performed for the benefit of visitors by the Maramba Cultural Dance Troupe.

More importantly, this is often used for important local meetings – as when the MP visits, for example, and holds a public meeting. Such events are more interesting than the dances, though go with a Zambian friend to ensure your safety as passions may run high.

Curio stalls

Just inside the Zambian border, next to the field museum, is an outstanding curio stand. The carvers and traders come mostly from Mukuni village, though the goods come from as far afield as Zaire and Malawi. This is an excellent place to buy wooden and stone carvings, drums, malachite bangles and the like. Similar carvings are for sale in Zimbabwe, but often at twice the price, so visitors to Zimbabwe who just cross the border to shop here are common enough for this to have become known as "the best place in Zimbabwe for curios".

There are usually about twenty or thirty separate traders, laying their wares out separately and all competing with one another. The best buys are heavy wooden carvings: hippos, rhinos and smaller statues, often made out of excellent quality, heavy wood. That said, you should consider the ethics of encouraging *any* further exploitation of hardwoods.

This is a place to bargain hard. When you start to pay, you will realise how sophisticated the traders are about their currency conversions, reminding you to double-check any exchange rates. Traders will accept most currencies and some credit cards, including American Express.

Victoria Falls Craft Village

Behind the main post office on Livingstone Way, this is Zimbabwe's more regulated answer to Zambia's curio stalls. Amongst this small complex of well-built curio shops, you'll find some excellent pieces. If you are shopping for very high quality pieces of art, then this may be the place for you. But if you're simply seeking good value curios you will find those here are invariably more expensive than the alternatives from just beyond the border.

Beside the shops is a very un-PC "native village", which can't be recommended at all.

Thrills and spills

The Falls area has become the adventure capital of Southern Africa in the last few years. There is now plenty of choice about how to get your sho of adrenaline: white-water rafting, canoeing, bungee-jumping or simply a flight over the Falls. There are also choices of operator for most of these – so if you book locally, shop around to find something that suits you before you decide. Prices won't change much by shopping around – but you will find the true range of what's available. Whatever you plan, expect to sign an indemnity form before your activity starts.

Flight of Angels

Named after Livingstone's famous comments, the "Flight of Angels" is a sightseeing trip by small aircraft over the Falls themselves. This is a good way to get a feel for the geography of the area, and is surprisingly worthwhile if you want to really appreciate the Falls. Various possibilities can be booked from most of the agents in the area, including:

Light aircraft The normal trip – typically in a six-seater plane – departing from Victoria Falls' own small runway. Options are available to extend the trip over the Zambezi National Park for game-viewing.
Rates: US$50 per person for a 15-minute trip

Seaplane Similar in view to the normal aircraft, this was brought over from the USA specially to take off and land on the Zambezi itself.
Rates: US$60 per person for a 15-minute trip.

Microlight Batoka Sky Ltd, PO Box 60305, Livingstone. Tel: 323672; fax: 324289
This is a totally different experience from a light aircraft: essentially sight-seeing from a propeller-powered armchair 500m above the ground. The microlights only take two people: one pilot, one passenger. Because the passenger sits next to the propeller, cameras cannot be carried; though you can arrange to be photographed above the Falls, from a camera on one wing, or even pictured on video.

The microlights are affected by the slightest turbulence, so when you book a flight in advance specify the early morning or late afternoon. Transport between the Livingstone base and the hotels is provided.
Rates: US$65 per person for a 15-minute trip; US$100 for 30 mins, including mini-safari upriver. No flying on Thursdays.

Helicopter Del-Air Ltd., PO Box 60012, Livingstone. Tel/fax: 321850
The most expensive way to see the Falls – but it is tremendous fun. Del-Air use a five-seat Squirrel helicopter, and are based at the new Taita Falcon Lodge, overlooking the Batoka Gorge.
Rates: US$55 per person for a 15 minute trip, taking 3-5 people. US$500 per flying hour for the whole helicopter.

Upper Zambezi canoeing

Canoeing down the upper Zambezi is a cool way to spend a few hot days. Periodically it becomes strenuous, but you will generally find it relaxing. All canoe trips must be accompanied by a qualified river guide. Once you are used to the water, the guides will encourage you to concentrate on the wildlife. The silence of canoes make them ideal for floating up to antelope drinking, elephants feeding, or crocodiles basking. Hippos provide the excitement, and are treated with respect and given lots of space. Trips on the Zambian side are run by *Makora Quest* and *Chundukwa Adventure Trails*. On the Zimbabwean side the main operator is *Shearwater*.
Rates: around US$60 for a half day, including lunch. US$70 for a full day

White-water kayaking

Similar to the canoeing, but including the rapids on the upper Zambezi, these trips are not nearly as reckless as the white-water rafting, but are more challenging than the normal Upper Zambezi canoe trips.

Bungee-jumping

There's only one company organising bungee-jumping – *African Extreme*, an offshoot of the original pioneers from New Zealand, Kiwi Extreme (Tel: Livingstone 324156, fax: 324157). You jump from the middle of the main bridge between Zambia and Zimbabwe, where the Zambezi is around 110m below you. It is the highest commercial bungee-jump in the world, and not for the nervous.

Masochists can jump, and then be lowered directly on to a white-water rafting trip rather than being brought back up on to the bridge. You can book in advance, through any of the agencies, or simply turn up at the bridge and pay there.
Rates: US$130 for one jump – no refunds if you change your mind

White-water rafting

The Zambezi below the Falls is one of the world's most difficult navigable stretches of white water. It was the venue for the 1995 World Rafting Championships, and rafting is now very big business here.

Experienced rafters grade rivers from I to VI, according to difficulty. Grade I is the easiest, and grade VI is impossible to run. The rapids below the falls are mostly graded IV and V. This isn't surprising when you realise that all the water coming slowly up the Zambezi's 1.7km width is being squeezed through a number of rocky gorges that are often just 50-60m wide. Fortunately for inexperienced rafters, the vast majority of the rapids are not "technical" to run – ie: they don't need the boat to be manoeuvred within the rapids, they just need it to be positioned properly before entering the rapid.

The operators

Two tour operators now dominate this lucrative trade, Shearwater and Sobek, though there has recently been a new arrival: Raft Quest. See page 163 for details.

All offer broadly similar experiences, at prices which are often identical. The rapids are numbered starting from the boiling pot, from one to twenty-three, so it's easy to make a rough comparison of the trips on offer. Raft Quest has a policy of only employing guides with a minimum of four years' rafting experience - which must be commended.

The trips

A typical rafting trip will start with an evening's briefing, covering safety issues and answering any questions. The following day will start with a short safety/practice session in the rafts, on a quiet section of the river, before the rapids are run. Participants are expected to cling on for dear life, and throw their weight around the raft on demand - but nothing more. A trained oarsman guides every raft. People often fall out, and the rafts sometimes capsize, but safety records are generally good. Serious injuries are uncommon, and fatalities thankfully rare.

Half-day trips will run about half of the rapids, but a full day is needed to get through all the rapids from one to twenty-three. Lunch is normally included, and the climb up and out of the gorge at the end can be steep and tiring. Given that it may take you half a dozen rapids, or more, to really start enjoying the trip, go on the full day trip if you go at all.

Sobek runs a couple of longer trips each year, which need booking several months in advance. The four-day expeditions go as far as the Batoka Gorge, while seven-day expeditions reach the mouth of the Matetsi River. These offer more than the adrenaline of white water, and are the best way of seeing the remote Batoka Gorge.

Note that when the river is highest, around February to July, the rafting is easiest. As the water gets lower from August to January, more rocks are uncovered and the rafting becomes more difficult and dangerous.

Rates: half-day trips, incl. breakfast and brunch - around US$70 per person. Full day trips - around US$ 80 per person. Both include transfers. Sobek's longer expeditions cost US$150 per person per day

Horse-riding

There are two operators offering horse-back safaris in the Falls area: in Zambia, *Chundukwa Adventure Trails*, and in Zimbabwe, *Zambezi Horse Trails*. Both can offer day trips for novices in search of game, as well as longer sojourns with overnight camps for more experienced riders.

Booze cruises

These used to be strictly at sundown, and the drinks were free. Now, sadly, they are more frequent and less generous – as drinks are normally bought from a bar on board. Nostalgia aside, floating on the upper Zambezi with a glass in one hand, and a pair of binoculars in the other, is still a pleasant way to watch the sun go down. You may even spot the odd hippo, crocodile, or elephant.

On the Zambian side these are organised by Bwaato Adventures (PO Box 60672. Tel: 324227, fax: 321490. They also have an office on the Zimbabwean side, tel: 5828; fax: 4375.) They cost around US$15-20 for a champagne breakfast cruise or an evening sunset cruise.

In Zimbabwe cruise normally leave from the jetty just before A'Zambezi River Lodge, at around 10.15, 14.15 and 17.00. Book in advance through one of the agents in town, who will also arrange for you to be picked up about half an hour before the cruise.

Safaris on the Zambian side

Mosi-oa-Tunya National Park

Study a map and you'll see that much of the Zambian area around the Falls is National Park. All of this is a protected area, but only a small section is fenced off into a game park, with a low entry fee. This small sanctuary is well worth a visit, and not just because it protects what are probably Zambia's only remaining rhino. In a few hours' driving you'll probably see most of the common antelope, including some fine giraffe, and have the chance to visit the old cemetery at Old Drift. You can drive yourself around easily, or go with one of Shungu Mufu's tours (see page 153).

Safaris on the Zimbabwean side

Victoria Falls National Park

Like the northern side of the river, a good section of Zimbabwe's land around the falls is protected – though only the rainforest area, criss-crossed by footpaths to viewing points, is actually fenced off. If you are feeling adventurous, then follow the river bank upstream from Livingstone's statue. (If the gate is closed beyond the statue, then retrace your steps out of the entrance to the rainforest; and turn right then right again, down Zambezi Drive, to reach the outside of that gate.)

This path runs next to Zambezi Drive for a while. After almost 2km Zambezi Drive leaves the river and turns back towards town, passing a famous baobab tree called the Big Tree. From there the path continues for about 8km upstream until it reaches the A'Zambezi River Lodge, just outside the gate to the Zambezi National Park. This is a very beautiful, wild walk but, despite its innocent air, you are as likely to meet hippo, elephant or buffalo here as in any other National Park. So take great care as you admire the view across the river.

Zambezi National Park

This park borders the Zambezi River, starting about 6km from Victoria Falls and extending about 40km upstream. You cannot walk here, so you need a vehicle, but there are several Zimbabwean operators running morning and afternoon drives through the park who will collect you from any of the main hotels.

The park is actually bisected by the main road from Victoria Falls to Kazungula/Kasane – along which even wild dogs are occasionally spotted. Better game viewing is to be had from the roads designed for it: the Zambezi River Drive, or the Chamabondo Drive.

The former is easily reached by driving out of town along Park Way, past the Elephant Hills Hotel and the Victoria Falls Safari Lodge. This road follows the river's course almost to the end of the park, and there are plenty of loop roads to explore away from the river.

The Chamabondo Drive has a separate entrance on the road to Bulawayo. Take a right turn just before the road crosses the Massive River, about 7km out of town. This leads past several pans and hides until it terminates at Nook Pan, from where you must retrace your steps as there are no loop roads.

The park has good populations of elephant, buffalo and antelope – especially notable are the graceful sable which thrive here. The river-front is beautiful, lined with classic stands of tall *acacia albida* trees.

Excursions from the Falls area

If you are seeking an excursion for four or five days from the Falls area, then there are a number of superb game parks within easy reach:

Kafue National Park, Zambia

The southern side of Kafue is actually quite close to the Falls, though the area is very undeveloped and you will need either a few 4WDs in convoy or the help of a local operator. Game viewing in this part of the park is mostly on foot, from either fixed or mobile camps. You are unlikely to meet anyone else in this remote area, so if you are feeling adventurous see *Chapter Sixteen* for more details. The obvious choice of operator is *Chundukwa Adventure Trails* (see page 162), who have several small walking camps in this area.

Chobe National Park, Botswana

This is sometimes suggested as a day-trip from the Falls, but is too far to be worthwhile. However, the Chobe river-front around Serondella has higher densities of wildlife than any of the other parks mentioned here –

and so is well worth a trip of a few days. Note that high park fees, and excellent lodges, mean that Chobe is never a cheap option.

If you have a 4WD then you can drive yourself around and camp at the basic, unfenced site at Serondella. Take your food with you, and watch for the baboons. Otherwise UTC does regular (if expensive) daily transfers from Victoria Falls to Kasane. You can arrange to stay at either the excellent Chobe Game Lodge (tel: Kasane 650340), or the smaller Chobe Chilwero Lodge (tel: Botswana 250324).

Hwange National Park, Zimbabwe

Zimbabwe's flagship national park has four established public camps which provide excellent value, basic accommodation and camping. It also has several more basic camping spots at picnic sites, with a host of more expensive, all-inclusive private lodges clustered around its borders. The cheapest serious safari option from Victoria Falls is probably to rent a vehicle from Victoria Falls, staying first at Main Camp, then Sinamatella. Note that most Zimbabwean car hire companies won't allow their vehicles near either Nantwich or Robins Camp due to poor road conditions.

If your budget is not so limited, then consider staying at one of the plusher private lodges, and arrive by plane or private transfer.

Chizarira National Park, Zimbabwe

One of Zimbabwe's wildest and least visited parks, Chizarira requires patience, lots of driving skill, and preferably a 4WD – and that's just to get there. Most visitors fly in, or are taken by an operator, and because the land is rugged and remote much of the game viewing is on foot. You won't see the quantities of game this way that you see elsewhere, but the wilderness experience is excellent.

One lodge operates – the Chizarira Wilderness Lodge, which is linked with Zambezi Wilderness Safaris in Victoria Falls (see page 163). Another possibility is to use *Backpackers' Africa,* a reliable operator concentrating on walking safaris, including options into Chizarira.

Kasuma Pan National Park, Zimbabwe

This small, little-visited National Park borders on to Botswana between the Zambezi and Hwange National Parks. Like Chizarira, it is used for walking safaris more than for driving, though the environment is very different. It consists of a huge depression – a grass-covered pan surrounded by forests which are dominated by the familiar *mopane* and teak trees.

Only two parties are allowed into the park at any time, each requiring a licensed guide – which effectively limits access to organised operators, usually *Backpackers' Africa* and *Kalambeza Safaris*.

USEFUL INFORMATION

Telephones

By a convenient arrangement, callers in Livingstone or Victoria Falls can telephone the other side using a local, rather than an international, telephone code. From Zambia just dial "6" before a Victoria Falls number; from Victoria Falls dial "8" before a Livingstone number. This makes huge savings on international call charges, but the few lines available are often busy. Just keep redailing – you will get through.

Tourist information

Both Livingstone and Victoria Falls have tourist information offices. You can expect pleasant, friendly staff with little useful information.

Livingstone's is situated next to the main Museum, where Mosi-oa-Tunya Road bends into the centre of town. The Victoria Falls office is a small bungalow opposite the Wimpy on Park Way.

Zambian operators with a base in Livingstone

Across Africa Overland PO Box 60420. Tel: 320823; fax: 320277 or 320732

Across Africa Overland is run by Di and John Tolmay and is based at *Thorn Tree Lodge* (see page 142). This has two very large trucks, and several 4WDs, which are deployed as one unit for large, self-contained expeditions around Southern Africa. These cost around US$1,800 per day for a group of up to eight people, and are usually chartered for long safaris or hunting trips.

Chundukwa Adventure Trails PO Box 61160. Tel: 324006; fax: 324006; tlx: ZA 24043

Owned and run by Doug Evans, this has its base at *Chundukwa River Camp* (see page 141). Doug is an experienced old Africa hand, with professional hunting and guiding licences in both Zambia and Zimbabwe: just the kind of chap to have on your side when the going gets tough. He organises and guides safaris from horseback, canoe and foot. When canoeing he concentrates on two- or three-day trips (covering about 90km) on the upper Zambezi, usually ending at Chundukwa. Horse-riding is usually just one or two days in the region around Chundukwa, though longer trails are possible for experienced riders.

If you're looking for a trip into the southern part of Kafue, then Chundukwa runs a couple of tented camps on the Nanzhila Plains in the southern part of Kafue National Park (see page 279). Chundukwa's walking and vehicle safaris are probably the best way of seeing this remote area. Itineraries are flexible, but eight days in total is popular: three canoeing, one riding, three walking in Kafue, and one relaxing.

Rates: Expect to pay around US$150 per person per night for a long trip, more for a shorter trip

Sobek (Livingstone) PO Box 60305. Tel: 320058 or 323672, fax: 324289

Sobek is a Zambian-based operator, sister-company of US-based rafting specialists Mountain Travel/Sobek. They are involved with white-water trips all over the globe, from Ethiopia to Papua New Guinea. In Zambia Sobek has bases in Livingstone, running their white-water rafting trips, and also in Lusaka, organising separate Lower Zambezi canoeing trips.

Makora Quest PO Box 60420. Tel: 320697, fax: 320732
Run by Colin Lowe, Makora Quest is based just downstream from Kubu Cabins. From here they run high quality, expert-guided canoe trips on the Upper Zambezi – half-day, full-day and two-day trips.

Raft Quest PO Box 60420. Tel: 320697, fax: 320732
Founded in 1996 by Zambezi veteran Colin Lowe (see Makora Quest, above), this company has come into existence as a reaction against the style of trips run by both Shearwater and Sobek. Colin aims for smaller groups and an overall higher quality of operation. Rafting is big business in the area around Victoria Falls, and many feel that safety standards have been compromised in the drive to increase the number of paying customers. It remains to be seen if his small operation, even if it is of a higher standard, can compete with the marketing power of Shearwater.

Zimbabwean operators with a base in Victoria Falls

There are many operators in Victoria Falls, but a couple of those which are best, and those which are biggest, would include:

Zambezi Wilderness Safaris PO Box 288, Victoria Falls. Tel: 4527 or 3371/2/3; fax: 4224 or 2020
Part of Southern Africa's Wilderness group, Zambezi Wilderness Safaris have sister-companies in South Africa, Namibia, Botswana and Malawi. They own several excellent lodges around the subcontinent, including the *Chizarira Wilderness Lodge* in Zimbabwe, and run long expert-guided safaris encompassing several National Parks. They offer a high quality service, and usually try to take a more ethical view on tourism than some of the other operators.

Backpackers' Africa PO Box 44, Victoria Falls. Tel: 4424 or 4510; fax: 4683
This is a long-established Zimbabwe-based safari operation running organised walking safaris around Zimbabwe – with a special emphasis on Chizarira National Park. Normally a vehicle will take your luggage ahead of you, and so you are free to walk with just your camera and binoculars.

Shearwater Adventures Victoria Falls Centre, PO Box 125. Tel: 4471; fax: 4341
Shearwater is a large Zimbabwe-based safari operator which has extensive canoe safaris operations. Their head office is in Harare, and an office in Victoria Falls oversees the white-water rafting that they offer from the Zimbabwean side of the river. This office is very prominent (near the Wimpy) and has a busy general booking desk, which can arrange Shearwater rafting trips and other day trips.

UTC (United Touring Company) Zimbank Building, Livingstone Way.
Tel: 4267 or 4268
UTC is a very large safari operator whose operations cover most of east and Southern Africa. Around the Falls area they run many day trips using conspicuous zebra-striped buses, including convenient airport transfers and a daily link with Kasane in Botswana.

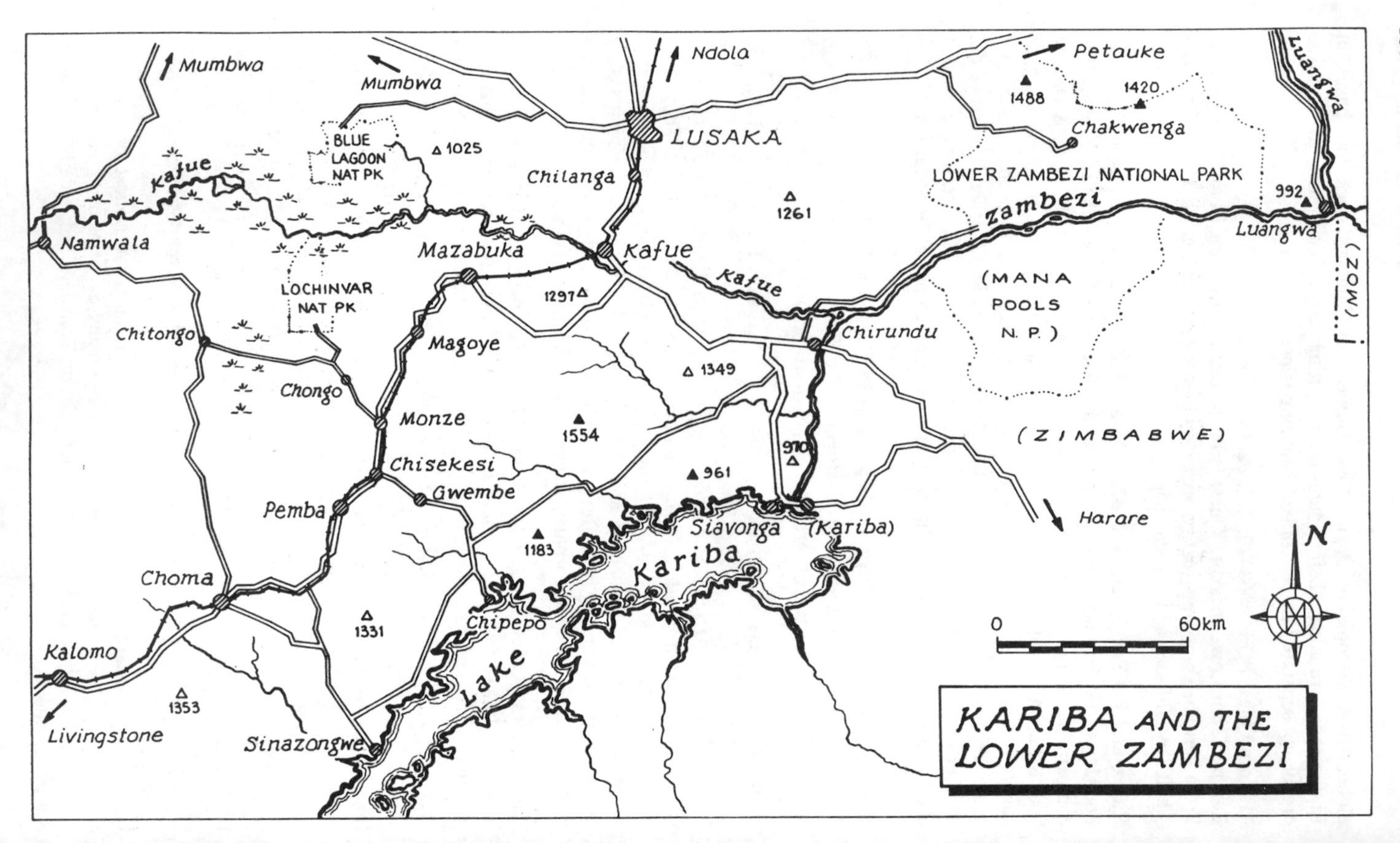
Mumbwa
Mumbwa
Ndola
Petauke
1488
1420
Chakwenga
LUSAKA
BLUE
LAGOON
NAT PK
1025
Kafue
Chilanga
LOWER ZAMBEZI NATIONAL PARK
1261
992
Luangwa
Zambezi
Luangwa
Namwala
Mazabuka
Kafue
Kafue
(MOZ)
LOCHINVAR
NAT PK
1297
(MANA
POOLS
N.P.)
Chitongo
Chirundu
Magoye
1349
Chongo
Monze
1554
(ZIMBABWE)
910
Chisekesi
961
Gwembe
Pemba
Siavonga
(Kariba)
Harare
1183
N
Kariba
Choma
1331
Chipepo
0
60km
Kalomo
Lake
1353
Livingstone
Sinazongwe
KARIBA AND THE
LOWER ZAMBEZI

Chapter Eleven

Lake Kariba and the Lower Zambezi

Zambia's border with Zimbabwe is defined by the course of the Zambezi, as it slowly meanders towards the Indian Ocean. Below the Victoria Falls, it flows east, sometimes northeast, and today's biggest features of this river are artificial: Lake Kariba, between Zambia and Zimbabwe, and Lake Cabora Bassa, in Mozambique.

Zambia's attractions on Lake Kariba are limited to Siavonga, which is a good place to relax. Few visitors will reach it, or take advantage of the chance to hire a boat for a few days on the lake, despite its proximity to Zimbabwe's busy town of Kariba.

Below the dam's wall, the Zambezi continues through the hot, low-lying Lower Zambezi Valley and some of the best game viewing in the country. On both sides of the river - Zambian and Zimbabwean - are important national parks. The game viewing is excellent, and this is the place to canoe down one of the world's great rivers, whilst game-spotting and avoiding the hippos. It should be on every visitor's list of things to do in Zambia.

LAKE KARIBA

Lake Kariba was created by the construction of a huge dam, started in November 1956 and completed in June 1959. It was the largest dam of its time - 579m wide at its crest, 128m high, 13-26m thick - and designed to provide copious hydro-electric power for both Zimbabwe and Zambia. It was a huge undertaking which turned some 280km of the river into around 5,200km² of lake. It has six 100,000kW turbo generators on the Zimbabwean side, and was designed to have another set on the Zambian side. The total construction cost was £78 million.

In human terms it immediately displaced thousands of BaTonga villagers, on both sides of the border, and took the lives of 86 workers in the process - around 18 of whom are entombed within the dam's million cubic metres of cement. It has opened up new industries relying on the lake, just as it closed off many possibilities for exploiting the existing rich game areas in that section of the Zambezi Valley.

It inevitably drowned much life, despite the efforts of Operation Noah to save and relocate some of the animals as the floodwaters rose. However, the lake is now home to rich fish and aquatic life, and several game reserves (and lodges) are thriving on its southern shores.

For the visitor, Zambia's side of the lake is less well developed than Zimbabwe's, and lacks a National Park – so there is very little big game around. However, the fishing is equally good and the resorts of Siavonga and Sinazongwe make good places to relax, or to base yourself for outings on to the Lake.

Health and safety around the lake

Bilharzia

Bilharzia is found in Lake Kariba, but only in certain areas. Unfortunately, it isn't possible to pinpoint its whereabouts exactly. That said, shallow, weedy areas that suit the host snail are likely to harbour the parasites, and you're unlikely to contract bilharzia whilst in deep water in the middle of the lake.

NYAMINYAMI STRIKES BACK

We now expect large projects with huge environmental impacts like the Kariba Dam to have equally big effects on local communities in their vicinity. Plans for dams frequently create political strife. Proponents argue the benefit to the whole country or region, and opponents cite the damage to the environment and the local communities which will be sacrificed for the project. Recent projects in Tasmania and China, to name but two, have resulted in similar arguments.

In the late 1950s, when construction on the dam was started, the world's environmental lobby was less influential than it is now. There was little effective resistance to the removal of thousands of the BaTonga people from the valley on to higher ground around the new lake. The BaTonga were amongst the least developed ethnic groups in the region, and so their physical resistance to their relocation was easily overcome. However, the BaTonga had inhabited the valley for centuries, treating the river with reverence as home to *Nyaminyami* – guardian of the river. Their elders were certain that the project would stir up Nyaminyami's anger, and he would then destroy the dam.

Work started in November 1956 and July 1957 saw a rare dry-season storm raise the river's level by a massive 30m to smash through the coffer dam and destroy months of work.

The following year, 1958, saw another momentous flood, as unusually heavy local rains combined with the flow from distant deluges in its catchment area to produce one of the greatest flows that the river has ever seen. Again, Nyaminyami's attempt to defeat the dam was only narrowly beaten.

It was officially turned on by the Queen Mother in May 1960, and has been producing power ever since, though Nyaminyami may still have the last word as there are concerns over cracks found in the dam's concrete.

See *Chapter Six* for more detailed comments on this disease. Local people who engage in water sports consider it as an occupational hazard, and are regularly treated to expel the parasites from their bodies (those who can afford the treatment, that is).

Animal dangers

The lake contains good populations of crocodiles, and also a few hippos. Both conspire to make bathing and swimming near the shore unsafe. However, it is generally considered to be safe to take quick dips in the middle of the lake – often tempting given Lake Kariba's high temperatures and humidity. The crocodiles have apparently not learned how to catch water-skiers. Yet.

Siavonga

The road to Siavonga leaves the main Lusaka-Chirundu road a few kilometres west of the Chirundu bridge over the Zambezi. From that turn-off, it is just over 65km of rolling road (excellent tarmac) to Siavonga, mostly through areas of subsistence farming. There are lots of small villages, and hence animals wandering over the road, so drive slowly. This is a marvellous area for baobab trees, and an excellent one for roadside stalls – selling a range of baskets from small decorative ones to large linen baskets.

During a visit at the end of the dry season, the problems of erosion and overgrazing seemed especially bad. Numerous gullies cut through the powdery, red soil, there was little green grazing to be seen anywhere, and even the goats were looking thin.

Approaching Siavonga, the road winds its way around the hills in steep spirals before finally dropping down into the town, on the edge of Lake Kariba. Like Kariba, its Zimbabwean neighbour over the dam, Siavonga has an artificial layout as the result of being built on the upper sections of three or four hills – the lake's recently created shorc.

Where to stay

Siavonga has a surprising amount of accommodation considering its small size and relatively few attractions. The reason is its proximity to Lusaka – just two and a half hours' drive away – encouraging conferences to come here: the stock trade for all of Siavonga's hotels. On a quiet night, you can find a good bed at a reasonable price. Because it is used to the conference trade, check the rates for dinner, bed and breakfast, and full board – these are often good value, and there are no sparkling local restaurants to compete. Campers have less choice, and will probably head to the Eagle's Rest.

Zambezi Lodge (30 rooms) PO Box 30, Siavonga. Tel: 511148; fax: 511103 (also contact at PO Box 31701, Lusaka)
This pleasant hotel perches slightly above the lake, with its rooms spread out between its main building and the slipway into the water. For the energetic, the Lodge has an excellent swimming pool and good facilities for water sports: two cabin cruisers, two speedboats, and the kit for water-skiing, windsurfing and paragliding. Inside the bar is open most of the time, and popular with locals. Try playing on the "winner stays on" pool table: an evening's fun for Kw500, if you are good with a cue. The kitchen serves good, inexpensive food until late.

The twin rooms are large, though not modern, with en suite bath/shower and toilet, and a ceiling fan. This is a good-value choice for a few days by the lake.
Rates: US$50 double, US$33 single, bed & breakfast

Lake Kariba Inn (35 rooms) PO Box 177, Siavonga. Tel: (01) 511358
Built about nine years ago, Lake Kariba Inn has recently been repainted and is now looking good. The rooms have a small entrance hall, space for two children's beds if needed, and a veranda. There's a ceiling fan, and an en suite shower (with instant water-heater) and toilet.

The main building has a large bar, buffet restaurant, and the requisite pool. A steep set of stairs leads down to the water, many metres below, where the inn's boats – *Chipembere* and *Matusadonna* – are usually moored. See page 170 for details of their operations and costs.
Rates: US$78 per double/twin, US$53 single, full board basis

Manchinchi Lodge (30 rooms) PO Box 115, Siavonga. Tel: 511599 or 511283; fax: 511218; tlx: ZA 70903
This hotel changed hands in late 1995 for US$1million, making it the most valuable of Siavonga's hotels, as well as the plushest. The gardens are certainly the best in town, with extensive manicured lawns, shrubby borders, and a main swimming pool with an adjacent shallow one for children. Non-residents can use these, and their nearby changing rooms, for Kw1,500 each, and there is a convenient public phone just beyond.

A few yards below, the hotel has a private sandy cove with thatched umbrellas and sun-loungers, if you must fry yourself. Inside, the small lounge has a well-stocked bar and a darts board. The rooms all have en suite facilities (shower only), air conditioning, CNN/M-Net colour TV, and private verandas. They are comfortable rather than plush, as their fittings are too old.
Rates: US$70 per double/twin, US$55 per single, bed & breakfast

Leisure Bay Lodge (17 rooms)
Set in a small cove with sandy beach and thatched umbrellas, the Lodge has a large patio area and adjacent bar (with TV) which is often busy with locals – and a good place to meet people. Most of the small twin rooms overlook the lake, and all have air conditioning and en suite toilet and shower. Though very clean, they still manage to appear rather dingy.
Rates: US$40 double, US$25 single bed & breakfast

Eagle's Rest Chalets (18 chalets) PO Box 1, Siavonga. Tel/fax: 511168
If Eagle's Rest is still poorly signposted, then turn left at the gate to Manchinchi Lodge, and follow the winding road for about 1km. It may be worth the trip, as

Eagle's Rest is the first place in Siavonga which tries to appeal more to tourists than to conferences.

Here 18 self-catering chalets have been built, each big enough to take four beds in one room with a ceiling fan, and an en suite shower and toilet. Outside each is a useful sheltered area for preparing food, including a fridge, sink, simple gas cooker, and basic cutlery and crockery.

There are plans afoot to get a small shop going, and a restaurant/bar for breakfast, snacks, and evening meals.

Rates: about US$15 per person bed & breakfast

Eagle's Rest Camping PO Box 1, Siavonga. Tel/fax: 511168

Immediately next to the chalets is a small camp-ground with ablutions block and points for electricity and water. Campers will be free to use the restaurant/bar and shop when they are completed.

Rates: camping US$5 per person

Lake View Guest House

This government resthouse is used by visiting officials, and not available for casual visitors.

Getting around

Siavonga is small, but is not easy to get around without your own vehicle. The roads curve incessantly, sticking to the sides of the hills on which the town is built. Each of the hotels is tucked away in a different little cove or inlet, and to get from one to another usually involves several kilometres of up and down, winding roads.

By ringing well in advance you may be able to arrange a lift here from Lusaka or Kariba, in Zimbabwe. Then you could ask around for lifts going out of town, and perhaps even hitch from the outskirts. Alternatively, you could get a bus in and walk around everywhere, which would be practical - but you'll find it much easier with your own transport.

Getting organised

Siavonga is quite a sleepy, relaxed place but it does have a bank (Zambia National Commercial Bank), a Caltex petrol station, a post office and a few shops. These, together with the civic centre (which includes a police station and a court room), form the "town centre" which is perched high on one of the hills.

The main (only) supermarket, Zefa Trading Ltd, has large stocks of an eclectically selected and very limited range of goods. Expect to find dry goods and various cold drinks, but few foodstuffs and lots of biscuits. Before you complain too loudly about anything, you should know that it is run by the area's MP. Next door, the Kool Centre Restaurant & Take-away serves cold soft drinks and the local *chibuku* alcoholic brew.

What to see and do

Most of the activities in Siavonga revolve around the lake: boating, fishing and watersports – note the comments on safety on pages 166-7.

Watersports

For windsurfing, paragliding or waterskiing, try the Zambezi Lodge and Manchinchi Bay first, as both have equipment.

Houseboats/fishing trips

There are several options for hiring boats or pontoons (essentially floating platforms):

Matusadonna is a proper houseboat, on which a 4-day, 3-night cruise will cost a total of US$1,500 (including food, drink and fishing tackle). This begins to sound good value when it is split between up to six passengers. Accommodation is in two private cabins with bunks and one double cabin. There's a kitchen, bar and shower/toilet on board, and a shaded upper deck you can sleep on to keep cool. You'll be accompanied by a small crew, including a chef.

Chipembere is a much simpler affair, little more than a pontoon about 5m x 7m in size, with an engine at the back. Fortunately there's a cool box, braai stand, and flush toilet on board. A 4-day, 3-night trip, bringing all your own food, costs US$500 split between up to ten people (though six would be more comfortable). There's virtually no privacy aboard – so make sure you charter with very good friends.

A third option is the *Hooligan* catamaran houseboat, which is booked from Lusaka. This is described as an 18m x 8m three-deck boat, with three crew and facilities broadly similar to the Matusadonna, described above. Contact Michelle in Lusaka on tel: 260989, or Daytrippers on tel: 262281, for more details.

A final avenue worth exploring would be Manchinchi Bay, which has a 17m cruiser (used sometimes for booze cruises) for rent at about US$140 per evening.

Visiting the dam

Whilst you're here, take a walk over the dam wall (despite the border controls on each side), and perhaps even up to the Observation Point on the Zimbabwean side. There's an excellent little craft shop here, well known for its Nyaminyami sticks on which the river guardian is represented as a snake with its head at the top of the stick. The local carvers have become adept at carving intricate, interlinked rings and cages containing balls out of just one piece of wood. They're not cheap, but make great souvenirs.

Note that both Zimbabwe and Zambia are acutely aware of the vulnerability of the dam to damage or terrorist attack. So don't appear "suspicious", and always ask before taking photographs - it may be just a wall to you, but it's of vital importance to them. There used to be tours available in the morning of the underground hydro-electric power station, so ask at the dam if these are still running.

Kapenta Rig Tour

Kapenta are small sardine-like fish introduced into Kariba in the 1960s from Lake Tanganyika. Fishing for them has become an important new industry around the lake, both in Zimbabwe and Zambia. When dried, Kapenta is tasty, high in protein, and very easy to transport: an ideal food in a country where poorer people often suffer from protein deficiency.

Look out over the lake at night and watch the fishing rigs use powerful spotlights to attract the fish into their deep nets. These are then brought back to shore in the early morning, sun-dried on open racks (easily smelled and seen), and packaged for sale.

Short tours lasting a couple of hours in the early evening can be arranged to one of these rigs, and you'll bring back fresh kapenta to eat. *Rates: around US$15 for a group, usually arranged by the hotel*

Crocodile Farm

There's a genuine, commercial crocodile farm near town, which welcomes visitors and charges only a few dollars entrance.

Sinazongwe

Zambia's second small town on the lakeside is roughly equidistant between Livingstone and Siavonga. It is used mainly as an outpost for kapenta fishing, and has even less to offer visitors than Siavonga.

FROM LUSAKA TO CHIRUNDU

The tar road from Lusaka to Harare, via Chirundu, is an important commercial artery and so it is kept in good repair. Leaving Lusaka, you soon pass the town of Kafue and, shortly before the busy turning to Livingstone, cross over the wide, slow Kafue river which is also heading to join the Zambezi. Then the road, gradually, consistently and occasionally spectacularly, descends. It leaves the higher, cooler escarpment for the hot floor of the Zambezi valley, before crossing the busy bridge at Chirundu into Zimbabwe.

Kafue

This small town is close to the Norwegian-built hydro-electric dam on the Kafue River. Tours of the plant are possible if arranged with ZESCO (Zambia Electricity Supply Corporation Ltd), which even has its own small lodge for accommodating visitors. Otherwise, there is little of interest here, though the town does have large concrete and textile factories. Outside town is the impressive Lechwe Lodge, and if you are stuck for somewhere to stay then the River Motel is always a possibility.

River Motel (10 rooms) PO Box 110, Kafue. Tel: (01) 311309
This small motel has basic accommodation, which is clean, though uninspiring.
Rates: around Kw 25,000 for a single or a double, including breakfast

Lechwe Lodge (four twin-bed chalets) PO Box 31522, Lusaka.
Tel: (01) 222083/4, fax: 222684, tlx: ZA 4132
On a working farm just west of Kafue Town, this small lodge has been running since 1990. To get here, turn west off the main road just north of Kafue Town, which passes the *Nitrogen Chemicals* factory immediately on the left, and later *Kafue Textiles*, before bending right. Take the next left turn, and stay on a gravel road for about 3.2km. Then take the left turn signposted to Bunelli and Lechwe Lodge, which is 6.5km from the turning.

There is game on the farm, re-introduced from Kafue and Lochinvar National Parks. However, the lack of major predators or very dangerous animals means that it is a place to just wander around. The lodge is on the edge of the Kafue River's floodplain, which can be explored on foot, horseback, with game drives, or with guided boat trip on the nearby river. The food is good, mostly home-produced, and so the lodge makes an excellent base for a few days in the vicinity of Lusaka. There is a private landing strip here and the transfer flight is so short that the lodge can be used as an overnight stop, in preference Lusaka's hotels.
Open: all year
Rates: US$120 per person, fully inclusive

Chirundu border area

A few kilometres before Chirundu, just after the turn-off to Siavonga and Kariba, keep a look out for a roadside plaque noting the *Chirundu Forest Reserve* – a small area around the road where the remnants of petrified trees can be seen strewn on the ground.

The border post at Chirundu always seems to be busy with a constant stream of trucks going through, or at least waiting to go through. There's a BP garage here, an office for the Manica Freight Company, and the Nyambandwe Hotel. This is a promising place to look for a lift if you are hitchhiking, but otherwise there is the slightly seedy, unsafe feel typical of a town where mant people come and go, but few ever stay.

About 2-300m north of the border at Chirundu is a road signposted northeast to Chiawa and Masstock Farms; this is the road to both Gwabi Lodge and the Lower Zambezi National Park.

Nyambandwe Hotel. Tel: (01) 515084/515088
This is convenient if you are unexpectedly stuck in town: the rooms are small (with frilly pink fabrics) and have tiny en suite shower/toilets. In Chirundu's heat, you will probably appreciate the electric fan on a stand, though perhaps not the noisy local disco which is held here on Friday and Saturday nights. There is often a live band – which could be fun, but if you want any sleep get a room as far from the bar as possible. It seems likely that some of the rooms are hired by the hour, as well as the night.
Rates: US$20 double, US$15 single, bed & breakfast

Gwabi Lodge (6 rooms) PO Box 30813, Lusaka. Tel: (01) 250772
This small lodge is set in impressively green lawns about 12km from Chirundu, and 3km up from the Kafue River's confluence with the Zambezi. It is used extensively by *Drifters*, for their participation safaris by overland truck, making it quite a busy place that is well prepared for campers and budget travellers. You'll find everything has its price here, from a bag of drinking-water ice to overnight use of the car park for non-residents – but these prices are generally reasonable.

The thatched chalets are comfortable: solidly built with stone floors, mains electricity, en suite showers/toilets and fans. There's a great pool here, overlooking the Kafue River some distance below, and a cool thatched bar area next to it serving sensibly priced drinks. Whilst game activities are offered here, you are nowhere near the National Park, so game densities are much lower than further down the river. So this is a good place to stop, but it's too far from the park to use as a safari lodge.
Rates: US$65 per person per night, for dinner, bed & breakfast

LOWER ZAMBEZI NATIONAL PARK

The Lower Zambezi valley, from the Kariba dam to the Mozambique border, has a formidable reputation for big game – leading UNESCO to designate part of the Zimbabwean side as a World Heritage Site. The Lower Zambezi National Park protects a section of the Zambian side, and much of the Zimbabwean side is taken up by either Mana Pools National Park or one of a number of game management and safari areas. Given that some of the game regularly crosses the river – notably the elephants and buffalo – this makes for a large wildlife area with a terrific amount of game.

However, take a look at a map of the Zambian bank and you'll realise that the land up to 55km east from the Kafue River (from Gwabi Lodge) is not in the National Park at all. Going past the Kafue, the first land that you arrive at is privately owned, then it becomes "game management area" which is leased from the chieftainess in the area. Finally, east of the Chongwe River, is the National Park.

As you might expect, the game densities increase as you travel east, with the best game in the National Park, and fewer animals on the privately owned land nearer to Chirundu. The situation is similar on the other bank of the river, in Zimbabwe, so if you want good game viewing then get into the park itself if you can.

Geography

From Chirundu to the Mozambique border, the Zambezi descends 42m, from 371m to 329m above sea-level, over a distance of over 150km. That very gentle gradient (about 1:3,500) explains why the Zambezi flows so slowly and spreads out across the wide valley, making such a gentle course for canoeing.

From the river, look either side of you into Zambia and Zimbabwe. In the distance you will spot the escarpment, if the heat haze doesn't obscure it. At around 1,200m high, it marks the confines of the Lower Zambezi Valley and the start of the higher, cooler territory beyond which is known as the "highveld" in Zimbabwe.

The valley is a rift valley, similar to the great rift valley of East Africa (though probably older), and it shares its genesis with the adjoining Luangwa valley. The original sedimentary strata covering the whole area are part of the *karoo* system, sedimentary rocks laid down from about 300 to 175 million years ago. During this time, faulting occurred and volcanic material was injected into rifts in the existing sediments.

One of these faults, the wide Zambezi valley, can still be seen. In geologically recent times, the Zambezi has meandered across the wide valley floor, eroding the mineral-rich rocks into volcanic soils and depositing silts which have helped to make the valley so rich in vegetation and hence wildlife. These meanders have also left old watercourses and ox-bow pools, which add to the area's attraction for game.

So look again from one side of the valley to the other. What you see is not a huge river valley: it is a rift in the earth's crust through which a huge river happens to be flowing.

Flora and fauna

Most of the park, made up of higher ground on the sides and top of the escarpment, is thick bush – where game viewing is difficult. This is broad-leafed *miombo* woodland, dominated by *brachystegia*, *julbernardia*, *combretum* and *terminalia* species. Fortunately, there's little permanent water here, so during the dry season the game concentrates on the flat alluvial plain by the river.

Acacia species and *mopane* dominate the vegetation on the richer soils of the valley floor, complemented by typical riverine trees like leadwoods (*combretum imberbe*), ebonies (*diospyros mespiliformis*) and figs (*ficus* species). Here the riverine landscape and vegetation are very distinctive: similar to the Luangwa Valley, but quite different from other parks in the subcontinent.

Perhaps it is the richness of the soils which allows the trees to grow so tall and strong, forming woodlands with carpets of grasses, and only limited thickets of shrubs to obscure the viewing of game. The acacia species include some superb specimens of the winterthorn, *acacia albida*, and the flat-topped umbrella thorn, *acacia tortilis,* (the latter being a great favourite with the game, as its tightly spiralled seed pods are very nutritious: 19% protein, 26% carbohydrate, 5% minerals). It all results in a beautiful, lush landscape which can support a lot of game, and is excellent for the ease of viewing which it allows.

Mammals

The Lower Zambezi has all the big game that you'd expect, with the exceptions of rhino (due to poaching), giraffe and cheetah. Buffalo and elephant are very common, and can often be seen grazing on the islands in the middle of the river, or swimming between Zimbabwe and Zambia. It is normally safe to get quite close by drifting quietly past these giants as they graze.

Giraffe are notable for their absence, but otherwise the valley is dominated by large herds of impala, and smaller numbers of kudu, eland, waterbuck, bushbuck, zebra, wildebeest and the odd duiker or grysbok.

Lion, leopard and spotted hyena are the major predators. There are plans afoot to reintroduce cheetah – obtained from the *Africat* project in Namibia – but these may not come to fruition. Even on a short visit, lion were very visible, with one marvellous pride having an excess of thirty animals. Many of the larger trees have branches that seem made-to-measure for leopards – these are sometimes seen on night drives, but rarely during the day.

In the river crocodile and hippo are always present, but look also for the entertaining Cape clawless otter and the large water monitor lizard, or *leguaan*, which both occur frequently though are seldom seen.

Birds

Around 350 species of birds have been recorded in the valley. By the river you will find many varieties of water-loving birds like kingfishers: pied, giant, woodland, malachite and brown-hooded kingfishers, to name the more common ones. Similarly, darters, cormorants, egrets and storks are common, and fish eagles are always to be found perching on high branches that overlook the river. Less common residents include ospreys, spoonbills and African skimmers.

Poaching

The original inhabitants of the valley, the Nsenga people, were moved out of the area during the colonial era. It was declared a national park in

1983. Poaching from the park was a major problem, initially because the surrounding peoples had always hunted for food in the valley, so they were not happy to stop. However in the 1980s commercial poaching for ivory and rhino horn completely wiped out the park's black rhino population, and threatened to do the same to the elephants.

The world ivory trade ban did much to stop this, and the elephant population in the park is now good. There now seems to be no difference between the populations on the two sides of the river, and the herds are not nervous of vehicles (a good sign). That said, poaching still occasionally occurs and there are game scouts stationed at Chilanga and in the park, who monitor it very closely.

Several honorary wildlife rangers are involved with safari camps in the valley, so supporting these camps helps to stop the poaching - both by supporting the livelihoods of these rangers, and keeping a presence of people in the park which makes it more difficult for poachers to operate.

Where to stay

There are three ways of getting into this area. Visitors can stay at one of the private camps as a base, and go for game-viewing drives, walks and trips on the river from there. This will involve being transferred from Lusaka by road or private plane.

Alternatively they can take part in one of the popular canoe safaris which run along both sides of the river, usually using sparse temporary "fly" camps each night. These will usually start at either Kariba or Chirundu, and you'll be driven out of the valley at the end by road.

The last option is for the adventurous and well-equipped - to drive in with their own vehicles, and all their own supplies and camping equipment. For safety's sake, in case of a breakdown, two 4WD vehicles would be a sensible minimum for such a trip.

Private camps and lodges

There are three main lodges in valley; all are good and have different styles of operating. With advance notice and a 4WD, you can drive yourself into any of these. However, most people will probably arrange for a road transfer, or a private plane transfer. Looking at the lodges from west to east:

Kayila Lodge (6 twin-bed chalets) Safari Par Excellence, Lusaka. Tel: 287748
This is the only camp run by Safari Par Excellence which is intended for a long stay of three or four days: the others are designed as overnight camps for canoeists.

Kayila is solidly built with furniture carved from heavy railway-sleepers, and has an air of permanence. Its central thatched lounge/dining area is built with open sides, and set in a small group of baobabs on a small rise next to the river. The inside of one of those great trees has been converted into a small toilet (complete with wash basin and mirror) for the bar, accessed by a small door in its trunk.

The rooms are all different and very comfortable. The Tree House is a favourite, built quite high in a sausage tree overlooking the river. There are two large single beds upstairs, covered by mosquito nets, and a private bathroom/toilet built solidly in stone at the bottom of the tree. The honeymoon suite is much larger, and has its king-size bed and large bath set in stone. It is open to the river on one side, which lends a feeling of space. Activities involve mainly driving into and around the park for game-viewing, or walking in the local area.
Open: all year.
Rates: US$240 per person full board & activities

Royal Zambezi Lodge (6 twin-bed tents) PO Box 31455, Lusaka.
Tel: 223952 or 223504, fax: 223504 or 223747, tlx: ZA 42520
Situated quite a few kilometres west of the National Park, Royal Zambezi is a beautiful lodge which has been well designed, though it feels quite formal. The rooms are very comfortable Meru-style tents; all have en suite facilities and are protected from the sun under a thatched roof. They look out on to well-watered green lawns, and the river beyond.

The "Kigelia Bar" is built around the trunk of a large sausage tree, *Kigelia africana*, and there's a small plunge pool for occasional cooling dips. Most of your activities here will be drives into the park, including night drives, but there are also opportunities to canoe and to go on short walking trips around the area or canoeing trips on the river.
Open: March to December.
Rates: US$250 per person, full board & all activities

Chiawa Camp (7 twin-bed tents) G&G Safaris, PO Box 30972, Lusaka.
Tel: 288290 or 261588, fax: 262683. E-mail: chiacamp@zamnet.zm
Chiawa is a small, friendly camp set beneath a grove of mahogany trees, about 8km (30 minutes' drive) within the National Park. Its rooms are Meru-style tents on raised wooden platforms, with en suite facilities (flush toilets and impressively hot solar water showers). Being in the park, it is a seasonal camp, used only during the dry season so mostly built of wood and reeds, giving it a pleasantly rustic air.

A full range of activities is offered here, from game walks and drives (including night drives), to motor-boat trips and canoeing along the river. Chiawa keeps a log of fishing catches, and has a good reputation for serious fishing trips – though few of its visitors just want to fish.

There are several ways of getting to the camp. Most people come by road transfer to Gwabi Lodge (2 hours), then are taken by speedboat along the river to Chiawa (1 hour 30 minutes) which is a fun way to arrive. This costs US$85 per person, one way. Alternatively you can fly in to the park's airstrip, Jeki, in 40 minutes, for US$110 per person, one way. With a 4WD, a map, and some determination you could always drive yourself.
Open: 15 April to 15 November
Rates: US$215 per person per day, full board, all activities and park fees

Chifungulu Camp (4 twin and 2 double tents) Tongabezi, P. Bag 31, Livingstone
Tel: Livingstone 323235, fax: 323224, tlx: ZA 24043
Chifungulu is a new camp set on a high bank inside the park, and it is accessible only by air. It offers the full range of day and night drives, canoeing, walking, and boat trips on the river, and promises to be of a high standard. The tents it uses are unusual being of an oval marquee design, though they have the customary en suite bathrooms. Local reed furniture is used throughout, as are linen sheets.

Visitors arrive by air. Transfers to Jeki airstrip by light aircraft cost around US$135 per person from Kariba, or US$85 from Lusaka, and Jeki is a 45-minute game drive from camp. There are plans to open a "luxury" fly camp about 20km downstream, planned as a base for longer canoeing trips.
Open: April to November
Rates: US$250 per person per day, full board, all activities and park fees, excluding transfers and alcoholic drinks

Visiting independently

The roads into the park need a 4WD vehicle (ideally two) but are not difficult driving in the dry season. Get detailed maps of the whole valley before you leave Lusaka, and pack a compass. It would be wise to get a permit before you arrive, from the National Parks office in Lusaka or Chilanga, though you may be able to get one at the scout's camp in the park itself.

To find the right track, take the turning off the main road just before Chirundu and follow the signs to Gwabi Lodge. Where the sign points left, indicating the lodge is 2km ahead, continue straight ahead to reach the pontoon which crosses the Kafue River. Then it's a simple case of sticking close to the river, and following the main track.

Masochists might like to know that there's a much more difficult approach possible via the Great East Road. You'll certainly need permission from the National Parks office in Chilanga to attempt this route, and it would be wise to take a guide for most of the way. The road starts just beyond the National Park's boundary (as indicated by a tsetse-fly barrier) and after about 22km leads to the park gate, and nearby scout's camp. You'll need to collect a guide from here if you wish to continue. The road soon heads for Chakwenga, about 60km inside the park, and then drops over the escarpment. It then becomes steep, little-used and very overgrown. This isn't an easy option at all, but the road does eventually lead down into the main game-viewing area on the valley's floor.

Canoeing on the river

Canoeing down the Zambezi is a terrific way to relax in the open air and see the river, whilst doing some gentle exercise and game-viewing at the same time.

Physically, you will feel tired at the end of a day, but canoeing downriver is not too strenuous (unless you meet a strong headwind) and no previous experience is demanded. All the operators use very stable Canadian-style fibreglass canoes about 5.7m long. These are large enough for two people plus their equipment, and very difficult to capsize.

Psychologically, it's great to view game from outside of a vehicle, and whilst moving under your own propulsion: it makes you feel in charge of your own trip, and an active participant rather than a passive passenger. That said, there is normally one guide to a party of four to eight canoes, so on occasions you will be much closer to a pod of hippos than to your trusty guide.

Which section to canoe?

Canoe safaris are run from the Kariba Dam wall right to the confluence of the Luangwa and Zambezi rivers – where Zambia and Zimbabwe end, and Mozambique begins. This whole trip is normally a 10-day/9-night canoe trip, costing around US$950 per person. However, most people are limited by either time, or money, or both, and so choose to do just a part of this.

Kariba to Chirundu is the easiest, shortest section, normally taking around 3 days/2 nights and costing around US$350. The first few hours of this, through the Kariba Gorge, are the best part, and after that there's little game around and no great attractions. Because both Kariba and Chirundu are easily reached by road, the transfers to and from these trips will be very cheap.

Going from Chirundu to the Lower Zambezi (or Mana Pools, if you're with a Zimbabwean operator) is the most popular section. Typically this also takes 4 days/3 nights, costs around US$590, and gradually the game viewing gets better and better as you go along. Obviously the more time afforded in the National Park areas, the more animals you're likely to see, so quiz your chosen operator on *precisely* where the trip finishes, and where the final camp is in relation to the National Park boundary.

The final section, through the lower Zambezi National Park and on to Luangwa River confluence, is the wildest, with the best game and the fewest other canoes. Eventually the river passes through the spectacular Mpata (sometimes called Mupata) Gorge, before reaching the border. As you would expect, the transfers into and (especially) out of this section are expensive: expect this trip to cost around US$800 for 5 days/4 nights.

These costs include transfers to and from the river from Kariba, but note that they do vary seasonally: expect prices in July, August, September and October to be about 30% higher than this.

Canoeing operators

With canoeing operators leading groups down both sides of the river, the Lower Zambezi can seem almost busy. That said, the river is wide, with many islands in the middle, so though you may spot people in the distance on the other side, you won't be within chatting distance. The southern side (Zimbabwe) has noticeably more visitors than the north (Zambia), which is quieter, and there is a greater choice of trips in Zimbabwe than Zambia.

As a limit on numbers (for the sake of maintaining some semblance of a wilderness atmosphere) the Zimbabweans do not allow more than one party of canoeists on each section of their side of the river at a time. This is an excellent policy to avoid groups meeting each other, and spoiling the isolated atmosphere.

Fortunately the Zambian side is much less busy than this, and the choice of operators here is as follows:

Safari par Excellence
Sold extensively through outlets in Zimbabwe, Saf par's trips concentrate on the section from Chirundu to the eastern end of the National Park, canoeing between established fly camps.

They have two different styles of trips, using different camps. Their "participation safaris" have very basic fly-camps and ensure that visitors get involved with the cooking and camp chores. Typically their trips operate from Kariba, driving to the pontoon and canoeing from there for about 15km to Dziva – the first night's stop. Next day they normally continue downriver to Chongwe Camp (still outside the park) and perhaps have a couple of nights there. They operate from 15 March to 15 January and cost about US$300 per person for 4 days/3 nights.

Saf par's upmarket canoe trips start in a similar way, but venture much further into the park, using Mutondo Camp outside the park, and then two others (Chifungulu and Chakwenga) within the park. These require no cooking or other help from the guests, and are more comfortable than the participation camps – but they are also more expensive. They operate from 15 March to 15 November and cost about US$850 per person for 4 days/3 nights.

Sobek (Lower Zambezi) PO Box 30263, Lusaka
Sobek organise 3-day/4-night trips from Kariba. Operate 1 April to end of November.

Tongabezi Canoeing P. Bag 31, Livingstone
Tel: Livingstone 323235, fax: 323224, tlx: 24043 ZA
Tongabezi used to run just an upmarket canoeing operation in the valley, but now with the opening of Chifungulu Camp they are moving towards a camp-based operation. Guests can still cover several different stretches of river in several days, but they will probably be staying at the one camp. Whatever the precise form of this new operation, you can be confident that it will be well run and very professional… just don't forget to dress for dinner.

Chiawa Camp G&G Safaris, PO Box 30972, Lusaka
Tel: 288290 or 261588, fax: 262683. E-mail: chiacamp@zamnet.zm
If you want a taste of canoeing on the Zambezi without committing yourself to a full four-day trip, then Chiawa Camp does half-day and one-day trips, completely within the park. At the end there's the option of a short nature-walk, before transferring back to camp. These are excellent trips and can be added to a minimum of three nights at the camp.

ZAMBIA MEANS GEMSTONES

Judi Helmholz

"Zambia means Gemstones" heralds the cover of the magazine, illustrated by a full-sized photo of a large, rough emerald. The article tells that Zambia is a major supplier of gemstones – emeralds, aquamarines, amethyst and tourmaline. Apparently, Zambia's high-quality emeralds are in great demand.

One source of Zambian gems lies in the hills and valleys near Lake Kariba, 200km from Lusaka. While en route to Lake Kariba, my husband, Arthur, encountered villagers displaying beautiful pieces of raw amethyst for sale along the road. Never one to pass up an opportunity, Arthur stopped and negotiated to purchase the best specimen. The amethyst was a bargain at the original price of US$5, and a steal at the final price of US$1.

As Arthur was leaving, an old man rushed to him clutching a little plastic bag. "Perhaps some of these," he said quietly, glancing cautiously around. Intrigued, Arthur examined the small, tightly sealed plastic bag containing some green stones. Emeralds!

"Only Kw5,000, special price for you," whispered the old man. Arthur offered Kw1,000 for the bag. The old man hesitated and then agreed, stipulating that Arthur must buy two bags for such a low price. He did.

In Kariba, Arthur proudly recounted the tale of his extraordinary gemstone purchase to a friend. "Funny thing," the man commented, "as soon as those green stones began appearing for sale, all the green traffic lights in Lusaka were smashed, their green glass stolen."

Ripping open one of the bags, Arthur examined the stones. Sure enough, you could even see ridges from a traffic light. Arthur had paid US$2, the equivalent of two days wages for the average Zambian, for smashed traffic-light glass from Lusaka.

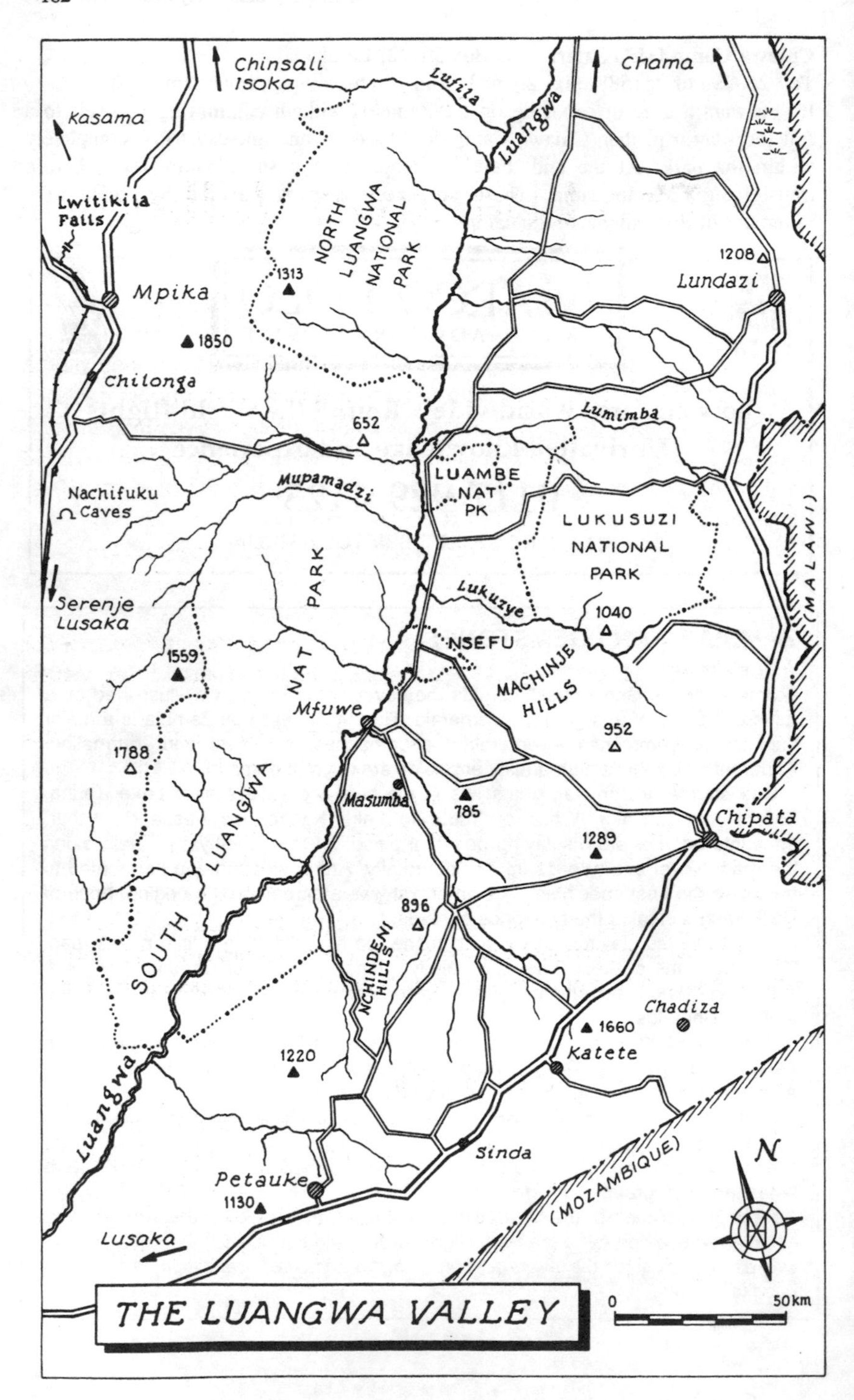

Chinsali
Isoka
Chama
Kasama
Lufila
Luangwa
Lwitikila Falls
NORTH LUANGWA NATIONAL PARK
1313
1208
Lundazi
Mpika
1850
Chilonga
Lumimba
652
Mupamadzi
LUAMBE NAT PK
Nachifuku Caves
LUKUSUZI NATIONAL PARK
Serenje
Lusaka
Lukuzye
1040
1559
NSEFU
MACHINJE HILLS
SOUTH LUANGWA NAT PARK
Mfuwe
952
(MALAWI)
1788
Masumba
785
Chipata
1289
896
NCHINDENI HILLS
Chadiza
1660
Katete
1220
Luangwa
Sinda
N
(MOZAMBIQUE)
Petauke
1130
Lusaka
THE LUANGWA VALLEY
0
50km

Chapter Twelve

The Luangwa Valley

This lush rift valley, enclosed by steep escarpment walls, is one of the continent's finest areas for wildlife. Four national parks protect parts of this area: South Luangwa, North Luangwa, Luambe and Lukusuzi. Separating these are Game Management Areas - which contain variable populations of game. All of this valley is remote, but for the enthusiast, the wildlife is well worth the effort made to get here.

For most visitors, South Luangwa National Park is by far the most practical park to visit in the valley. This is the largest of the parks, with superb wildlife and many excellent camps to choose from. Communicating with South Luangwa is not difficult, and its infrastructure is easily the best. This is the only park in the valley that can easily be visited independently.

The more intrepid might organise a safari from there into North Luangwa, which is even more remote and exclusive. Its wildlife is now flourishing, thanks to some intensive conservation efforts over the last decade, and the few safaris that run concentrate on taking small groups for walking trips. Luambe National Park is much smaller than the South or North parks, and there are no longer any camps there. The bird-watching is good, as with the other parks, though there is less game.

Finally Lukusuzi National Park is something of an unknown quantity, as there are no facilities or camps there at the moment; few people have even visited this park.

FROM LUSAKA TO CHIPATA

Chipata is about 570km from Lusaka along a road which is good tar in places, and potholed in others. It's a long drive. Hitchhiking is possible, though even leaving Lusaka early in the morning might not get you to Chipata by evening. Buses leave Lusaka for Chipata frequently, from early morning through to late afternoon, and take 10-12 hours. Expect them to cost around Kw6,000.

Chipata

This tidy, busy town is more than just a gateway to South Luangwa; it is also a border-town just 19km from Malawi. Arriving from Lusaka, there is a useful AGIP petrol station on your right, just after the welcome arch, which also has one of the best little supermarkets in town attached to it. The police station is about 1.5km after this on your left, after which there is a left turning which leads down to the main township – from which all the local buses depart. The road then bends to the right, and shortly after that the main post-office is on your left. Continuing, there is a Barclays Bank and a BP petrol station on the right as you leave for Malawi. It's not a large town, but because of its position near Malawi it has easy access to supplies from there which may be unobtainable elsewhere in Zambia.

Chipata Motel

Mfuwe Road, PO Box 510020, Chipata. Tel: 22340

Just on the left as you turn off the main Lusaka road on the way to Mfuwe, this is a very basic motel used mainly by low-budget local business-people. That said, it is convenient as the bar will sell you Cokes if you are hitchhiking, and you can always sleep here if traffic is scarce.

Mfuwe

Mfuwe doesn't seem to have a centre there is just an airport and, almost 20km away, a bridge which crosses the Luangwa River into the park, at the heart of the park's all-weather road network. This is frequently referred to as a local landmark. As you approach the bridge there's a left turn to Nkwali, Kapani, Chinzombo and the camps on the southern side of Mfuwe, then immediately on the right are Flatdogs and Lukonde budget camps. Around this area you will pass the occasional local farm stall for vegetables, and there's a school, church and clinic – but don't look for a small town as there isn't one. Yet.

SOUTH LUANGWA NATIONAL PARK

Park fees: US$15 per person per day. US$5 per vehicle per day

There are many contenders for the title of Africa's best game park. The Serengeti, Amboseli, Ngorongoro Crater, Etosha, Kruger, Moremi and Mana Pools would certainly be high on the list. But South Luangwa has a better claim than most. A few of the above parks will match its phenomenally high game densities. Many others – the lesser known of Africa's parks – will have equally few visitors. But none have the combination which allows South Luangwa to entertain its visitors with remarkable wildlife spectacles amidst isolation and a true feeling of wilderness – which is, perhaps, the test of a great game park.

Above: *Hippos in Kafue - perhaps Africa's most dangerous animals* (PM)

Below: *Elephants crossing the Luangwa, near the Nsefu sector* (PH)

Above: *Lion relaxing on the Busanga Plains* (PM)

Below: *A leopard - spotlit on a night-drive in South Luangwa* (PH)

Top: *Female impala jumping* (PM)
Centre left: *Male bushbuck* (PM)
Centre right: *Puku, one of Zambia's most common antelope* (PM)
Bottom: *Zebra in the Luangwa Valley* (PM)

Above left: *Watching elephants on foot in South Luangwa* (CM)
Above right: *Zambia's game viewing vehicles have open tops and sides* (PM)
Below left: *Dining room and viewing platform, Shumba Camp* (PM)
Below right: *Lufupa Lodge, one of Kafue's main lodges* (PM)

History

In the 19th century the area was crossed by many European explorers who came to hunt, trade, or bring the gospel; or simply out of curiosity. Around 1810 to 1820, a trading post was opened at Malambo, some 100km north of Mfuwe. This was on the main trade route from Tete to Lake Mweru which had first been established by Lacerda as early as 1798. Later, in December 1866, when Livingstone crossed the Luangwa at Perekani – a place north of Tafika and south of Chibembe – he was just one of many Europeans exploring the continent.

In 1904 a Luangwa Game Park was declared on the eastern bank of the river, but this was not maintained and came to mean little. Then on May 27 1938 three parks were defined in the valley: the North Luangwa Game Reserve; the Lukusuzi Game Reserve; and the South Luangwa Game Reserve – which corresponded roughly to the present park, though without the Chifungwe Plain or the Nsefu Sector.

In 1949 the Senior Chief Nsefu, prompted by Norman Carr, established a private game reserve on the Luangwa's eastern bank, between the Mwasauke and Kauluzi Rivers. This became the Nsefu Sector, which was absorbed into the boundaries of the present park – along with the Chifungwe Plain, north of the Mupamadzi River – when new legislation turned all game reserves into national parks on February 15 1972.

Geography

The South Luangwa National Park now covers about 9,050km² of the Luangwa valley's floor, which varies from about 500m to 800m above sea level. On its western side the park is bounded by the Muchinga Escarpment, and from there it generally slopes down to the eastern side of the park, where it is bounded by the wide meanders of the Luangwa River.

Near the banks of the Luangwa the land is fairly flat, and mostly covered with mature woodlands. These are few dense shrubberies here, but many open areas where beautiful tall trees stand perhaps 10-20m apart, shading a mixture of small bushes and grassland. Occasionally there are wide, open grassland plains. The largest are Mtanda Plain in Nsefu, Lion Plane just opposite Nsefu, Chikaya Plain north of there, Ntanta around the Mupamadzi's confluence with the Luangwa, the huge Chifungwe Plain in the far north of the park, and the little-known Lundu Plain, south of the Mupumadzi River. These are not the Serengeti-type plains with short grass: they usually have tall species of grasses and often bushes. It is their lack of trees that makes them open.

Understandably, most of the animals – and hence the camps – are concentrated around the Luangwa River. However, increasingly camps are being set up on elsewhere in the park. Norman Carr's trio of bush camps are located along the Lubi River, one of the Luangwa's smaller tributaries, and Robin Pope's Zebra Pans Bushcamp is situated on a large pan well away from any of the rivers.

Geology

The Luangwa Valley is a rift valley, similar to the great rift valley of East Africa, though probably older, and it shares its genesis with the adjoining Lower Zambezi Valley. The original sedimentary strata covering the whole area is part of the karoo system, sedimentary rocks laid down from 175 to 300 million years ago.

During this time, faulting occurred and volcanic material was injected into rifts in the existing sediments. One of these faults is the wide valley which the Luangwa now occupies. In geologically recent times, the Luangwa has meandered extensively across the wide valley floor, eroding the volcanic rocks and depositing mineral-rich silts. These meanders also left behind them old watercourses and ox-bow pools. The most recent of these can still be seen, and they are an important feature of the landscape near the present river.

Flora and fauna

Vegetation

To understand the Luangwa Valley's vegetation, the base of its productive ecosystem, consider the elements which combine to nurture its plants: the water, light, heat and nutrients. The rainfall in the valley is typically 800 to 1100mm per annum - which is moderate, but easily sufficient for strong vegetation growth. Occupying a position between 12° and 14° south of the equator, the valley lacks neither light nor heat. (Visit in October and you will probably feel that it has too much of both.)

However the key to its vegetation lies in the nutrients. The Luangwa's soils, being volcanic in origin, are rich in minerals, and the sediments laid down by the river are fine, making excellent soils. Thus with abundant water, light, heat and nutrient rich soils, the valley's vegetation has thrived: it is both lush and diverse.

Animals

Because of its rich vegetation, the Luangwa supports large numbers of a wide variety of animals. Each species has its own niche in the food chain, which avoids direct competition with any other species. Each herbivore has its favourite food plants, and even species which utilise the same food plants will feed on different parts of those plants. This efficient use of the available vegetation - refined over the last few millennia - makes the wildlife far more productive than any domestic stock would be if given the same land. It also leads to the high densities of game that the valley supports.

The game includes huge herds of elephant and buffalo, commonly hundreds of animals strong, which are particularly spectacular if encountered whilst on foot. Despite the Zambia's past poaching problems, South Luangwa's elephants are neither scarce nor excessively skittish in the presence of people, and the buffalo herds are amongst the largest anywhere in Africa.

The dominant antelope species are impala and puku. Whilst impala are dominant in much of Southern Africa, puku are rare south of the Zambezi. They stand a maximum of 0.8m high at the shoulder and weigh in at up to about 75kg. These form the small breeding groups which are exceedingly common in their favourite habitat – well-watered riverine areas – dominated by a territorial male adorned by the characteristic lyre-shaped horns. Impala do occur here but are not the most numerous antelope, as they are in the Zambezi Valley and throughout Zimbabwe.

Other antelope in the park include bushbuck, eland, kudu, impala, roan, wildebeest and zebra. The delicate oribi antelope occur occasionally in the grassland areas (especially Chifungwe Plain), while the small grysbok are often encountered on night drives. Reedbuck and Lichtenstein's hartebeest also occur, but not usually near the river, whilst sable are occasionally seen in the hills near the escarpment.

Luangwa has a number of "specialities" including the beautiful Thornicroft's giraffe. This rare subspecies differs from the much more common southern giraffe, found throughout Southern Africa in having a different – darker and more striking – body pattern. Unlike its more common neighbours, this does not extend down its legs, which are almost white.

Cookson's wildebeest are endemic to the valley and a subspecies of the blue wildebeest which are found throughout the subcontinent.

In contrast to these examples, the common waterbuck is found in the valley. Its rarer subspecies, the defassa waterbuck, is found over most of the rest of Zambia. This has a white circular patch on its rump, rather than the common waterbuck's characteristic "toilet seat" white circular ring.

A special mention must go to the hippopotami and crocodiles found in the rivers here, and especially the Luangwa: their numbers are remarkable. Look over the main bridge crossing the Luangwa at Mfuwe – sometimes there are hundreds of hippo there. Towards the end of the dry season, when the rivers are at their lowest, is the best time for this. Then these semi-aquatic mammals are forced to congregate, and you'll appreciate their sheer numbers.

Predators

The main predators in the Luangwa Valley are typical of sub-Saharan Africa: lion, leopard, spotted hyena and wild dog. During the day, the visitor is most likely to see lion, *Panthera leo*, which are the park's most common large predator. Their large prides are relatively easily spotted, and their hunting trips make gripping spectacles.

South Luangwa seems to have made a name for itself amongst the safari community as an excellent park for leopard, *panthera pardus*. This may be because leopard hunt by night, and South Luangwa is one of Africa's few National Parks which allows operators to go on spotlit game drives at night. That said, estimates made whilst filming a BBC documentary about leopards in the park suggest an average leopard density of one animal per 2.5km² – roughly twice the density recorded in South Africa's Kruger National Park. So perhaps the reputation is justified. In the author's experience, night drives in Luangwa with experienced guides do consistently yield excellent sightings of these cats – at a frequency that is difficult to match elsewhere on the continent.

In contrast to this, cheetah and wild dog occur here, but are very uncommon, and rarely sighted.

Hunting and poaching

South Luangwa has always been Zambia's "most favoured park". Over the years it has been given a disproportionately large share of the resources allotted to all of the country's National Parks. Many would argue that this has been to the detriment of the other parks, though it did enable it to fight the plague of commercial poaching, which hit the country in the 1980s, with some success. The poachers came for rhino horn – which is sold to make dagger-handles in the Middle East and Chinese medicines for the Far East – and of course ivory.

Sadly the valley's thriving black rhino population was wiped out, as it was throughout Zambia. (There are still said to be one or two animals left in the country, but this is probably just wishful thinking.) Fortunately, the elephant populations were only reduced; and in recent years, thanks in part to the CITES ban on the ivory trade, they have bounced back.

Today there is minimal poaching in the park, as demonstrated by the size of the animal populations, and certainly no lack of game.

Birds

The Luangwa has the rich tropical birdlife that you would expect in such a fertile valley. This includes species that prefer a dry habitat of plains and forests, and those which live close to water. It is difficult to mention more than a few of the Luangwa's 400 species, but note that in *Further Reading*, page 308-9, are books which cover the region's birds.

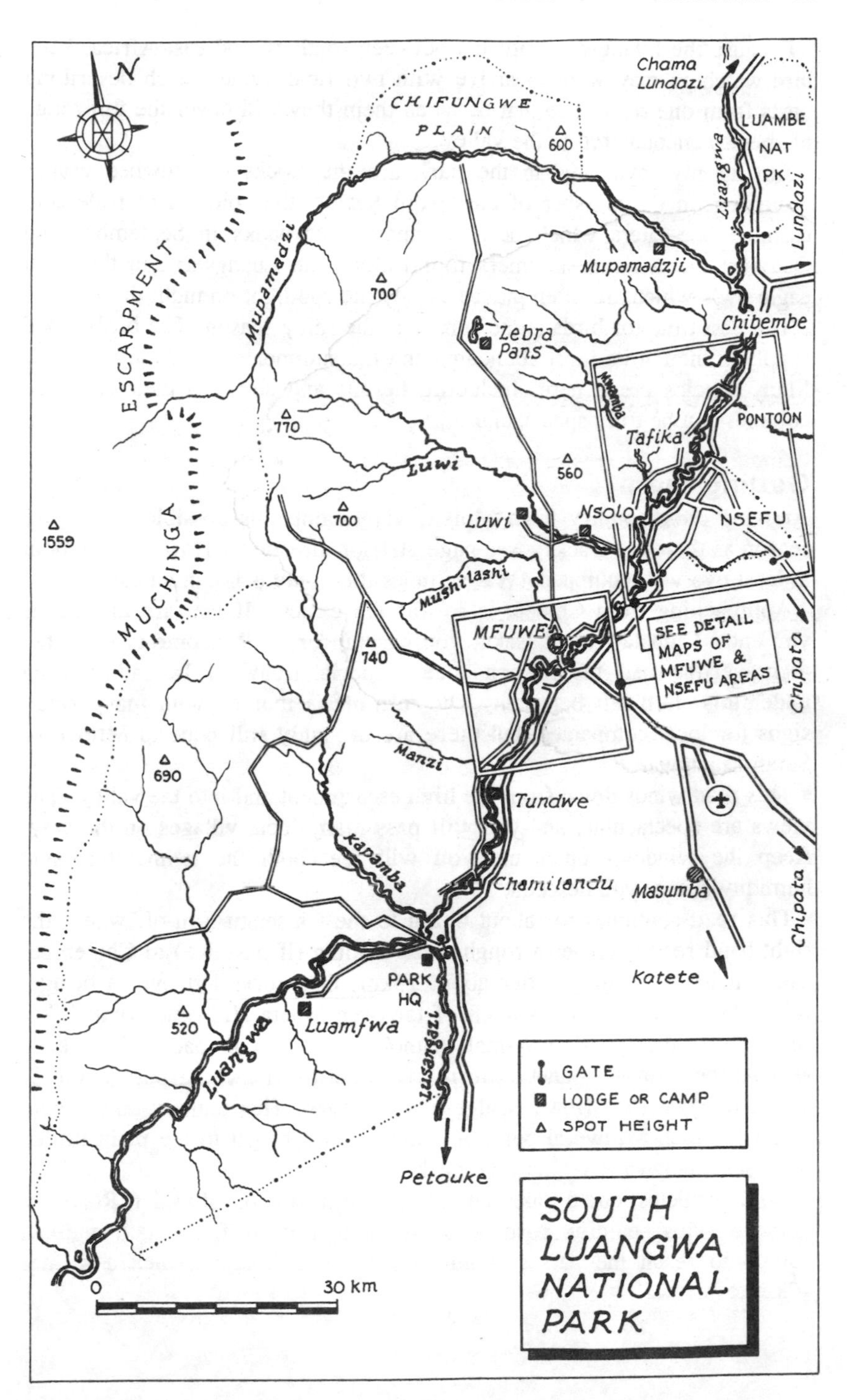
N
CHIFUNGWE
PLAIN
600
Chama
Lundazi
LUAMBE
NAT
PK
Luangwa
Lundazi
ESCARPMENT
Mupamadzi
Mupamadzji
700
Chibembe
Zebra
Pans
Nkwenba
PONTOON
Tafika
770
560
Luwi
700
Luwi
Nsolo
NSEFU
1559
MUCHINGA
Mushilashi
MFUWE
SEE DETAIL
MAPS OF
MFUWE &
NSEFU AREAS
740
Chipata
690
Manzi
Tundwe
Kapamba
Chamilandu
Masumba
Chipata
PARK
HQ
Katete
520
Luamfwa
Luangwa
Lusangazi
GATE
LODGE OR CAMP
SPOT HEIGHT
Petauke
SOUTH
LUANGWA
NATIONAL
PARK
0
30 km

Because the Luangwa is situated between southern and east Africa, keen bird-watchers may want to arrive with two field guides, each describing birds from one region, so that between them they will cover the full range of species encountered in the valley.

Among my favourites in the park are the flocks of crowned cranes occurring on the marshes of the Nsefu Sector; the colonies of iridescent carmine bee-eaters which nest in sandy river banks in September and October; the African skimmers found along the Luangwa; and the giant eagle owls which are often picked out by the spotlight on night drives.

The best time for birds is the summer: the rainy season. The birds' food supply is then at its most abundant, and the summer migrants are around. Many species breed here, including herons and storks – their riverside colonies can be truly spectacular.

Getting there

Arriving cross-country from Mpika, via Luambe, is possible in the dry season as there are tracks – see page 207 for directions. However, without at least two well-equipped 4WD vehicles this route is not practical.

Approaching from Chipata is by far the easiest. If you are driving as you enter Chipata from Lusaka, you pass under a "Welcome to Chipata" arch over the road (the independence memorial archway). Instead of going under this, turn left before it. The turn-off is marked with many small signs for local companies, but there are probably still none to Mfuwe or South Luangwa.

This road winds down from the high escarpment and into the valley. The views are spectacular, and you will pass many local villages on the way. Keep the windows open and you will feel both the temperature and humidity rise as you descend.

This road continues for about 67km to the Chisengu turn-off where the right-hand road becomes a rough track leading (if passable) to Chibembe. The left leads to Jumbe after about 16km, then forks left over a bridge. After this there's a short stretch of tar over Mpata Hill, and some 15km further on, after passing a small catholic church, the road forks – keep left. At the tarmac T-junction turn left to get to Mfuwe Airport (about 3-4km), or right for Mfuwe Bridge and the park. This journey takes about 95km to reach Mfuwe airport, or about 115km to get to the main bridge over the Luangwa River into the park.

4WD vehicles could take an earlier turn off the Lusaka Road, at Petauke. This beautiful road is slower and more difficult, taking about 150km to reach the park's southern gate at Chilongozi, then a further 40km to Mfuwe.

Hitchhiking

With plenty of water and stamina, getting to Mfuwe from Chipata is not difficult. Start hitching early at the turn-off, or outside the Chipata Motel. (You can always sleep there if necessary.) Don't accept local lifts going just a few kilometres, there's no point – better to wait for a vehicle going at least to Mfuwe airport. Most of the camps have trucks doing supply-runs to Chipata, though the upmarket camps will rarely be enthusiastic about helping "penniless" backpackers. I took five hours to get a lift from here one October morning, so expect a long wait.

Getting around

In your own vehicle

South Luangwa's network of roads is not as extensive as you might expect. A few all-weather roads (mostly graded gravel) have been built in the park around the Mfuwe area – accessible over the main bridge into the park. Only these roads that can be relied upon during the wet season.

Elsewhere, the park has seasonally passable roads which are (optimistically) marked on some of the maps. Such tracks follow both banks of the Luangwa, north and south of Mfuwe, and a few penetrate westwards into the park. In the areas near camps, there are numerous "loop" roads, which leave these main tracks and return to them. These are just side roads for game viewing, and trying to be precise about their position is pointless – they are usually made simply by the passage of a few vehicles, and will disappear again very swiftly once the vehicles stop.

Without a vehicle

If you do not have a vehicle of your own, then you must rely on the game trips organised by the Wildlife Camp or Flatdogs. If you can get up to Chibembe, then that opens up a bigger area for you – otherwise consider really splashing out on one of the upmarket camps. After all, it is such a waste to get all the way here and then not make the most of the park.

Maps

Two different maps of the South Luangwa National Park are available in Lusaka. One showing South Luangwa and Luambe National Parks was compiled for the National Tourist Board, and is useful in giving the general scheme of the area's roads. Otherwise the information on its reverse side is fairly dated, and so not very valuable.

A second very different map concentrates on just the South Luangwa National Park. This was produced in 1989 using aid donations, and shows the landscape and vegetation in considerable scientific detail. Its reverse side details the various land systems in the area: the different combinations of land form, rock, soil and vegetation in the park. This is a

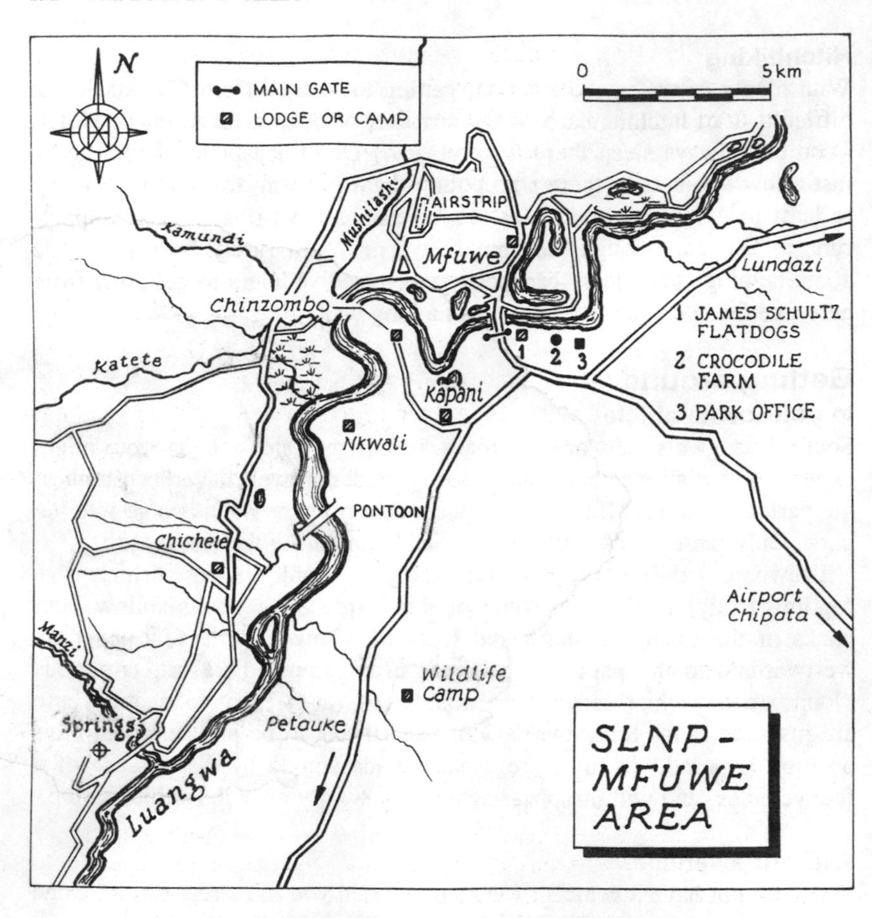
N
MAIN GATE
LODGE OR CAMP
0
5 km
AIRSTRIP
Mushilashi
Kamundi
Mfuwe
Lundazi
Chinzombo
1 JAMES SCHULTZ FLATDOGS
2 CROCODILE FARM
3 PARK OFFICE
Katete
Kapani
Nkwali
PONTOON
Chichele
Airport Chipata
Manzi
Wildlife Camp
Springs
Petauke
Luangwa
SLNP - MFUWE AREA

ELEPHANTS - E.H

fascinating map which has many of the camps marked (some are even in the correct place), but few of the roads.

If you need to navigate yourself at all, get both of these, and consider also buying more detailed Ordnance Survey-style maps available from the Surveyor General's office in Lusaka. Such detailed maps would be essential for visits to Luambe or Lukusuzi.

Upmarket camps and lodges

Most of South Luangwa's camps aim at upmarket visitors from overseas. Given the park's remote location, this is not surprising. They have great difficulties (and costs) in communicating, organising supplies, and actually getting clients into the valley. Then remember that many of them can only operate for six months of the year, and they have to pack up and re-build their camps after every rainy season. Thus, they do have some plausible reasons to be expensive.

The rates at these camps generally include your meals and activities for around US$200-260 per person per day. Some will also include your bar bill and park fees in this. Often, especially at the larger camps, there are discounts if you are a resident of Zambia, or even sometimes of another Southern African country.

The camps may cost about the same, but their atmospheres and styles differ greatly – so choose carefully:

Kapani Safari Lodge (8 twin-bed rooms) Norman Carr Safaris
PO Box 100, Mfuwe. Tel: 062 45015, fax: 062 45025, tlx: ZA 63008
Founded by the legendary Norman Carr, the present camp was built as recently as 1985, though Kapani's solid, quality accommodation feels as if it has been here for ever. The rooms are brick-built, with tiled roofs, heavy wooden furniture and 24-hour electricity which powers efficient (and quiet) ceiling fans. Each has a veranda for sitting out, and its own drinks fridge, making this probably the best appointed camp in the valley.

Activities here are mainly game drives into the park, for which the guiding is excellent. It also acts as base camp for its two smaller sister-camps in the park, and for *Traditional Walking Safaris*.
Rates: US$240 per person per night, full board, activities and park fees
Open: all year

Nsolo Camp (4 twin-bed reed chalets) Norman Carr Safaris
PO Box 100, Mfuwe. Tel: 062 45015, fax: 062 45025, tlx: ZA 63008
Nsolo is a small, reed and thatch camp built overlooking a bend in the seasonal Lubi River. The chalets are basic thatch, with reed blinds for windows, twin beds under mosquito netting, and en suite showers and flush toilets. Solar lights are used in the evenings. The central bar/dining area is open to the surrounding bush, and the camp has a very relaxed, rustic feel about it.

Nsolo is nine or ten kilometres inside the park from the main Luangwa River, directly west of the Nsefu sector in a sandy area dominated by *mopane* trees.

Though game drives during the day and evening are possible, walking is the major attraction. On my last visit here the ranger accompanying our walks was Rice Time, a sprightly Zambian hunter who strode through the bush with the speed and confidence of a youth – despite being over 70 years of age.
Rates: US$240 per person per night, full board, bar, activities and park fees
Open: 1 June to 31 October

Luwi Camp (4 twin-bed reed chalets) Norman Carr Safaris
PO Box 100, Mfuwe. Tel: 062 45015, fax: 062 45025, tlx: ZA 63008
A further 10km up the Lubi River from Nsolo, Luwi Camp is a slightly more rustic camp set under a group of tall shady trees (*vitex*, *breonadia* and *khaya nyusica*), looking out over a small plain. The chalets are reed and thatch, with mosquito-netted twin beds and small solar-powered lights. Toilets and showers are in another reed building nearby. A very short walk leads to a hide perched over a small lagoon – frequented by hippos – at a bend in the river. This is primarily a camp for walking: either for day walks based here, or for walks linking with Nsolo and Kakuli Camps.
Rates: US$240 per person per night, full board, bar activities and park fees
Open: 1 June to 31 October

Kakuli (4 twin-bed chalets) Norman Carr Safaris
PO Box 100, Mfuwe. Tel: 062 45015, fax: 062 45025, tlx: ZA 63008
This camp is situated almost opposite Tena Tena, over the Luangwa River, and opens in 1996. It is linked to Nsolo (10km away) and Luwi camps (20 km away) by the seasonal Lubi River, which makes three-day walks between these three sister-camps a very interesting option.

The buildings will probably be simple reed-walled, thatched chalets with simple solar lights and en suite facilities, and activities will probably centre on walking, with the occasional drive or night-drive. (Note that there used to be a camp on this site run by Savannah Trails.)
Rates: US$240 per person per night, full board, bar, activities and park fees
Open: 1 June to 31 October

Nkwali (6 twin-bed rooms) Robin Pope Safaris
PO Box 80, Mfuwe. Fax: 062 45051, Tel: 062 45090.
Situated a few kilometres southeast of the main bridge over the Luangwa River at Mfuwe, Nkwali overlooks the Luangwa and the park beyond from a private game management area which includes some beautiful tall acacia and ebony woodlands, a favourite haunt for giraffe and elephant.

Each of Nkwali's rooms has a thatched roof resting on white-washed bamboo walls, and contains two beds surrounded by one large mosquito net. The en suite facilities are partially open to the sky – making showers much more fun. There is no electricity, but there is a generator for recharging videos. The bar is spectacularly built around an ebony tree, and the food is excellent.

Most trips from here will be drives into the park, which is accessed by boat, a nearby pontoon, or over the main Mfuwe Bridge. Walks are led into the park, and in the surrounding game management area.
Rates: US$210 per person per night, full board, bar, activities and park fees
Open: April until early January

Tena Tena (6 twin-bed tents) Robin Pope Safaris
PO Box 80, Mfuwe. Fax: 062 45051, Tel: 062 45090.
Tena Tena overlooks the Luangwa River at the southern end of the Nsefu sector of the park, about 20km northeast of the bridge at Mfuwe. Tena Tena is a widely recognised name, and certainly one of the best camps.

Accommodation is (unusually for Luangwa) in large tents - each set on a solid base with twin beds inside, and en suite shower and toilet at the rear. These tents are very comfortable, and insect-proof. There is a separate dining area, including a well-stocked bar and small library of books, lit by a generator in the evening. (This is usually switched off as the last person goes to bed.)

Tena Tena activities concentrate on morning and afternoon walks and game drives (including night drives). The quality of guiding, like everything else here, is first-class - it ranks with the best on the continent.
Rates: US$260 per person per night, full board, bar, activities and park fees
Open: June until end October

Zebra Pans Bush Camp (6 twin-bed chalets) Robin Pope Safaris
PO Box 80, Mfuwe. Fax: 062 45051, Tel: 062 45090.
This small bush camp lies deep in the north of the park, about 30km from either the Luangwa River to the southeast or the Mupamadzi River to the north. It is situated on the edge of the Kabvumbu Pans, in a low, undulating landscape covered in *miombo* woodland. As the park's only camp in this type of environment, and the only one not near a river, this original choice of site provides the visitor with a contrasting range of plants and trees: a welcome departure from the norm.

Accommodation is in basic reed chalets, with outside facilities and long-drop toilets. The food is good, the bar is well-stocked, and the camp is geared towards walking safaris. The surrounding area is noted for different wildlife, including some of the less common antelope, like hartebeest, roan, reedbuck and eland.
Rates: US$210 per person per night, full board, bar, activities and park fees
Open: June until late October

Chinzombo (9 twin-bed chalets) Chinzombo Safaris
PO Box: 30106, Lusaka. Tel: 211644, fax: 226736, tlx: ZA 44460
Coming from Mfuwe, Chinzombo is a few kilometres past Kapani Lodge, again overlooking the river a little downstream. Its thatched rooms have twin beds, with individual mosquito nets, and en suite facilities. They are spread around quite a large camp, which is dwarfed by a beautiful stand of Natal mahogany (*Trichilia emetica*) trees.

Next to the river there's a large thatched bar, and small swimming pool, and nearby is the separate dining room. Game drives (and night drives) in the park are the main activities here.

The land on which Chinzombo stands is controlled by the "Save the Rhino Trust", to which the camp's management pay rent - thus effectively making a "donation" to the charity.
Rates: July to October US$250 per person per night, otherwise US$200, full board, bar, activities and park fees
Open: April to early January

Chamilandu (4 twin-bed chalets) Chinzombo Safaris
PO Box: 30106, Lusaka. Tel: 211644, fax: 226736, tlx: ZA 44460
About two hours drive southwest of Mfuwe, Chamilandu was set up in 1988 as a bush camp for walking safaris. It is in a very quiet southern area of the park, where there are few other roads or camps.

The chalets, made of thatch and reeds, have en suite showers and separate outside toilets. The twin beds have mosquito nets and small solar-powered reading lights.

Rates: July to October US$200 per person per night, full board, bar, activities and park fees
Open: May to late October

Kuyenda (4 twin-bed chalets) Chinzombo Safaris
PO Box: 30106, Lusaka. Tel: 211644, fax: 226736, tlx: ZA 44460
This is a small bush camp concentrating on walking safaris, and is similar to its sister, Chamilandu. The chalets, made of thatch and reeds, have en suite showers and separate outside toilets. The twin beds have mosquito nets and small solar-powered reading lights.

Rates: July to October US$200 per person per night, full board, bar, activities and park fees
Open: May to late October

Chibembe (12 twin rooms, 5 two-bed huts and camping) Wilderness Trails
PO Box 35058, Lusaka. Tel: 220112-5, fax: 220116, tlx: 40675 ZA
Chibembe is a large and busy camp in the northwest of the park. It stands on the high river bank, though each rainy season eats into the soft sand bank and the water's edge moves closer. This means that the bar, which sits in the shade of a magnificent Natal mahogany (*Trichilia emetica*), has a better view of the river every time you visit.

The camp dates from 1974 and its rooms are solid wood-and-brick, though not modern. The beds are covered by good mosquito nets, and the shower and toilet are en suite. There's a swimming pool also, which is unusually large for a Luangwa camp.

A full range of activities are possible, including day and night game drives, and walking safaris lasting from a few hours in the afternoon up to a few days. The longer walks utilise two small, basic trail camps, and luggage is carried for you between these in advance.

Chibembe is unusual for also having a campsite, with basic self-catering huts (sharing the campers' ablutions). This makes it the obvious spot in the north of the park for campers with a vehicle. It is this uncommon mix of campers and upmarket-safari visitors which makes Chibembe such a busy, lively camp. It also means that there are always groups going walking or out on game drives – and so it is easy to join in.

Rates: US$205 per person per night, full board, bar, activities and park fees
Camping: US$5 per person per night. Breakfast/lunch/supper: US$6/12/18
Open: 1 May to 31 October

Nsefu Game Lodge (6 twin-bed rondavels) Wilderness Trails
PO Box 35058, Lusaka. Tel: 220112-5, fax: 220116, tlx: ZA 40675

Nsefu is well situated on the Luangwa River, on the edge of the Nsefu Sector. It was first opened in the late 1940s – probably the park's oldest camp – and was moved to its present location in 1953.

The solid brick rondavels are entered via a few steps, and inside there are twin beds, each with a mosquito net, on the reed-matted floor. The shower and toilet have their own small section of the rondavel. These rondavels, and in fact the whole camp, have a very permanent feel.

Near the bar dining area is a small *boma* (a circular area for sitting) for a communal fire at night, and if the buffalo haven't eaten it then there is usually a reed fence around the camp. There's a water-hole to be seen from the bar – or a small hide if you want to take a closer look. Activities include day and night game drives and walking in the morning and/or afternoon.

Rates: US$215 per person per night, full board, bar, activities and park fees
Open: 1 May to 31 October

Tafika (4 twin-bed reed chalets) Remote Africa Safaris
PO Box 5, Mfuwe. Tel/fax: 062 45059.
Founded by John and Carol Coppinger, Tafika stands on the bank of the Luangwa, overlooking the national park. It is a fairly new, small camp, with four reed-and-thatch chalets. Each has two large three-quarter-size beds with twin mosquito nets, and en-suite facilities – including a flush toilet, wash basin, and excellent shower which is open to the skies. Lighting is by solar-powered storm lanterns.

The bar/dining area has a large, circular dining table, though dinner is a relaxed affair, eaten together outside – Tafika is an unpretentious camp.

Game activities include drives and walks. John used to manage *Wilderness Trails* in the valley, before starting Tafika in 1995. His years of experience in the valley (and his partner, Bryan's) ensure that the guiding is excellent. I remian impressed by his skill in locating three leopards on just one night drive. Tafika is not luxurious, but the food is excellent, the atmospherc relaxed, and the guiding truly expert.

John keeps a microlight aircraft nearby, which can take a passenger. Flights can be arranged at the camp for US$60 per 15–20 minutes, so if you stay here then don't miss seeing the park from an eagle's point of view.

Remote Africa Safaris also use Tafika as a base for the park's only river safaris (see pages 202-3), which are a very exciting option during February or March. It also operates two-centre trips including Mwaleshi Camp, in North Luangwa National Park (see page 204).

Rates: US$240 per person per night, full board, bar, activities and park fees
Open:15 May to 30 November (plus 10 February to 10 April for river safaris)

Kaingo (4 twin-bed chalets) Shenton Safaris
PO Box 810064, Kapiri Mposhi. Tel/fax: 05 362188
Just north of the Nsefu section, Kaingo is a small camp built where the old seasonal lion camp used to be. The chalets are brick with a thatched roof, and inside are twin beds with mosquito nets, and an en suite shower/toilet. The dining room is a large brick and thatch building, with an amazing bar made from a tree-trunk – which adds to the solid feeling of the camp.

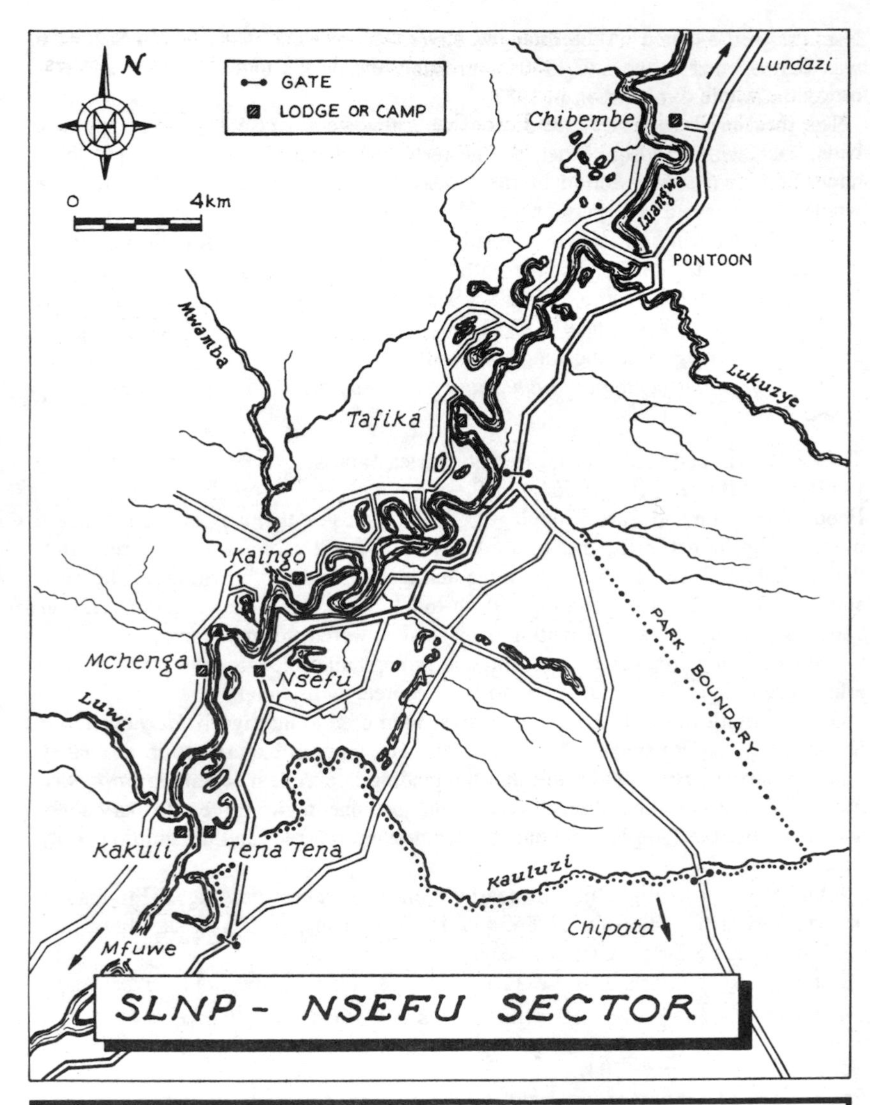
N
GATE
LODGE OR CAMP
0
4km
Chibembe
Lundazi
Luangwa
PONTOON
Mwamba
Lukuzye
Tafika
Kaingo
PARK BOUNDARY
Mchenga
Nsefu
Luwi
Kakuli
Tena Tena
Kauluzi
Chipata
Mfuwe
SLNP - NSEFU SECTOR

Kaingo is run by Derek Shenton and his family, and activities include day and night drives, walks, picnics in the bush and fishing in the river by camp. Drives lasting the whole day are also possible.

Note that the Shentons also run Forest Inn, near Mkushi (see page 224).

Rates: US$200 per person per night, full board and activities
Open: 21 May to 5 November

Mchenja (5 twin-bed rondavels) Savannah Trails
PO Box 30983, Lusaka. Tel: 215417, fax: 216848, tlx: ZA 45210
In the National Park, opposite the Nsefu section between Nsefu Camp and Tena Tena, Mchenja is not a well-known camp. The accommodation is in thatched reed rondavels with outside facilities, and the camp seems to market itself mostly to Italian clients.
Open: 1 June to 31 October

Mupamadzi River Camp (3 twin-bed tents) Wilderness Trails
PO Box 35058, Lusaka. Tel: 220112-5, fax: 220116, tlx: ZA 40675
About 12km up the Mupamadzi River from its confluence with the Luangwa, this small tented camp makes a good base for walks in a seldom-visited area of the park.

Accommodation is in large tents, each with en suite toilet and shower – though the Mupamadzi River itself is often shallow and clear enough for a cooling dip in the heat of the day.
Rates: US$200 per person per night, full board, bar and activities
Open: 1 May to 31 October

Kapamba
This basic camp does not usually accept overseas visitors. It is run by, and for, some of the more affluent members of Chipata's business community, and does not have a very good reputation among other local operators.

Mfuwe Lodge
Just inside the park, Mfuwe has a superb position overlooking the Mfuwe Lagoon – an old ox-bow channel of the river. Until recently, it was owned by the large National Hotels group and so, effectively, it was a nationalised asset. However, in recent years it had become increasingly neglected, and its pre-fabricated chalets with tin roofs had become very shabby. In late 1995 its management was put up for "tender" and new owners were found (said to be a large company with a very successful tourist lodge in Malawi). Thus it is hoped that within a few years Mfuwe will, once again, be a prime lodge in an excellent location.

Chichele Lodge
About 15km southwest of Mfuwe, Chichele was another camp owned by National Hotels which has now been put under private management with one of the larger operators in Luangwa. It is hoped that this, too, will soon be refurbished and open again.

Luamfwa Camp
Well away from any other camp, in the south of the park, Luamfwa Camp overlooks the Luangwa River. Little is known about the current state of the camp, and although work seems to have been carried out on it for several years, it still

appears to be closed. Given its remote position, it seem likely that guests will arrive direct by light aircraft, and hence it would only be viable as an upmarket, expensive camp.

Budget camps

South Luangwa National Park is not an ideal safari destination for the impecunious backpacker. Hitchhiking into the park from Chipata is surprisingly difficult, supplies are far from easy to find, park fees are relatively high (US$15 per person per day), and few of the camps have anything but all-inclusive rates.

A more practical way to arrive is in your own fully-equipped 4WD – because then you can see the park for yourself. If you do come with a vehicle, bring all your supplies, and the best maps that you can find in Lusaka, as you probably will not find any for sale here.

For both backpackers and overlanders, Luangwa's less-expensive options include:

Flatdogs Camp (camp-site) Chibuli Guides and Tours
PO Box 100, Mfuwe. Tel: 062 45074
"Flatdog" is a local nickname for a crocodile, hence when a camp-site opened around the location of an old crocodile camp, the choice of name was no surprise. To reach it, turn right about 1km before the Mfuwe bridge across the Luangwa into the park; Flatdogs is signposted about 1km away.

This is the nearest that this area gets to a camp for budget travellers. There is a pleasant site by the river, clean showers and toilets, some small thatched roofs for shelter, a few braai stands for BBQs, and even lights in the evening. (Watch out for crocs and hippo.) Camping costs US$5 per person.

As well as camping, Flatdogs has four thatch-and-brick four-bed chalets, which come with mosquito nets, coils and table lamps. Showers and toilets are private, but a few metres away. They cost around US$20 per person.

At the front there's a small take-away (and a curio shop), and within a few kilometres' walk there's a local market selling basic vegetables – otherwise bring all your food from Chipata. The camp will also arrange airport transfers for US$10 per person, and game drives for US$25.

Wildlife Camp Box 510190, Chipata. Tel: 062 21781, tel/fax: 062 21606
Operated by the Wildlife Conservation Society of Zambia, this is an excellent, inexpensive camp. Its main drawback is that its popularity leads to it being busy, and its game drives are often positively packed.

It is well signposted about 7km from the Mfuwe bridge – just turn towards Kapani and Nkwali and the wildlife camp is signposted left in about 6km. It makes a good base if you have your own vehicle – camping is US$5 per person, and the chalets are basic but clean and pleasant for US$20 per person. Zambians, Malawi residents, and members of the WCSZ qualify for discounts off these rates. The camp is set in a large grove of mopane trees, and thatched roofs, without walls, are available to pitch tents under.

The bar/restaurant is relaxed, there's a deep-freeze available for storing food, and the activities are cheap enough to be good value – at US$20 for a game drive or a walk, and US$25 for a night drive – even when they are over-subscribed.

Lukonde
Situated virtually next to Flatdogs (follow the directions to Flatdogs), the ownership of Lukonde has been in dispute for some time. Now it appears to be up and running again, although when I last saw it there were very few guests.

However there were six basic brick chalets with tin roofs and en suite facilities available. Each had three beds and cost US$35 per person. The camp overlooks the Luangwa and has green lawns, a nice bar, and several spectacular *acacia albida* trees.

Chibembe (12 twin rooms, 5 two-bed huts and camping) Wilderness Trails
PO Box 35058, Lusaka. Tel: 220112-5, fax: 220116, tlx: ZA 40675
Chibembe (see page 196) is unusual for an upmarket camp as it also has a camp-site, and some basic self-catering huts (sharing the campers' ablutions). This makes it *the* obvious spot in the north of the park for campers with a vehicle. Its uncommon mix of campers and upmarket-safari visitors makes for a busy, lively camp. It also has plenty of groups going out on game drives or walking, which are easy to join, and good facilities – like a swimming pool which campers can use.
Camping: US$5 per person per night. Breakfast/lunch/supper: US$6/12/18
Open: 1 May to 31 October

Tundwe Camp (6 chalets, each with 4 beds)
Contact Simon Phiri at Busanga Travel, PO Box 37538, Lusaka. Tel: 221681
Limited information is available on this camp, though it has a beautiful situation on the banks of the Luangwa, about 25km southwest of Mfuwe. Previously it was run by Sobek Adventures, though it has now been taken over by owners associated with the Busanga Trails camps in Kafue, and currently aims to attract similar medium-budget clients.

Each chalet is on two levels, with two smaller beds on an upper level, and two down below. All have en suite shower/toilets, mosquito nets, and electricity for a few hours in the evening. There is a separate dining/lounge area, self-service tea and coffee, and an area for quiet reading with reference books on the area's flora and fauna. Walks and drives are possible.
Rates: US$80 per person per night, full board and activities.
Open: 1 May to 31 October

Mobile safaris and river safaris

Traditional Walking Safaris (aka Wild Zambia Safaris)
c/o Kapani Safari Lodge, PO Box 100, Mfuwe
Tel: 062 45015, fax: 062 45025, tlx: ZA 63008
Based at Norman Carr's Kapani Lodge, these small safaris are run by Giles and Ruth Trotter. They operate in South Luangwa, Lake Bangweulu and rarely in North Luangwa (one of the few companies that do). The camp is packed up and moved each day by the camp staff – to meet the small party of walkers with their guide and armed game scout. These take a maximum of six people, last three days

or more, and are usually organised on a tailor-made basis, though a few scheduled tours leaving on fixed dates are available each year.
Rates: around US$300-350 per person per night

Robin Pope Safaris PO Box 80, Mfuwe. Fax: (062) 45051, Tel: (062) 45090
Between late June and late September, Robin Pope Safaris organises about twelve mobile walking safaris into the far north of the park, along the Mupamadzi River. The trip itself lasts five days and nights, and participants are requested to spend at least one night prior to the trip at Nkwali, and one at the end at Tena Tena – though a few more to acclimatise would be ideal.

The walks are about 10km per day, and while you walk the camp is moved by the back-up vehicle to meet you. The camp has comfortable walk-in tents (each with twin beds), hot and cold showers, and a staff of eight or nine. These trips are organised on fixed dates each year, and take a minimum of four people, a maximum of six.

Tailor-made and individually priced expeditions to Nyika Plateau, Kasanka and the Bangweulu Swamps, and the Liuwa Plains of the Western Province, can also be arranged with Robin Pope's team. These trips are expensive, but probably the best around. All of these options should be booked as far in advance as possible.
Rates: around US$320-370 per person per night whilst walking, plus costs at Nkwali and Tena Tena

Chinzombo Safaris PO Box: 30106, Lusaka
Tel: 211644, fax: 226736, tlx: ZA 44460
Chinzombo can arrange what it describes as "portered walks", for between four and six people per group.
Rates: around US$370 each for 6 people, or US$550 each for 4 people, per night

Wilderness Trails PO Box 35058, Lusaka
Tel: 220112-5, fax: 220116, tlx: ZA 40675
North of Chibembe, Wilderness Trails have three basic "walking camps" set a convenient distance apart: Nakalio, Kasansanya and Mbulu. Each has a small staff (a cook, a waiter, and a bedroom attendant!) to cater for a maximum of seven clients at a time. Expect basic thatch and reed chalets with outside toilets and showers.

A typical Wilderness "Walk on the Wild Side" will start with a night at Chibembe, and then walk from camp to camp over a three-day period. These whole-day walks are accompanied by the normal armed National Parks scout, professional walking guide, and inevitable tea-bearer. All your personal belongings will be transferred for you, so you need just your binoculars, camera, and sense of adventure. Though the camps are semi-permanent, and so not truly mobile, these trips are good value.
Rates: around US$200 per person per night

Remote Africa Safaris PO Box 5, Mfuwe. Tel/fax: (062) 45059
Remote Africa Safaris operate the park's only river safaris, which take place during February and March, and use Tafika as a base. Strictly for the fit and adventurous, these trips utilise five-man inflatable dinghies and canoes during the Luangwa's flood. They start with a night on arrival at Kapani Lodge, then a long journey upriver on the following day, to Tafika. This becomes a base for four days

of exploration on the river and its tributaries, before finally returning on the river to Kapani.

This adventurous trip is probably the only way to take a good look at the park during the rainy season, when the heronries and other bird colonies are at their most spectacular. Given that most of the park's roads are unusable during this time, you should not underestimate what an unusual and adventurous trip this is.
Rates: around US$240 per person per night

NORTH LUANGWA NATIONAL PARK

Park fees: US$15 per person per day
North Luangwa National Park shares the same origin as South Luangwa, as it is part of the same rift valley. Like South Luangwa, its western boundary is the steep escarpment, and its eastern boundary is the Luangwa River. It has the same geology, soil types and vegetation as South Luangwa, and so its landscapes are very similar. The native game species found in the two parks, and their ecosystems, were originally virtually identical. Perhaps the north park had some East African bird species that don't occur further south – like the chestnut-mantled sparrow weaver, or the white-winged starling. But the differences were very minor. However, the north park differs greatly in the impact that people have had on the ecosystem.

Recent history

Without the conservation efforts and funds that were devoted to South Luangwa, the country's premier game park, the North Luangwa National Park has been a "poor relation" for many years. Poachers hunting rhino and elephant met less resistance there, and local people crossed its boundaries freely in search of food. The impact on the game was inevitable.

However, in 1986 a couple of American zoologists – Mark and Delia Owens – arrived in the park in search of an African wilderness in which to base their animal research. They came from a project in Botswana's Central Kalahari Game Reserve, with an uncompromising reputation for defending the wildlife against powerful vested interests. They also had behind them an international best-selling book about their experiences – *The Cry of the Kalahari*. This had brought conservation issues in Botswana to a popular audience, and had indirectly resulted in considerable financial backing for their conservation efforts.

Their presence here was to have a profound impact upon the park, which continues to the present day. In the early 1980s, elephant poaching was estimated at about 1,000 animals per year. Their second best-seller, the highly readable *Survivor's Song* (called *The Eye of the Elephant* in the US, see *Further Reading*), relates their struggles to protect this park from the poachers, and their efforts to find alternatives for the local people, so that they would support the anti-poaching work. Read it before you arrive, but don't be alarmed: the place is much safer now.

Present situation

With the dedication of the Owens, amongst others, and the financial assistance that they can direct, poaching has been virtually eliminated. The park's game scouts are now well paid and properly housed, and so have become amongst the most zealous and effective in the country. More importantly, a series of local education and development programmes have been initiated in the local villages around the park. These aimed to raise awareness about conservation and to provide alternatives for people who relied upon poaching for food.

Camps and lodges

At present, only a couple of safari operators are allowed into the park, all of whom run small, specialist trips, concentrating on walking rather than driving. Two (detailed below) have semi-permanent camps in the park. No private visitors, however self-sufficient, are allowed. This makes the experience here even more remote and isolated than the rest of the valley: you can guarantee that you won't be disturbed by anyone else whilst walking here.

Mwaleshi Camp (4 twin-bed chalets) Remote Africa Safaris
PO Box 5, Mfuwe. Tel/fax: 062 45059.
John Coppinger set up Mwaleshi Camp for Wilderness Trails some years ago, and so retained control of it when he set up his own operation: Remote Africa Safaris. Transfers from Tafika Camp (in South Luangwa) to Mwaleshi take about six hours by road, and pass through Luambe National Park, so a minimum stay of about four nights at Mwaleshi is insisted upon. Alternatively, there are two airstrips within reach of Mwaleshi camp: Waka Waka is three hours away by road, and Luelo is about two hours' drive.

Mwaleshi is a basic bush camp, with chalets constructed from reeds and grasses, set on a scenic stretch of the Mwaleshi River, a perennial stream of clear water that feeds the Luangwa. There are two communal toilets (one flushes) and each chalet has a hand basin. The two shared showers have open views across the river. Though there are a few roads in the area, walking is the main activity. The wildlife is abundant, and there is a particularly good population of lion in the camp's vicinity.

Rates: US$240 per person per night, full board, bar, laundry, activities, park fees and transfers from South Luangwa
Open: mid-June to 31 October

Mimbulu Camp (4 twin-bed chalets) Shiwa Safaris
P Bag E395, Lusaka. Tel: 04 370064, fax: 04 370040
or arrange via Grand Travel in Lusaka – see page 131

Situated at a bend in the Mwaleshi River, this small camp is set under some beautiful Natal mahogany trees, *Trichilia emetica*, which provide welcome shade. It is surrounded by plains areas, and all the chalets have basic private facilities. Hammocks are available for relaxing during the heat of the day, and when it is cooler game viewing is done on foot - with only the occasional drive. A minimum stay of four nights here is required in Mimbulu/Buffalo camps, with one night before, and one after, spent in South Luangwa or Shiwa N'gandu.
Rates: US$150 per person per night, full board. Return transfers from Shiwa N'gandu are around US$400 per group
Open: mid-June to 31 October

Buffalo Camp (4 twin-bed chalets) Shiwa Safaris
P Bag E395, Lusaka. Tel: 04 370064, fax: 04 370040
or arrange via Grand Travel in Lusaka - see page 131
Similar to Mimbulu Camp, Buffalo is set under trees and all its chalets have basic private facilities. Game viewing is on foot, with only the occasional drive. A minimum stay of four nights here is required in Mimbulu/Buffalo camps, with one night before, and one after, spent in South Luangwa or Shiwa N'gandu.
Rates: US$150 per person per night, full board. Return transfers from Shiwa N'gandu are around US$400 per group
Open: mid-June to 31 October

Mobile trips

Aside from the two operators above, it is possible to visit the park with one of two mobile operators which have been allowed access:

Wild Africa Safaris c/o Kapani Safari Lodge, PO Box 100, Mfuwe
Tel: 062 45015, fax: 062 45025, tlx: ZA 63008
Run by Giles and Ruth Trotter, and based at Norman Carr's Kapani Lodge, these small safaris operate in South Luangwa, Lake Bangweulu and North Luangwa. They take a maximum of six people and are usually organised on a tailor-made basis - though a few scheduled tours leaving on fixed dates are available each year.
Rates: around US$300-350 per person per night

Mwaleshi Safaris Tel: 01 252452 or 251149
Run by Chris and Beatrice Weinand, this operation used to run safaris into North Luangwa, but it is unknown if they still do.

LUAMBE NATIONAL PARK

Park fees: US$15 per person per day. US$5 per vehicle per day
This small park, just 247km², is situated between North and South Luangwa National Parks and only reachable between about May and October. The first serious rains turn the area's powdery black cotton soil into a impassable quagmire - impossible even for the best 4WD. Even in the dry season the roads are bad, as the black cotton soil seems to set into bumps with the onset of the dry season.

CROWNED CRANE - E.H

Getting there

You'd be foolish to drive to Luambe with fewer than two 4WD vehicles, with spares, and plenty of food and water. Some form of reliable emergency back-up is vital in case of accident or breakdown.

From South Luangwa

The entrance to the park is about 80km north of Mfuwe. Just take the track north that passes Chibembe heading towards Chama and continue driving – there's a small scout camp and a boom across the road at the entrance to the park. This road continually deteriorates beyond South Luangwa, and little traffic ever gets this far.

From Mpika

Take the Lusaka road southwest from Mpika, and then take a left on to a track after about 40km. After 26km, this track passes the Bateleur Farm where camping is possible (arranged in advance with Mr and Mrs Stone at Northern Meat Products in Mpika, see page 226. About 46km from the main road you reach the Ntunta Escarpment, with its breathtaking view over the whole Luangwa Valley.

The road now becomes very rough as it descends down the escarpment, and after about 11 kilometres (it feels longer) you will reach the Mutinondo River. Cross this, and after 8km there's a turning to the left which would take you to the Nabwalya Village in the middle of the Munyamadzi Game Management Area. In the dry season there's a pontoon across the Luangwa just south of Nabwalya village (near Nyamphala Hunting Camp), and once across you can join the "main" road linking Chibembe and South Luangwa with Luambe.

If you continue straight on and don't turn left to Nabwalya, then after about 15km you will reach the Chifungwe Game Scouts' Camp on the Mupamadzi River – the boundary to South Luangwa National Park. Crossing the Mupamadzi and heading due south will take you right across the heart of the park, skirting around the western side of Zebra Pans. About 55km after the Mupamadzi you will reach the Lubi River (usually just deep sand) and then some 10km after that you will join one of the all-weather roads in the Mfuwe area.

Flora and fauna

Luambe is mostly *mopane* woodland, though with areas of *miombo* and grassland. It is a small park in the middle of a large Game Management Area – where hunting is allowed. Thus, although the ecosystem is virtually identical to the North and South Luangwa parks, the game densities are less than in these other parks. There is game left, but a trip here is worthwhile for the bird-watching, which is excellent, and the sense of isolation.

Where to stay

There used to be a camp called Chipuku Camp here, run by *Chibote Safaris (26C Leopard's Hill Road, PO Box 32946, Lusaka. Tel: 01 261661, fax: 01 261626)*. This was the only camp in the park, but recent reports indicate that it has closed. There is a new development planned just north of the park, but currently no camps near the park.

LUKUSUZI NATIONAL PARK

This remote park is on the eastern side of the Luangwa Valley, slightly higher in altitude than the other parks in the valley. There are no facilities here at all – just a game scouts' camp at the gate, and an exceedingly poor track leading through the park. Equally, it is uncertain how much wildlife has survived the poaching here, though it is thought that the dominant predator here is the spotted hyena, rather than the lion. The vegetation is mostly miombo woodland, dotted with grassland. Visiting the park requires an expedition.

Getting there

There is a track which turns east from the "main" Chibembe–Luambe track, and then continues through Lukusuzi National Park until it reaches the Great East Road. This will almost certainly be in very poor repair, and may be impassable. The easiest approach to the park would be to take the Great East Road to Chipata, then turn north towards Lundazi. About 110km beyond Chipata there is a track on the left to Lukusuzi. There is a game scouts' camp at the park's entrance, so stop and ask them for advice about the park before you go any further.

LOCAL SAFARI OPERATORS

Chinzombo Safaris

PO Box: 30106, Lusaka. Tel: 211644, fax: 226736, tlx: ZA 44460

Run by the tall, brusque Phil Berry, who is renowned for his knowledge of leopards, Chinzombo Safaris operates Chinzombo Camp, as well as two smaller bush camps, Kuyenda and Chamilandu, which are designed mainly for small parties going on walking safaris.

Norman Carr Safaris

PO Box 100, Mfuwe. Tel: 062 45015, fax: 062 45025, tlx: ZA 63008

The safaris are now managed by a capable team led by Nick Aslin. Operations encompass Kapani Safari Lodge, three bush camps (Nsolo, Luwi and Kakuli) and include the occasional Traditional Walking Safari. All are excellent products, and have justly given Norman Carr Safaris one of the best reputations of any company in the valley.

Norman Carr himself lives at Kapani, having played a pivotal role in the history of the valley by pioneering commercial walking safaris, upon which South Luangwa has founded its reputation. He remains an important and highly outspoken figure, though now he devotes most of his time to development projects helping the surrounding local communities to benefit from the park. He is especially involved with projects involving local schools: encouraging the next generation of Zambians to value their wildlife heritage. The private operators in South Luangwa have not, with one or two notable exceptions, been over-zealous in instigating similar forward-thinking development projects – so once again Norman Carr is ahead of his time.

Remote Africa Safaris
PO Box 5, Mfuwe. Tel/fax: 062 45059. Email: remote@fido.zamnet.zm
Founded by John and Carol Coppinger, Remote Africa Safaris is a small but high-quality operator with some excellent, truly innovative ideas. John used to run Wilderness Trails in the valley, so he is a very experienced guide who knows the valley well. Remote Africa's main camp is Tafika, just north of South Luangwa's Nsefu sector. They also run Mwaleshi in North Luangwa (one of this park's only two camps), South Luangwa's first (and only) river safaris (during February and March) and the park's only microlight aircraft, which is based near Tafika and available to give guests a unique view of the park.

Robin Pope Safaris PO Box 80, Mfuwe. Fax: 062 45051, Tel: 062 45090.
Email: popesaf@zamnet.zm
Robin Pope was raised in Zambia, trained by Norman Carr, and is one of the best wildlife guides in the valley. His English wife, Jo, is also trained as a walking guide but it is her efficiency with the marketing and business side of the camps which makes her legendary. Together with a good team they run Tena Tena, Nkwali, Zebra Pans camps, and a range of mobile walking safaris in South Luangwa and throughout Zambia.

Wilderness Trails
PO Box 35058, Lusaka. Tel: 220112-5, fax: 220116, tlx: ZA 40675
Wilderness Trails run The Adventure Centre in Lusaka (see page 130), which acts as a general bookings and operations centre, as well as Chibembe Safari Lodge, Nsefu Game Lodge, Mupamadzi River Camp and several small trails camps in the north of South Luangwa National Park.

Note that this operation is not connected with the Wilderness Safaris group operating in Namibia, Botswana, South Africa, Zimbabwe and Malawi.

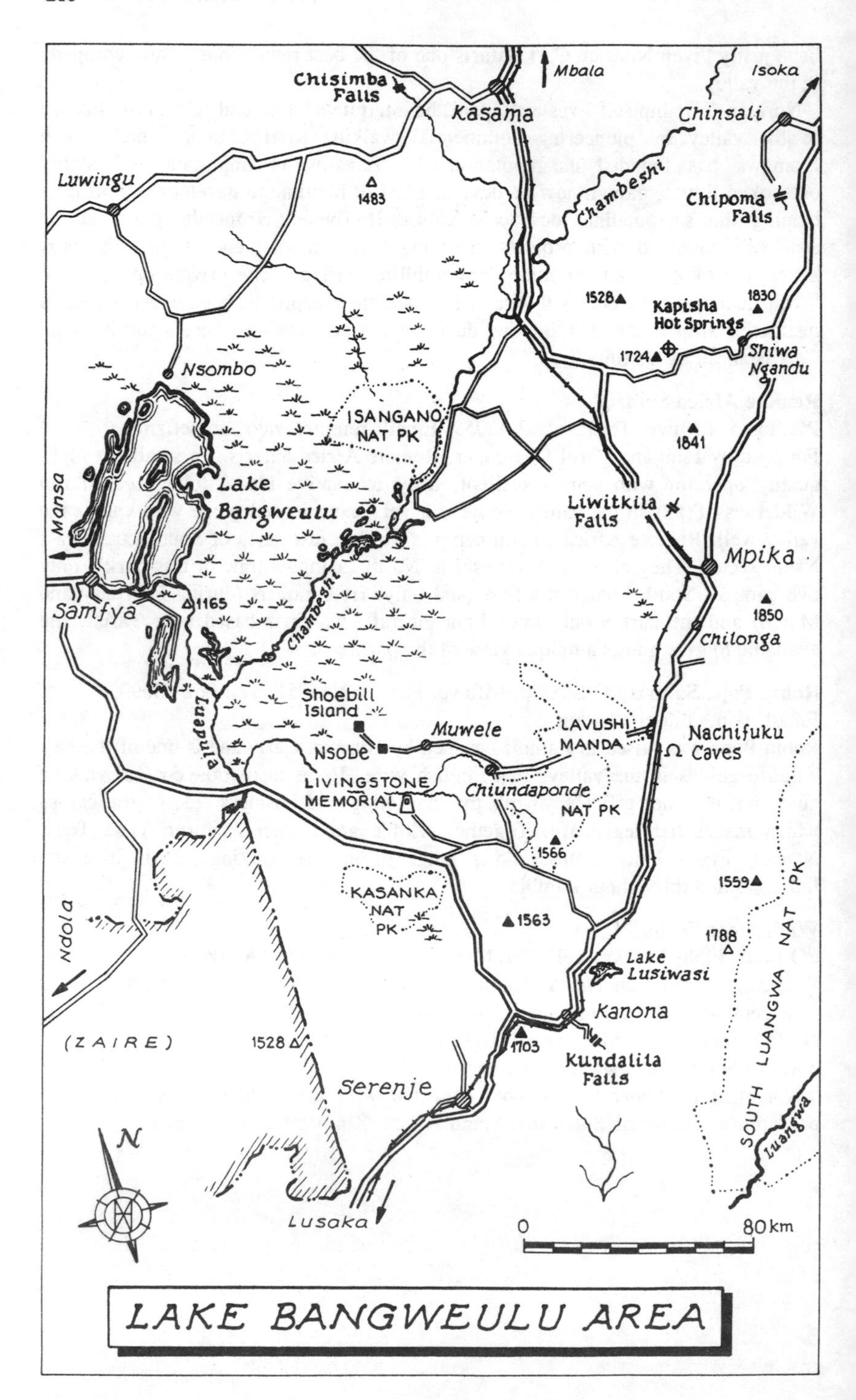
Chisimba Falls
Mbala
Kasama
Isoka
Chinsali
Luwingu
1483
Chambeshi
Chipoma Falls
1528
1830
Kapisha Hot Springs
1724
Shiwa Ngandu
Nsombo
ISANGANO NAT PK
1841
Mansa
Lake Bangweulu
Liwitkila Falls
Mpika
Samfya
1165
Chambeshi
1850
Chilonga
Shoebill Island
Luapula
Muwele
LAVUSHI MANDA
Nachifuku Caves
Nsobe
LIVINGSTONE MEMORIAL
Chiundaponde
NAT PK
1566
1559
KASANKA NAT PK
1563
Ndola
1788
Lake Lusiwasi
Kanona
SOUTH LUANGWA NAT PK
(ZAIRE)
1528
1703
Kundalila Falls
Serenje
Luangwa
N
Lusaka
0
80km
LAKE BANGWEULU AREA

Chapter Thirteen

Bangweulu Area

The spectacular Bangweulu Swamps are, after the rains, a fascinating water-wilderness of a similar size to Botswana's Okavango Delta. A huge swamp with its own endemic species of antelope, it is the breeding place for one of Africa's strangest and rarest birds: the shoebill.

Nearby Kasanka National Park is a jewel of a reserve, proving beyond doubt that small can be beautiful, while the manor house and estate at Shiwa N'gandu are a must for anyone seeking an insight into Zambia's colonial history. Aside from these three main attractions there are several fascinating stops to be made in this area where David Livingstone, literally, left his heart.

KASANKA NATIONAL PARK

Park fees: Kw5,000 (or US$5) per person per day

This small park is the first privately managed national park in Zambia. It is only 420km² in area, but encompasses a wide variety of vegetation zones from dry evergreen forests to various types of moist forest and permanent papyrus swamps. The park and its camps are so well kept that is really is a delightful place spend a relaxing few days, and keen bird-watchers will find many more pressing reasons to visit.

History

Kasanka was made a national park in 1972, but it was poorly maintained and poaching was rife until the late 1980s. Then an initiative was started by David Lloyd, a former district officer, and Gareth Williams, a local commercial farmer. With the support of the National Parks Department and the local community, they started to put private money into revitalising the park.

In 1990 the National Parks Department signed a management contract with the Kasanka Trust, giving the latter the right to manage the park and develop it for tourism in partnership with the local community. The trust is a registered charity based in London (28 Bolton Street, London; tel: 0171 352 2481, fax: 0171 912 1712), which appears to be trail-blazing a model for the successful private management of a Zambian National Park.

It has been fortunate in gaining the financial backing of the European Union, through the British Council.

The Kasanka Trust aims to manage the area's natural resources for the benefit of both the wildlife and the local people. Thus the local chief, Chief Chitambo IV, who rules over the communities in the park's immediate area, is represented on the committee that runs the park.

Geography, flora and fauna

Kasanka is on the southern fringes of the Bangweulu Swamps, and just 30km from the border with Zaire. It is almost completely flat and, lying at an altitude of about 1,300m, it gets a high rainfall during the wet season - about 1,200mm - which results in a lush cover of vegetation.

Although there are several small rivers flowing through the park, the evenness of the land has caused an extensive marsh area known as the Kapabi Swamp. There are eight lakes in the park, though seven of these are really just small permanently flooded dambos.

The park's natural flora is dominated by *miombo* woodland, in which *brachystegia* species figure heavily. Because local people use fire as part of their cultivation cycles, and it can spread into areas of the park, some of this is less tall than it might be - perhaps reaching only 5m rather than its normal 20m.

There are also sections of much taller dry evergreen forest, where the tallest trees have an interlocking canopy, and the *mateshi* undergrowth is dense and woody. A good area for this is near the Kasanka River around the Katwa guard post.

Elsewhere you will find evergreen swamp forest, with some superb tall specimens of water berry and mululu trees (*Syzygium cordatum* and *Khaya nyasica*). Around the Fibwe guard post is one such area, and the Machan Sitatunga Hide is perched in a huge mululu tree. Similar species also occur in the areas of riparian forest found by Kasanka's small rivers. Interspersed in these forested areas are open grasslands and swamps. The latter include large areas of permanent beds of papyrus and phragmites, often with very little open water to be seen. The wild date palm, *phoenix reclinata*, is one of the most common species of tree found here.

Mammals

Poaching in the 1970s and 80s caused drastic reductions in the numbers of animals in the park, but seems to have had only a few long-term effects on the species present. Many of these move into and out of the park quite freely, and as they gradually learn that the park is a safe haven, they are staying longer or becoming resident, and seem less shy.

The puku is the most common antelope here, and other relatively common residents include bushbuck, reedbuck, defassa waterbuck,

Sharp's grysbok and the common duiker. Lichtenstein's hartebeest occur in good numbers, while sable, roan, zebra and buffalo are more scarce. A small herd of elephant has recently moved into the park.

Of particular interest are the shy sitatunga antelope, which can often be spotted in the very early morning from the Machan Sitatunga Hide – near Fibwe guard post. This offers one of the subcontinent's best opportunities for viewing these beautiful creatures in an undisturbed state – far superior to simply getting a fleeting glance of the back of one as it flees from the speedboat in which you are travelling.

Leopard are the dominant predator, and only the occasional lion has been recorded as passing through the park. None is known to be resident. Other smaller carnivores include spotted hyena, honey badgers, and the Cape clawless otter. Mongooses are well represented: the water, slender, white-tailed, banded, and large grey mongoose are all found here.

In the lakes, rivers and swamps, hippo and crocodiles are common. The slender-snouted crocodile – a typical resident of Zaire's tropical rainforest rivers – occurs here, though it is less common than the "normal" Nile crocodile. Because of the park's proximity to Zaire, other species which are typical of those equatorial rainforests (and very rare for Southern Africa) can be spotted in Kasanka. For example, the blue monkey is often sighted on the western side of the park, occurring with the area's more common primates: baboons and vervet monkeys. Whilst the skin of a Moloney's monkey has been found nearby, no positive identifications of these primates have yet been made inside the park. The status of the shy, forest-dwelling yellow-backed duiker is less certain, but it is believed to be resident.

Probably the most spectacular sight occurs only around the start of the rains (in November and December) when an enormous colony of fruit-bats roosts near the centre of the park. Each night they pour out of their resting place just after sunset like a column of smoke, filling the sky as they fly in search of food. The bats have wingspans of up to 1m, making a grand spectacle which is probably best observed from the Machan Sitatunga Hide.

Birds

With lush vegetation and a wide range of habitats, Kasanka is an excellent place for quiet, undisturbed bird-watching. The rivers and wetland areas have excellent populations of ibis, storks, herons, kingfishers and bee-eaters as well as many waterfowl. The larger birds include wattled cranes and saddle-billed storks, and occasionally the rare shoebill stork, which breeds in the Bangweulu swamps to the north. Reed cormorants and African darters are common on the more open stretches of water.

PIED KINGFISHER - E.H

Many species common in East or Central Africa occur here, on the edges of their ranges, like the grey apalis, green sunbird, the red and blue sunbird, green loerie or Boehm's flycatcher. Equally, it is a good area in which to seek generally uncommon birds, like Lady Ross's touraco (also known, more prosaically, as Ross's lourie), the African finfoot and the half-collared kingfisher. The park was the site for a recent study of hornbill species by a team organised jointly by the universities of Manchester (in the UK) and Lusaka.

The more common raptors in the area are the bateleur, martial, crowned, and steppe eagles, plus the snake eagles (black-breasted, western-banded and brown) and the chanting goshawks (pale and dark). Kasanka's fish eagles are often seen, but its Pel's fishing owls are not.

Getting there

The main entrance to Kasanka, on its eastern border, is fairly obvious. Coming from Kapiri Mposhi, refuel if necessary in Serenje, as there is no fuel available in the park. Then take the main road signposted to Samfya and Mansa – often referred to as the "Chinese Road" because, like TAZARA, it was built by the Chinese. Drive for between 54 and 55km (watch the milestones on the left of the road) then turn left, where shortly you will find the Mulaushi guard post at the entrance to the park.

If you are heading to Kankonto Camp, then you may still like to check in here on arrival, but you must then continue towards Mansa until the 91km marker, where there is another turn that leads directly to the camp.

Alternatively the park has a seasonal airstrip for light aircraft.

Camps

All the camps in the park are run by Kasanka Wildlife Conservation Ltd. They can (and should) be booked in advance by contacting PO Box 36657, Lusaka; tel: 01 260106 or 01 362164. Failing that try Gareth Williams himself on Mkushi 05 362164. If you arrive without a booking, and space is available, then pay at the main Wasa Lodge.

Wasa Lodge (6 twin-bed rondavels)

This delightful spot on the shore of Lake Wasa is the park's main camp and the first one reached when you enter from the main road. Its thatched rondavels are very well maintained, and the shared toilets and bucket-showers are among Zambia's best. It has small solar lights and no generator.

The camp is well staffed and equipped, so bring your own supplies and the camp's staff will cook them for you. They will also prepare hot water for showers, and are generally around for any reasonable help that you might need.

Rates: US$10 per person per night self-catering. US$80 per person per night full board & all activities (which must be pre-arranged)

Open: all year – but access can be difficult in the wet season

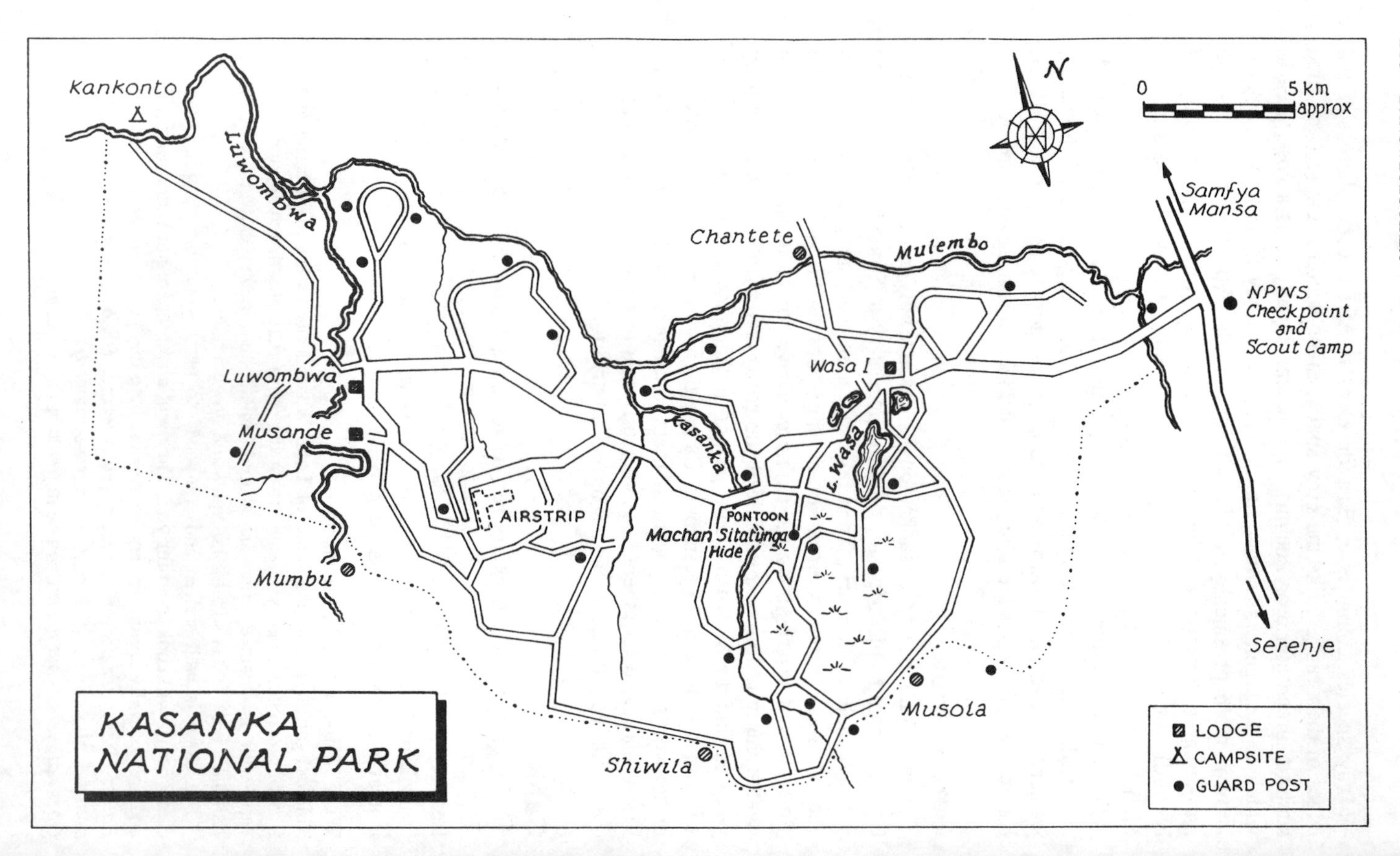
KASANKA
NATIONAL PARK
LODGE
CAMPSITE
GUARD POST
N
0
5 km
approx
Kankonto
Luwombwa
Samfya
Mansa
Chantete
Mulembo
NPWS
Checkpoint
and
Scout Camp
Wasa I
Luwombwa
Musande
Kasanka
L. Wasa
AIRSTRIP
PONTOON
Machan Sitatunga
Hide
Mumbu
Serenje
Musola
Shiwila

Luwombwa Fishing Lodge (5 twin-bed rondavels)
This sits on the bank of the Luwombwa River in the western half of the park. Its accommodation is equally good, with simple thatched huts, two separate showers and long-drop toilets. There is a bar and dining area made of reeds and thatch. The camp works on a similar basis to Wasa Wasa – you bring your supplies and the camp's staff look after you. Motor boats (5 seats) with guides are available for hire here, as are canoes (3 seats).

Musande Tented Camp (6 twin-bed tents)
Just a few kilometres south of Luwombwa, Musande is also on the bank of the Luwombwa River and is staffed and equipped. It is run on the same basis as the others, though the accommodation is in tents rather than rondavels. Motor boats with guides are also available for hire here.

Kankonto Camp (camping only)
If you have all your own camping equipment, as well as supplies, then camping here is an option. To reach it take the separate access road which branches off southwest from the main road to Mansa, near the 91km marker. The camp stands at the northwestern tip of the park, on the northern bank of the Luwombwa River. It has basic cooking and washing facilities, but nothing else.

What to see and do

During the dry season Kasanka's roads are generally good, and accessible with a high-clearance 2WD. There are manually operated pontoons for crossing the Luwombwa River, at the fishing lodge and the Kasanka River in the centre of the park.

Driving yourself around is easy, though walking is more pleasant. A few places within the park are worth specific mentions:

Machan sitatunga hide

A magnificent mululu tree, *Khaya nyasica*, near to the Fibwe guard post, can be climbed using a basic ladder, to reach two platforms almost 18m above the ground. The views over a section of the Kapabi swamp are excellent, and if you reach this in the early morning and climb silently then your chances of seeing sitatunga are excellent. (Leisurely risers can take heart, I have seen sitatunga from here as late as midday.) This must be one of the best tree-hides on the continent!

Lake Ndolwa

This quiet spot on the southern side of the park is the best place to seek the rare shoebill stork. The guard post here has good views over the lake, which has a small resident population of sitatunga, and some excellent birdlife.

Chikufwe Plain

This is a large open area of seasonally flooded grassland, which is a favourite place to spot sable, hartebeest and reedbuck. There is a little-used, but still serviceable, airstrip here, and a small hide on a loop road around the southern side of the plain.

Fishing

Fishing is allowed within the park, and the best waters are normally the Luwombwa River, so head for the Luwombwa or Musande camps if you want to do much fishing. The camp's cooks will prepare your catch for dinner, if you wish. The main angling species found here are tigerfish; largemouth, small-mouth and yellow-belly bream; and vundu catfish. There are strict rules which only allow large fish to be removed for eating.

Further information

Finally, if possible, get hold of a copy of *Kasanka – A Visitor's Guide to the Kasanka National Park* before you arrive if possible. It is a delightful and very comprehensive little guidebook which covers the park in great detail – see *Further Reading*, pages 308-9.

LAVUSHI MANDA NATIONAL PARK

This park is potentially interesting for its hilly and very pleasant landscape, though sadly it has lost most of its animals to poachers over the last few decades. Until tourism picks up in Zambia, there will probably be little incentive for anyone to try to rejuvenate its fortunes by restocking it with game, and its rocky, undulating land would be difficult to farm.

Geography

Lavushi Manda is over three times the size of Kasanka, and covers 1,500km^2 of the Lavushi hills. It is easily reached from the Great North Road, almost equidistant from Serenje and Mpika, and the landscape is attractive and undulating. To the north the land slopes away, and the park's streams all drain into the Lukulu or Lumbatwa Rivers and thence ultimately into Lake Bangweulu.

Miombo woodland covers most of the park, with some areas of riparian forest nearer the larger streams and many grassy dambos. Though this is very pleasant and attractive, there is very little game here. It has virtually all been poached.

Getting there

The turning off the main Mpika–Serenje road is about 141km beyond the turn to Mansa (also the Kasanka turn-off), and about 64.6km from Mpika.

This road goes across the railway line, and 12km later enters the park via a checkpoint. It leads directly east–west through the park, and on the eastern side of the park it intersects an ungraded road just before a small village called Chiundaponde. This ungraded road runs from Muwele, Ngungwa and Chikuni (and also Nsobe Camp) in the Bangweulu GMA, to the main Mpika–Serenje road. South of this intersection, a turn-off allows a short-cut to Kasanka National Park, and it is a short drive to the Livingstone Memorial.

Where to stay/what to see and do

There are no camps, but camping should be possible if you come with all your food, water, and equipment. Ask the scouts on the gate.

Driving through the park makes an interesting diversion; it is a convenient route into the Bangweulu Game Management Area and few regard it as a destination in itself. That said, it might make a good area for exploration if you are a very dedicated hiker.

ISANGANO NATIONAL PARK

East of Lake Bangweulu, Isangano National Park covers 840km² of flat, well-watered grassland. The western side of the park forms part of the Bangweulu Flats, which are seasonally flooded.

The park's ecosystem is apparently the same as that of the Bangweulu GMA's. However, it is reported that the game in Isangano has mostly disappeared because of poaching, and there is no internal road network within the park at all.

Thus visitors are generally advised to look toward Bangweulu GMA instead, if they want to visit this type of area. At least there is some infrastructure, and the local communities will derive some positive benefit from a visit.

LAKE BANGWEULU AND SWAMPS

This area is often described, in clichéd terms, as one of Africa's last great wilderness areas – which might be overstating its case a little, but it is certainly a very large and very wild area, which very few people really know and understand.

Under the RAMSAR Convention of 1991 it was designated as a Wetland of International Importance, and since then the WWF has been involved in helping the local communities in the GMA to sustainably manage it, as their own natural resource.

Though most visitors' image of a wilderness area is an unpopulated, barren tract of land, this GMA area does have small villages. It remains as home to many local people, who still hunt and fish here, as their ancestors have done for centuries. The old way of conserving an area by displacing the people and proclaiming a National Park clearly hasn't worked in much of Zambia: witness the minimal game left in Lavushi Manda or Isangano. This new approach of leaving the people on the land, and encouraging them to develop through sustainable management of their natural resources, is the more modern way to attempt to preserve as much of the wildlife as possible.

Geography

The low-lying basin containing Lake Bangweulu and its swamps receives one of the highest rainfalls in the country – over 1,400mm per annum. On the northwestern edge of the basin is Lake Bangweulu itself, about 50km long and 25km wide at its widest point. This is probably the largest body of water within Zambia's borders, and an excellent spot for watching the local fishermen. It is easily reached at Samfya, on the main road from Serenje to Mansa, but is of little interest to most visitors.

The more fascinating area is the seasonal swamp to the southeast of the lake, which covers an area two to three times the size of the lake. Here is a very wild area with few roads and lots of wildlife. This is one of the few areas in the country where the local communities are beginning to use the wildlife in their GMAs as a really sustainable source of income. There is little development here, just one or two small lodges and a simple community-run camp for visitors who arrive on their own. The area still has many residents who continue to fish and eke out a living directly from the environment, but gradually the community development schemes are beginning to tap into tourism as a way to fund sustainable development.

Flora and fauna

Towards the end of the rains, and for a short time after them, this area becomes a water-wilderness of low islands, reed-beds, floodplains and shallow lagoons. From March through to about June/July, the birdlife can be amazing and the animals impressive. This is the best time to visit, because towards the end of the dry season the southern side of the swamps dries out. Then the waters recede towards the lake, and the wildlife gradually moves after them.

Animals

The speciality here is the black lechwe, an attractive dark race of the lechwe said to be endemic to the Bangweulu area. (The only other place where they have been recorded is the swamps on the southern side of Lake Mweru, and their status there is now uncertain.) They are much darker than the red lechwe found throughout Southern Africa, or the race known as the Kafue Flats lechwe which occur in the Lochinvar area.

Their current population in this area is estimated at 30,000 animals, and herds measured in their thousands are not uncommon. Among these herds of black lechwe are other animals including sitatunga, tsessebe, reedbuck, common duiker and oribi. Elephant and buffalo are frequently seen; predators are uncommon but hyena, leopard and jackal are sometimes observed.

Birds

The big attraction here is the chance to see the unusual and rare shoebill stork (also called the whale-headed stork). This massive, grey bird, whose looks are often compared to a dodo, breeds in the papyrus beds here and nowhere else in Southern Africa. Its population is estimated at about 1,500 individual birds, making Bangweulu a vital refuge for this very threatened species.

Aside from the elusive shoebill, the birdlife after the rains is amazing. Migrants which stop here while the floodwaters are high include flamingos, pelicans, spoonbills, cranes, storks, ibises, ducks and geese. Bangweulu is also an important reserve for wattled cranes, which occur here in large flocks: greater numbers than almost anywhere else, with the possible exception of the Kafue Flats. The swamp's shallow waters are ideal for smaller waders, like sandpipers, godwits and avocets. The whole area is remarkable, and worth the effort required to get here.

Getting there

The easiest way into the area –the only wet-season access – is via Lavushi Manda National Park. Take the turning to the west about 65 km from Mpika. This goes across the main TAZARA railway line and 12km later reaches the park gate. You will need to sign in before driving across the park.

About 68km later, a few kilometres before the village of Chiundaponde, there is a turning to the right. Recognise this by noting that the soil colour on the road is light brown, while you are turning onto a track with a grey substrate. If you need to ask directions, the local people know this as the road to Chikuni and Nsobe Camp.

From here it is about 48km to Muwele village. Just before this, the road forks. Take the left fork through the village, and remember to drive very slowly for safety's sake. About a kilometre after the village is a left turn signposted to the Nsobe Safari Camp. Continue straight without taking the turn, and you will reach the National Parks and Wildlife Camp at Chikuni Island, the airstrip, and finally, about 10km later, Shoebill Island Camp.

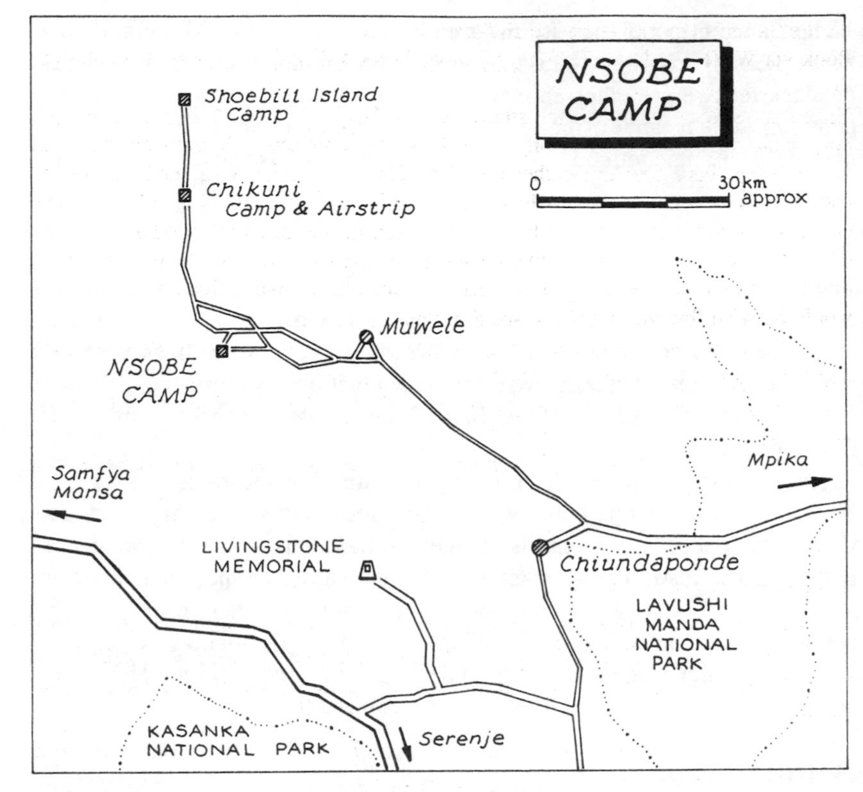

Camps

There are two camps in the area: Shoebill and Nsobe. If you're flying in on a luxury trip, then you'll probably be staying at Shoebill, which is an excellent camp. If you're driving in to see the swamps, then bring all your supplies and consider staying at Nsobe, which is more used to independent visitors – and much more Zambian in feel. It will cost you less, and more of the money will go directly to supporting the local community.

Shoebill Island Camp (4 twin-bed tents)

Accessed down a causeway, Shoebill Island Camp is built just outside the woodland, with a fine view over the swamps. There are large mosquito-proofed walk-in tents and two separate bucket showers, a long-drop toilet and a bar/dining area. During your stay do make the effort to see camp's best view over the swamps – by climbing the water tower.

If there isn't enough water to travel through the swamps by canoe, the usual form of water transport, then the guides will take you walking over the floating reed-bed in search of shoebills and other wildlife. Alternatively the camp will organise drives on to the drier areas of the plains, and into the surrounding woodlands.

Rates: US$250 per person per night
Open: 1 June to 31 December

Nsobe Safari Camp (5 twin-bed chalets)
Book via WWF Wetlands Project, National Parks & Wildlife, P. Bag 1, Chilanga. Tel: 01 278231
Nsobe is the local name for the sitatunga, and Nsobe Camp is billed as Zambia's only safari camp which is wholly owned by the community. It must certainly be one of very, very few in Southern Africa. The community developed, maintains and runs the camp with the help of the WWF, who are closely involved in the efforts to preserve these wetlands. Nsobe is built in Mandamanta woodlands on the edge of the floodplain, and its five chalets have shared ablutions. Supplies must be brought with you, but there is a kitchen with a deep-freeze available. Booking would be wise, but you may find space if you just turn up.

Game viewing is possible on foot, by boat or by vehicle, and boats (with two boatmen) can be hired here for about Kw1,000 per hour. For walking safaris, very experienced trackers are also available for around Kw2,000 per hour, and for the less energetic there are secluded hides nearby.
Rates: US$30 per person; US$5 per person for campers. Reductions possible for Zambian residents
Open: 1 June to 31 December

What to see and do

Driving, walking and canoeing are the activities here, and all are better done with guides. While the black lechwe are spectacular, the birdlife is Bangweulu's main attraction, and the ungainly shoebill is a particular favourite among visitors.

As you might expect from an area which is seasonally flooded, and whose name translates as "where the water meets the sky", Bangweulu is a largely trackless wilderness. It is exceedingly easy to get lost if you simply head into it yourself, and indiscriminate driving does much damage to both the soil structure and the ground-nesting birds. It is strongly recommended on safety and conservation grounds that 4WD owners use one of the camps as a base for their explorations, and take the local advice that they are given about where to go and how to minimise their environmental impact.

Note that during some of the year lechwe flies and other insects can become a nuisance; the wet season from November through to March is especially difficult. Bring insect repellent here: it is vital. Arriving with a head-net, covering your face and neck below your hat, would certainly not be going too far. Both camps supply mosquito nets, and guests are advised to take all possible anti-malaria precautions.

MKUSHI

On the way from Kapiri Mposhi up the Great North Road, Mkushi is not just another stop on the TAZARA line, it is also the centre for a prosperous farming area, with a number of large commercial farms in the vicinity keeping cattle and cultivating cash crops. There are shops, fuel, a post office and a police post, as you'd expect in a small town this size.

Forest Inn (3 twin-bed chalets) Shenton Safaris
PO Box 810064, Kapiri Mposhi. Tel/fax: 05 362188
This is a small new camp run by the Shentons, owners of Kaingo Lodge in the South Luangwa (see page 197). Here there are three very comfortable thatch-on-stone chalets with electricity and hot showers, and a good campsite. The farm's fresh produce is available, and there is a small snack bar selling food. This is well signposted about 30km south of Mkushi, just off the main road.

SERENJE

Northeast of Mkushi, Serenje has a TAZARA station, a couple of banks, a catholic convent, a Baptist mission, a small teachers' college, fuel, a post office, a police post, two basic local motels (with little to choose between them), and a marvellously named shop: Aunt Flo's Fast Foods. Otherwise, it is of very limited interest to most visitors.

MPIKA

Though not much bigger than either Mkushi or Serenje, Mpika is a busy crossroads of a place which seems to have an importance outweighing its size. Here the Great North Road forks: one branch going to Kasama, Mbala, and Mpulungu on Lake Tanganyika, the other heading directly for the Tanzania border at Nakonde. It is also about a day's travel from either Lusaka, Mpulungu or the Tanzanian border, which perhaps explains why one often ends up stopping here overnight.

Getting there

Getting to Mpika is easy; it is getting away that always seems to be tricky. Fortunately there are is a choice of public transport if you are not driving:

By bus

Daily local bus services link Mpika with Lusaka, Mbala and (to a lesser extent) Isoka. These all pass by the main central *boma* of town (the central, circular meeting place), so if you wait there you shouldn't miss any of them. Sometimes, the same buses will pick you up if you wave them down whilst hitchhiking, but not always.

By train

The TAZARA station is about 5-6km out of town, almost on the road to Kasama, and private pick-up trucks operate shuttle runs between there and the central boma in Mpika, fitting as many people on to the vehicles as they can carry. If you arrive by train in the early hours of the morning then your options are to get one of these shuttles quickly, or sleep rough on the station until daybreak and then try to get one. At times like this, the station is crowded but fairly clean and safe.

The TAZARA train connects Kapiri Mposhi with Dar es Salaam in Tanzania, and Mpika is one of the stops between. Mpika to Kapiri Mposhi costs around Kw10,700.

Hitchhiking

With clear roads and a reasonable amount of traffic, hitching is a very practical form of transport to and from Mpika. There is probably more traffic going towards Mbala than Nakonde, but if you're heading towards Lusaka hitch around the BP station where both roads join.

If you're going towards Kasama and Mbala, then hitch on the turn-off by the BP station. Alternatively, and especially if it is late in the day, walk a further 2-3km down that tarred turn-off road, until you reach a smart, fenced compound on your right. This is known as the DDSP compound, or the MLGH (Ministry of Local Government and Housing) compound - it houses offices for various aid and semi-governmental groups, small businesses, and a nice resthouse with a simple bar and restaurant. You may pick up a lift from one of its workers, who travel widely in the district. You'll certainly see them come and go in a variety of plush 4WDs, and if the worst happens and no lift appears then you can wander across the road and sleep comfortably.

Where to stay

The best place to stay by far is the DDSP compound mentioned above. The sign outside details many of the offices here, including the Development Organisation for People's Empowerment - more usually known by its acronym.

DDSP's communal rooms are the cheapest: two separate bedrooms which share a single toilet/washbasin/shower are Kw8,000 per bed. These rooms are clean and the beds are OK, though the shower/toilet area is less sparkling. Self-contained rooms with their own shower/toilet are Kw10,000. If you are likely to arrive after about 21.30 then reserve a room in advance by telephoning Mpika (04) 370400 during the day. The key to your room will then be left at the gate-house.

There are houses available, each with a comfortable sitting room, kitchen, and two bedrooms which sleep four people easily for a total of Kw20,000.

The alternatives to the DDSP are the Musikanga Resthouse and the Government Resthouse, both of which are on the side of the boma away from the main road. Rooms at these are about Kw5,000 each, but are much less pleasant.

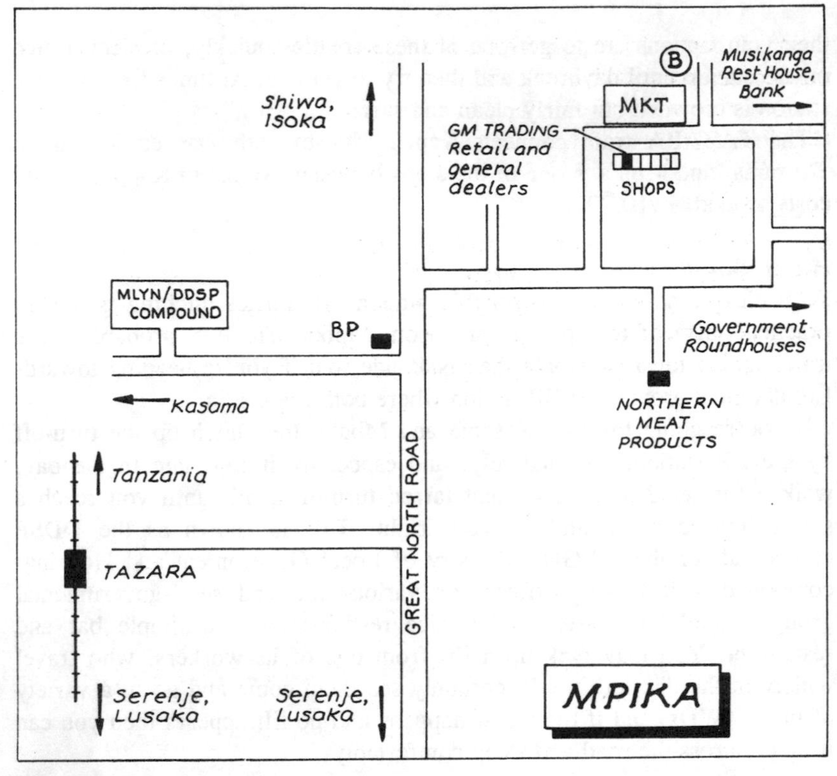

What to see and do

For supplies, GM Trading/Retail & General Dealers facing the boma is probably the best store in town. It has most of the supplies that you're likely to find east of the Copperbelt – from curry powder and canned foods, to South African wine, chocolates, and a fine selection of beautiful chitenjes for about Kw2,300-2,700 each.

Southwest of there, just a few hundred yards, is the Northern Meat Products butchery (tel: 04 370599), which sells the area's best fresh meat and sausages. The managers of this also own Bateleur Farm, where you can camp if you are taking the bush route from Mpika into the Luangwa Valley described on page 207.

If you need to change any money then the only bank in town able to do this is the TAZARA bank, which is off on the right as you head towards the TAZARA station – ask for local directions, and watch for the "Zamtel" sign.

SHIWA N'GANDU

Of all the colonial legacies in Africa, the historic manor at Shiwa N'gandu is one of the most remarkable. It tells of an English aristocrat's gracious vision of how Africa might have been, while its gradual subjugation over the decades speaks of how Africa is.

It is certainly worth making a special effort to see Shiwa, and the nearby Kapishya Hot Springs make an excellent base from which to do so.

Getting there

Shiwa N'gandu is reasonably well signposted off the main road to Isoka and Nakonde, about 87km northeast of Mpika. The main Shiwa N'gandu house is about 13km from this turn-off. The road then continues to Kapishya Hot Springs and on to the Mpika-Kasama road.

Alternatively it can be reached directly from the Mpika-Kasama road; again turn off about 87km from Mpika, and pass Kapishya Hot Springs before finally reaching the house.

With a post office at Shiwa, the estate is due to be linked to Mpika by a post bus. Inquire at Mpika about the latest situation.

History

Shiwa N'gandu was founded by Stewart Gore-Browne, who was born in England in 1883, and first came to Africa in 1911 as a member of the military commission. Whilst surveying the boundary between Northern Rhodesia and the Belgian Congo, he saw Shiwa N'gandu: the "Lake of the Royal Crocodiles". After World War I, Gore-Browne returned to buy the lake and surrounding land, using his inherited income and with help from his aunt. Then it was 70 miles on foot or horseback from Ndola to the Luapula River, followed by ten days in a canoe across the Bangweulu Swamps, followed by another 70-mile march.

Having spent time in South Africa, after the Boer war, Gore-Browne knew the attitude of white South Africans to blacks – and it appalled him. He based his views, especially with regard to Africa and the Africans, soundly on his own experiences, and refused to accept the prejudices of the resident white community. His vision for a utopian mini-state in the heart of Africa translated into an estate run with benevolent paternalism, and by 1925 Shiwa N'gandu was employing 1,800 local people.

Gore-Browne passed on skills to them, and with their help built neat workers' cottages with slate roofs, bridges, workshops, a school, a dispensary, and finally a magnificent manor house, set on a hill above the lake. All that could not be made locally was transported on the heads and backs of porters along the arduous route from Ndola. Simply look at all the heavy English furniture, the paintings, ornaments, and the walls of books to appreciate the determination with which Gore-Browne pursued his vision.

He also built a distillery for the essential oils which he hoped make into a profitable local industry. Given Shiwa's remote location, Gore-Browne knew that the estate's produce had to be easily transportable: a non-perishable, valuable commodity of low bulk. He had several failures, trying roses, geraniums, eucalyptus, peppermint and lemon grass with no success. Eventually, he found success with citrus fruit, which flourished and at last brought a good income into the estate.

In 1927, when he was 44, he married Lorna - a "ravishing" young lady from England who was just eighteen years old. She came to Shiwa, and threw herself into her husband's projects, and the estate and its inhabitants prospered. Then, in the 1950s, a tristezia virus killed off the fruit trees, hitting the estate hard and forcing it to turn to more conventional, less profitable, agriculture - possible because the main road which passes near the estate had then been completed.

Gore-Browne had become a rare, political figure in Northern Rhodesia, an aristocratic Englishman with excellent connections in London who commanded respect both in the colonial administration and with black Zambians. He was elected to Northern Rhodesia's Legislative Council as early as 1935, and was the first member of it to argue that real concessions were needed to African demands for more autonomy. He was impatient with the rule of the Colonial Office, and resented the loss of huge amounts of revenue through taxation paid to Britain, and "royalties" paid to the British South Africa Company.

Stewart Gore-Browne was knighted by George VI of England, but also trusted by Zambia's first president, Kenneth Kaunda. When he died, an octogenarian, in 1967, he was given a full state funeral and allowed to be buried on a hill overlooking the lake at Shiwa - an honour only bestowed on the Bemba chiefs. In the words of Kaunda, "He was born an Englishman and died a Zambian". Perhaps if Africa had had more like him, the transition from colonial rule to independence would have been less traumatic.

On his death, the estate at Shiwa passed to his daughter Lorna and her husband, John Harvey, a farmer from near Lusaka. However, with just the income of the farm and without the lucrative essential oils, both the manor house and the estate proved difficult to maintain. John and Lorna were both murdered in the early 1990s, allegedly because of what they knew of a high-ranking official's misdeeds. The incident has never had a satisfactory investigation.

Lady Lorna Gore-Browne returned to England and now lives in Highgate, London - she never returned to Shiwa after her husband's death. The estate is now run by David Harvey, Sir Stewart Gore-Browne's grandson.

Shiwa N'gandu manor house

Today the estate is a monument to Gore-Browne's utopian vision for this verdant corner of Africa. As you approach from the main road, the rectangular cottages built for farm workers come into view first, their white-washed walls and tiled roofs saying more of England than Africa. Then a red-brick gate-house appears, perhaps of Italian design. An old clock-tower rises above its tiled roof, and through its main arch is a long straight avenue, bordered by eucalyptus, leading to the stately manor house.

Climbing up, the avenue leads through the very English gardens – designed on several levels with bougainvillaea, frangipani, jacaranda and neatly arranged cypresses. Above the front door is a small carving of a black rhino's head: a reminder that Gore-Browne had earned the local nickname of Chipembele, black rhino.

At the centre of the manor is the square tiled Tuscan courtyard, surrounded by arches, overlooking windows and a red tiled roof. Climbing one of the cold, stone-slab staircases brings you into an English manor house, lined with wooden panelling and rugs hung on the walls, and furnished with sturdy chests, muskets, and all manner of memorabilia, including pictures of old relatives and regiments. Two frames with certificates face each other: one from King George VI, granting "our trusty and well-beloved Stewart Gore-Browne, esq" the degree, title, honour and dignity of Knight Bachelor, while opposite President Kaunda appoints "my trusted, well-beloved Sir Stewart Gore-Browne" as a Grand Officer of the Companion Order of Freedom, second division – dated 1966.

The library remains the manor's heart, with two huge walls of books, floor-to-ceiling, which tell of Gore-Browne's interests – Frouede's *History of England* in at least a dozen volumes, *Policy and Arms* by Colonel Repington and *The Genesis of War* by the Right Honourable H H Asquith. His wife was very keen on poetry: there is a classic collection of works by Byron, Shelley, Coleridge, Eliot and others. Central to the room is a grand fireplace, surmounted by the Latin inscription: *Ille terrarum mihi super omnes anculus ridet* – this corner of the earth, above all others, smiles on me.

Shiwa today

Today the estate has a luxuriance, even at the height of the dry season, which is seldom found elsewhere in Zambia. David Harvey studied agriculture in England and returned to manage the estate, which now farms both animals and crops. Despite success in updating production methods, and diversifying into chickens, pigs, groundnuts, and dairy produce, there isn't the income from such a farm to maintain the manor house to Gore-Browne's original standards.

As you walk around, the peaceful atmosphere is one of an ancient country estate which is gradually slipping back into the African bush. It is almost as if Africa's rampant vegetation were accelerating the manor's decline, having aged it by centuries in a mere 70 years. The working farm now at its core will probably survive into the next millennium, though much of Gore-Browne's vision will not.

Kapishya Hot Springs

P Bag E395, Lusaka. Tel: 04 370064, fax: 04 370040

About 20km from Shiwa N'gandu, the Harveys have built a small camp beside some natural hot springs. This is the best place to stay in the region, though you will need your own transport in order to reach it. There's a pool of hot spring water, and a cool rocky river, both of which make great sites for bathing. All is surrounded by combretum bushes and gently curving raffia palms, making for a very relaxing spot.

The solid thatched chalets have mosquito-netted windows and are furnished inside with reed mats, comfortable beds and shelves. They have en suite flush toilets and nice large showers and wash basins – plus individual mosquito nets for the beds. Nearby the grassy campsite has soft earth that's easy on tent-pegs, bucket showers and long-drop toilets. If you just turn up here then bring your own food, otherwise meals can be provided if you request them in advance.

Rates: US$30 per person self-catering, US$50 per person full board
Camping: US$5 per person

What to see and do

If you come to stay at Kapishya Springs, which are an attraction in their own right, then ask there to arrange a tour of the house – which normally includes afternoon tea and costs a few dollars per person.

Other than that, a stay here can easily be combined with a visit to North Luangwa National Park, as David Harvey runs Shiwa Safaris who own *Mimbulu Camp* there (pages 204-5), and knows the park and the wildlife well.

If you've time to spare then take a slow wander around the estate, and perhaps down to the lake. As ever, you will find the local people very welcoming and friendly, and usually happy to talk about what they are doing.

OTHER ATTRACTIONS

The Bangweulu area has a number of smaller attractions – caves and waterfalls – which are worth stopping off the road to have a look at. Here is a small selection of the best:

Nachikufu Caves

This cave complex contains excellent San/bushmen rock paintings: when excavated in the 1940s it was estimated to have been occupied intermittently from about 10,000BC until just 1,000 years ago.

The caves are in three storeys: a main cave at the bottom, one above that, and another again above that. Both of the higher ones need a little climbing to reach them.

Rates: entry Kw150 per person per day

Getting there

About 60km south of Mpika, just before the Lavushi turn-off, is the signposted turning to Nachikufu.

Nsalu Cave

This semi-circular cave, cut into Nsalu Hill, contains some excellent San/bushmen rock paintings. Sadly there have been graffiti in the cave, though many of the paintings can still be seen.

Rates: entry Kw150 per person per day

Getting there

Head north on the Great North Road and there is a left turn to the cave about 30km north of Kanona, between Serenje and Mpika. The caves are 15km down this track, and the caretaker's house is half way along. They are fenced off to deter vandalism, so stop there to get the caretaker's help.

The Livingstone Memorial

This plain stone monument, under a simple cross, marks the place where David Livingstone's heart was buried in 1873. He died from dysentery and malaria in the village of Chitambo, where his followers removed his heart and internal organs, and buried them under a mupundu tree which stood where this monument now stands.

In an amazing tribute, his two closest followers, Susi and Chuma, salted and dried his body before carrying it over 1,000 miles to Bagamoyo (now on Tanzania's coast). This journey took them about nine months. From there they took Livingstone by ship to London, and he was finally buried with full honours in Westminster Abbey on April 18 1874.

In 1899, after fears that the mupundu tree was diseased, it was cut down and a section of its trunk which had been engraved with Livingstone's name, and the names of three of his party, was shipped to the Royal Geographical Society in London. There it remains to this day. The village has since moved, but a memorial now stands to mark the spot where Livingstone's heart was buried.

The present Chief Chitambo, Freddy Chisenga, is the great grandson of the Chief who received Livingstone, and he will now guide visitors from his home in Chalilo village to the memorial at Chipundu. He is also involved with the community's participation in the Kasanka National Park.

You should stop at the clinic on the way to the memorial to sign the visitor's book, where you must pay an entry fee of Kw150 per person.

Getting there

The monument is clearly marked on most maps. The easiest route is to take the "Chinese" road from Serenje to Mansa, then turn right about 10km after the entrance to Kasanka National Park. This is about 65km after you turned off the Great North Road. The memorial is clearly signposted down a left turning, about 8km later.

NAMES

Judi Helmholz

During your travels you may have the good fortune to meet a Wireless, a Handbrake or an Engine. If you are really lucky, you may encounter a Cabbage. These are names of people I have met in Zambia.

Looking for Fame and Fortune? Look no futher than twin boys living in the Western Province. Beware of Tempation though, he is a money-changer known for calculating exchanges solely to his advantage.

Working with Sunday and Friday got rather amusing, "Sunday, can you work on Saturday with Friday?" Working with Trouble was another matter entirely, as we had to frequently enquire, "Where can I find Trouble?" Gift, true to his namesake, felt compelled to ask for one, while Lunch took on a whole new meaning and Clever is a friend who is true to his name.

Unusual names aren't limited solely to English. For example, there is Mwana Uta which literally means "son of a gun", and Saka Tutu meaning "father of an insect". Pity the local man named Mwana Ngombe or "child of a cow".

Kundalila (Nkundalila) Falls

Kundalila means "cooing dove," and this is one of Zambia's most beautiful waterfalls, set in an area of scenic meadows and forests on the edge of the Muchinga escarpment. The clear stream drops 65m into a crystal pool below, and makes a great place for a picnic and a cooling dip. Look out for blue monkeys which are said to inhabit the forests here.

Note that the falls are in an area of military sensitivity, where camping has not been allowed in the past. Because of this, make sure that the caretaker is clear about how much this costs. Pay in advance, and obtain a full receipt, as misunderstandings are often said to arise here.

Rates: entry Kw150/camping Kw500 – per person per day/night

Getting there

Drive to Kanona on the Great North Road, about 10km from the turn-off to Mansa, and 180km southwest of Mpika. A track turning southeast is clearly signposted as "Kundalila Falls National Monument", so follow this for about 13km (15 minutes) to a grassy car park and campsite. You should sign in with the caretaker before you enter. At the bottom of the site there is an old bridge across the Kaombe River. The path then splits and the right branch leads you to the top of the gorge – with no safety fences. The left takes you to the bottom, where there's a beautiful pool for swimming, if you can bear the water's chill.

Lwitikila Falls

This small waterfall is a good place for a dip and lunch, though don't expect to have it all to yourself as it lies in a local community area.

Getting there

Take the road to Chinsali and Isoka from Mpika for about 15km, until you see a right turn signed to the Lwitikila Girls Secondary School. Continue along this track, which bends round slowly to the left and then goes uphill, before you see some houses on the right. In front of the first house is a smaller track goes off to the right – this leads directly to the falls.

Chipoma Falls

The Lubu River drops 40m over a distance of 500m at this large set of rapids, southwest of Chinsali.

Getting there

Turn northwest off the Great North Road about 144km northeast of Mpika, and 27km southwest of the Chinsali turn-off. Follow this road for around 6km, taking left turns at all the forks and junctions, until you reach the caretaker's house by the falls.

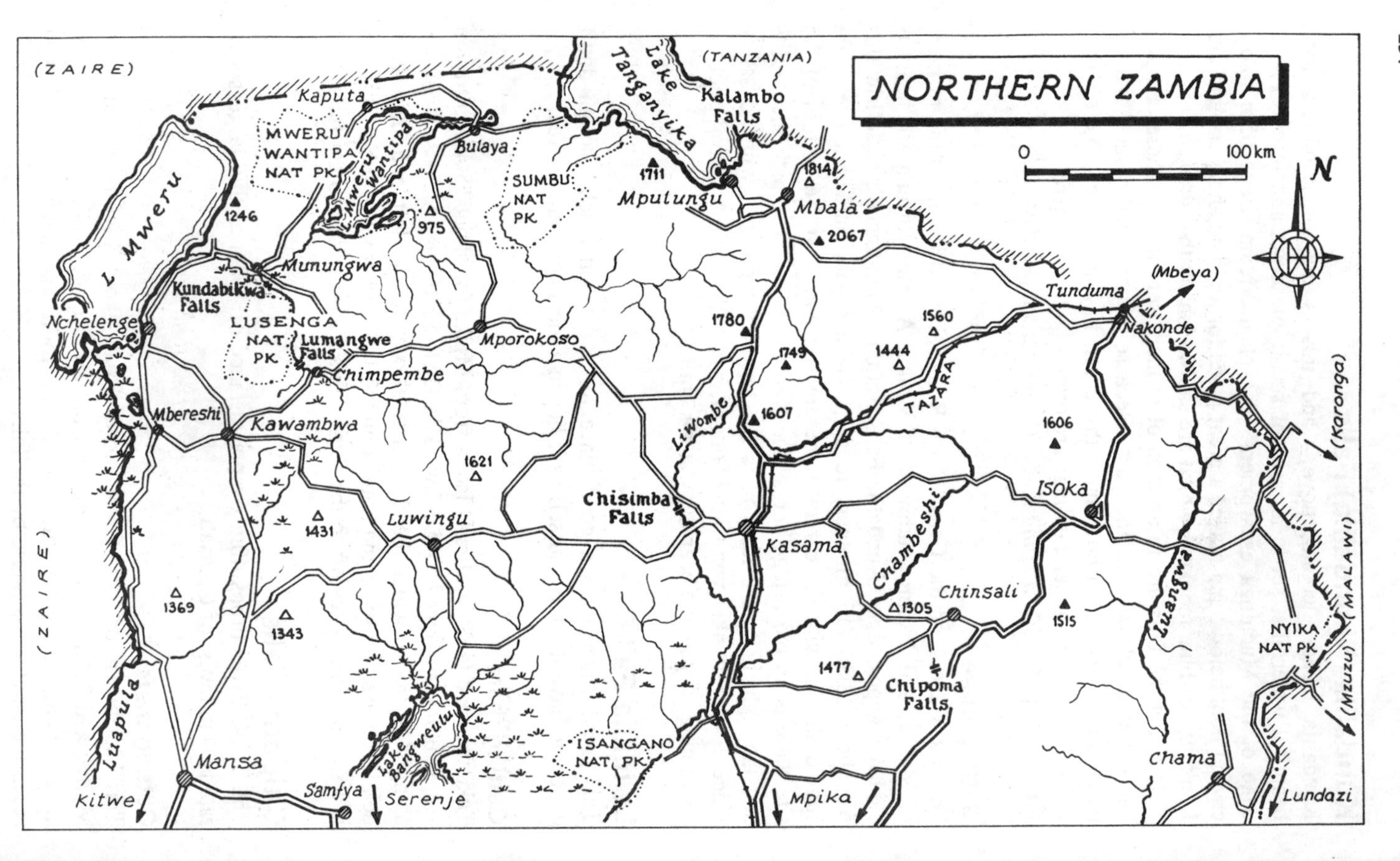
NORTHERN ZAMBIA
0
100 km
N
(TANZANIA)
(ZAIRE)
(ZAIRE)
(MALAWI)
(Karonga)
(Mbeya)
(Mzuzu)
Lake Tanganyika
Kalambo Falls
Mpulungu
Mbala
Tunduma
Nakonde
Isoka
Chinsali
Chipoma Falls
Chama
Lundazi
NYIKA NAT PK
Luangwa
Chambeshi
TAZARA
Kasama
Mpika
Liwombe
Chisimba Falls
Mporokoso
SUMBU NAT PK
Bulaya
Kaputa
L. Mweru Wantipa
MWERU WANTIPA NAT PK
Mununga
Chimpembe
Lumangwe Falls
LUSENGA NAT PK
Kundabikwa Falls
Kawambwa
Mbereshi
Nchelenge
L. Mweru
Luwingu
Lake Bangweulu
ISANGANO NAT PK
Samfya
Serenje
Mansa
Kitwe
Luapula
2067
1814
1711
1560
1444
1749
1607
1780
1606
1515
1305
1477
1621
975
1431
1343
1369
1246

Chapter Fourteen

Northern Zambia

To explore Northern Zambia properly, and to visit the national parks here, requires a small expedition. The area's three main national parks have all suffered from neglect. They are not prepared for visitors, and an almost total lack of roads or facilities does not make for easy travelling. Years of poaching have reduced the populations of game animals within them, and what animals are left remain shy and understandably wary of mankind.

The biggest attractions in the region are the Nyika Plateau and Lake Tanganyika. Nyika is mainly in Malawi, and its wildlife has been well conserved. Most of its animals are non-threatening, and so it is a superb place for hiking.

Tanganyika is one of the largest lakes in East Africa's Great Rift Valley, and a gateway to Tanzania and Burundi. It also has a rich aquatic life found nowhere else, and several small lodges are being established on its shores to attract visitors to stay for a few days. The snorkelling and fishing are good, and it's a pleasant place to relax.

KASAMA

Kasama is centrally located, and visitors to northern Zambia will invariably end up spending some time here – even is only to refuel and buy a few soft drinks. It is a busy little town, with lots going on. As it acts as a supply centre for much of the north of the country, there are some well-stocked stores, and a relatively large amount of traffic coming into, and leaving, town.

Getting there

By train

The TAZARA station is a few kilometres from the centre of town, on the right as you enter from Mpika. This is your last chance to disembark at a major town before the railroad turns east, and away from Lake Tanganyika.

By bus

The bus services here are generally very good. The post bus reaches here from Lusaka (ask at the post office), as do numerous normal buses, and there are good links with Luwingu, Mbala and Mpulungu – though hitching may be faster than taking a bus if you're heading for the lake.

Hitchhiking

Kasama is a good place for hitching. If you want to go north, to Mbala or Mpulungu, walk on past the Zambia National Commercial Bank and the BP garage, to beyond the roundabout and start hitching – there is a convenient lay-by.

If you're heading south towards Mpika then you need to walk out past the Chibuku Distribution Centre, or perhaps a little further, hitching as you walk.

Heading eastwards is more difficult, as there is less traffic. That said, a traveller going in that direction is something of a rarity, so novelty value will encourage potential lifts. Most drivers will not have a clue where you're heading for.

Where to stay

There isn't much choice here. Try the Modern Kwacha Relax Hotel, PO Box 410053, tel: 221124.

Where to eat

For a bite to eat there are lots of small cafes – the J. J. Restaurant set back from the main crossroads serves typical nshima and chicken/meat/fish, and it is very basic, but friendly.

On the Mpika side of the crossroads is the Starlight Shop which is one of the town's best for supplies. You can sit down for a Coke, and their stock even runs to bottles of imported (South African) wine.

Chisimba Falls

These falls partially run an unobtrusive hydro-electric station, but the water that is left makes for a pleasant waterfall, and there is a good campsite nearby.

Getting there

Turn off the main road to Kasama, and head west towards Luwingu for about 19km, before taking a right turn on to the road to Mporokoso. About 5km later a sign directs you off the road to the power station – down a small track leading left and down to the camp site.

MBALA

This is a small town just off the road from Kasama to Mpulungu. There is a BP station, a few shops, a Standard Chartered Bank amongst others, and a fairly cool, relaxed air. The road to Mpulungu descends into the merciless heat of the rift valley beyond here – so enjoy the relative cool whilst you can.

Mbala is notable for the Moto Moto museum, described below, which is one of the country's best museums and well worth stopping for.

Where to stay

There are two options here. The New Grasshopper Inn (which used to be merely the Grasshopper Inn) has 14 rooms, and can be contacted at PO Box 93, tel: 04 291.

The alternative is the Arms Hotel (tel: 450585) which has 10 rooms. This used to be called the Abercorn Arms, but changed when the town changed its name from Abercorn to Mbala.

Moto Moto Museum

This museum opened in 1974 and has an excellent reputation as perhaps the best place in the country for Bemba history and artefacts. It was originally assembled by a missionary stationed here, Father Corbell, who amassed a very extensive collection of tools, craft instruments, and exhibits connected to traditional ceremonies and witchcraft. These have been housed with the help of some aid money, and the museum is now well signposted and well known to the locals.

Opens: 09.00 to 16.45 Mon-Fri

MPULUNGU

Sitting in the heat of the rift valley, about 40km from Mbala, Mpulungu is Zambia's largest port. It's a busy place and visited by many travellers, most of whom are Africans but with the odd backpacker mixed in too. The atmosphere is very international, a mix of various Southern, Central and East African influences all stirred together by the ferries which circle the lake from port to port.

There is a strong local fishing community, and a small but thriving business community complete with a small contingent of white African, expat and even aid workers. Mpulungu's runway is, apparently, capable of taking international jets, though permission has yet to be obtained to enable this to happen. So though Mpulungu might seem like the end of the earth when you get off a bus in the pitch-black, it isn't.

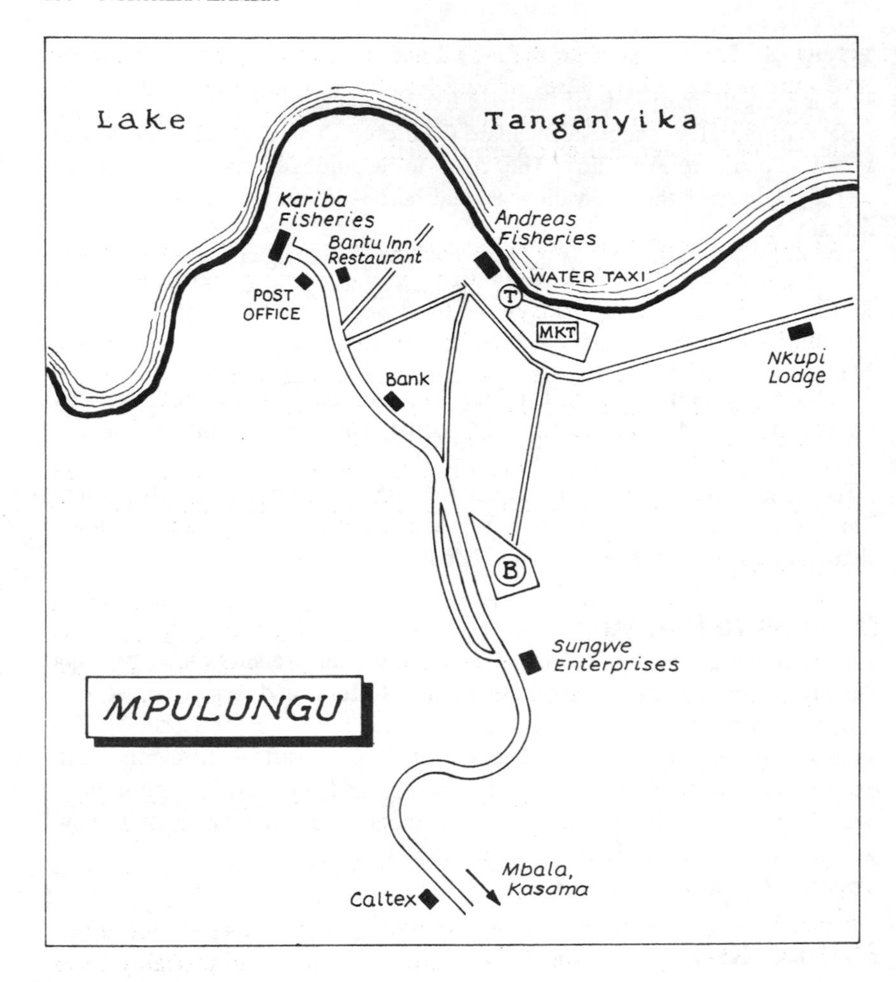

Getting there

By bus

As Mpulungu is the end of the route, most of the buses from Mbala tend to arrive in the afternoon and evening, and those departing tend to leave in the morning. The "terminus" is the main road, beside the market area – you cannot fail to go through it.

Hitchhiking

Hitching here from Mbala in the afternoon is very easy, with lots of lifts. However, getting out again in the morning is virtually impossible. Everybody who has a little space in their vehicle goes to the area for buses and fills up with paying passengers, so few are at all interested in a stray hitchhiker walking away from the main station. So, if you want to get out of here then go with the crowd and hang around the main market area quizzing any likely buses or vehicles. Because of the steep, twisting road out of the valley, heavy or under-powered vehicles can be painfully slow, so get a lighter, more powerful vehicle if you can.

By ferry

There are two large international Tanganyika ferries each of which calls at Mpulungu once every week. Both arrive in the morning and leave in the afternoon: the *Liemba* on Fridays and the *Mongosa* on Mondays.

From Mpulungu they sail over the Tanzanian border to Kasanga, then to Kigoma in the north of Tanzania, and then on to Burundi. (This last stop was omitted whilst the country was in turmoil.) The ferries stop at countless places in between these more major ports.

First class is comfortable with videos for entertainment and meals of rice and fish or chicken, while second class is considerably more basic.

By boat-taxi

If you need a short trip out to one of the lodges on the lake then hire a boat-taxi from the beach-side market, next to Andreas Fisheries Ltd. You will need to make sure that the driver knows the lodge that you want, and exactly where it is, and you may want to bargain over the rate a little.

Where to stay

There are several options if you are staying to relax and snorkel by the lakeside, though few of these are particularly cheap. If you are just passing through, or have arrived late in the afternoon or evening and need a basic place to sleep, then go for Nkupi Lodge.

If you want to stay longer then you need to organise transport out to one of the lake-side lodges, in which case your first call should probably be to Mrs Neilson, who runs the Caltex petrol station. This is on your left about 1km before you reach the main bus station/market area of town. She has radio contact with most of the lodges, and will advise you on where is open and how to get there. Bear in mind that these lodges are new to tourism, and so details of their operations and services are very likely to change before you read this.

Nkupi Lodge This relaxed backpackers' retreat has become something of a legend with overlanders, largely because of its total lack of competition in Mpulungu and its laid-back owner, Denish. There are very basic chalets here and camp-sites. Both showers and toilets are shared and separate. Beer is available, as is scrupulously boiled water, but no food.

To find this either ask one of the locals, or follow the tar road past the main bus/market area. This climbs a hill, so follow one of the paths to your right which goes up and over to Andreas Fisheries Ltd and the beach-side market on the other

side. Then turn right and follow the road, keeping the sea reasonably close to you on your left. You'll find Denish's place on your right in a few hundred yards, surrounded by a good fence.
Rates: Camping is Kw2,000 per night. A bed with a mosquito net in a basic curtained chalet costs Kw4,000

Lake Tanganyika Lodge Reached by a short boat-taxi ride, this is a basic lodge on the lake aimed at backpackers where you can swim and snorkel. There are chalets for around Kw10,000 per person, though it is possible to camp for only about Kw250 per day. Breakfast costs Kw2,500, lunch is Kw3,500 and dinner is around Kw5,000.

Kalambo Lodge *(6 twin chalets)*
PO Box 34065, Lusaka. Tel: 061 235382, fax: 235381
Run by Toby Veall, and often referred to simply as Toby's Lodge, this is Zambia's first upmarket lodge on the lake and it is still in the experimental stages. It started as Toby's base for catching aquarium fish for export, and that is still what finances it. He is gradually developing six twin-bed thatch-on-stone chalets, each with its own flush toilet, shower and solar-powered lighting.

The main activities here are fishing and snorkelling, and the under-water visibility in the lodge's area is excellent, with a good variety of fish-life and some steep drop-offs underwater. Hence, scuba diving is planned, and walks from the lodge to the Kalambo Falls (about 90 minutes away) are also popular.

The lodge is about 16km from Mpulungu, close to the Kalambo River, and is reached by a short boat transfer or water-taxi. Toby is in frequent contact with Mrs Neilson at the Caltex station, so check with her first if you want to go there.
Rates: around US$100 per person per night

LAKE TANGANYIKA

Lake Tanganyika is one of a series of geologically old lakes that have filled areas of the main East African Rift Valley. Look at a map of the continent and you will see many of these in a "string" down the continent: Lakes Malawi, Tanganyika, Kivu, Edward and Albert are some of the larger ones. Zambia just has a small tip of Tanganyika within its borders, but it is of some importance to the country. Access to Tanganyika grants Zambia a real port with transport links to a whole side of Tanzania and direct access to Burundi.

It also makes this one corner of Zambia totally different from the rest of the country, with a mix of peoples and a "tropical Central Africa" feel. There are also a few lake-side lodges if you need to relax, though these cater for very few visitors at the moment.

Geography

Lake Tanganyika is the deepest of the Rift Valley Lakes of Central/East Africa, with a maximum depth of about 1,470m. It has an area of around 34,000km^2 and is estimated to be about 10 to 15 million years old. The surface layers of water are a tropical 24°C to 28°C and support virtually all of the known life in the lake.

Well below these, where it is too deep for the sun's light to reach, are separate, colder waters. Below about 200m, these are deprived of oxygen and hardly mix with the upper layers. They are currently the subject of much scientific study.

The lake has a variety of habitats around its 3,000km-or-so of shoreline, ranging from flat sands to marshy areas and boulder-strewn shores. Most of the fish species live within about 30m of the surface – where the water is generally very clean and clear, with a visibility of up to 20m in places.

Flora and fauna

The geology of the rocks around the lake has led to the water being unusually hard (between 7° and 11° dH), alkaline (average 8.4 pH) and rich in minerals for a freshwater lake. It is not an ideal environment for normal aquatic plants, and so these are generally found near the entry of rivers into the lake but not elsewhere. Various species of algae have adapted to fill this ecological niche, and extensive "lawns" of grass-like algae cover many of the lake's submerged rocks.

Animals

The water's excellent clarity, the lack of cover and the rocky shores do not encourage either hippo or crocodile. However they are occasionally seen, especially near mouths of rivers. The lake is a reliable source of water for the game, which often come to drink during the dry season.

Birds

The birdlife on the shoreline is generally good, though will seldom match the variety to be seen around one of the big tropical rivers – Zambezi, Luangwa or Kafue, for example. The species found there also tend to represent many more of the typical East African birds than can be found elsewhere in Zambia.

Fish

Lake Tanganyika, and the other lakes in the rift valley, continue to fascinate both zoologists and aquarists as they have evolved their own endemic species of fish. So far, just under 200 have been identified in Tanganyika, mostly from the *Cichlidae* family – cichlids (pronounced sick-lids) as they are known. Many of these are small, colourful fish which live close to the surface and the shoreline. Here they inhabit crevices in the rocks and other natural cavities, avoiding the attention of larger, predatory fishes which patrol the deeper, more open, waters.

These are generally easy to keep in home aquaria being small, colourful, and fairly undemanding; several operations have sprung up in recent years to catch specimens for the pet trade, and fly them out to Europe and America. One or two of the lake's lodges make their living out of this, and tourism is just an emerging side-line for them.

For anglers, who will find most of the cichlids too small to be of interest, the lake is the furthest south that the goliath tigerfish or Nile perch can be found, and an excellent place for the *nkupi* which are the largest cichlids in the world. All are eagerly sought by fishermen, with the best time for fishing between November and March. This is taken very seriously as Nile perch can reach an impressive 80kg in weight.

Safety in Lake Tanganyika

Tanganyika is a marvellous lake in which to go snorkelling, or even scuba diving, as the numerous fish are beautifully coloured and there is seldom any need to dive deeply. That said, you must be aware of the risks – mainly from bilharzia (see page 68), but also from crocodiles and hippos. Both can be very localised, with one bay noted for bilharzia, and the next bay being disease-free but with the odd crocodile. There is also an endemic fish-eating snake, the Tanganyika cobra, which usually avoids swimmers like terrestrial snakes avoid walkers... but watch out for them anyhow.

The locals obviously know the area, so if you are considering taking a swim then ask their advice about the precise place that you have in mind. They may not be infallible, but will give you a good idea of where is likely to be safe, and where is not.

KALAMBO FALLS

The Kalambo River, for a short distance, marks the boundary between Zambia and Tanzania. At the Kalambo Falls, it ceases to flow on the plateau and plunges over the side of the Great Rift Valley in one vertical drop of about 221m. This is the second highest waterfall in Africa, about double the height of the Victoria Falls, and the twelfth highest in the world.

On either side of the falls there are sheer rock walls, and a large colony of marabou storks breed in the cliffs during the dry season. The falls themselves will be at their most spectacular towards the end of the wet season, in February or March, though are worth visiting in any month.

Rates: entry Kw150/camping Kw500 – per person per day/night

Archaeology

Though few visitors realise it, the Kalambo Falls are also one of the most important archaeological sites in Southern Africa. Just above the falls, by the side of the river, is a site that appears to have been occupied throughout much of the Stone Age and Early Iron Age. The earliest tools discovered there may be over 100,000 years old, a semi-circle of stones suggests some form of wind-break, and three hollows lined with grass were probably where the inhabitants slept.

It seems that the earlier sites of occupation were regularly flooded by the river, and each time this deposited a fine layer of sand – thus preserving each layer of remains, tools and artefacts in a neat chronological sequence. Much later, the river cut into these original layers of sand and revealed the full sequence of human occupation to modern archaeologists.

Kalambo's main claim to fame is that the earliest evidence of fire in sub-Saharan Africa was found here – charred logs, ash and charcoal have been discovered amongst the lowest levels of remains. This was a tremendously important step for stone-age man as it enabled him to keep warm and cook food, as well as use fire to scare off aggressive animals. Burning areas of grass may even have helped him to hunt.

The site is also noted for evidence of much later settlement, from the early Iron Age. Archaeologists even speak of a "Kalambo tradition" of pottery, for which they can find evidence in various sites in Northern Zambia. The Kalambo site is unusual, and thus important, because it is a place which has had a number of settlements throughout the centuries. Thus the remains of each can be found on top of the last, and a reliable time-scale can easily be established.

It seems that the early Iron Age farmers displaced the area's Stone-Age people around the 8th century BC: no further Stone-Age remains are found after that date. After that there is evidence of at least four different Iron-Age settlements between the 5th and 11th centuries AD.

Getting there

By boat-taxi

The river's mouth is around 17km from Mpulungu, so adventurous backpackers get private water-taxis to boat them upstream to near the base of the falls, and often ask to be collected the following day. From there it is a strenuous climb to the top of the falls, where camping is allowed. You will need to bring all your own food and equipment.

Alternatively, small boats which ply between Mpulungu and Kasanga, in Tanzania, may drop you off one day, and pick you up on the next.

Driving
To get to Kalambo take the road to Zombe and the Tanzanian border from Mbala, then a few kilometres out of town the falls are clearly signposted to your left. The falls are about 33km from Mbala, and this track deteriorates towards the end. Because of Kalambo's border position, policing it is difficult. Vehicles left unattended are likely targets for theft, so consider taking extra safety precautions, like having someone with you to look after the vehicle.

SUMBU NATIONAL PARK
Sumbu National Park covers about 2,020km², and borders on Lake Tanganyika. It protects (to some extent) remnant populations of elephant, buffalo, and a range of antelope including blue and yellow-backed duiker, Lichtenstein's hartebeest, roan, sable, waterbuck and a good number of puku. The main natural predators are lion and leopard, though poachers continue to have more effect on the game populations than either.

In the lake itself, there are plenty of hippos and a very healthy population of crocodile. Some are sufficiently large to dissuade you from even thinking of dipping your toe in the lake. Game viewing is limited by the lack of a good road network in the park.

Getting there
By air
There is an airstrip at Kasaba Bay, which used to be regularly visited by Zambia Airways. The failure of the airline was probably the catalyst for the final decline of the lodges.

Driving
The easiest approach to the park is from Mporokoso, from where you head north. This road continues roughly northwest, and then northeast, passing close to the eastern shores of Lake Mweru Wantipa, before taking a right turn, to go southeast, at Bulaya. From there the track enters the park, deteriorates, and continues to Nkamba Bay and Kasaba Bay. There is just one "road" in the park. The Lufubu River, which marks the park's south-eastern boundary, prevents any access to this directly from Mbala.

Camps and lodges
There are two lodges in the park, Nkamba Bay and Kasaba Bay. Both were government-run, and both were in terminal decline in the mid-1990s: expensive, and very poorly maintained. Eventually they were put up for tender in late 1995, and their position at the moment remains very uncertain. The most recent news suggested that the tender for Nkamba

Bay had been won by a group connected with a hunting concession area in the Luangwa valley – which, if true, is probably not good news for the conservation of the area. By the time that you read this there may have been more positive developments.

What to see and do

Fishing was really the main reason for coming to Sumbu, although some game did come to the lake-shore in the dry season to drink. The road is not extensive enough to make for good game-viewing, and neither is the remaining population of animals.

MWERU WANTIPA NATIONAL PARK

This is another large tract (3,134km²) of Zambia which was once a thriving national park. It was renowned for having large elephant and crocodile populations. Now poaching has much reduced these, though reports suggest that some big game remains – perhaps including a strong population of buffalo. The lake shores are said to be dense papyrus beds, and claims are even made that sitatunga can be found here.

Getting there

There are no passable roads in the wet season, and any dry-season trip there will need the back-up of a small expedition. Approach via Nchelenge and then north to the Kaputa/Chiengi area, where there is a track east into the park.

LUSENGA PLAIN NATIONAL PARK

Again, Lusenga Plain was a good idea for a national park, but without enough support it is now a park in name only. Poaching has reduced the game considerably, and with no internal roads in the park, there are few reasons to visit. Lusenga Plain was originally designated as a park to protect a large open plain, fringed by swamp and dry evergreen forest and surrounded by ridges of hills.

On its northeastern side the park is bordered by the Kalungwishi River, on which three beautiful waterfalls can be found: Kundabikwa, Kabweluma and Lumangwe Falls. Two of these are relatively easy to visit – see below for directions.

Getting there

Recent visitors have had success in reaching the park by getting the assistance of a game scout for a guide from the National Parks and Wildlife Office in Kawambwa. Otherwise the park is hard to find. It is usually approached from the Kawambwa-Mporokoso road, and you should be very well equipped for any attempt to reach it.

Kundabikwa Falls

To reach these take the Mporokoso road for about 65km towards Kawambwa, before taking the main turning off to the northwest, towards Mununga. About 42km after the turning is a track off to the left, which leads down to the falls.

Lumangwe Falls

These are reached directly from the Mporokoso-Kawambwa road. At Chimpembe there is a pontoon across the river, and a few kilometres east there is a track heading northwest, following the direction of the Kalungwishi. After about 14km you reach the falls and it is possible to camp here.

If you have the energy to walk downstream from here for three or four kilometres then you will reach the third set of falls, the Kabweluma Falls. Before arriving at Lumangwe you must sign in, so get advice about the best route to take from the guard on the gate.

NCHELENGE

This is a small town near the shores of Lake Mweru, which is the base for a thrice-weekly ferry service out to the two populated islands in the lake: Kilwa and Isokwe.

There are two places to stay here. The Lake Mweru Water Transport Guest House (tel: 02 97201) is down by the waterfront and its clean rooms have en suite facilities. No meals are provided, so look to eat out at one of the cafés – nshima and fish is the normal dish. The nearby Nchelenge Resthouse (tel: 02 972045) is a slightly less attractive alternative, run by the Nchelenge District Council.

SIGN OF THE TIMES

Judi Helmholz

When it comes to creativity and marketing, Zambian entrepreneurs are unsurpassed. Take the "Just Imagine Grocery Store & Bottle Shop". Unfortunately customers often have to do just that, as there are often no groceries or bottles to be found there. Similarly, the "Good Neighbour Grocery Store & Bottle Shop" doesn't always live up to its name, as its assistants are no strangers to price disputes.

Catchy slogans like "We Admit We Are The Best" or "Choice Restaurant - For All Your Super Feeding Requirements" adorn stores and shop fronts. "No Sweat, No Sweet", the Zambian equivalent of "no work - no reward", appears to be popular for everything from roadside stalls to school mottos to butchers' shops.

NYIKA PLATEAU NATIONAL PARK

With thanks to Philip Briggs

Nyika Plateau is a marvellous area for hiking, and has some unusual wildlife. It lies mostly in Malawi, with just a slim Zambian National Park hugging the border, and is best approached from the Malawian side. For this reason, below is a description of the plateau as a whole, and how to see it, including directions within Malawi.

Geography

Nyika Plateau National Park is a tiny Zambian national park of only 80km². However, it adjoins Malawi's Nyika National Park, which is the country's largest national park. This was established in 1965 and extended to its present size of 3,134km² in 1978. At the heart of both parks lies the gently undulating Nyika Plateau, which averages over 2,000m in altitude.

In addition to the main plateau, the Malawian National Park also protects part of the eastern slopes of the Nyika range, where grassland and forest are replaced by thick brachystegia woodland.

Flora and fauna

Nyika is notable for its wonderful montane scenery, and as being an ideal hiking destination. The lower slopes harbour brachystegia woodland, which is replaced by more open grassland at the higher altitudes.

Of particular interest to botanists are the roughly 200 orchid species recorded in the park, of which 11 species are endemic to Nyika.

Mammals

Nyika protects a rich diversity of mammals – almost 100 species have been recorded – including an endemic race of Burchell's zebra, *Equus burchelli crawshayi*, and a very high density of leopard.

Game viewing is good all year round, and the open nature of the plateau ensures excellent visibility. In the area around Chilinda, the main camp, visitors are practically guaranteed to see roan antelope, scrub hare, Burchell's zebra, reedbuck, bushbuck and (in the rainy season only) eland. Your chances of seeing leopard around Chilinda are excellent.

The lower slopes of brachystegia woodland support good populations of buffalo and elephant, though these animals only rarely move up to the grassland of the plateau. Lion and cheetah are also infrequent visitors to the plateau.

Birds

With well over 400 species recorded, Nyika supports a great diversity of birdlife. However, this figure is rather deceptive as many of the species included on the checklist are found only in the inaccessible brachystegia woodland of the lower slopes, and are thus unlikely to be seen by visitors who stick to the plateau.

Nevertheless, the grassland around Chilinda Camp is inhabited by several tantalising birds. Foremost are the wattled crane, Denham's bustard and the exquisite scarlet-tufted malachite sunbird (distinguished from the commoner malachite sunbird by its much longer tail). More rewarding than the grassland for general birding are the forests, particularly the large Chowo forest near the Zambian Resthouse, where localised species such as Sharpe's akalat, bar-tailed trogon, olive-flanked robin, white-breasted alethe and a variety of other robins and bulbuls may be seen.

Four birds found at Nyika (yellow mountain warbler, churring cisticola, crackling cloud cisticola and mountain marsh widow) have been recorded nowhere else in Malawi, while the Nyika races of red-winged francolin, rufous-naped lark, greater double-collared sunbird and Baglafecht weaver are all endemic to the plateau. There are also three butterfly species endemic to the plateau, and one species each of chameleon, frog and toad which are found nowhere else.

The rivers and dams on the Nyika Plateau are stocked with rainbow trout, and are thus popular with anglers.

An entrance fee of US$5 per person per day is charged for visiting the Malawian side of Nyika.

Getting there and away

Coming from Malawi, Chilinda Camp lies roughly 120km from Rumphi, and is reached along roads which shouldn't present any problem to a 2WD in the dry season but which may require a 4x4 vehicle after heavy rains. The route is clearly signposted: from Rumphi you need to follow the S85 westwards for roughly 60km, then turn right into the S10 to Chitipa. Thazima Entrance Gate is 8km along the S10. About 30km past the entrance gate, a signposted left turn-off leads to the Zambian Resthouse, which lies about 2km from the S10. Perhaps 500m further towards Chitipa, you'll see the turn-off to the right signposted for Chilinda Camp. Chilinda lies about 30km from this turn-off.

The best place to stock up on food before you reach Nyika is Mzuzu, and the last place where you can buy fuel is Rumphi. The drive between Lilongwe and Nyika cannot be done in a day during the rains, and it's a long slog even in the dry season.

There is no public transport all the way through to Chilinda. In the dry season, a daily bus between Rumphi and Chitipa can drop you at the turn-off to the Zambian Resthouse or else at the turn-off towards Chilinda Camp. This means that, unless you plan on staying at the Zambian

Resthouse, you will have either to walk the last 30km to Chilinda - it's reasonably flat - or else try to hitch. In the rainy season there is no bus but you can get easily get a lift from Rumphi along the S85 (ask for a vehicle heading to Katumbi), and then walk the 8km from where you will be dropped to the entrance gate. Provided you have a tent, you are allowed to camp at the entrance gate, though facilities are basic.

Considering the vagaries of public transport, the ideal would be to hitch a lift in Rumphi heading all the way to Chilinda. From various travellers' reports, it seems like your chances of getting a lift the whole way are about 50/50 on any given day. The best days to hitch are Fridays and Saturdays, which is when Malawian residents tend to head to the park (but also when accommodation is most likely to be fully booked - not a problem, of course, if you have a tent).

Another option is to ask the Wildlife Office in Mzuzu (next to the bus station) whether they have any vehicles heading to Chilinda, bearing in mind that such vehicles are infrequent and very often too loaded with park staff for tourists to be offered a lift.

If you really don't have any luck hitching through to Nyika, Vwaza Marsh and its elephants are far more accessible and should offer considerable consolation.

One of the options for backpackers leaving the park is to hike to Livingstonia over two or three days.

Where to stay

Backpackers can pitch a tent at the entrance gate, but there are several more interesting options:

Chilinda Rest Camp This overlooks a small dam encircled by extensive pine plantations. The main camp consists of six double rooms, with semi-private toilets and hot baths, at a cost of US$10 per room. There are also a few single rooms for US$6, but these can be permanently occupied by staff. Alongside the rooms are four private chalets, each of which costs US$20 for up to four people. Guests staying in the rooms can use a communal kitchen (fully equipped, with resident chef) and dining room/lounge, while each of the chalets has a private kitchen and chef. Visitors should bring food with them (there is a shop but it is not reliable). A bar in the main building serves sodas, beer and spirits.
Rates: US$4 per person
Open: all year

Youth hostel/camping site About 2km from the main Chilinda Rest Camp is a camp-site, where you can either rent a standing tent with beds and bedding, or else pitch your own tent. Near the camp-site is the youth hostel, where a bed costs US$3.50 per person.
Rates: US$5 per person for their tents, US$3 per person to use your own
Open: all year

Juniper Forest Lodge The Malawian national nark maintains a rustic cabin on the edge of a juniper forest in the southeast of the park, 43km from Chilinda. Staying in a rustic cabin like this is only practical if you have your own transport. The cabin must be booked as a unit.
Open: all year
Rates: US$3 per person

Zambian Resthouse Robin Pope Safaris
PO Box 320154, Lusaka. Fax: 062 45076, Tlx: ZA 63007
This is the only private accommodation on the Nyika Plateau, and it is run by the excellent South Luangwa operator, Robin Pope Safaris.

This resthouse has four double bedrooms, hot showers, an equipped kitchen with a fridge, a stove and a resident cook. Unlike Chilinda Camp, the Zambian Resthouse is situated near some extensive patches of indigenous forest, and thus it is very popular with birdwatchers. If you arrive at the Zambian Resthouse without a booking, there is a large risk that it will be full, especially over weekends – so book in advance if possible. Contact Robin Pope Safaris (see page 209), or book in Lilongwe, Malawi, through Central African Wilderness Safaris.
Rates: US$4 per person
Open: all year

What to see and do

Nyika National Park has many very scenic spots, archaeological sites, and an extensive network of roads and trails. There are many different hiking and driving options. The following synopsis of major attractions serves as a taster only:

Walks around Chilinda

Plenty of roads radiate from Chilinda Camp, and it would be quite possible to spend four or five days in the area without repeating a walk. A good short walk for visitors with limited time is to the two dams near Chilinda. The road here follows a dambo and the area offers good game viewing (reedbuck and roan antelope), as well as frequent sightings of wattled crane. The round trip covers 8km and takes two hours. The dams offer good trout fishing in season.

Another good short walk (about an hour) is from behind chalet four to the Kasaramba turn-off and then left along Forest Drive through the pine plantation back to Chalet Four. At dusk there is a fair chance of seeing leopards along this walk.

A longer walk is to Lake Kaulime, which lies 8km west of Chilinda. This is the only natural lake on the plateau and is traditionally said to be the home of a serpent which acts as the guardian to Nyika's animals. More certain attractions than legendary serpents are migratory waterfowl (in summer) and large mammals coming to drink.

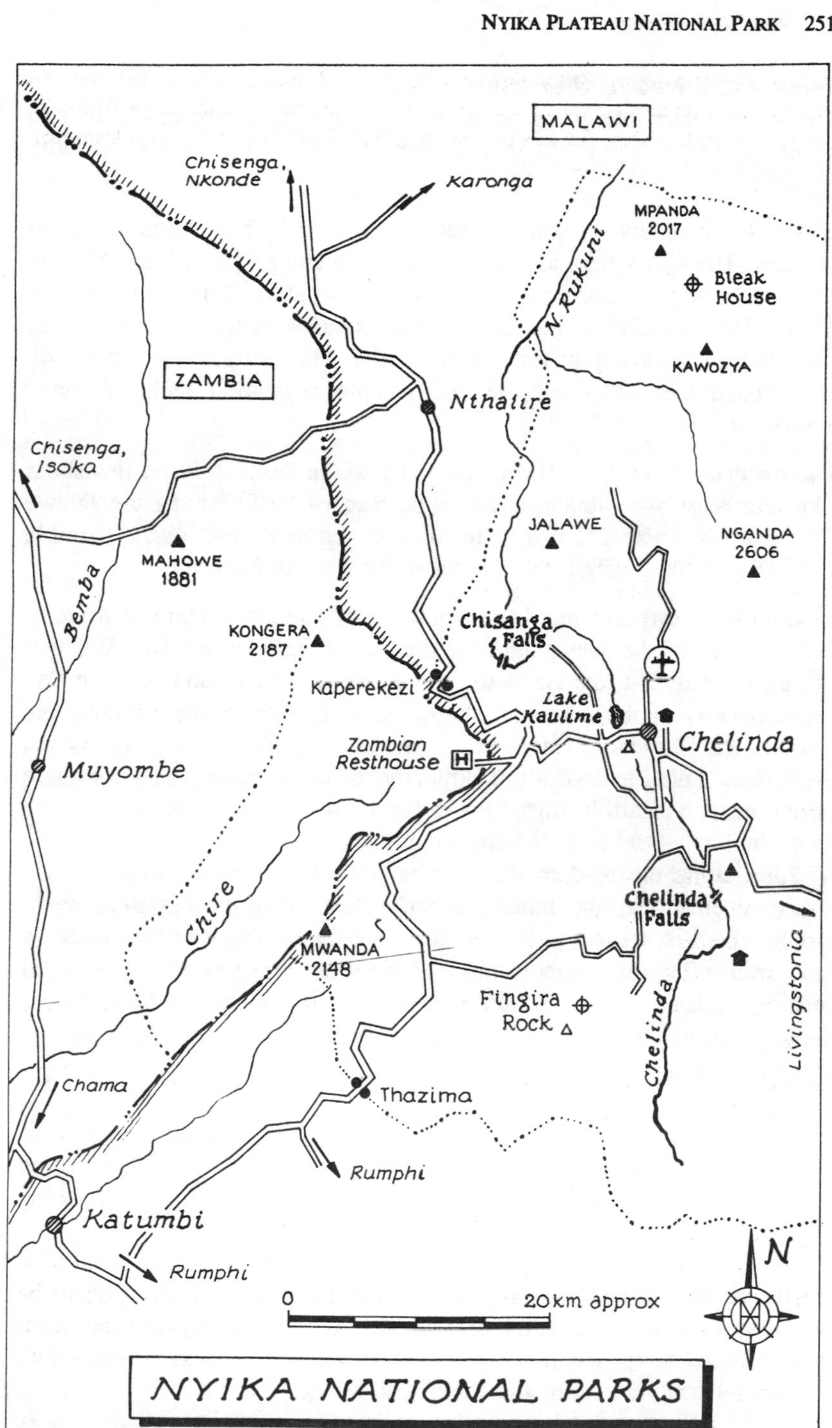
MALAWI
ZAMBIA
Chisenga, Nkonde
Karonga
N. Rukuni
MPANDA 2017
Bleak House
KAWOZYA
Nthalire
Chisenga, Isoka
JALAWE
NGANDA 2606
MAHOWE 1881
Bemba
KONGERA 2187
Chisanga Falls
Kaperekezi
Lake Kaulime
Chelinda
Zambian Resthouse
Muyombe
Chire
Chelinda Falls
MWANDA 2148
Fingira Rock
Chelinda
Livingstonia
Chama
Thazima
Rumphi
Katumbi
Rumphi
N
0
20km approx
NYIKA NATIONAL PARKS

Walks and drives further afield

Many of the more interesting points in Nyika are too far from Chilinda to be reached on a day walk, though they are accessible to visitors with vehicles.

Jalawe Rock is about 1km on foot from a car park 34km north of Chilinda. The views here are spectacular, stretching across Lake Malawi to the mountainous Tanzanian shore. With binoculars, it is often possible to see buffaloes and elephants in the brachystegia woodland of the Mpanda Ridge below. A variety of raptors, as well as klipspringer, are frequently seen around the rock, and the surrounding vegetation includes many proteas.

Nganda Peak is, at 2,605m, the highest peak on the plateau. It lies about 30km northeast of Chilinda, and can be reached by following the Jalawe Rock road for about 25km then turning left on to a 4km long motorable track. It's a 1.5km walk from the end of the track to the peak.

Kasaramba Viewpoint lies 43km southeast of Chilinda. You can drive to within 1.5km of the viewpoint and then walk the final stretch. When it isn't covered in mist, the views to the lake are excellent, and you can also see remnants of the terraced slopes built by the early Livingstonia missionaries. The most extensive rainforest in Nyika lies on the slopes below Kasaramba, and visitors frequently see the localised crowned eagle and mountain buzzard in flight. From Kasaramba, a 3km road leads to the top of the pretty 30m-high Nchenachena Falls.

Further along the road to Kasaramba, also 43km from Chilinda, is a large juniper forest, the most southerly stand of *Juniperus procera* in Africa. There is a rustic cabin on the edge of the forest, from where a short trail offers the opportunity of sighting forest animals such as leopard, elephant shrew, red duiker, bushpig and a variety of forest birds. The forest can also be explored from the firebreaks which surround it.

Zovo Chipola Forest, near the Zambian Resthouse, is of special interest to birdwatchers, and also harbours several mammal species, the most commonly seen of which are bushbuck, blue monkey and elephant shrew. The larger Chowo Forest lies in the Zambian part of the park, and is also easily visited from the Zambian Resthouse. A 4km trail runs through Chowo.

Fingira Rock is a large granite dome lying 22km south of Chilinda. On the eastern side of the rock, a cave 11m deep and 18m long was used as a shelter by humans around 3,000 years ago – excavations in 1965 unearthed a complete human skeleton and a large number of stone tools. Several schematic rock paintings can be seen on the walls of the cave. A reasonable track runs to the base of the rock, 500m from the cave.

The brachystegia woodland around Thazima entrance gate is rich in birds and noted for unusual species. Walking in this area you are also likely to see mammal species which are rare at higher altitudes.

Horseback trails

Horseback day trails can be arranged at the private stables near Chilinda.

Wilderness trails

Six wilderness trails have been designated within Nyika National Park, ranging from one to five nights in duration. Visitors wishing to use these trails must supply their own camping equipment and food, and are required to hike in the company of a National Park guide. Porters can be arranged on request. It is recommended that trails are booked in advance through the National Parks office in Lilongwe. That said, most travellers who use the hiking trail to Livingstonia manage to arrange it at Chilinda without complication.

Of particular interest for wildlife viewing is the four-night Jalawe and Chipome River Trail, which passes through the brachystegia woodland in the northern part of the park and thus offers the opportunity to see elephant, buffalo, greater kudu and a variety of other mammals which are generally absent from the plateau.

The most popular of Nyika's wilderness trails leads from Chilinda all the way to Livingstonia on the Rift Valley escarpment east of the national park. Depending on which route you select, the hike can take between one and four days (though the one-day route is, at 42km, only a realistic option if you're exceptionally fit). Note that it is not permitted to hike this route in reverse, as a guide and park fees cannot be organised at Livingstonia.

Note on guidebooks

If you have the opportunity, buy a copy of Sigrid Anna Johnson's book: *A Visitor's Guide to Nyika National Park, Malawi*. It is often available at the park reception at Chilinda, and is an excellent guide to the plateau. See *Further Reading* for more details. A small booklet containing a detailed map of the Chilinda area is also sold at the park reception for a nominal charge.

The above description of Nyika Plateau has been edited from an original section in the excellent *Guide to Malawi* by Philip Briggs, published by Bradt Publications. If you plan an extended visit to Malawi, then get hold of a copy of this before you travel.

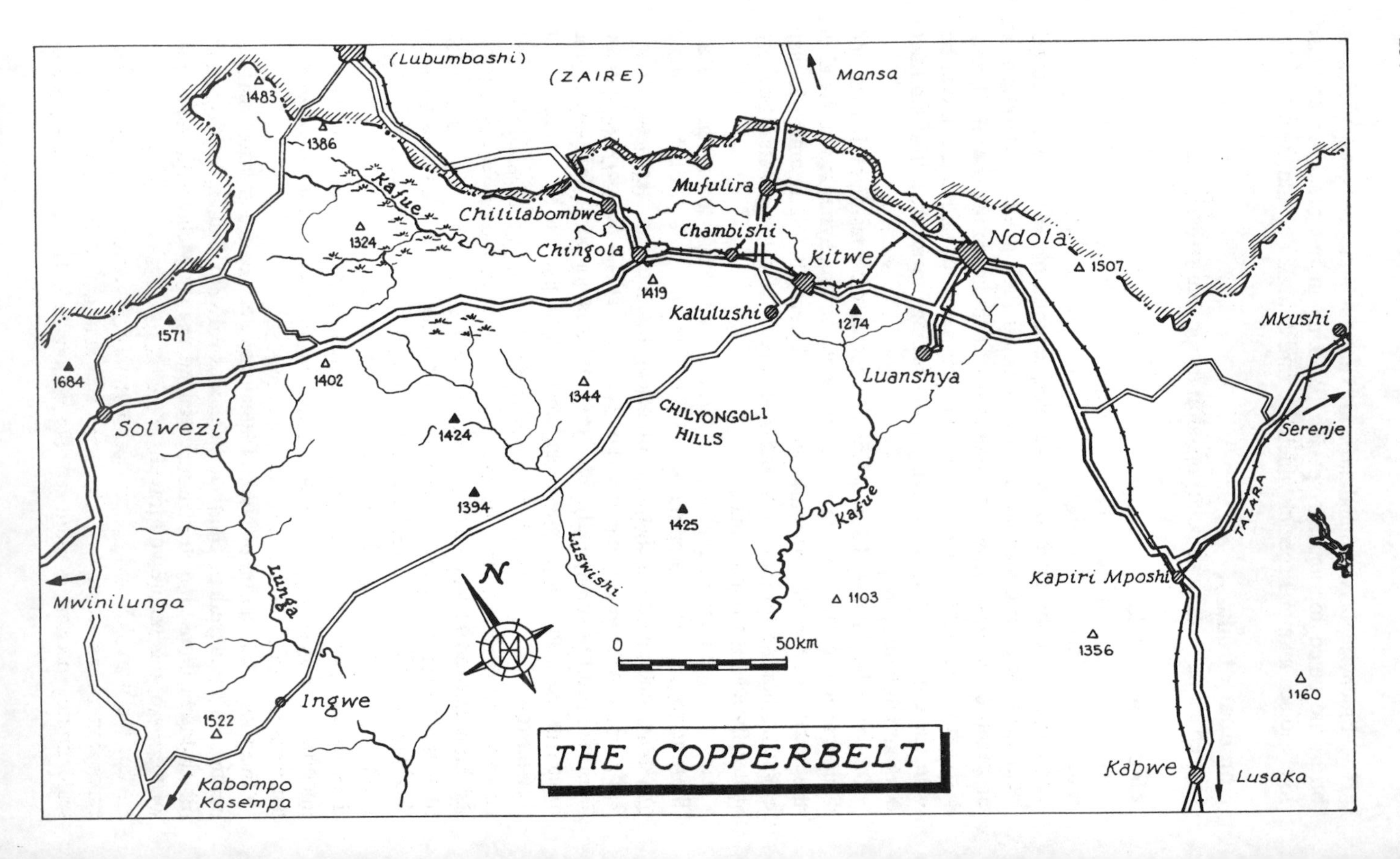
(Lubumbashi)
(ZAIRE)
Mansa
1483
1386
Kafue
Mufulira
Chililabombwe
Chambishi
1324
Chingola
Kitwe
Ndola
1507
1419
Kalulushi
1274
Mkushi
1571
1684
1402
Luanshya
1344
CHILYONGOLI
HILLS
Solwezi
1424
Serenje
1394
TAZARA
1425
Kafue
Luswishi
Lunga
N
Kapiri Mposhi
Mwinilunga
1103
0
50km
1356
1160
Ingwe
1522
THE COPPERBELT
Kabwe
Lusaka
Kabompo
Kasempa

Chapter Fifteen

The Copperbelt

The Copperbelt is Zambia's industrial base, a prosperous area around Ndola, Kitwe and Chingola dotted with mines – the area's production of copper and cobalt are of global importance. The population density here is high, and the environmental impact of so many people can clearly be seen. Despite this, the centres of the Copperbelt's cities are pleasant and not the sprawling industrial wastes that might be expected.

For the normal visitor, these areas have very few attractions and so this chapter is deliberately concise. For simplicity's sake, this text also aims to cover three of the main towns around the Copperbelt – Kabwe and Kapiri Mposhi to the south, and Solwezi to the west – even though these are not strictly part of the Copperbelt.

The history of the copper

Zambia's rich copper deposits have been exploited since around the 6th or 7th century AD. There is evidence that the early Iron-Age inhabitants of Zambia mined, smelted and even traded copper with their neighbours – bracelets and bangles have been found at several sites.

However, large-scale exploitation of these reserves waited until the 20th century. Around the turn of the century, the old sites where native Africans had mined copper for centuries, like Bwana Mkubwa southeast of Ndola, were being examined by European and American prospectors. The demand for metals was stimulated from 1914 to 1918 by World War I, and small mines opened up to satisfy this need. They worked well, but these small-scale productions were only viable whilst the price of the raw materials remained high. Copper, zinc, lead and vanadium were among the most important of the minerals being mined.

Given Zambia's location, and the high costs of transporting any produce out of this land-locked land, it made economic sense to process the mineral ores there, and then export the pure metal ingots. However, this would require considerable investment and large-scale operations.

After the war, demand for copper continued to increase, fuelled by the expansion in the worldwide electrical and automotive industries. Large-scale mining became a more feasible option. In 1922 the British South

Africa Company, who claimed to have bought all of the country's mining concessions in various tribal agreements, started to allocate large prospecting areas for foreign companies. Exploration skills from overseas flowed into the country, locating several large deposits of copper – well beneath the levels of the existing mining operations.

By the early 1930s, four large new mines were coming on stream: Nkana, Nchanga, Roan Antelope and Mufulira. These were to change Northern Rhodesia's economy permanently. Despite a collapse of the prices for copper in 1931, the value of the country's exports increased by 400% between 1930 and 1933 – leaving copper accounting for 90% of the country's exports by value. Thus began the mining industry which still accounts for 20% of Zambia's GDP and 90% of Zambia's export earnings, and employs about 15% of the workforce.

KAPIRI MPOSHI

Kapiri Mposhi's main claim to fame is that it stands at one end of the TAZARA railway. There is a constant flow of people, buses and trucks through town which makes it lively, but not safe. Kapiri is a town which visitors often pass through, but where they seldom linger. Expect people around at all times of the day and night, and be on your guard against opportunist thieves.

Getting there

Kapiri Mposhi is hard to avoid if you're travelling northwards from Lusaka; and its links to the rest of the country are excellent:

By bus

Kapiri Mposhi is very easily reached by bus, as it stands on the main routes between Lusaka and both Northern Zambia and the Copperbelt. There are very frequent arrivals and departures, especially to/from Lusaka and the Copperbelt. If you enter the town travelling north, then the bus terminus is in the centre, on your left behind a variety of market stalls.

By train

If you continue along the road going north, it will soon cross a railway line. Turn right just after this and follow the road for about 1km to reach the bustling and quite imposing TAZARA terminus.

If you did not buy one in Lusaka, then this is the place to buy your ticket to Dar, or to find an easy way to get as far north as Kasama. It gets exceedingly busy around train departure times, and foreigners will encounter considerable hassle. To avoid this, arrive well before the train is due to depart and take great care of your belongings. If you need to buy a ticket, then allow at least an extra hour.

Express trains run all the way to Dar, and leave at 13.00 on Tuesdays and Fridays. Ordinary trains run only to the border – where Nakonde and Tunduma are on opposite sides of the Zambia/Tanzania border. They depart at 17.00 on Mondays, Thursdays and Saturdays. All of these services have an excellent reputation for time-keeping, which is almost unrivalled in Africa. As a guide, the express trains cost:

From Kapiri/US$	1st class	2nd class	3rd class
To Nakonde / Tunduma	23	14	7
To Dar es Salaam	48	29	15

An ordinary train costs only a little less than an express, about US$20 for a first class ticket to Nakonde – instead of US$23 for the express.

Hitchhiking

Alternatively, hitching there is fairly easy. Trying to hitch from within town would be difficult, so walk out a kilometre or so until you find space. Alternatively ask around the truckers in town for a lift. If you are going north, then get a short lift or taxi to take you the 6km to where the road to the Copperbelt proper splits off the Great North Road which continues on up to Mpika and beyond. This is an excellent hitching spot.

Where to stay

There are a few small hotels here, including the **Unity Motel** and the **Kapiri Motel**. All are basic and noisy, and rooms are rented by the hour as well as the night. Kapiri not a town to stay in unless you have to.

Where to eat

There are lots of take-aways, though relatively little fresh food seems to be available at the market. Several stand out by virtue of their names. The **Try Again Restaurant** is surely be an invitation to unhappy customers, whist the **Combahari Steak House and Clinic** is one to watch.

The **Malila Restaurant**, which is on the left if you are travelling north, just after the bus station, is not much of a restaurant but is probably the best shop for food supplies – tins, packets and the like.

If you are driving then look out for the excellent bakery and Coke-shop just to the south of where the roads split, about 5km north of Kapiri. It also sells a good selection of pirate videos and cassette tapes.

KABWE

This pleasant town is situated little more than 60km south of Kapiri Mposhi and about 130km north of Lusaka. It is built on the old colonial model of a perpendicular road-grid central business area, surrounded by pretty, spacious suburbs and with "satellite" townships containing lots of high-density housing for poorer people.

These divisions have now melted a little, but the centre still has pleasantly wide streets lined with a variety of busy-looking shops. The town's economy has always been closely linked with mining, which recently has been for zinc and cobalt. The mine is only about 2km south of the centre. Reports claim that it has recently closed.

History

Kabwe, when under colonial rule, was known as Broken Hill. In 1921 an almost complete human skull was unearthed here during mining operations, at a depth of about 20m. Together with a few other human bones nearby, these are estimated to be over 125,000 years old – making them the oldest human remains which have come to light in Southern/Central Africa to date. Scientists christened the specimen *Homo rhodesiensis,* but it has always been called "Broken Hill Man".

Where to stay

Elephant's Head Hotel (35 rooms)
PO Box 80410, Kabwe. Tel: 222521/2/3
On the corner of Freedom Way and Buntungwa Street, on the southern side of town, this is the town's main hotel. It's not an exciting place to stay, but the rooms are clean, the TVs work, and there's a basic restaurant.
Rates: Kw 50,000 per twin, including breakfast

Hotel Horizon Tel: 223398; fax: 221019
On the corner of Independence Avenue and Buntungwa Street, this is a less impressive than the Elephant's Head Hotel, but also a bit cheaper.
Rates: Kw 35,000 per twin, including breakfast

NDOLA

About 320km north of Lusaka, Ndola is Zambia's second largest city and the heart of the Copperbelt. Considering its strong industrial base, it is a pleasant city with broad, leafy streets and little to indicate its industry apart from a certain air of prosperity.

Getting there

By air

Ndola's airport is on the southern side of the centre of town, and well signposted off to the right as you enter town from the south. It used to be well-served by Air Zambia, and it is now a major hub for the private airlines, with excellent links to Lusaka. A few more distant flights are gradually appearing, to/from places like Mfuwe and Livingstone, but it remains to be seen if these will be economic to maintain. Don't trust anything but the latest airline schedules for the current services.

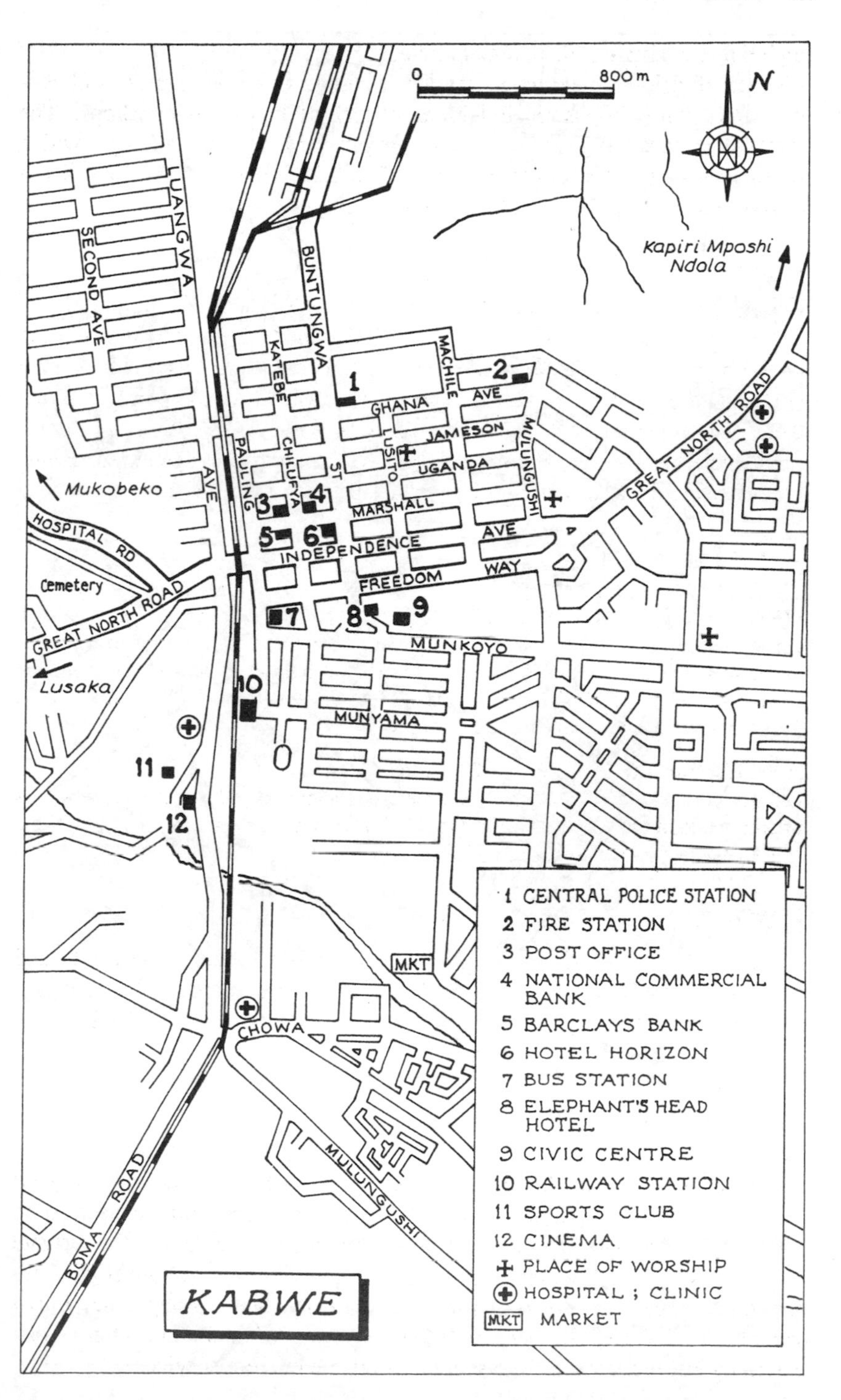
KABWE
0
800m
N
Kapiri Mposhi
Ndola
Mukobeko
Lusaka
LUANGWA
SECOND AVE
BUNTUNGWA
KATEBE
MACHILE
GHANA
AVE
JAMESON
LUSITO
MULUNGUSHI
CHILUFYA
ST
UGANDA
PAULING
AVE
MARSHALL
INDEPENDENCE
AVE
FREEDOM
WAY
GREAT NORTH ROAD
HOSPITAL RD
Cemetery
GREAT NORTH ROAD
MUNKOYO
MUNYAMA
MKT
CHOWA
MULUNGUSHI
BOMA ROAD
1 CENTRAL POLICE STATION
2 FIRE STATION
3 POST OFFICE
4 NATIONAL COMMERCIAL BANK
5 BARCLAYS BANK
6 HOTEL HORIZON
7 BUS STATION
8 ELEPHANT'S HEAD HOTEL
9 CIVIC CENTRE
10 RAILWAY STATION
11 SPORTS CLUB
12 CINEMA
PLACE OF WORSHIP
HOSPITAL ; CLINIC
MKT MARKET

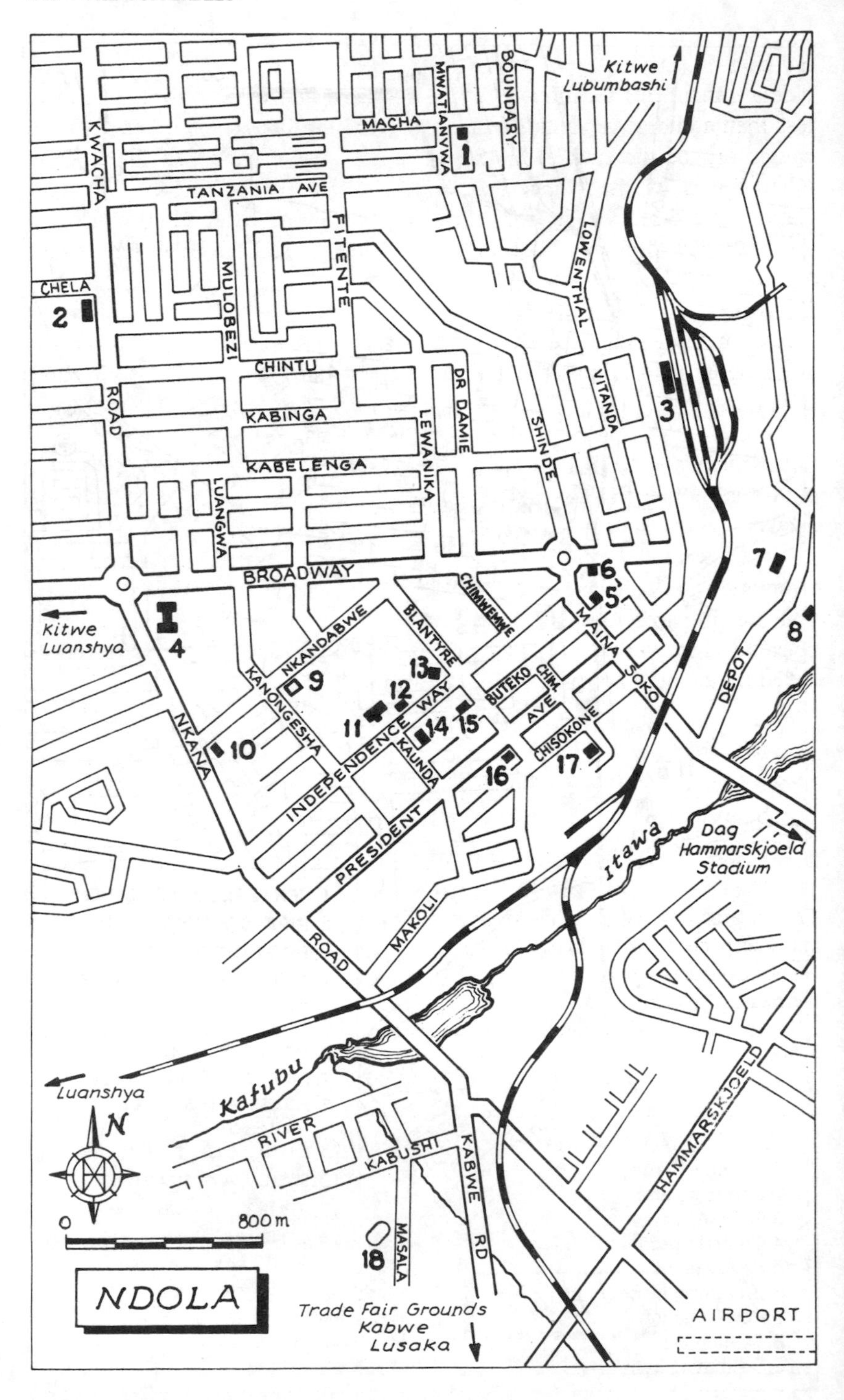
NDOLA
Kitwe
Lubumbashi
MACHA
MWATIANVWA
BOUNDARY
KWACHA
TANZANIA AVE
FITENTE
MULOBEZI
CHELA
LOWENTHAL
CHINTU
DR DAMIE
VITANDA
SHINDE
KABINGA
LEWANIKA
ROAD
KABELENGA
LUANGWA
BROADWAY
CHIMWEMWE
MAINA SOKO
Kitwe
Luanshya
NKANDABWE
BLANTYRE
KANONGESHA
BUTEKO AVE
CHIM.
DEPOT
INDEPENDENCE WAY
KAUNDA
NKANA
CHISOKONE
PRESIDENT
Itawa
Dag Hammarskjoeld Stadium
MAKOLI
ROAD
Kafubu
Luanshya
RIVER
KABUSHI
KABWE RD
HAMMARSKJOELD
MASALA
0
800m
Trade Fair Grounds
Kabwe
Lusaka
AIRPORT
1 2 3 4 5 6 7 8 9 10 11 12 13 14 15 16 17 18

By bus

Ndola's main bus terminus is at the southern end of Chimwemwe Road, less than a kilometre south of the Savoy Hotel – though some buses can be caught around the back of the Savoy. There are very frequent links to the other towns of the Copperbelt, and also Lusaka. To reach Northern Zambia (accessed via the road through Mkushi and Serenje) then first get a southbound (probably Lusaka) bus and change at Kapiri Mposhi.

By train

There are regular departures from Ndola to Livingstone, and back, stopping at all stations – but these are too slow to be of use to many travellers.

Hitchhiking

Ndola is quite a big town, so good hitch spots are a long walk from the centre – so consider getting a taxi for a few kilometres.

If you want to get to Northern Zambia, via Mansa, then resist the temptation to "cut the corner" by crossing into and out of Zaire – unless you are prepared to spend time placating border officials. It is perfectly possible, but you may find the demands for bribes outweigh any time saved by taking that route.

Where to stay

There is a small choice of hotels here, but they aim at visiting business-people and prices are correspondingly high.

Savoy Hotel (145 rooms) PO Box 71800, Ndola.
Tel: 02 611097/8, fax: 02 614001, telex ZA 30020
This is probably the most lavish hotel in Zambia, and prides itself on its casino and "suspended swimming pool situated on the mezzanine floor." It stands on Buteko Avenue, just off Maina Soko Road, near the eastern end of Broadway, in the heart of Ndola. There is a secure car park here and its rooms boast CNN and 24-hour video on demand. They are comfortable and functional, but lack originality.
Rates: US$80 single, US$90 double, including breakfast

KEY TO NDOLA MAP OPPOSITE

1.Shopping area
2.Shopping area
3.Railway station
4.Central hospital
5.Savoy hotel
6.Broadway cinema
7.Power station
8.Boating club
9.Swimming bath
10. Central fire station
11. Civic centre
12. Lowenthal theatre
13. High court
14. Boma
15. Central police station
16. Plaza cinema
17. Central bus terminal
18. Musa Kaonka stadium

Mukuba Hotel (52 rooms plus suites) PO Box 72126, Ndola
Tel:02 655545/655738/655763, fax: 02 655729
This reasonable hotel is inconveniently located about 6km from the centre, on the southern side of town adjacent to the grounds used for the annual Trade Fair. To get there head south towards Kabwe, then take a right into the industrial area, on to Arkwright Road, then Crompton Road.

That said, if you have transport, then it's worth the trip. The rooms all have tea/coffee makers, two telephones and a fridge. The televisions in the rooms are very well served with video channels, CNN, M-Net and various other TV stations, whilst outside there is a 9-hole golf course, with a small resident herd of impala. For a drink there is a choice of three bars, and for dining the excellent Chondwe Restaurant. If you can live with the 10-minute drive from the centre of town, this is better value than the more flashy Savoy.
Rates: US$75 single, US$80 double, including full breakfast

The New Ambassador (30 rooms) PO Box 71198, Ndola
Tel: 02 617071
The New Ambassador is found on President Avenue, fairly near the Plaza Cinema, and is more basic than either the Savoy or the Mukuba.
Rates: Kw 40,000 per twin, including a basic breakfast

Where to eat

There are plenty of take-aways around town, but for evening meals the main hotels are best. The Mukuba's restaurant is good, though not cheap, and there is a choice of three bars if you feel in need of a drink.

KITWE

Situated a few kilometres southwest of the large Nkana Mine, Kitwe is another large town which relies for its prosperity on a nearby copper mine. Getting to or from Kitwe is easiest by bus, and is only about 60km from Ndola.

Getting there

By air

Kitwe does have an airport, but it is mostly local mine traffic. Ndola is much better served by regional flights.

By bus

Kitwe's main bus terminus is in the "second class trading area" in the middle of town. Here you'll find many departures for Ndola, plus some for Solwezi and Lusaka.

By train

Kitwe is the end of the line from Livingstone which passes through Ndola and Lusaka, so slow trains connect it to Livingstone and Lusaka daily.

Hitchhiking

Like Ndola, Kitwe is a large town, so good hitch spots are a long walk from the centre. It is best to get a taxi for a few kilometres.

Where to stay

Edinburgh Hotel (78 rooms) PO Box 21800
Tel: 02 222188, fax: 225036
This is less impressive than the Ndola hotels – though all rooms have en suite shower and toilets, air-conditioning, colour televisions and telephones. There are two restaurants, a bar and a swimming pool. The hotel is situated on the corner of Independence and Obote Avenues, a few blocks north of the Oxford/Kantanta Road, and has a small shopping mall, the Edinburgh Centre, on its ground floor.
Rates: US$70 single, US$85 double, including breakfast.

Nkana Hotel (65 rooms) PO Box 20664
Tel: 02 226586
Standing opposite the Edinburgh on Independence Avenue, the Nkana attracts more Zambians than the Edinburgh, and its bar can become very lively at times.
Rates: US$70 single, US$85 double, including breakfast.

CHINGOLA

Chingola is the end of the Copperbelt, beyond which you either proceed north towards Lubumbashi in Zaire, or head west towards Solwezi and Mwinilunga.

Where to stay

Lima Motel (35 rooms) PO Box 10497. Tel: 311894
This is the only hotel in town itself, but most visitors try to get out to the Chimfunshi Orphanage, below.

Chimfunshi Wildlife Orphanage
Run by David and Sheila Siddel, Chimfunshi is part of the Siddels' 20,000-acre farm. Their involvement with chimps began in 1987 when they received an orphaned chimpanzee whose parents had been shot, and started to look after it. Now they have about twenty chimps, and accept a limited number of visitors to see the chimps; the money raised goes to supporting the orphanage.

The chimps are mostly animals that are being illegally smuggled out from Zaire on their way to being exported to Europe or America. The orphanage is probably the highlight of the Copperbelt for most visitors. To get there take the tar road from Chingola towards Solwezi for about 65km until there's a sign pointing right to the orphanage, which is just a short drive from the main road.

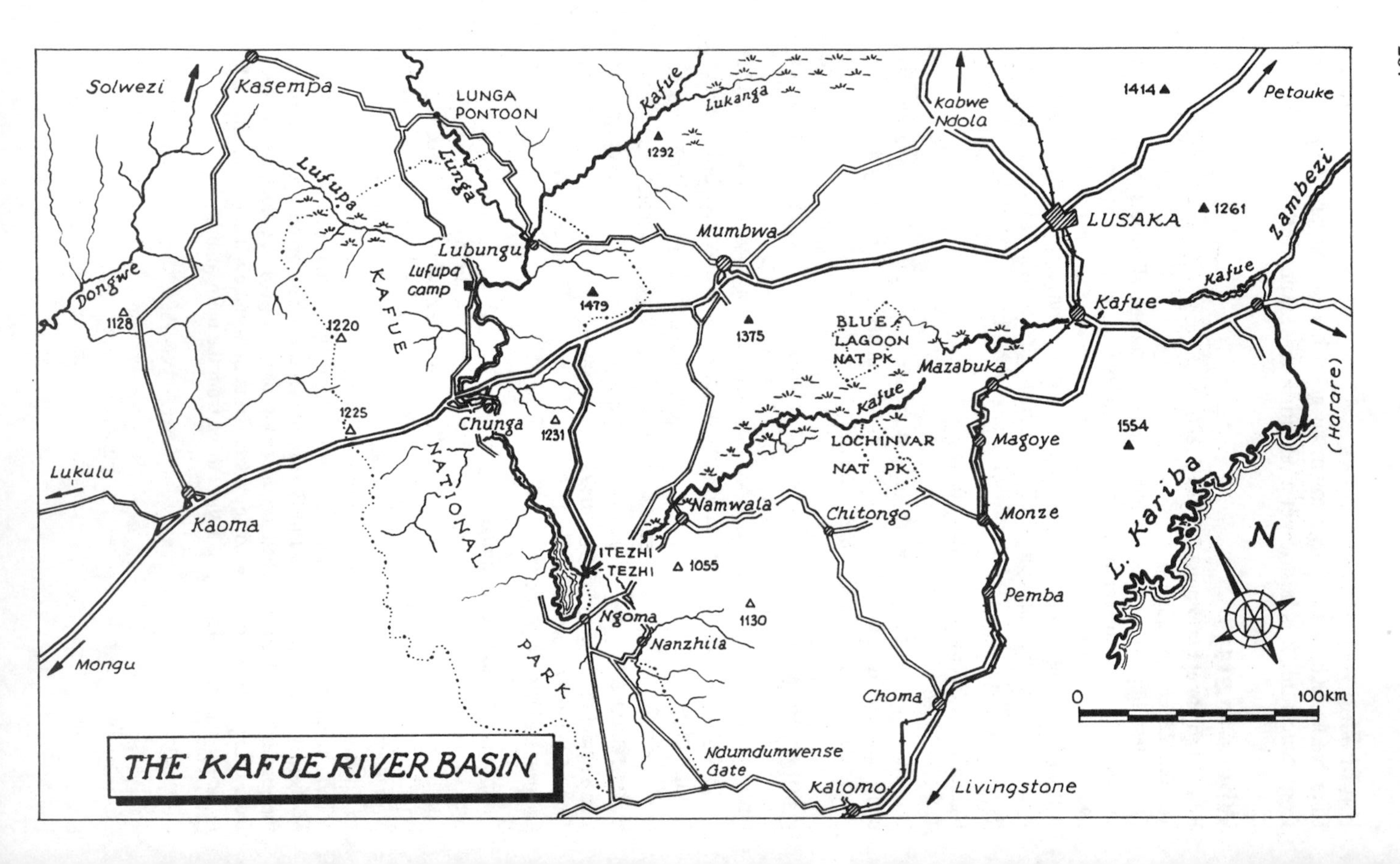
Solwezi
Kasempa
LUNGA PONTOON
Kafue
Lukanga
Kabwe
Ndola
1414
Petauke
Lufupa
Lunga
1292
LUSAKA
1261
Zambezi
Mumbwa
Lubungu
Dongwe
KAFUE
Lufupa camp
1479
Kafue
Kafue
1128
1220
1375
BLUE LAGOON NAT PK
Mazabuka
(Harare)
1225
Chunga
1231
Kafue
LOCHINVAR NAT PK
Magoye
1554
Lukulu
NATIONAL
Namwala
Chitongo
Monze
L. Kariba
N
Kaoma
ITEZHI TEZHI
1055
Pemba
Ngoma
1130
Nanzhila
Mongu
PARK
Choma
0
100km
THE KAFUE RIVER BASIN
Ndumdumwense Gate
Kalomo
Livingstone

Chapter Sixteen

The Kafue River Basin

Southwest of the Copperbelt, which is discussed in Chapter Fifteen, the Kafue River Basin covers a large area of central Zambia stretching from the border with Zaire to the west of Lusaka. It includes the Kafue, Blue Lagoon and Lochinvar National Parks.

Much of this central swathe of the country is difficult to visit, consisting of endless seasonal bush tracks which link occasional farming settlements. At its heart lies the huge Kafue National Park, which has some superb game viewing areas within its boundaries. The best of these, the Busanga Plains, take time to reach, but at times it ranks with the subcontinent's most impressive game areas.

Elsewhere, there are seasonal floodplains which sustain game and attract a rich variety of birdlife – like the Lukanga Swamps and the Kafue Flats. Part of the latter is protected by two small National Parks – Blue Lagoon and Lochinvar – but most such areas remain outside the parks. The Kafue River Basin is a wild area, with some excellent game and endless possibilities for exploring, but very little development.

MUMBWA

After about three hours' drive from Lusaka (148km), on the Great West Road to Mongu, a large modern factory looms next to the road. Orderly warehouses stand behind well-watered lawns. This hive of activity at Mumbwa is perhaps the country's biggest cotton ginnery.

A few kilometres west is a turning off the road to the north, which leads to the thriving township of Mumbwa, about 5km north of the ginnery. This busy little centre is a place with petrol stations, a Barclays Bank, a "medi-test" laboratory – and lots of small local shops.

Getting there

On the far side of the shops, in the township, is the local bus station. All the buses passing through Mumbwa – heading west to Mongu or east to Lusaka – will stop here. Being a relatively busy route, you'll find these arriving and departing at all times of the day, though the highest frequency of buses is the middle of the day, when buses that departed from Lusaka or Mongu in the morning will pass through Mumbwa.

Where to stay

La Hacienda Hotel is the only place here. It is fairly clean though very uninspiring.

KAFUE NATIONAL PARK

Park fees: US$10 per person per day. US$10 per vehicle per day

Kafue is a huge national park: two and a half times the size of South Luangwa. Sadly, until recently, few resources were devoted to its upkeep and anti-poaching efforts were left to a couple of dedicated souls from the few safari lodges which remained in the park.

Now the situation is better. Although many of the camps named here are not fully operational, those that are bring a steady trickle of visitors into the park - which help add weight (and finance) to the ongoing effort to build the park back up to its former glory. It will be a while before elephant numbers recover, but it is very heartening to see that the rest of the game is already thriving, and occurring in numbers that lead one to question the existence of any problems.

The camps here are generally not as plush or well-oiled as the better camps in the Luangwa, but the game-iewing can be just as good. Game viewing in the Busanga and Nanzhila Plains can be stunning, so don't visit without at least a side-trip into one of these remarkable areas.

Geography, flora and fauna

Established in 1924, the Kafue National Park covers about 22,400km² (about the size of Wales, or Massachusetts) and is still one of the world's largest parks. Naturally, its geography varies considerably.

The map clearly shows that the park is bisected by the tarred Lusaka-Mongu Road. This provides the easiest route into the park, and also a convenient split which allows us to refer to "northern" Kafue and "southern" Kafue as simply meaning the areas to the north, and to the south, of the road. Surrounding the park are no fewer than eight Game Management Areas (GMAs), which do provide some element of a buffer zone for the park's wildlife.

Northern Kafue

The northern section of the park is a slightly undulating plateau, veined by rivers - the Lufupa, the Lunga, the Ntemwa, the Mukombo, the Mukunashi, and the Lubuji - which are all tributaries to the main Kafue, whose basin extends to the border with Zaire. The main Kafue

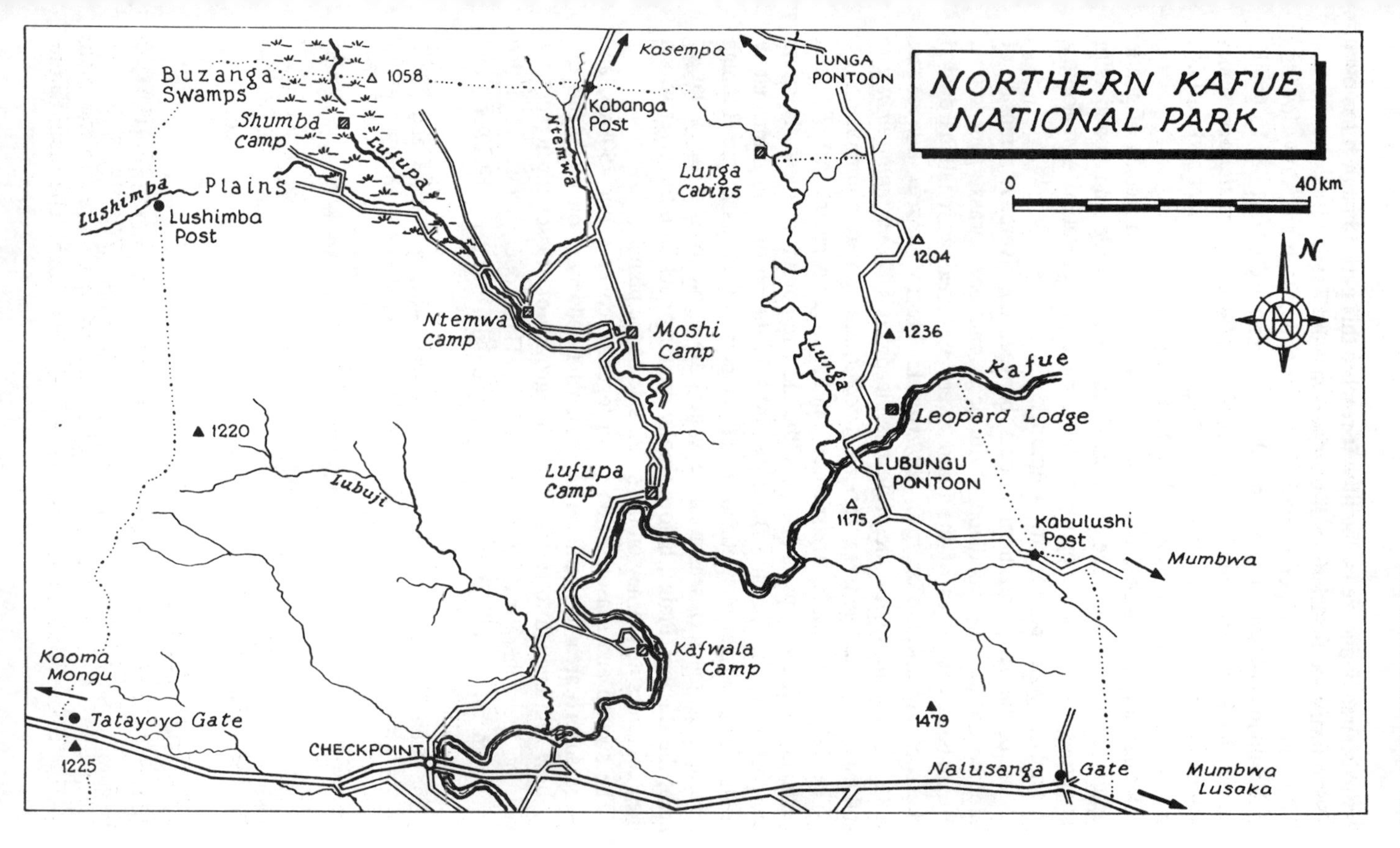
NORTHERN KAFUE
NATIONAL PARK
0
40 km
N
Buzanga
Swamps
1058
Kasempa
Kabanga Post
LUNGA PONTOON
Shumba Camp
Lufupa
Ntemwa
Lunga Cabins
Lushimba
Plains
Lushimba Post
1204
Ntemwa camp
Moshi Camp
1236
Lunga
Kafue
Leopard Lodge
1220
Lufupa Camp
LUBUNGU PONTOON
Lubuji
1175
Kabulushi Post
Mumbwa
Kafwala Camp
Kaoma
Mongu
Tatayoyo Gate
1479
1225
CHECKPOINT
Nalusanga
Gate
Mumbwa
Lusaka

River is already mature by the time it reaches this park, though it has over 400km further to flow before discharging into the Zambezi.

Thus in the park its permanent waters are wide, deep and slow-flowing, to the obvious pleasure of large numbers of hippo and crocodile. Its gently curving banks are overhung by tall, shady hardwoods, and the occasional islands in the stream are favourite feeding places for elephant and buffalo. In short, it is a typically beautiful large African river.

Occasionally it changes, as at Kafwala. Here there is a stretch of gentle rapids for about 7km. The river is about 1,000m wide and dotted with numerous islands, all supporting dense riverine vegetation – making a particularly good spot for bird-watching.

Most of the park's northern section, between the rivers, is a mosaic of miombo and mopane woodlands, with occasional open grassy pans known as dambos. The edges of the main rivers are lined with tall hardwood trees: raintrees, *lonchocarpus capassa*; knobthorn, *acacia nigrescens*; jackal berry, *diospyros mespiliformis*; leadwoods, *combretum imberbe*; and especially sausage trees, *kigelia africana*, are all very common.

The Kafue's tributaries are smaller, but the larger ones are still wide and permanent. The Lufupa is probably the most important of these. It enters the park from the Kasonso-Busanga GMA in the north, and immediately feeds into a permanent wetland in the far north of the park: the Busanga Swamps. In the wet season these waters flood out over a much larger area, the Busanga Plains, before finally draining back into the river which then continues its journey on the south side of the plains.

The swamp and seasonal floodplain together cover about 750km², and are a superb area for game. The seasonal floodwaters on the plains are shallow, but enough to sustain a healthy growth of grasses throughout the year on the mineral-rich black-cotton soil. These open plains are dotted with numerous small "islands" of wild date palms (*phoenix reclinata*) and various wild fig trees (various *ficus* species).

The area is perfect for huge herds of water-loving lechwe and puku, which are joined by large numbers of zebra, wildebeest, and other plains grazers, as the waters recede at the end of the wet season.

However, the Busanga Plains are very remote, and normally impossible to reach by vehicle until about June. Thus few people (even in the safari business) have heard about them, let alone visited them, and so this remarkable area continues to go largely unknown and unrecognised.

Southern Kafue

South of the main road, the park is long and thin; and stretches about 190km southwards, although only about 85km wide at its broadest point. On the park's eastern boundary is the Itezhi-Tezhi Dam: 370km² of water.

The vegetation and geography of the southern side are similar to the north – mostly a mosaic of miombo and tall mopane woodlands – although stands of teak are increasingly common. Underfoot, much of Southern Kafue, especially towards the western side, stands on Kalahari sand. Open grassy dambos retain the moisture of small streams and so sustain green grass throughout the year.

In the far south of the park, the Nanzhila Plains are a fascinating area. Wide expanses of grassland are dotted with islands of vegetation and large termitaria – often with baobabs, *Adansonia digitata*, or jackal berry trees, *Diospyros mespiliformis*, growing out of them.

Animals

Covering such a large area, with a variety of habitats, Kafue is rich in wildlife and many of its species seem to exhibit strong local variations in their distribution.

Antelope

Kafue has a superb range of antelope, but you will have to travel throughout the park if you wish to see them all. In the park's far north the permanent waters of the Busanga Swamps are home to the secretive sitatunga, which is uniquely adapted to life in the swamps. These powerful swimmers will bound off with a series of leaps and plunges when disturbed, aided by their enlarged hooves which have evolved for walking around on floating reed islands. They will then stand motionless until the danger passes, or even submerge themselves leaving just their nostrils above the water for breathing.

A little further south the Busanga Plains have large herds of red lechwe and puku, with smaller groups of zebra and blue wildebeest. Oribi are locally common here, as they are on the Nanzhila Plains, and you also have a good chance of seeing roan and the beautiful sable antelope.

In the main body of the park, kudu, bushbuck, tsessebe, eland, Lichtenstein's hartebeest, reedbuck, common duiker, grysbok and defassa waterbuck (a subspecies without the distinctive white ring on the rump) are all frequently seen. Numerically, puku dominate most of the northern side of the park, though this gradually cedes to impala as you move further south. Tsessebe are found in the southern side of the park, on the Nanzhila Plains, but not in the north, while giraffe are not found anywhere in the park.

Predators

Lion and leopard are common in the park. Spotted hyena also occur, and whilst cheetah and wild dog (cape hunting dogs) are seldom common anywhere, Kafue National Park is an important refuge for them.

Lion are widespread all over the park, and are easily spotted on the plains. On the Busanga Plains, large prides stalk through nervous herds of puku and lechwe nightly, using the natural drainage ditches for cover with deadly efficiency. There are currently at least five different prides in this area, and they seem to be thriving. Elsewhere they are probably equally common, though less easily spotted.

Leopard are common throughout the main forested areas of park, though they are seldom seen on the open plains. They are most easily observed on night drives, and continue with their activities completely unperturbed by the presence of a spotlight trained upon them. They appear particularly common in the area around Lufupa - though this is probably due to the success of Lufupa Camp's guides in locating these elusive cats.

Spotted hyena are seen regularly, though not often, throughout the park, apparently occurring in smaller numbers than either lions or leopards.

Cheetah are most frequently spotted on the Nanzhila plains, and occasional sightings of wild dog occur all over the park, but the packs of these nomadic animals range so widely that they are not common in any locale.

Other animals

Elephants occur in Kafue, though their numbers are still recovering from intensive poaching. On the northern side of the park small herds are only seen infrequently, and they are very skittish and wary of humans. In 1995 they were seen often around Lufupa - the first time that this had happened in eight years. The situation is better in the south, where elephants now commonly occur around the Kafue River, in the Chunga and Ngoma areas.

Buffalo are widely distributed throughout the park, but do not seem to be common, though herds do frequent the Busanga and Nanzhila Plains. Sadly, black rhino appear to be extinct throughout the park after sustained poaching.

The Kafue River, and its larger tributaries like the Lunga, are fascinating tropical rivers - full of life - and infested with hippo and crocodile, which occur in numbers to rival the teeming waters of the Luangwa.

Hunting and poaching

For many years there were few efforts or government resources devoted to protecting Kafue, and poaching was rife. This ensured the extermination of black rhino, and a sharp reduction in elephant numbers at the hands of organised commercial poachers. Fortunately the park is massive, surrounded by GMAs, and not easily accessible, so although the smaller game was hunted for meat, this was not on a large enough scale to threaten the population of the smaller game.

Organised commercial poaching is now virtually unknown, and the remaining incidence of smaller scale poaching by locals (for food) is being tackled by a number of initiatives.

Some concentrate on increasing the physical policing of the park. Others try to tackle the underlying reason for this poaching, and attempt to offer practical alternatives for the local people of the surrounding areas which are more attractive than shooting the game. For example, one such project allows local people in neighbouring areas to come into the park to collect natural honey. Both types of initiatives work with the help and support of some of the more enlightened local safari operators.

With the exceptions of elephant and rhino, the park's game densities appear to have been restored to normal levels in most areas, and the situation is continuing to improve.

Birds

The birding in Kafue is good, and about 450 species have been reliably recorded here. Near the Kafue and the larger rivers expect the full range of water-birds, from fish eagles through to darters and cormorants. Even for a casual observer, many species are common and an afternoon's observation by the river would probably include several species of kingfishers, bee-eaters, geese, ducks, cranes, storks, ibises, and vultures. The brochures are fond of mentioning the existence Pel's fishing owl – though these are resident in Kafue, they are neither common nor easily spotted wherever they occur in Southern Africa.

Specialities worth noting are the skimmers which nest on sandy beaches of islands in the middle of the river, and the shy African finfoot, which frequents the shady fringes of the slower rivers, swimming under the overhanging trees with part of its body submerged.

On the drier, southern side of the Busanga Plains you'll often find wattled cranes and the uncommon Stanley's bustard, as well as the kori bustard – the world's heaviest flying bird.

Getting there

Aside from the obvious entrances into the park, off the main Lusaka-Mongu road, a number of more adventurous, and more difficult, approaches are possible:

From the north

There are reasonable gravel roads from either Kitwe (via Ingwe) in the Copperbelt, or Solwezi (via Mwelemu) in the north, to Kasempa – which is just 50km north of the park. From here gravel roads lead southwest towards Kaoma, and southeast towards Mumbwa. No fuel and only minimal supplies are available at Kasempa.

Take the Mumbwa road leading southeast from Kasempa for about 82km until a track turns right from the road. Taking this smaller track will lead, after about 19km, to the National Park's Kabanga Post – from where a road proceeds southwards into the park keeping on the east bank of the Ntemwa River until around Ntemwa Camp. This is the easiest way to enter the park from the north.

Alternatively, if you ignore the right turning and continue, then you will reach the Lunga Pontoon (across the Lunga River) after about 16km. If you turn right just before the pontoon, then keep left (near the river) as the track divides, this will lead eventually to Lunga Cabins.

Crossing the Lunga Pontoon it is then an 80km drive to Lubungu Pontoon, along a route which skirts the eastern boundary of the National Park. Leopard Lodge is about 3km upstream from this pontoon, on the north side of the river. See the route described below, *from Mumbwa*, for the tracks beyond the pontoon.

From Mumbwa

If you are heading to the western side of the northern section of the park, then leaving the main road at Mumbwa is an option. Turn north into Mumbwa township, then left at the Total garage. At the top of the next rise is a right turn marked by an old sign to Hippo Mine. This track continues for 30km, then forks. Keep left, and battle on for another 30km until you reach the park's Kabulushi Post. This is 20km from the Lubungu Pontoon. If the Lubungu's waters are very low, then the pontoon will not be in operation and you will have to ford the river a few kilometres upstream – ask at the village for a guide to help you find this. Leopard Lodge is a kilometre or two further upstream, on the north bank of the river.

From Kalomo on the Lusaka-Livingstone Road

From Kalomo, which is about 126km from Livingstone on the way to Lusaka, there is an old sign to Kafue pointing roughly north. This track divides several times, so keep heading left – after a few kilometres you should be travelling northwest. After about 74km you will reach the Dumdumwenze Gate where the game scouts will sign you into the park.

From here, keep right as the road forks if you are heading for Ngoma, which is about 100km away. Nanzhila is only about 60km from the gate, but to camp there you must have permission in advance (from the headquarters at Ngoma, or even head office at Chilanga).

This approach is impassable in the wet season, so from Dumdumwenze Gate ask the scouts for the best route. You will probably be directed almost due west, skirting the southern side of the park, until you meet the cordon road which crosses the road and leads you straight to Ngoma. Given the occurrence of black-cotton soils in the area, travelling alone in the wet season would be very inadvisable.

From Monze on the Lusaka-Livingstone Road

From Monze take a turning on the north side of town towards Chongo, heading northwest towards Lochinvar National Park. You may need to ask local directions to get on the right track. After 7-8km you will pass Chongo - keep left there as the track divides after the village. (The right fork, about 8km after Chongo, leads to Lochinvar National Park.) About 35km later you will reach Chitongo, and a T-junction. Take the right turn and then about 18km later keep left as the track gradually turns from heading slightly west of north, to heading due west. The track forking right here, heading northwest, is less reliable but goes the same way. About 50km after Chitongo you will reach the larger village of Namwala, on the southern edge of the Kafue's floodplain, from where the track leads west into the park, entering past the site of the old Nkala Mission, and about 2km north of Ngoma Lodge.

Where to stay

Camps in the north of Kafue

Lufupa Camp (14 rondavels) Busanga Trails, PO Box 37538, Lusaka
Tel: 221683 / 224971 / 223628 / 221694, fax: 274253
This large camp overlooking the confluence of the Lufupa and Kafue is the centre of activity in the northern Kafue, and the main base for operations of Busanga Trails. The accommodation is in basic thatched, brick rondavels. These are large (having 3-5 beds) and have en suite showers, toilets and wash basins - but no frills or excessive comforts.

The dining room serves buffet-style meals and whilst there is little choice, the food is good. Tea and coffee are always available (help yourself) and there is a good, comfortable bar near to the small swimming pool. The camp's atmosphere is very casual and relaxed.

Activities are mostly by 4WD, though walking can be organised. The camp is large enough to run several activities at once, and an afternoon boat trip up either of the Lufupa or Kafue rivers is excellent.

The guides are good and adept at locating leopards in the area, so exciting night drives are the camp's chief attraction. Watching a leopard stalk by night is unforgettable, and Lufupa offers visitors a much better than average chance of spotting these cats.

Access to Lufupa is easy, though not quick. Enter the park by turning north from the tar road on the western side of the main bridge, past a game scouts' check-point. Follow that dirt road about 44km northeast, where a right turn, heading east to Kafwala Camp, should be ignored. Keep heading roughly northeast for about a further 26km to reach the camp. This track is good in the dry season (fine for a high-clearance 2WD) but becomes impassable when wet due to the black-cotton soil. Road transfers between Lusaka and Lufupa are included in the price of safaris here. They take about five hours, and are usually scheduled to connect with BA flights between Lusaka and London.

Lufupa is an unusual camp. It attracts an international clientele, whilst having fairly basic accommodation and facilities. Its secret lies in sensible pricing, access which is easy to arrange, and a reputation for leopards. In the UK, Sunvil Discovery (see page 58) are currently the only company to feature trips here.

For those with a 4WD there is a campsite here. Wood is supplied and there is a slipway for launching boats.

Rates: £750/US$1125 per person for seven nights, full board, including transfers from Lusaka & game activities. Camping: US$5 per person per night
Open: 1 May to around 31 November

Shumba Camp (4 twin-bed chalets) Busanga Trails, PO Box 37538, Lusaka
Tel: 221683 / 224971 / 223628 / 221694, fax: 274253
Shumba is the permanent bush-camp of Busanga Trails on the Busanga Plains. It is set on a picturesque "island" of large fig trees, in the middle of the plains about 75km (2½ hours drive) north of Lufupa, and some 15-20 minutes drive south of the base of the permanent swamps.

Accommodation is in one of four thatched, reed-walled chalets, each of which has twin beds, a shelf and a mirror. Shared showers and toilets are nearby. There is a two-storey look-out lounge, with excellent views across the floodplain and a waterhole nearby. Below this is a dining area where buffet meals are served.

Activities here revolve around driving: little game is seen if you walk around an area this open. As with Lufupa, the highlights are the night drives, and Shumba's guides are expert at spotting distant prides of lion.

Rates: Shumba can only be visited as part of a trip including Lufupa. Add about £40/US$60 per night to Lufupa's cost, for each night spent here instead of Lufupa
Open: 15 July to around 31 November

Lunga Cabins (6 twin-bed cabins) African Experience, PO Box 31051, Lusaka.
Tel: Johannesburg (2711) 462 2554, fax: (2711) 462 2613
Standing on the bank of the Lunga River, just outside Kafue's northern boundary, in the GMA, Lunga Cabins has a good reputation as a very comfortable, even luxurious, bush camp.

Accommodation is in well decorated, solid thatched cabins with en suite showers and toilets. Facilities include a thatched dining area, a bar with a sundeck which extends over the river, a small pool and even a steam bath. Activities include short walking safaris, 4WD and motor boat trips, and also guided canoe trips down the river.

Because of the camp's location most visitors arrive by private charter plane from Lusaka, and because of African Experience's connections, many guests come from South Africa.

Open: 15 April to around 31 December
Rates: US$250 per person per night.

Lupemba Camp (3 twin-bed igloo tents) African Experience, PO Box 31051, Lusaka. Tel: Jo'burg (27.11) 462 2554, fax: (27.11) 462 2613

This is a small, temporary satellite camp of Lunga Cabins, which sits on bank of the Lunga River. Accommodation is basic: small igloo tents with two bucket showers and a long-drop toilet outside. Meals are prepared over an open fire – so this is just bush camping with a couple of competent helpers and a guide.

The camp is accessed from Lunga Cabins by motor boat, and so activities are limited to short walking safaris and motor boat trips – though it is also possible for Lunga to arrange a similar fly-camp on the Busanga Plains.
Rates: US$250 per person per night
Open: 15 April to around 31 December

Hippo Camp (6 twin-bed tents) Lubungu Wildlife Safaris, PO Box 30796, Lusaka
This is a small tented camp within the National Park east of Lufupa, on the bank of the Kafue River – about 110km from Mumbwa. It is run by Mark Evans, who trained in South Luangwa, and concentrates on walking and photographic trips.

Leopard Lodge Outside the National Park's northeast boundary, Leopard Lodge is a few kilometres north of the Lubungu Pontoon, which crosses the Kafue river just on the edge of the park. It is uncertain if this is still open to visitors.

Treetops Conservation School Camp Busanga Trails, PO Box 37538, Lusaka
Tel: 221683 / 224971 / 223628 / 221694, fax: 274253
This run-down camp has a permanent presence of National Park scouts, and accepts local school children in groups for short stays. Like the schools camp at Kafwala, it is an important step towards educating the next generation of Zambians about the bush.

Ntemwa Camp 105km north of the main bridge over the Kafue, Ntemwa has a beautiful situation overlooking the Lufupa River from just south of the Busanga Plains. It now consists of four concrete rooms with tin roofs, and two thatched cottages – all of which are disused and in various stages of dereliction. This camp was offered for private tender in late 1995, so may be developed again in the future. It would be a superb spot for a "new" camp.

Moshi Camp This is slightly south of Ntemwa, about 90km north of the bridge. It also has a great spot overlooking the Lufupa, and it is also totally derelict. Moshi was offered for private tender in late 1995, so may be developed again in the future.

Camps near the road: Kafwala and Chunga

Mukambi Safari Lodge (10 twin-bed chalets) P. Bag E523, Lusaka
Tel: 01 228185, fax: 01 228184
5km east of the main bridge over the Kafue, this camp is signposted just south of the tar road. It is easily accessed in a normal 2WD vehicle. The thatch-on-brick chalets are solidly built using beautifully carved wooden doors. Inside, the windows are effectively mosquito-netted, and the decor is consciously ethnic with the odd carving or *object d'art*, and murals on the walls. The spotless tiled bathrooms have showers heated by gas geysers.

The central dining/bar area is also well designed, though quite formal – almost like a new hotel. It overlooks the Kafue River, and there's a good pool on the terrace outside. A range of walking, boating and 4WD game-viewing trips are

available. This is a well-built lodge which appears to have concentrated its efforts, successfully, on being comfortable. The option of a private fly-camp on the Busanga Plains is promised.
Rates: US$70 per person per night, full board
Open: all year
Excursions: walking US$30pp, boating US$25pp, driving US$20pp

Kafwala Camp (4 two/three bed huts) Wildlife Conservation Society
Book through the WCSZ branch in Kabwe – PO Box 80623, Kabwe. Tel: 05 223467; fax: 05 224859 – or see *Zambia Today*, page 102, for their head office.
This camp is built on the bank of the Kafue about 700m below the start of the Kafwala Rapids, northeast of the main bridge over the Kafue. Simply enter the park by turning north from the tar road on the western side of the main bridge, past the game scouts' check-point. Follow that dirt road about 44km northeast, then take the right turn which leads to Kafwala.

Access to the camp itself is restricted to members of the Wildlife Society, and it must be booked in advance. If you're thinking of staying here then join the society in Lusaka: it does a lot of good and needs more support.

Accommodation is in basic huts, with a total of eleven beds: Huts 1 & 2 have three beds each; Hut 3 has two beds; Hut 4 has just one bed; and there's a semi-open "Breezeway" with two beds and limited privacy. Toilets, shower and bathroom are communal, and there is a lounge and a braai area.

Deep freezes, fridges, lamps, crockery, cutlery and bedding are all provided – but you must bring all your own food and drink. The camp's staff will cook for you, so include some flour and yeast, for excellent bread. If you bring light fishing tackle then the cook will fillet and prepare your catch for dinner. The staff will also service the rooms, do the washing, and help with anything else that is reasonable. (You should tip them at the end of your stay.)
Rates: around US$15-20 per person per day
Open: all year.

Kafwala Safari Camp (Schools Camp) Busanga Trails, PO Box 37538, Lusaka
Tel: 221683 / 224971 / 223628 / 221694, fax: 274253
Near to the Wildlife Society camp is a small and very basic camp used by Busanga Trails for local schoolchildren. Educating Zambia's next generation about the country's remaining wildlife is vital if it is to be conserved throughout the next century, so initiatives like these are essential to the park's future.

Chunga Safari Lodge (6 twin-bed chalets) Njovu Safaris, PO Box 35058, Lusaka.
Tel/fax: 221681
On the other side of the river from the Chunga Safari Village and the National Parks Camp is a new camp which is nearing completion as this goes to press. It will stand in the GMA, just south of the main road, and six rustic chalets with en suite facilities are planned for here – with a small lounge, dining room, pool, and a bar overlooking the river. This has been under construction for some time, and is reached from a road between the road to Mukambi and the bridge – so look out for new signs.

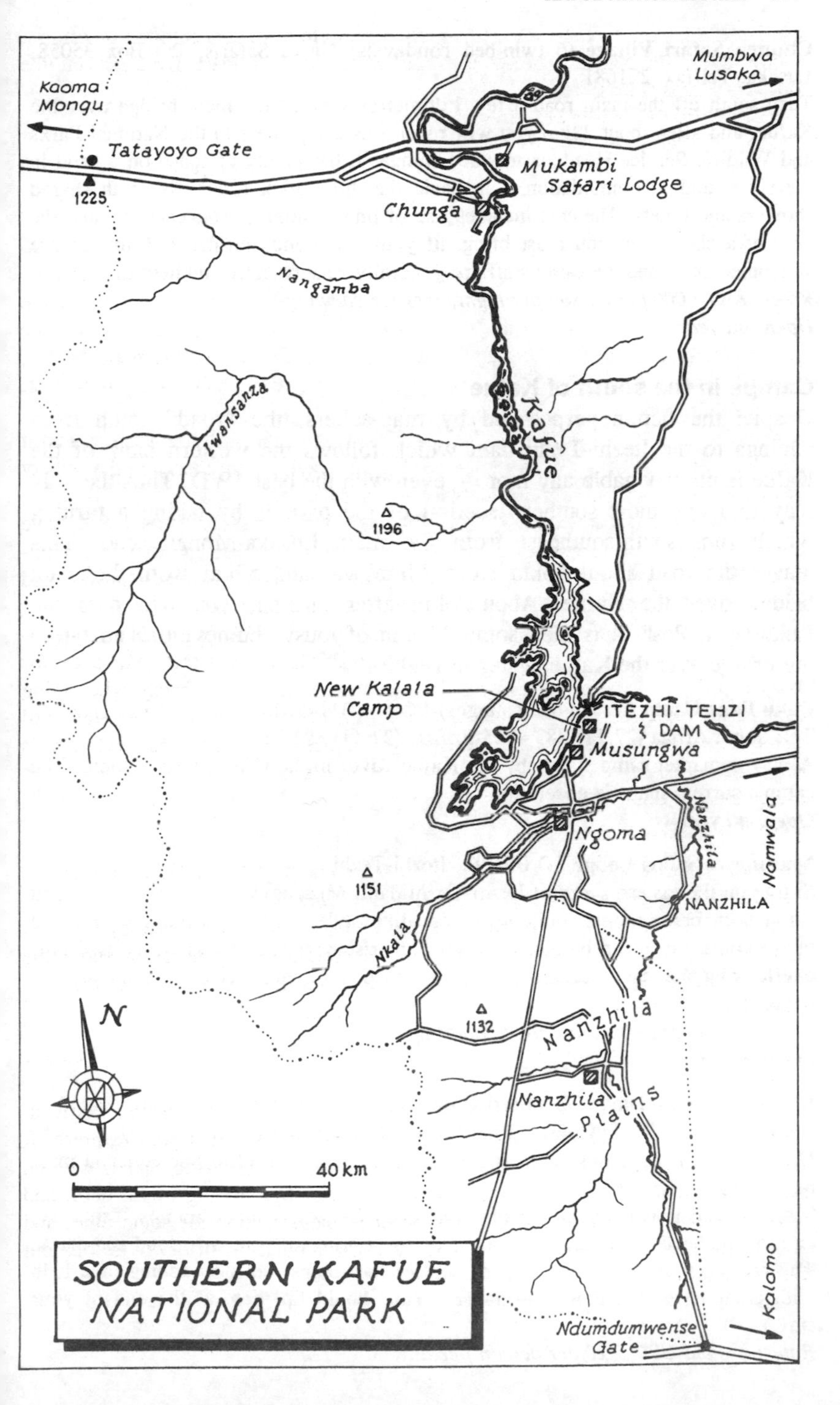
Mumbwa
Lusaka
Kaoma
Mongu
Tatayoyo Gate
1225
Mukambi
Safari Lodge
Chunga
Nangamba
Iwansanza
Kafue
1196
New Kalala
Camp
ITEZHI-TEHZI
DAM
Musungwa
Ngoma
Nanzhila
Namwala
1151
NANZHILA
Nkala
N
1132
Nanzhila
Nanzhila
Plains
0
40 km
SOUTHERN KAFUE
NATIONAL PARK
Kalomo
Ndumdumwense
Gate

Chunga Safari Village (6 twin-bed rondavels) Njovu Safaris, PO Box 35058, Lusaka. Tel/fax: 221681
Turn south off the main road a few kilometres west of the main bridge over the Kafue, and after about 22km you will reach this camp, next to the National Parks and Wildlife Service Headquarters at Chunga. It has plenty of space on a bend in the river, and accommodation is in basic thatch-on-brick rondavels, with shared showers and toilets. The cost includes use of linen, cutlery, crockery, etc, and the help of a chef – but you must bring all your own food and drink. Campers are welcomed here, and the camp staff are generally very friendly and helpful.
Rates: Kw10,000 per person per night, less for camping.
Open: all year

Camps in the south of Kafue

Despite the fiction perpetrated by map-sellers, the "road" south from Chunga to the Itezhi-Tezhi dam which follows the western bank of the Kafue is not navigable any more – even with the best 4WD. Thus the only way into this most southern section of the park is by taking a turning which runs south-southeast from the main Lusaka-Mongu road. This leaves the road about 66km from Mumbwa, and 59km from the main bridge over the Kafue. About 6km after turning, you will pass the Lukomeshi Post. It is then some 110km of lousy, bumpy, broken tar to the bridge over the Kafue at Itezhi-Tezhi.

Puku Pans Camp (8 twin-bed cottages) PO box 31149, Lusaka
Tel: South Africa (27.11) 883 4345-9, fax: (27.11) 883 2556
A new upmarket camp stands by the Kafue River in the GMA, near Ngoma. The camp's current status is uncertain.
Open: all year

Musungwa Safari Lodge PO Box 92, Itezhi-Tezhi
Sitting on the eastern shore of Itezhi-Tezhi dam, Musungwa is a large, established camp with brick rooms, built in a hotel-like style, with a swimming pool and tennis courts. It is run by Ros Kearney, an Irishman, and stands on a small hill, overlooking the dam. Campers are welcomed here, and petrol is available for residents.
Rates: US$5 per person per night camping
Open: all year

Wildlife Camp – David Shepherd Camp Tel: 324006; fax: 324006; tlx: 24043
Book with the Wildlife Conservation Society (see *Zambia Today*, page 102)
Near Ngoma Lodge, this camp is for members of the Wildlife Society, and must be booked in advance.

Accommodation is in basic huts, but deep freezes, fridges, lamps, crockery, cutlery and bedding are all provided. You must bring all your own food and drink. The camp's staff will cook for you, service the rooms, do the washing, and help with anything else that is reasonable. (You should tip them at the end of your stay.)
Rates: around US$15-20 per person per day

Nanzhila Tented Camps Chundukwa Adventure Trails, PO Box 61160, Livingstone. Tel: 324006; fax: 324006; tlx: ZA 24043 (see page 162)
Chundukwa Adventure Trails runs two tented camps here on the Nanzhila Plains in the far south of the park, about five hours' drive from Livingstone. Activities are mainly on foot, though day and night drives are available. Chundukwa is probably the best way of accessing this area, as Doug Evans, or one of his guides, escorts all these safaris and knows the area very well.

Chundukwa also organises more basic, completely mobile trips around the Nanzhila Plains, with participants carrying their own backpacks and just a few staff to help with setting up the camp and the chores.
Rates: US$220 per person per night full board (min. of 4 pax.), including transfers & park fees. US$185 for backpacking trips
Open: all year

New Kalala Camp In a busy spot, overlooking the Itezhi-Tezhi Dam from its eastern bank, this camp has recently ceased operating.

Nanzhila Camp Situated in a great position in the centre of the Nanzhila Plains, this used to be the main National Parks Camp. Now it is so run down that the scouts there will often allow you to camp anywhere in the vicinity. Water is sometimes available in the season.

Camping

Camping is possible in the park, and easily arranged at some of the larger camps like Lufupa, Chunga, and Musungwa. The two wildlife camps also make excellent value stops, and are only a little more expensive than camping. Elsewhere it may be possible to camp at some of the old sites of National Parks camps, which are now in disrepair. Ask for the latest news on this, and for permission, at the National Parks and Wildlife Service camps – either at Chunga or Ngoma in the park, or at the National Parks headquarters in Chilanga.

Getting around independently

If you are not seeing Kafue as part of an all-inclusive trip, then you will need two good 4WD vehicles, the most detailed maps you can buy, and all your provisions for the duration of your stay. Camping is possible (see below) but proper facilities are few and far between. If you have problems, you must be able to solve them yourself, as you can expect little help. Despite the fact that almost twenty camps are listed above, several are derelict and only a handful would be capable (and willing) to offer any help in an emergency.

That said, if you come well-equipped, then the park is wonderful. Camps like Musungwa, Chunga Safari Village and Lufupa will be happy to help you with advice on the area, and will probably even sell you a bed and a cold beer. If you do come well-equipped, then you can be assured of seeing very few other vehicles during your stay in this impressive area.

LOCHINVAR AND BLUE LAGOON NATIONAL PARKS

Further down the Kafue's course, about 120km east of Ngoma, are two small National Parks which encompass opposite sides of the Kafue River's floodplain. Their geography and ecosystems are very similar, although Lochinvar's wildlife has probably fared better over the last few decades than that of Blue Lagoon. Neither receives many visitors, and those who do visit should arrive with a 4WD and their own supplies, prepared to camp.

Geography, flora and fauna

Both parks are very flat, and the sections nearer the river are seasonally flooded. The resulting level grassy plain reflects the sky like a mirror, for as far as you can see. It is quite a sight, and a remarkable environment for both animals and waterfowl.

The parks are home to huge herds of Kafue Flats lechwe – a little-known subspecies of the red lechwe, endemic to the Kafue's floodplain – and a sprinkling of buffalo, zebra, wildebeest and other antelope.

The landscapes in both parks change with proximity to the river, and as you move further from the river, above the "high flood" line, the environment becomes different. The grassland here does not receive an annual flooding, and so termitaria can exist – their occupants safe from drowning. These sometimes form areas known as "termite cities" where many termitaria rise up from the plain, often with nothing else in sight, but sometimes accompanied by a distinctively shaped *Euphorbia candelabra*, or even the odd baobab. This open grassland is the typical habitat for the delightful, diminutive oribi antelope, as well as the larger grazers – zebra, wildebeest and buffalo.

Further from the water, the plains gradually merge into woodland, where *albizia* species of trees occur with typical species from munga woodlands like *acacia* and *combretum*. Here you may find kudu, baboon, or buffalo hiding in the thickets.

Birds

The best season for birds on the Kafue's floodplain is the summer rains. Then the river floods and the resulting lagoons attract a great variety of migrant birds – from flamingos and pelicans to large flocks of cranes, storks and ibises. Species which are otherwise uncommon can often be seen here in fairly large numbers, like spoonbills and wattled cranes.

Because of their shallow depth, these floodwaters also prove a great attraction for the smaller waders – sandpipers, godwits and avocets – and many species of ducks and geese can be found here in large numbers.

KUDU BULL ~ E.H

Lochinvar

Lochinvar's northern boundary is the Kafue River, and this area was a cattle ranch from 1913 until 1965 when the government, helped by the World Wide Fund for Nature, purchased it to make it a National Park.

Subsequently the park has been designated by the WWF as a "Wetland of International Importance", and a WWF team has been working with the local people on a project to manage the park on a sustainable basis for the benefit of both the people and the wildlife. Details of the project are available within the park – though there are a lot of settlements in the area, and conservation here is not proving to be an easy task.

Getting there

Lochinvar is easiest to approach from Monze, on the Livingstone-Lusaka Road – about 282km from Livingstone and 186km from Lusaka. The road heading northwest from Monze is signposted for Namwala just north of the grain silos. It passes Chongo village and forks about 8km afterwards – perhaps 25km from Monze. Ask local advice to find this if necessary. Take the right fork, or you will end up in Kafue. The gate to Lochinvar is about 48km from Monze.

Maps

An excellent 1:50,000 visitors' map to Lochinvar was published by the Surveyor General in 1986, and is still available at their main office in Lusaka. It indicates the vegetation types and also gives photographs and short descriptions of some of the park's interesting features and wildlife. Most of the "camps" depicted are now disused, and some of the roads now seem as if they were figments of a cartographer's imagination.

Where to stay

The original state-run Lochinvar Lodge was put up for tender to private safari operators in 1996, but no buyers were found. This may change, but until then the only option is the park's basic campsite, for which you must bring all your supplies. There were three or four small camps here, but none remains open.

What to see and do

The birds and animals are not the only attractions here; there is also a historical interest and some relaxing hot springs:

Gwisho Hot Springs Near the southern edge of the park, Gwisho Hot Springs are well signposted 2km west of the old lodge. These occur because of a geological fault, which has an associated deposit of gypsum – the mineral used to make plaster of Paris. This was mined here from 1973 to 1978.

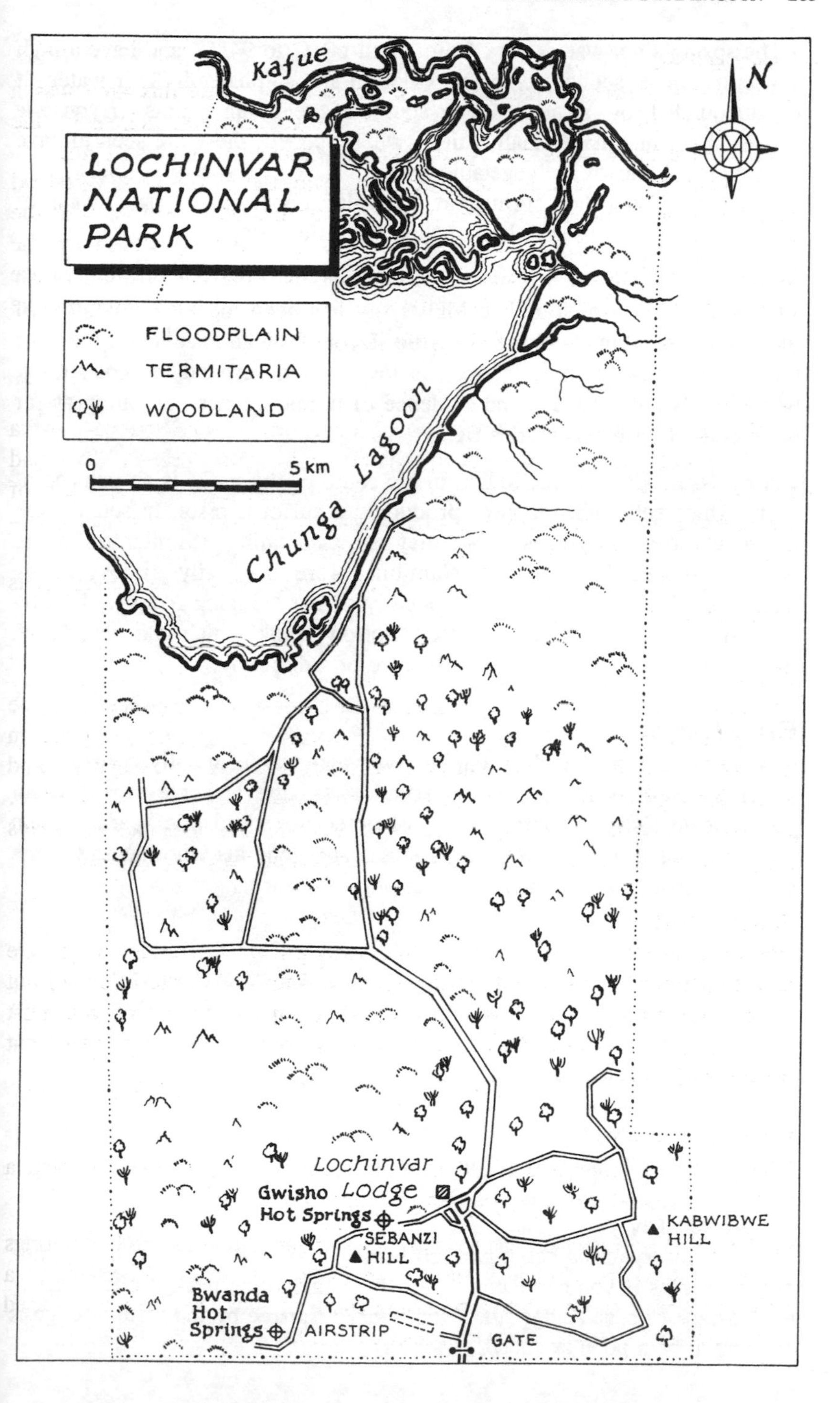

Kafue
N
LOCHINVAR NATIONAL PARK
FLOODPLAIN
TERMITARIA
WOODLAND
0
5 km
Chunga Lagoon
Lochinvar Lodge
Gwisho Hot Springs
SEBANZI HILL
KABWIBWE HILL
Bwanda Hot Springs
AIRSTRIP
GATE

The spring's hot waters vary from about 60°C to 94°C, and have a high concentration of sodium, chlorine, calcium and sulphates in their water. It is surrounded by a picturesque stand of real fan palms (*Hyphaene petersiana*) which have small fruits – when opened, these are seen to have a hard kernel known as "vegetable ivory".

There are other hot springs at Bwanda, about 4.4km southwest of Gwisho, near what used to be Lupanda Wildlife Camp.

Sebamzi Hill This is a National Monument marking the position of an Iron-Age village which archaeologists say has been inhabited for most of the last millennium. Looking out from it you have an excellent view over the park and the springs. Notice the low mounds around the hot spring, where excavations have found evidence of human settlement dating as far back as the first few centuries BC.

Drum Rocks Close to the lodge, in the south of the park, is an outcrop of rocks which echo when tapped, producing a curious, resonant sound. Ask the scouts to direct you to these: they are fascinating. (Similar rocks, on the farm called Immenhof in Namibia, were originally discovered by San/bushmen and are now known locally as the "singing rocks".) Nearby is a large baobab with a completely hollow trunk which can be entered from a crack in the side which is the size of a doorway.

Blue Lagoon

Blue Lagoon is to the north of the river and was originally owned by a farming couple who turned conservationists, the Critchleys. In recent years the Ministry of Defence has restricted access to this "park" to the military, plus a few privileged politicians and generals who have used the old farmhouse intermittently as something of a retreat.

Getting there

Blue Lagoon is not well signposted, and there are several ways to reach it. The easiest is to take the Great West Road from Lusaka to Mongu, then turn left about 28km from Cairo Road – opposite a small shop called Bancroft Supermarket.

This track will lead you to the National Park's scout camp at the gate. After signing in with them, you will then need to be guided by a scout on to another road to actually get into the park.

Where to stay

There is no organised camp here so bring all your supplies with you, and ask the scouts if you can camp somewhere inside the park itself. There is no shortage of spectacular sites, and a large fig tree by the water's edge is proving to be a popular spot.

What to see and do

Aside from the birds and animals, ask to be shown around the old farmhouse that used to be owned by the Critchleys. The interior has been very well preserved - complete with the family's furniture - and is fascinating to see.

THE PRICE OF LOVE

Judi Helmholz

People who say you can not put a price on love have obviously never been to Zambia. Like many African countries, Zambia maintains its tradition of *lobola* or bride price, which must be negotiated and paid to the bride's parents before two people are permitted to marry. *Lobola* is paid in cows or cash or a combination thereof. Some entrepreneurial new in-laws might consider a "pay as you earn" scheme, but often it is a case of no money, no marriage.

When we planned a trip to the Western Province, Victor, a friend, asked if he could come. He wanted to find a wife from his home village to bring back to Livingstone. Could we also loan him some money with which to pay the *lobola*? We agreed.

We dropped Victor off at his village, leaving him to initiate his search for a prospective wife. Two hours later we returned to find him with a huge smile on his face. "I have found one!" he exclaimed. He had found two, as it turned out. "Come and see," he said excitedly, grabbing our hands and dragging us through the village to meet his prospective brides. "OK!" he commanded, pointing to two young woman, neither of whom he had met before this morning. "Choose one for me!" he said, smiling and pushing the women forward for our inspection. The girls looked at us blankly. "Victor, we are merely loaning you the money. You must choose your own wife."

A few hours later, we heard the wailing of women from the village. Victor must have made his decision. He came into camp with one of the girls in tow. "This is Brona – my new wife!" he exclaimed. Brona was not smiling. She knew only that she would be leaving her village for a place she'd never been to, with a man she'd never met before, for possibly the rest of her life.

After some negotiation, Victor had paid Brona's father a deposit of Kw50,000, about US$50, for his daughter. Driving back to Livingstone, Victor and Brona sat in the back seat holding hands. We hoped things might work out for the two of them.

Two British friends living in Zambia got a big surprise when they approached the council for a marriage licence. "How much *lobola* did you pay?" the official asked. "Nothing," replied John. The official was aghast.

"You are telling me you paid nothing. You must have paid something!" Sue finally commented, "John purchased my air ticket from the UK." The official smiled, satisfied at last. "Ah yes, you see, you did pay. What is the value of this?" "Approximately US$1,000," replied John. The official was aghast. Taking John aside, he whispered into his ear, not wanting Sue to overhear, "You paid too much!"

Arthur and I? We also got married in Zambia. *Lobola*? Of course! Arthur paid ten cows for me. My parents live in the USA, so Arthur arranged for a herd of ten small cows to be carved out of wood for my father. The herd sits on my father's mantelpiece at home and he proudly tells all visitors, "That's what I got for my daughter."

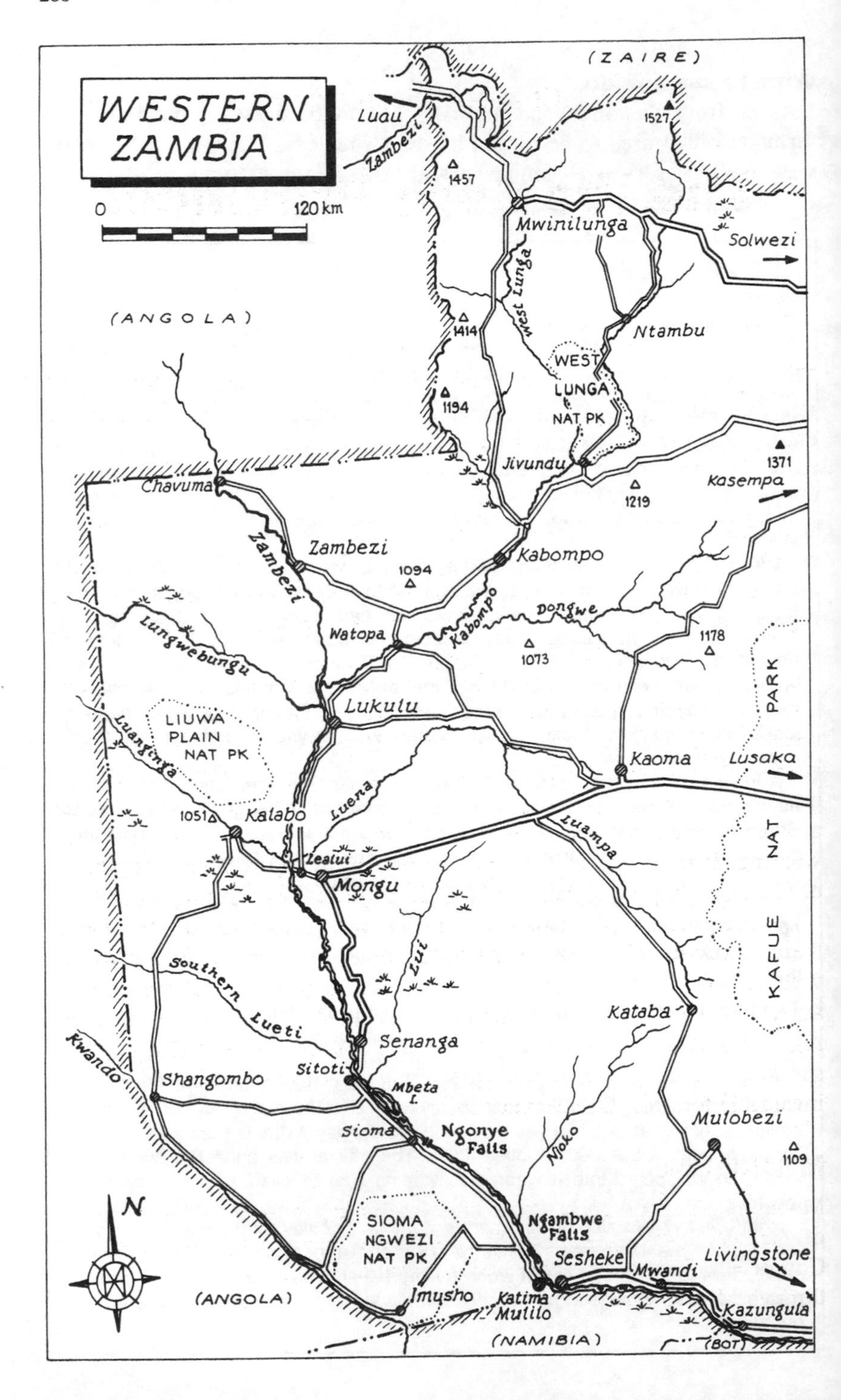
WESTERN
ZAMBIA
0
120 km
(ZAIRE)
(ANGOLA)
Luau
Zambezi
1527
1457
Mwinilunga
Solwezi
West Lunga
Ntambu
1414
WEST
LUNGA
NAT PK
1194
Jivundu
1371
Kasempa
1219
Chavuma
Zambezi
Zambezi
Kabompo
1094
Kabompo
Dongwe
Lungwebungu
Watopa
1073
1178
Lukulu
LIUWA
PLAIN
NAT PK
Luanginga
Kaoma
Lusaka
KAFUE NAT PARK
1051
Kalabo
Luena
Luampa
Lealui
Mongu
Lui
Southern
Lueti
Kataba
Senanga
Kwando
Shangombo
Sitoti
Mbeta
I.
Mulobezi
Sioma
Ngonye
Falls
Njoko
1109
N
SIOMA
NGWEZI
NAT PK
Ngambwe
Falls
Sesheke
Livingstone
Mwandi
(ANGOLA)
Imusho
Katima
Mulilo
Kazungula
(NAMIBIA)
(BOT)

Chapter Seventeen

The Western Provinces

This remote area of western Zambia is difficult to visit, but can reward intrepid travellers with some of the country's most interesting experiences. The Barotseland floodplains, near Mongu, offer a glimpse of rural Zambian life that is still largely untouched by the 20th century, while the Liuwa Plain National Park has excellent game and few visitors. It is the venue for one of Africa's last great wildlife migrations, which has remained largely unknown because of the difficulty of getting into the area. Other parks, Sioma Ngwezi and West Lunga, do not have the same reputation for wildlife, but are still very wild placcs to explore with a well-prepared group of 4WD vehicles.

Common to the whole region are the related problcms of supplies and transport. Much of the region stands on deep Kalahari sand, and vehicles need a high-clearance 4WD capability. If you are going off the main roads, then a small expedition is needed: consisting of several vehicles, in case one runs into problems. During the rainy season, many of the roads are impassable, and even the ferries across the rivers will often stop working. Being stranded is a very real possibility. Thus the area's paucity of visitors is largely explained by the sheer difficulty of getting around.

The best established network here is that of the missions. On the whole, these do remarkable work for the communities in the area, being involved with schools, hospitals, churches, development projects and many other aspects of local life. The courteous traveller can learn a lot about the region from these missions, and they are also good places to find English-speaking guides to accompany you on your travels – who will prove invaluable for around US$2 per day.

MWINILUNGA

Mwinilunga is an outpost, the main town in the remote northwest corner of Zambia. It is easily reached using the tar road from Solwezi and the Copperbelt. This degenerates into a gravel/dirt road shortly after passing through Mwinilunga.

In the town you'll find petrol, shops with basic supplies, a couple of banks, a few outposts for aid agencies, a small Franciscan mission, and two basic local resthouses – one council and one government. Beyond the tar, a good track leads north into Zaire via Ikelenge and Kalene Hill. The border at Jimbe Bridge is just over 100km away.

WEST LUNGA NATIONAL PARK

150km northwest of Kafue, as the pied crow flies, West Lunga is another of Zambia's parks which is ideal for small expeditions to explore, although not practical to visit casually. Check with the National Parks and Wildlife Service for the latest news about the park (there is an office at Solwezi if you are approaching from the north) and don't arrive without the backing of several vehicles for safety in the event of an emergency. There are no camps here, or commercial operators, or even scouts inside the park – so you must get around independently.

Geography, flora and fauna

West Lunga National Park covers 1,684km^2 of forests, dambos, open grasslands and papyrus swamps. It is bounded by the Kabompo River to the south (adjacent to which are most of the park's swamps) and by the West Lunga River to the west.

Despite persistent local poaching, the park still harbours elephant, buffalo, lion, leopard, hippopotamus and a wide range of antelope including puku, sitatunga, blue, common and yellow-backed duiker, sable, bushbuck and defassa waterbuck.

Getting there

The easiest ways to get to West Lunga are to approach from the Copperbelt or by skirting Kafue National Park's eastern boundary and proceeding through Kasempa. Approaching from Mongu is very time-consuming and slow going – with a good 4WD essential even in the dry season.

From the Copperbelt

Take the tar road through Kitwe and Chingola to Solwezi, from where it turns south until crossing the Mutanda River at Mwelemu. On the other side of the river, the road splits and the main tar surface continues to the right, heading west to Mwinilunga. The gravel road to the left continues south, towards Kabompo and Kasempa – so take this road. After almost 90km the road is joined from the east by a gravel road coming from Kitwe (which would have made a shorter, but more time-consuming, approach), via the village of Ingwe. About 16km later there is a road left to

Kasempa, and one right to Kabompo. Take the road to the right. After 140km there is a signposted right turn to the small village of Jivundu, which is on the south bank of the Kabompo River. The park is on the north bank and there is a pontoon which will take you across the river.

From Kafue

See the directions in *Chapter Sixteen* for details of approaching Kasempa from Mumbwa via the Lubungu and Lunga Pontoons, then head north from Kasempa on to the road from Mwelemu to Kabompo.

ZAMBEZI

The road from Kabompo, which is sometimes referred to as the "M8", is a remarkably good gravel road, with relatively few villages and lots of thick teak forests along its route. In the dry season the smoke from occasional bush fires will be seen drifting in the sky, above scorched areas of blackened ground that the fire has already consumed.

Zambezi is a small town with a few very basic shops, a mission, a telecommunications centre (Zambia's PTC), and a small local market. There is one simple hotel here, the Zambezi Motel (tel: 08 371123), which costs around US$12 per night, and an even more basic government resthouse which charges US$5 per night. Note that the town, like many regional centres in Zambia, is referred to locally as "the boma".

Zambezi has just one fuel station, but this is very unreliable and often empty. There are disturbing reports from this area of watered-down petrol from illicit sources – known as "bush fuel" – being sold to unsuspecting travellers. This makes it even more essential that if you head west from Mongu or south from Mwinilunga, then you do so with very large reserves of fuel.

Note on security: Because tourists are rare, and the border with Angola is a sensitive one, travellers going west or north from Zambezi should report to the local police– just to let them know that you're here. Perhaps going in to the police station to inquire "if it is safe to proceed" is the easiest way to do this. It will allow them to ask you any questions that occur, and reassure the police that you are not there to cause problems and mean no harm.

Getting there from Lukulu

From Lukulu follow the road north towards Watopa Ferry, which is about 70km away (1.5 hours drive). This will be on the left side, just after entering the two-shop town of Watopa. The Kabompo is a major tributary of the Zambezi and is crossed there with a manually-operated cable ferry, which is free. From here it is about 20km north to the junction with the road from Kabompo to Zambezi, and turning left it is a further 75km to Zambezi. This good M8 road actually continues on to the Angolan border, at Chavuma.

What to see and do

Traditional dancing

A few kilometres north of town are the palaces of the Lunda and the Luvale senior chiefs, on the east and west sides of the road respectively – as you might predict from the rough distribution of languages mapped out at the start of *Chapter Three*. The Luvale chief's palace is not only the venue for the Lykumbi Lya Mize (see page 26), but also for traditional dancing which is held here several times per week.

Chinyingi Mission

About a third of the way from Zambezi to Chavuma, just after the Makondu River, is a major track heading west and leading to the Chinyingi Mission. If you miss this turning then there is another better-signposted turning a few kilometres later.

The Mission is located on the east side of the river, and runs a school and a rural health centre. It is perhaps most famous for the Chinyingi suspension bridge – one of only four bridges to span the width of the Zambezi anywhere along its length. (The others are at Chirundu, Tete and the railway bridge near Livingstone.) The mission is run by Capuchin brothers, who are helpful and very jovial – they will happily tell you more about the area and the mission if you ask them.

CHAVUMA

Chavuma stands about 6km south of the Angolan border and the place where the Zambezi re-enters Zambia. The land around here is arid, and the soil mostly grey in colour, which makes villages in this area look dull compared with those further south. The road here from Zambezi is very

THE CHINYINGI BRIDGE

Judi Helmholz

The suspension bridge at Chinyingi was built in the mid-1970s by Brother Crispin Baleri of the mission after four people drowned whilst trying to ferry a sick person to the health centre. The tragedy happened in a *mekoro* (dug-out canoe) on the river late at night, and brother Crispin was so determined that it would never happen again that he decided to build a bridge.

Despite his lack of technical training, Baleri read all he could find on bridge construction and elicited donations of cables from the mines of the Copperbelt. Locals worked for second-hand clothes to construct the bridge, which is still used today, bouncing and swaying as you walk across it. Below there is now a pontoon operated by cables which is capable of ferrying a vehicle across.

good gravel.

As in Zambezi, paying your respects to the local police is a wise move, just so that they know who you are and what you are doing in their area.

The same goes for the Brethren Missionaries, who will also be able to help you with advice on camping or accommodation. They are found in a large compound up on the hill by town. They have their own camping spot by the river, which they may allow you to use, and they will certainly be able to direct you to any other suitable places.

What to see and do

Chavuma Falls

This is not nearly so spectacular as the Zambezi's later drops at Ngonye and Victoria Falls, but makes a good picnic site for an afternoon – the falls are found by taking the footpath near the pontoon.

No man's land

Every morning there is a small market here in no man's land, between the territories of Zambia and Angola. Both Zambians and Angolans come to barter for goods, under the watchful eyes of the armed border guards. As a foreigner, make sure you have very clear permission from the border guards before you even consider joining in, and don't take any photographs without permission. That said, it is a fascinating occurrence.

KALABO

This small town by the Luanginga River is the gateway to Liuwa Plain National Park. It is about 82km from the ferry over the Zambezi at Lealui, which is around four hours' drive. Allow five hours from Mongu. Here there are a few small shops and a National Park Office, which can issue permits for the park and a scout to accompany you. However, note there is no fuel available here – you must bring all you need from Mongu.

Kalabo also has a mission, and a basic government resthouse. The former is a good source of information on the whole area, and can direct you to the resthouse if you need it.

Getting there

Kalabo is not easy to reach, and travelling anywhere west of the Zambezi is really expedition territory. The roads are usually just tracks in the Kalahari sand, which need days of low-range driving. This not only requires a 4WD (or preferably several, in case of emergency), but also large quantities of fuel. Fuel cannot be replenished outside of Mongu, so long-range extra fuel tanks and lots of jerry cans are the normal solution. Note also that if there is any risk of the ferries going out of operation, then your only way back out is to keep west of the river, and drive south to Senanga. If you were forced to do this, it would take much more time and fuel than going straight from Kalabo to Mongu, but you need to bear the possibility in mind.

Water is also a problem, as it tends to seep through the Kalahari sand rather than forming pans on the surface. Hence no potable water can be relied upon outside Kalabo, so take some good containers and fill up at Mongu and Kalabo.

In the wet season the town is cut off, and the only way to reach here is using the postboat from Mongu. This can take one vehicle at a time: enquire locally to find out how it can be arranged. During the rest of the year, several approaches are possible:

From Mongu via Lealui

From Mongu, the best route for most of the year is to start by crossing the Zambezi using the Sandaula ferry, at Lealui. After this the tracks diverge as they cross the floodplains - which can be confusing. However, if you pick up any local hitchhiker going to Kalabo, then s/he should be able to direct you on to a navigable track. Wherever you drive, you are likely to encounter lots of semi-naked herd-boys waving sticks furiously at cattle to move them out of the vehicle's path.

From Mongu via the Libonda ferry

If the ferry at Lealui has problems, then the one at Libonda, higher up the river, may be working. This is reached by driving upstream from Lealui for about two hours. Leaving the ferry on the western bank, there is a direct track to Kalabo, but it is difficult to locate. Again, taking a local guide (hitchhiker) is the best way to travel - and you will see plenty of these throughout the area. You will pass men, women and children carrying everything from luggage to mattresses and supplies on their heads. Given the area's lack of transport, it you have room in your vehicle then you should offer lifts whenever possible.

From Senanga to Kalobo

There is a track on the western side of the river, but the difficulties of over 150km of low-range driving, with no access to fuel, should not be underestimated. Approaching from Mongu is best, although if the river is high and the ferries are not operating, then this may be your only option.

MICROLIGHTING - E.H

LIUWA PLAIN NATIONAL PARK

"Liuwa" means "walking stick" in the local language, and a legend relates how a Litunga (a Lozi king) planted his walking stick here on the plain, where it grew into a large *mutata* tree. The tree in question can still be seen from the track which leads from Minde to Luula: after leaving the first tree belt, look in the distance on your left side when you are half-way to the next tree belt.

Liuwa Plain is certainly the most fascinating park in the region, but getting here requires an expedition, or possibly the use of the new safari camp in the area.

Geography

Except for the sandy track leading through the park, passing the game-scout camps of Minde and Luula (which is on the northern boundary of the park), there are no roads at all in Liuwa Plain National Park. That, however, is part of the park's attraction: around 3660km² of untouched Africa. Most of this is a vast honey-coloured sea of grass, with just the occasional pan, island of raffia palms, or small tree-belt interrupting the flatness. The environment is unlike any other park in Zambia, and the game is prolific.

Unfortunately Angola's civil war has ensured that guns are available in Angola, and the park's proximity to the border means that armed poachers are occasionally encountered in Liuwa. Provided that you travel with an armed game scout, they will try to avoid you anyhow and should not be a problem.

The best time to visit Liuwa is certainly August to December, with November being the ideal month. Then the land is dry, and the game is at its most prolific.

Flora and fauna

Liuwa's attraction lies mainly in the great herds of blue wildebeest which amass here at the start of the rainy season, around November and December. Thousands of wildebeest, with zebra, tsessebe and buffalo, group together, joining the more static resident roan antelope, red lechwe and reedbuck. The open plains are particularly good for oribi – a diminutive and very beautiful antelope.

With these come the predators: mainly lion, hyena and wild dog, though the odd leopard also occurs here. For some reason Liuwa's lionesses, which blend superbly into the golden grass, have a reputation for charging vehicles, so be careful.

For bird-watchers, crowned and wattled cranes are obvious specialities, as are the rare resident palmnut vultures, though pelicans, open-billed storks and fish eagles are also found when the pans in the area contain water.

Camps and lodges

There are just two operators who run trips in this park at the moment. Robin Pope Safaris is based in the South Luangwa (see page 209), but runs one or two mobile trips per year up here, normally in November. These small expedition are very popular despite their high cost (around US$3-400 per person per day), as the operators take all the pain out of the organising. Visitors just fly in to have a marvellous week or more in one of the world's most fascinating and isolated parks. You will need to book well in advance in order to secure a place on one of these trips. The second option is a new camp:

Royal Barotse Safari Camp (4 twin-bed tents) Tukuluho Wildlife Ltd
PO Box 1120, Ngwezi, Katima Mulilo, Namibia.
Tel: Johannesburg (2711) 705 3201/2; fax: (2711) 705 3203
This is a new camp for 1997 and will be best reached by flying into Kalabo's airstrip on a private charter plane, and the camp will then collect you. All meals, drinks and activities will be included in the tariff, and the camp aims to match the best in the country. If this camp delivers what it promises, then it will have a busy future as part of any adventurous trip around Zambia. Note that Tukuluho's other camp in the region is Maziba Bay, near Sioma.
Rates: US$250 per person per night all-inclusive. Transfers from Kalabo US$30 per person

Getting around independently

Venturing into Liuwa Plain National Park should really be left to the experts. However, if you have several vehicles and the equipment, and insist on your own trip, then you can go in with an armed National Park scout from Kalabo. You will need to supply all of his provisions (cigarettes and other extras are greatly appreciated). It is wise to contact in advance the head office of the National Parks and Wildlife Service in Chilanga (see page 101), or the office in Mongu, to arrange for the permits and a guide. They will also be able to advise you of the costs in advance.

The park is approached from the National Park office in Kalabo by crossing the Luanginga River on a pontoon. This crossing can be tricky if your vehicle is heavily loaded, when recruiting some strong local help to get your vehicle on and off the pontoon is a good idea.

From there the park is about 30km of soft-sand driving. The entrance is marked by some cut wooden poles, and there are no tracks in the park other than the one leading to the Minde and Luula scout villages. The only water in the park is at Minde – where the red-brown water is fine for washing but unappealing to drink.

MONGU

The former British protectorate of Barotseland – now often referred to as simply the Western Province (WP) – covers the upper reaches of the Zambezi. It is the homeland of the Lozi king and his people, a group who have retained much of their cultural heritage despite the ravages of the last century. They were granted more autonomy by the colonial authorities than most of the ethnic groups in Zambia's other regions, and perhaps this has helped them to preserve more of their culture.

For the traveller this means that life here has altered relatively little since pre-colonial times. Most of the local people still follow lifestyles of subsistence farming, hunting and gathering, and when rains are good the people must still move to higher ground to escape the floodwaters.

On the edge of these floodplains, Mongu is the provincial centre for western Zambia and, because it is easily reached from Lusaka on a tar road, this is the best place in the region to get fuel or supplies.

Geography

Mongu stands about 25km from the Zambezi, and is set on a ridge overlooking the north of the Barotse plains. The town is spread out over several kilometres in a giant arc, which follows the ridge. It has two petrol stations, a bakery, a few grocery stores, a garage, several small hotels, and a large local market. Government administration has a strong presence here, and most departments are represented in a rather ramshackled collection of offices.

The views north over the floodplain are spectacular: a myriad of waterways snaking through apparently endless flat plains. Small villages and cattle dot the dusty plains during the dry season, but when wet it is all transformed into a haze of green grass on a mirror of water that reflects the sky.

Getting there and away

By bus

Several buses link Lusaka to Mongu every day – expect a minibus to cost Kw8,500 and a larger, slower bus to be about Kw5,500. There is also a postbus that services this route, so ask at the post office for details.

A very slow service also plies between Livingstone and Mongu, via Sesheke, during the dry season. Ask at the bus station for details.

Mongu to Lukulu

By far the best route to Lukulu is from just after the Kaoma turn-off, on the Lusaka-Mongu road. This is an all-weather road. However, if you are travelling in the dry season then there are two other routes.

One starts by heading west from Mongu towards Kalabo. Several kilometres before the Sandaula ferry over the Zambezi, at Lealui, a road turns off north. This passes the Barotseland Fishing Tours and Safaris Camp, then the Libonda ferry, and continues towards Lukulu on the eastern bank of the Zambezi. Nearer to Lukulu it passes Tiger camp and Bahati Lodge, before finally reaching Lukulu after about 120km.

The alternative, which is easier, is to go from Limulunga towards Mbanga. For this you should cross the dambo at the end of the Limulunga Road, and then ask for the road to Mbanga. This is a bush track through small villages across the floodplain, and even driving carefully you can expect scrawny multi-coloured chickens with chicks in tow to be scattered everywhere as you pass, and emaciated village dogs to bark wildly and show an unnatural interest in your tyres. If you are heading for Tiger Camp then pick up a guide at Mbanga, who will show you the camp. Otherwise continue through Mbanga in the same direction to reach Lukulu.

Hitchhiking

Hitching to Mongu is possible for the determined, but hitching to get around the area outside Mongu is very slow and difficult.

Getting around

By boat

Boat transport is the best way to see the immediate area around Mongu, and it is the only way if the flood is high. For a few dollars you can hire a mekoro (dug-out canoe) to take you out on the waterways, and perhaps down towards Lealui and the main channel. Spend a few hours like this, on the water, and you will appreciate how many of the locals transport themselves around. You will see everything from people to household goods, supplies, live animals and even the occasional bicycle loaded on to boats and paddled or poled (punted) from place to place.

By postboat

Given that boats are the only way to reach some settlements in this area during the wet season, there is a "postboat" on the Zambezi which carries passengers, cargo, and even the mail. It is large enough to also take the odd vehicle, though this may need a special arrangement. Ask at the Mongu District Council offices, or telephone 07 221175, for more details.

Driving

Apart from the main roads from Lusaka to Mongu, and to Lukulu, most of the area's gravel roads degenerate into patches of deep sand occasionally. Thus they require a 4WD even in the dry season, and the worst of them will require almost constant low-range driving through tracks of Kalahari sand.

During the wet season, the whole area north of the Ngonye Falls is subject to flooding. Then the Barotse floodplain becomes a large, shallow lake – much of the population moves to higher ground to live, and boats are the only options for getting around.

Where to stay

There are several small hotels in Mongu, and all are basic. Because of the town's bad reputation for crime, especially theft, you should take maximum precautions against losing your belongings, even when staying in one of the hotels.

Lyambai Hotel (17 twin-bed rooms) PO Box 910193. Tel: 07 221271
This is the town's largest hotel, and preferred by many.
Rates: Kw25,000 per person

Ngulu Hotel (16 twin-bed rooms) PO Box 910308. Tel: 07 221028
This is definitely a step up from the Mongu Lodge, though costs a little more. It is sometimes used by aid-workers in the area.
Rates: Kw23,000 per person

Mongu Lodge Tel: 07 221501/221606
This is the town's most basic accommodation. The rooms do have their own en suite bathrooms, though these are rarely sparkling.
Rates: Kw15,000 per person

Aside from these, camping is really the only option. Given the problems of theft around Mongu, any campsite should be chosen with care. If you can't make it to Bahati Lodge, below, then the compound at Limulunga is probably the best place to camp. There is also a small guest house there that sometimes operates.

Where to eat

The hotels will sometimes serve food if requested but for the town's best food try the Bisiku Restaurant, in the centre of town near the main market. With an afternoon's notice they will serve up an excellent dish of bream. Otherwise the grocery stores and the main local market are your best source of ingredients, though the variety is often limited.

Fishing camps

Between Mongu and Lukulu there are several good bush-camps which specialise in fishing trips on the Zambezi. These are certainly more comfortable than the hotels in Mongu, though also more expensive.

Bahati Lodge (5 twin-bed tents) PO Box 10122, Chingola
Tel: 02 312477/312603/312208/312071, fax: 02 312396. Alternatively, contact Nkwazi Africa Tours, in Johannesburg, on tel: 27 11 678 0862
30km downstream from Lukulu and 60km north of Mongu, Bahati Lodge is the most northern of the fishing camps on the Upper Zambezi. It has five large, well-made tents each with en suite facilities (basic showers) and a sun-deck.

Its main appeal is for fishermen who charter a plane for a few days and fly in for some big-game fishing, paying US$75 each per day, plus drinks. Because the camp gets most of its supplies from Chingola – about 700km away – it welcomes other guests who arrive in their own vehicles and with their own supplies and alcohol. Thus a much reduced "self-catering" rate is also available. There is usually a limited bar available, of mineral water and local beer.

Camping is also possible here, with use of showers and a flush toilet. Firewood is supplied, and you can rent a motor boat for US$35 per day. Limited fishing tackle is available for hire, but it is better to bring your own.
Rates: US$75 per person per day, including full board and use of a motor boat for fishing. Self-catering rate: US$25. Camping US$5 per person
Open: May to November

Tiger Camp (6 twin-bed tents) Tiger Fishing Tours, PO Box 31730, Lusaka. Tel/fax: 01 262810. Email: tiger@zamnet.zm
This upmarket fishing camp is on the eastern side of the Zambezi, about 32km from Lukulu and just downstream from Bahati Lodge. Accommodation here is in large tents with en suite (hot & cold) showers, flush toilets, and the protection from the sun of individual thatched roofs. The meals are extensive, and the three-course dinner is usually served with wine.

Boats, with skippers, and tackle are included in the rates, as are laundry and fishing licences – though you will have to pay for any fishing lures that you lose. Ideally, you should book in advance to stay here, and there is an airstrip for small charter planes. The camp is in daily radio contact with its Lusaka offices.

This camp comes highly recommended for its outstanding hospitality, helpfulness, personal attention and friendliness. "The best in the west."
Rates: US$130 per person per day, including full board and activities.
Open: May to November

Barotseland Fishing Tours and Safaris PO Box 30172, Lusaka
Tel: 01 261768/283983, fax: 01 263557, or book in Lusaka via African Tour Designers, page 130.
This company has a camp between Lealui and the Libonda ferry, on the bank of the Zambezi. From here it operates fully-inclusive fishing trips on the river. As for Tiger Camp, these should be booked in advance.

It also offers a special trip to see the spectacular Ku'omboka Ceremony, between the end of February and the beginning of March. (See page 25 for more details.) This is a three-night, four-day trip with road transfers from Lusaka included. Because of the uncertainty of the festival's date, participants need to be in Lusaka on stand-by, available to leave for Barotseland at very short notice.

Rates: US$180 per person per day, including full board and activities. Road transfers from Lusaka are US$80 return – min. 4 people, max. 8 people
Open: May to November

What to see and do

Aside from wandering around the local market, in the town centre, there are no specific sights to see in Mongu. The two obvious attractions are both excursions from the town:

The Litunga's summer palace at Lealui

About an hour from Mongu, on the floodplains, the summer palace is set in a large grove of trees which is easily seen from the escarpment on which Mongu stands. Driving takes about an hour, or it is possible to hire a mekoro to bring you out here from Mongu.

Don't expect a western-style "palace" as the Litunga's will simply appear to be a normal small African village with thatched huts. However, this is not only the King's summer residence, but also the main Lozi administration centre. Visitors are warmly welcomed, though are strongly advised to show the utmost politeness and courtesy to their hosts.

Museum at Limulunga

Just outside Mongu, near the Litunga's summer palace, is a small museum housing some interesting exhibits on the history and culture of the Lozi people. There is also a small craft shop – excellent for basketware from the area.

The Ku-omboka

If the rains have been good, and the floodwaters are rising, then around February or March, often on a Thursday, just before full moon, the greatest of Zambia's cultural festivals will take place. The Ku-omboka is the tradition of moving the Litunga, the Lozi king, plus his court and his people, away from the floodwaters and on to higher ground.

This spectacular ceremony is described in detail in *Chapter Three*, page 25, and it involves a flotilla of boats for most of the day, plus an impromptu orchestra of local musicians and much celebration. Don't miss it if you are travelling in western Zambia at the time.

MAKISHI DANCERS

Judi Helmholz

Sometimes in Mongu, or whilst travelling in the north of the Western Provinces, you will encounter colourfully clad characters adorned with fearsome costumes – Makishi dancers. To the uninitiated (defined as women and children in Luvale society), these are traditionally believed to be female spirits from the dead, and most will talk in high voices and even have "breasts" made of wire.

The creative and artistic skills of the Luvale people are reflected in the wide variety of mask styles worn by the Makishi. These are huge constructions, often made of bark and wood and frequently coloured with red, white and black. Even helicopter blades are sometimes spotted in the designs – a memory of the war in Angola.

Each Likishi (the singular of Makishi) dancer is distinctive and plays a specific role within the various ceremonies and festivals. For example, the Mungali, or hyena, depicts manacing villains, whilst the Chikishikishi, a monster with a boiling pot, represents discipline – and will consume mischievous members of society.

Apart from their occasional appearances throughout the land, the Makishi dancers play important roles during two of the most important ceremonies of Luvale culture: the Mukanda and the Wali. These are the initiation rites for boys and girls respectively.

The Mukanda, also known as circumcision camps, are traditional "schools" for local boys, aged from 12 to 17, where they are introduced to adult life and circumcised. The dancer known as "Chileya cha Mukanda", which literally means "the fool of the school", serves as a jester by mimicking the participants so as to relieve tension and anxiety before the circumcision ceremony. The girls attend a similar ceremony, though there is no physical clitoridectomy operation, as occurs in other cultures.

Sancta Maria Mission

This Catholic mission near Lukulu was founded in the 1930s and has a lovely setting high on one bank of the Zambezi, overlooking palm-fringed woodlands opposite. This is a stunning place from which to watch the sunset. It is run by the Sisters of the Holy Cross whose projects include community education and a leprosy clinic.

There is a Sunday service in Lozi which offers a fascinating blend of Catholicism and Lozi culture – with lots of singing and dancing. Being just over the river from Liuwa Plains, the sisters tell of one day, in the 1950s, when the bell in the tower started ringing wildly. On investigation it turned out to be caused by a spotted hyena which had seized the raw-hide bell-pull in its jaws, and was trying to pull it off and eat it.

SESHEKE

Sesheke actually consists of two small towns located on opposite sides of the Zambezi. The bigger town is on the east side, reached by driving from Livingstone, or taking the pontoon over the river. There is a service station here, a few stores, a simple hospital, and a small government resthouse.

The smaller western section, located next to the border with Namibia, has a police post and a small local store. Across the border in Namibia's Katima Mulilo fuel is cheaper and supplies more plentiful, so Sesheke can be very quiet.

Getting around

Sesheke is most easily reached from Katima Mulilo in Namibia, which has excellent roads (easily navigable by 2WD vehicles) linking it to the rest of Namibia and also to Kasane in Botswana. However, the route north, from Sesheke to Mongu, is worthy of special mention.

Sesheke to Mongu

The route from Sesheke to Mongu is fairly straightforward, following the western bank of the river for the first 188km, to Situate. After about 60km you pass through Kalobolelwa, where a track leads off left into Sioma Ngwezi National Park. Later, at about 110km, there is a sign for the camp at Maziba Bay (see below) before the Ngonye Falls are reached. These are marked by a National Parks and Wildlife Service office, near which there is a basic campsite. If you are not stopping at Maziba, then ask the National Parks office for guidance in seeing the falls, which are very spectacular. Alternatively, Maziba Bay offers white-water rafting trips below them if you are feeling adventurous.

At Sitoti, the track continues straight – to Kalabo – but the easier route is to take a right turn down to the ferry across the Zambezi. This is expensive for a foreign-registered vehicle, US$25 or 90 South African Rand, but only US$10 for a Zambian vehicle. From there it is about 30km to Senanga, where petrol is usually available. The road from Senanga to Mongu is about 110km and has recently been tarred, so it is now one of the best roads in this part of the country.

If you take the direct road to Kalabo from Sitoti then driving is much slower as you will just be ploughing through the Kalahari sand at a very slow speed.

SIOMA

The main reason for visiting Sioma is for the Ngonye Falls (often referred to as the Sioma Falls), and the Sioma Ngwezi National Park. The falls are spectacular, and the park is interesting, so the nearby camps on the Zambezi have a wider range of activities than just fishing. With travel in the area often taking much time, these are also good places at which to rest for a few days if you are travelling between Sesheke and Mongu.

Camps and lodges

There are just two camps in this area, both concentrating on fishing. In the near future it is likely that more will start up, and place a greater emphasis on game-viewing trips into Sioma Ngwezi.

Maziba Bay River Safaris (6 twin-bed tents and camping) Tukuluho Wildlife Ltd PO Box 1120, Ngwezi, Katima Mulilo, Namibia.
Jo'burg tel: 2711 705 3201/2; fax: 2711 705 3203. (Alternatively contact via Sunlink International Ltd, Harare, Tel: 2634 729025, fax: 2634 728744/883418.)
Maziba Bay is just a few years old and situated on the western side of the Zambezi, south of the Ngonye Falls and near to the Sioma Ngwezi National Park. It is about 110km north of Sesheke – about two and a half hours' driving along a graded gravel road – and is run by David and André Van de Merwe.
Accommodation is in simple tents (chalets under construction), or alternatively on the campsite – ablution blocks are shared between all of the guests. There is a small swimming pool, a lounge/bar area, and an outdoor "boma" for braais. Food is normally South African style, reflecting the character of the camp.
Maziba Bay offers an impressive range of activities including white-water rafting, kayaking and canoe safaris on the river, as well as game drives and walks into the National Park. See below for more details.
If you are not driving yourself, then access here is best by private plane – from either Livingstone or Katima Mulilo in Namibia. Note that this is a sister-camp to the Royal Barotse Safari Camp, on page 295.
Rates: US$150 per person full board and river activities, US$10 per person camping

Mutemwa Lodge (6 twin-bed tents) Fauna Afrika
Mutemwa is a very new camp about 50km north of the border with Namibia, almost half-way between Sesheke and Ngonye Falls. Few details of its operations arc available at present. It has an airstrip for access by private charter planes, and offers fishing and bird-watching trips. Canoes and boats can be hired, and the camp boasts a honeymoon suite built on its own private island. Campers are welcome at a campsite 1km downstream from the main lodge, and tents can be hired.
Rates: US$100 per person full board, US$10 per person camping

What to see and do

Although not as impressive as Victoria Falls, the Ngonye Falls are spectacular, and if the former didn't exist then they would certainly draw visitors. The geology of the area is the same as that of Victoria Falls, and these falls are formed in a similar process with erosion taking advantage of cracks in the area's basalt rock.

Sioma's main falls form a rather spectacular semi-circle of water, with lots of smaller streams around the edges. Some of these form little pools, ideal for bathing, though be careful to remain here as the main river has too many crocodiles to be safe. They are at their most spectacular when full, from January to around July.

Viewing access is difficult, as the main falls cannot be seen from the bank; you must cross on to the island in the river in front of them for a good view. There are two ways to do this. The first possibility is to venture downstream a little and cross on to one of the islands using a small metal boat/ferry – which was made by Brother Hugh at the Sioma Mission. The track leading to this isn't easy to locate, though a local guide can usually be found to help you. Using this you will still need to cross a small side-stream before reaching the island nearest the falls. The other way to see them is to take a boat. Maziba Bay, for example, offers half-day trips to the falls by canoe or raft for US$12 per person, including lunch. Other activities in the area include:

White-water rafting

The rapids below the falls are graded as a class III white-water run, and Maziba Bay takes rafting trips here which run them in a couple of hours. Usually such trips will include a visit to the main falls themselves, and the cost is US$20 per person.

Microlighting

Maziba Bay has a microlight which you can hire to take you over the falls, and also west to see the Sioma Ngwezi National Park. Wherever you go, this costs about US$25 for 15 minutes in the air.

Fishing

The *raison d'être* of coming to the Upper Zambezi always used to be fishing – for bream and tiger fish. Now more activities are offered, but still most visitors come primarily for the excellent fishing.

SIOMA NGWEZI NATIONAL PARK

Of all of Zambia's remote and seldom-visited parks, Sioma Ngwezi is probably the one to watch for interesting developments. The Victoria Falls /Livingstone area is fairly close and full of visitors, while Namibia's tourism in the Caprivi Strip is rapidly taking off – with the help of excellent lodges like Lianshulu, in Namibia's Mudumu National Park. Ngonye Falls are relatively close to Katima Mulilo in Namibia, and hence well connected to both Namibia and Botswana (and thus Cape Town and Johannesburg) with excellent roads.

Geography, flora and fauna

Positioned in the far southwestern corner of Zambia, Sioma Ngwezi National Park shares a long border with Angola, along the Kwando River, and also a short border with Namibia in the south. This corner is less than

50km from northern Botswana, and its vegetation and landscape owes much to the Kalahari sand which lies beneath it.

Most of the park is flat, dry and quite densely wooded - covered with a mosaic of *miombo* and *acacia* woodland, with the occasional area of teak forest and a few open dambos surrounding rare pools in the bush.

Sioma Ngwezi is the only Zambian park, outside the Luangwa valley and the Mosi-oa-Tunya park, where giraffe are found. They are certainly not of the same subspecies as those in Luangwa, Thornicroft's giraffe. It is claimed that they are an "Angolan" subspecies, which is different again from the normal "southern" variety found throughout the subcontinent.

The park's other antelope include roan, sable, tsessebe, blue wildebeest, zebra, and possibly lechwe on the Kwando River. The major predators are lion, leopard and spotted hyena.

Poaching is common, especially on the eastern side where there are a number of villages and the wildlife is generally very shy. However, the park is large and remote, so considerable wildlife still exists in this dense bush, especially in the central and western areas of the park.

Getting around independently

This is difficult and would require the backing of a couple of 4WDs. The Kalahari sand can be slow going, and there is only one decent road through the park. The driving is also very heavy on fuel - so remember that this is only available at Sesheke or Katima Mulilo in the south, or Senanga or Mongu to the north.

The main route through the park is the track which comes from the northwest, keeping close to the Kwando from Shangombo. A little short of the Namibian border, this turns sharply left and heads northeast through the middle of the park. Around the park's eastern boundary, at Ngweze Pools, there is a poor track southeast to the Zambezi, via Cholola, and another track leading northwest, roughly along the park's boundary - as well as the continuation of the original track which leads directly to the Zambezi at Kalobolelwa. You may need local help to find these, but there are villagers in the area who can help.

Better still, if you intend to explore this area independently then get a guide from the National Parks and Wildlife Service office at Sioma (which is signposted from the main road), which will make exploring much safer and more productive. Access to the park from Sioma is via the tsetse-fly control barrier (a dirt track), which bisects the Maziba Bay airstrip.

Alternatively, a more practical way for most people to visit is probably with an organised game-drive from one of the lodges. Maziba Bay does half-day drives into the park for about US$20 per person - and David and André at the lodge know the park better than most people.

LANGUAGES

Zambia's main language groups are briefly outlined in *Chapter Three*. This section will try to note down just a few useful phrases, and give their local translations in six of the most frequently encountered languages: Nyanja, Lozi, Luvale, Lunda, Tonga and Bemba. The visitor will probably find Nyanja the most useful of these. However, in the more remote areas – like the Western Province – where Nyanja is not spoken, the other languages will prove invaluable.

Space is too short here, and my knowledge too limited, to give a detailed pronunciation guide to these six languages. However all are basically phonetic and by far the best way to learn the finer nuances of

	Nyanja	**Lozi**	**Bemba**
how are you?	*muli bwanji?*	*muzuhile cwani?*	*mwashibukeni?*
I am fine	*good bwino*	*lu zuhile hande*	*eyamukwayi*
yes	*inde*	*kimona*	*eya ye*
no	*iyayi*	*baatili*	*awe*
thank you	*zikomo*	*nitumezi*	*twa to te la*
hey you!	*iwe!*	*wena!*	*iwe!*
I want	*ndifuna*	*nabata*	*ndefwaya*
there	*kunja*	*kwale*	*kulya*
here	*apa*	*faa*	*Hapa*
stop	*imilira*	*yema*	*iminina*
let's go	*tiyeni or tye*	*aluye*	*natuleya*
help me	*niyetizipita*	*nituse kwteni*	*ngafweniko*
how much?	*zingati?*	*kibukayi?*	*shinga?*
it is too much!	*yadula!*	*kihahulu!*	*fingi!*
where can I find…	*alikuti…*	*uinzi kai…*	*kwisa…*
the bank	*kosungila ndalama*	*kwa kub ukela mali*	*inanda yakusungila indalama*
the doctor	*sing'ang'a doctoro*	*mualafi/muwalafi*	*shinganga*
the police	*kapokola*	*mupokola*	*kapokela*
the market	*kumusika*	*kwamusika*	*ekobashita fyakulya*
drinking water	*mazi akumwa*	*mezi a kunwa*	*amenshi ayakunwa*
some food	*chakudya*	*sakuca*	*ichakulya*

pronouncing these phrases is to find some Zambians to help you as soon as you arrive. As a minor point, asking a Zambian to help you with a local language is also an excellent way to break the ice with a new local acquaintance, as it involves them talking about a subject that they know well, and in which they are usually confident.

As noted in *Cultural guidelines*, pages 28-9, learning a few simple phrases in the local language will go a long way towards helping the independent traveller to have an easy and enjoyable time in Zambia. Just remember to laugh at yourself, and have fun. Most Zambians will be very impressed and applaud your efforts to speak their language, no matter how hard they may laugh!

	Lunda	**Tonga**	**Luvale**
how are you?	*mudi nahi?*	*mwabuka buti?*	*ngacili?*
I am fine	*cha chiwahi*	*kabotu*	*kanawa*
yes	*ena*	*inzya*	*eawa*
no	*inehi*	*pepe*	*kagute*
thank you	*kusakililaku*	*twalumba*	*gunasakulila*
hey you!	*enu!*	*yebo!*	*enu!*
I want	*nakukena*	*ndiyanda*	*gikutonda*
there	*kuna*	*okuya*	*haaze*
here	*kunu*	*aano or awa*	*kuno*
stop	*imanaku*	*koyima or ima*	*imana*
let's go	*tuyena*	*atwende*	*tuyenga*
help me	*kwashiku*	*ndigwashe*	*gukafweko*
how much?	*anahi?*	*ongaye?*	*jingayi?*
it is too much!	*yayivulu!*	*chadula!* or *zinji!*	*yayivulu!*
where can I find...	*kudihi...*	*ulikuli...*	*ali kuli...*
the bank	*itala dakuswekamu mali*	*kubanka*	*chisete cha jimbongo*
the doctor	*ndotolu*	*mun'g'anga*	*ndotolo*
the police	*kapokola*	*kappokola*	*kapokola*
the market	*chisakanu*	*musika*	*mushika*
drinking water	*meji akunwa*	*maanzi akunywa*	*meya a kunwa*
some food	*chakuda*	*chakulya*	*kulya*

FURTHER READING

Historical

A History of Zambia by Andrew Roberts. Published by the Africana Publishing Company, a division of Holmes & Meier Publishers, 30 Irving Place, New Your, NY 10003, 1976. ISBN 0-8419-0291-7. A detailed and complete history of Zambia, from prehistory to 1974.

Travels and Researches in Southern Africa, by David Livingstone. 1857. This classic is fascinating reading, over a century after it was written.

David Livingstone and the Victorian Encounter with Africa, published by the National Portrait Gallery, London, 1996. ISBN 1-85514-185-X. Six essays on Livingstone's life, concentrating on not only what he did, but also on how he was perceived in the UK.

The Lake of the Royal Crocodiles by Eileen Bigland. Hodder and Stoughton, 1939.

Black Heart – Gore-Browne & the Politics of Multiracial Zambia by Robert I. Rotberg published by the University of California Press, Berkley, 1977 ISBN 0-520-03164-4

Guidebooks

Kasanka – A Visitor's Guide to Kasanka National Park by Lucy Farmer. First published July 1992 by the Kasanka Trust. A superb little 36-page guide, which includes comprehensive sections on the geography, vegetation, wildlife, birdlife, and the facilities for visitors at Kasanka. Get hold of a copy if you can – try the Kasanka Trust in the UK, the Wildlife Shop in Lusaka, or the main Wasa Lodge in the park.

A Visitor's Guide to Nyika National Park, Malawi by Sigrid Anna Johnson. Published by Mbabazi Book Trust, Blantyre. Length 150 pages; costs around US$4. It is available at most good bookshops in Blantyre and Lilongwe, and at the park reception at Chilinda. The book provides a detailed historical and ecological background to Nyika, 20 pages of special interest sites and notes on recommended walks and hikes, as well as complete checklists of all mammals, birds, butterflies and orchids which are known to occur in the park. In short, an essential purchase.

Travelogues

Survivor's Song: Life and Death in an African Wilderness by Mark & Delia Owens. First published in the UK by HarperCollins 1993. Published as *The Eye of the Elephant* in the USA. ISBN 0-00-638096-4. This relates the authors' struggles to protect the wildlife of North Luangwa National Park from poachers, and their efforts to develop viable alternatives to poaching for the local people. It is excellent reading, though insiders complain of sensationalism, and that it ignores valuable contributions made by others.

Pole to Pole by Michael Palin. This has an excellent section on Zambia, and Shiwa N'gandu in particular is covered well from pages 248 to 253.

Reference books

Bugs, Bites & Bowels by Dr Jane Wilson Howarth. Published in the UK by Cadogan Books Plc, London House, Parkgate Road, London SW11 4NQ. Distributed in the US by Globe Pequot Press. ISBN 0-86011-045-2. An amusing and erudite overview of the hazards of tropical travel which is small enough to take with you.

Common Trees, Shrubs and Grasses of the Luangwa Valley by P.P. Smith. Published in 1995 the UK by Trendrine Press, Zennor, St. Ives, Cornwall. ISBN 0-9512562-3-8. This small, practical field guide has pictures to aid identification at the back, and includes a small section on the value to wildlife of the various plants.

A Guide to Common Wild Mammals of Zambia published by the Wildlife Conservation Society of Zambia, 1991. ISBN 9982-05-000-1. A small field guide to the more common species, obtainable from the Wildlife Shop in Lusaka, or direct from the WCSZ.

A Guide to Reptiles, Amphibians & Fishes of Zambia published by the Wildlife Conservation Society of Zambia, 1993. ISBN 9982-05-001-X.Another good guide to the more common species, obtainable from the Wildlife Shop in Lusaka, or direct from the WCSZ.

Common Birds of Zambia published by the Zambian Ornithological Society of Zambia, revised 1993. ISBN 9982-9901-0-1. A good small field guide to the more common species, obtainable from the Wildlife Shop in Lusaka, or direct from the WCSZ.

A Guide to the Common Wild Flowers of Zambia and Neighbouring Regions published by Macmillan Educational Ltd, London, 1995. ISBN 0-333-64038-1. This is a good small field guide to the more common species, obtainable from the Wildlife Shop in Lusaka, or direct from the WCSZ.

Zambia – Debt & Poverty by John Clark. Published by Oxfam, 274 Banbury Road, Oxford, OX2 7DZ, 1989. This slim volume looks at Zambia's international debt, its causes and its consequences with clarity.

INDEX